Graduate Education for a Thriving Humanities Ecosystem

Graduate Education for a Thriving Humanities Ecosystem

EDITED BY
Stacy M. Hartman
and Yevgenya Strakovsky

The Modern Language Association of America
New York   2023

© 2023 by The Modern Language Association of America
85 Broad Street, New York, New York 10004
www.mla.org

All rights reserved. MLA and the MODERN LANGUAGE ASSOCIATION are trademarks owned by the Modern Language Association of America. To request permission to reprint material from MLA book publications, please inquire at permissions@mla.org.

To order MLA publications, visit www.mla.org/books. For wholesale and international orders, see www.mla.org/bookstore-orders.

The MLA office is located on the island known as Mannahatta (Manhattan) in Lenapehoking, the homeland of the Lenape people. The MLA pays respect to the original stewards of this land and to the diverse and vibrant Native communities that continue to thrive in New York City.

Library of Congress Cataloging-in-Publication Data

Names: Hartman, Stacy M., editor. | Strakovsky, Yevgenya, editor.
Title: Graduate education for a thriving humanities ecosystem / edited by Stacy M. Hartman and Yevgenya Strakovsky.
Description: New York : The Modern Language Association of America, 2023. | Includes bibliographical references.
Identifiers: LCCN 2023025327 (print) | LCCN 2023025328 (ebook) | ISBN 9781603296403 (hardcover) | ISBN 9781603296410 (paperback) | ISBN 9781603296427 (EPUB)
Subjects: LCSH: Humanities—Study and teaching (Graduate)—United States. | Universities and colleges—United States—Graduate work. | BISAC: EDUCATION / Schools / Levels / Higher | EDUCATION / Administration / General
Classification: LCC AZ183.U5 G69 2023 (print) | LCC AZ183.U5 (ebook) | DDC 001.3071/1—dc23/eng/20230705
LC record available at https://lccn.loc.gov/2023025327
LC ebook record available at https://lccn.loc.gov/2023025328

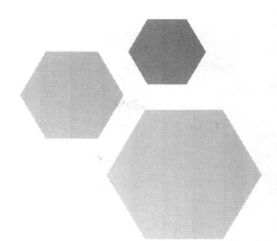

Contents

Introduction   1
  Stacy M. Hartman and Yevgenya Strakovsky

Part One: Engaged Curriculum   21

A Twenty-First-Century Doctoral Curriculum: Praxis, Scholarly Communication, and Capacity Building   25
  Sidonie Smith

Collaborative Ethics: Practicing Engagement in Our Academic Communities   41
  Jenna Lay and Emily Shreve

Reforming and Revalidating the Humanities Master's Degree at a STEM-Driven University   57
  Anna Westerstahl Stenport and Richard Utz

Purpose and Vocation: Rethinking the First-Year Graduate Proseminar   75
  David Pettersen

Experiential Learning and the Humanities PhD   91
  Tiffany Potter and Elizabeth Hodgson

Part Two: Civic Engagement — 107

New Pathways for Access, Inclusion, and Public Engagement in the Land-Grant Humanities PhD — 113
Todd Butler, Tabitha Espina, and Richard Snyder

Graduate Students and Their Communities: The Obermann Institute — 133
Teresa Mangum and Jennifer New

Generative Collaboration and the Digital Humanities — 151
Will Fenton

Working Knowledge: Narrative Theory in the Real World — 165
Marcia Halstead James

Sustainability and the Posthumanities — 179
Alex Christie and Katie Dyson

Humanities in Action: Centering the Human in Public Humanities Work — 195
Veronica T. Watson and Laurie Zierer

Part Three: Joy and Well-Being — 213

Cultivating a Joyful Workplace through Trust, Support, and a Shared Mission — 219
Katina L. Rogers

The Agony and the Ecstasy of Literary Study at the Graduate Level — 233
Donald Moores

Finding Joy in the Graduate Internship — 245
John Lennon

Bodies of Knowledge: Toward an Embodied Humanistic Praxis — 259
Manoah Avram Finston

Humanities under Quarantine: A Reflection on Isolation and Connectivity in Graduate Education — 275
Yevgenya Strakovsky

Joy and the Politics of the Public Good — 291
Stacy M. Hartman and Bianca C. Williams

Radical Collegiality and Joy in Graduate Education 309
  *Paul W. Burch, Brooke Clark, Sonia Del Hierro,
  Meredith McCullough, Kelly McKisson, and S. J. Stout*

Notes on Contributors 327

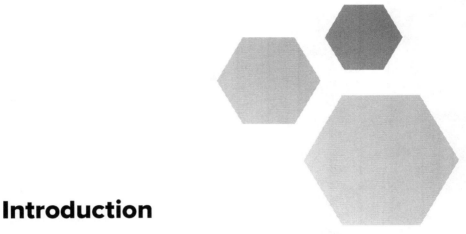

Introduction

Stacy M. Hartman and Yevgenya Strakovsky

The search for meaning is at the root of the humanities. It is their raison d'être. In a society that brushes the search for meaning aside, the humanities understandably struggle to thrive. But a renewed interest among society at large in finding meaning—in creating meaningful lives for ourselves—should renew broader interest in the humanities. This can happen if those of us who consider ourselves to be humanities scholars rise to meet the moment.

Concentric Crises and the Search for Meaning: The Humanities in the Time of COVID

In many ways, this volume is predicated upon a series of crises: the "crisis of the humanities," the crisis of the academic job market, and—most recently and most acutely—the global crisis brought on by the COVID-19 pandemic. The "crisis of the humanities"—a phrase we use advisedly and with significant reservations—does not have a definitive origin point, though Wayne Bivens-Tatum notes that the first use of the phrase in *JSTOR* dates back to 1922. Throughout the twentieth century, and into the first two decades of the twenty-first, there have been periodic resurgences of crisis rhetoric around the humanities, such that scholars have felt called to "defend" their disciplines. These earnest defenses of the humanities have revealed a defensiveness, or perhaps a nervous ambivalence, about what we do as humanities scholars and why we do it. Furthermore, the overwhelming rise of critical theory within the disciplines beginning in the 1980s rendered enjoyment and pleasure highly suspect, such that serious students needed to be disciplined away from such approaches. In a system of higher education in which undergraduates are likely to think of themselves more as consumers than as students, a path of study that has been stripped of enjoyment is an understandably hard sell.

The academic job market crisis that followed the 2008 global recession revealed deep fissures in the structure of graduate education. Graduate school in the humanities demands that students make sacrifices that are, first, unevenly distributed across boundaries of race, gender, class, health, and family status; second, not always conducive to producing high-quality intellectual work; third, not reasonable to expect in most professions; and, finally, only ever partially acknowledged by the profession itself. This model was easier for many to accept during the brief postwar period when there was a nearly a one-to-one ratio of academic jobs to graduates, but half a century later, in the context of far fewer jobs and far more graduates,[1] it can only be described, in Lauren Berlant's terms, as cruelly optimistic.

What, then, has the COVID-19 pandemic revealed? It is impossible now to think about a volume dedicated to graduate education in the humanities without also thinking about the ways in which COVID-19 has disrupted the landscape—not just of graduate education or higher education but also of the world around us. The pandemic has revealed the fragile scaffolding that held together our social infrastructure and has given rise to a wave of reflection about what is meaningful, what we create and cocreate as human beings, and what is worth preserving if we have a choice. It has revealed that many of us were not living lives we enjoyed before the pandemic—that we had commutes, jobs, and social lives that were draining us. It has revealed that the lifestyle of infinite ambition, aspiration, and acquisition that capitalism demands of us is, when we are confronted with our own mortality and death on a mass scale, devoid of meaning. It has revealed the importance of the humanities more powerfully than several decades of debate. In the midst of a multilateral societal reckoning, the demands of this moment—namely, the ability to see from the perspectives of others, the ability to critically analyze texts of all kinds and engage in productive modes of critique, the ability to engage in ethical reasoning and moral decision-making, and the ability to pause and sit inside ambiguity—are decidedly humanistic.

But the moment also demands bravery and a bold, affirmative vision for the future. This is where the academic humanities—embedded within overly cautious institutions and more accustomed to criticizing than to creating—have sometimes fallen short. This volume therefore aims to put into practice a language of affirmation through which the humanities can be reimagined. This hermeneutics of thriving, we hope, will also allow us as humanists to imagine the kind of world we would like to inhabit.

The essays in this volume speak to a broad conversation about how to imagine a graduate education that is driven by thinking rooted in abundance rather than scarcity; by collaboration rather than competition; by a commitment to others, both inside and outside the university; and by a belief in the collective ability to create change. This reimagining is reflected in the three key concepts that guide the volume: engaged curriculum, civic engagement, and joy and well-being. These essays envision humanities scholarship as an engaged and joyful endeavor that rises to meet the challenges of what—judging by the first two decades—may prove to be a very long twenty-first century.

Responding to the Academic Job Market Crisis: The Career Diversity Turn

Before we can begin to tackle the crises of today, we must revisit the crises of a dozen years ago. In 2010, the editors of this volume were both newly minted graduate students in German studies at Stanford University. The consequences of the 2008 crash were visible, haunting our libraries with the shadows of advanced graduate students who should have finished their degrees and embarked on their careers. Instead, they were lingering in the halls, taking on part-time teaching appointments, research assistantships, and postdoctoral fellowships. They were the lucky ones; Stanford is a well-funded, private university that had the resources and bureaucratic flexibility to keep them on while they waited for the academic market to recover.

And so they waited. And waited.

By the time we were curating our job market materials five years later, even Stanford was not in a position to offer this safety net anymore. The academic job market had crashed before, but it had always at least partially recovered. This time was different. Subsequent editions of the Modern Language Association (MLA)'s *Job List* show how steeply the numbers of jobs in these fields have declined since the 2008 recession.

The most recent report available as of this writing is from 2018–19, in which only 839 jobs in English and 751 jobs in modern languages were posted to the MLA's *Job List* (Lusin 1). These numbers represent an increase of 1.3% in the number of jobs posted in English over the previous academic year—the first increase in over half a decade—while other language and literature fields experienced their seventh straight year of decline. Both numbers are at or near the lowest number of jobs posted since the MLA began issuing its report in 1975 and represent a roughly 55% drop since 2007–08, the last year before the recession (1).

It wasn't yet possible in 2010 to know that jobs would continue to decline so precipitously, but it was possible to see the advanced doctoral students and recent graduates at departmental events and to realize that their lack of prospects would be a serious problem for some time to come. To the credit of our department's faculty, we began having a conversation about the issue through various forums. One of the most important for both of us was the Humanities Education Focal Group (HEFG), which Jenny (Yevgenya) supported as graduate coordinator for several years under the directorships of Russell Berman and Lisa Surwillo. Hosting speakers on the state of humanities education, HEFG offered an early space to discuss some of the difficult truths facing the profession: the lack of meaningful public engagement, the inequities in access to both graduate education itself and stable employment thereafter, and the pedagogical practices that might be holding us back from addressing these challenges. These discussions were an early example of the kind of proactive para-curriculum that we advocate for in this volume. Indeed, some of the contributors to this volume—namely, Katina Rogers and Sidonie Smith—were once guests of HEFG.

These events also made it increasingly clear that awareness and discussion were not enough. We needed alternative models of professional pathways for humanists. In our third year, Stacy began an internship at the Office of the Vice Provost for Graduate Education, working with Chris M. Golde in an early and decidedly ad hoc version of what has now become a somewhat established practice of administrative internships in some doctoral programs. In this volume, John Lennon's "The Joy of the Graduate Internship" and Jenna Lay and Emily Shreve's "Collaborative Ethics: Practicing Engagement in Our Academic Communities" both address such internships.

In discussions with then associate vice provost Golde, Stacy realized she was not alone in wanting more information about careers beyond the professoriate and, moreover, that there were people with PhDs in nearly every office on campus. Over the fall quarter of her third year,

Stacy conducted interviews with thirty such PhDs, and from those interviews the Alt-Ac Speaker Series was born. Although "alt-ac" as a term is now falling out of favor, and we prefer to think of "career pathways," at the time, defining one of those pathways as "alternative academic," as opposed to "nonacademic," was a necessary first step. The series brought together panels of staff members with PhDs for lunchtime talks, providing a forum for them to speak openly about their experiences and articulating a metaphorical map of where PhDs were concentrated in administrative positions at Stanford.

The alt-ac conversation at Stanford was part of a larger discourse that was emerging nationally at the time. Although discussion of "alternative" careers for PhDs had been percolating intermittently since at least 1980,[2] Anthony T. Grafton and Jim Grossman's landmark 2011 op-ed, "No More Plan B," is often cited as having kicked off the most recent and perhaps most enduring iteration of what we in this volume refer to as the *career diversity turn*, or the legitimization of expanded and diverse career pathways for humanities PhDs. "No More Plan B" addressed the field of history, but the conversation quickly grew. That same year, the Andrew W. Mellon Foundation and the American Council of Learned Societies (ACLS) announced the first round of the Mellon/ACLS Public Fellows Competition, a postdoctoral fellowship specifically designed to place humanities PhDs in high-impact roles at nonprofits, NGOs, and other nonacademic organizations. In 2013, the Mellon Foundation funded Humanities without Walls, a consortium of Midwestern universities focused on humanistic approaches to grand challenges and on expanding career pathways for PhDs.

As this network of initiatives and projects expanded, it created a vibrant community of practice—faculty members, students, administrators, and practitioners connected by an evolving conversation about the purpose of doctoral education, the relationship of higher education to the broader public, and the role of the humanities in an increasingly STEM-driven world. This volume includes many members of this community. Teresa Mangum and Jennifer New, for example, have been doing the work of doctoral education transformation at the Obermann Center for the Humanities at the University of Iowa since 2006. Sidonie Smith, a past president of the MLA, published her *Manifesto for the Humanities*, which called for increasing flexibility in the dissertation and deeper training in scholarly communication, in 2016. Jenna Lay, professor of English at Lehigh University, implemented increased support for job seekers, intensive tracking of alumni, and an administrative internship program for doctoral students. Todd Butler, an English professor and dean at Washington

State University, created a program to encourage students to engage with members of the rural communities that surround their campus. Lay's and Butler's projects were both supported by the National Endowment for the Humanities (NEH)'s NextGen Challenge Grants (2016–18)—a short-lived but crucial program that jump-started the conversation at many institutions.

In our own field of literature, the conversation intensified in 2014, when the MLA's Task Force on Doctoral Study in Modern Language and Literature, chaired by our mutual adviser Russell Berman, issued a report. In this report, the members of the task force—all faculty members, albeit from a diversity of institutions—made two recommendations that were explicitly related to the issue of careers beyond the professoriate: first, that doctoral programs should "expand professionalization opportunities" for doctoral students, and second, that they should "validate diverse career outcomes" ("Report" 16, 18). A third recommendation, that programs "use the whole university community," was less explicit in its prescriptions but no less important (17). This recommendation resonated with the campus-wide approach that Stacy's Alt-Ac Speaker Series had taken not long before.

This report provided the basis for the MLA's Mellon-funded Connected Academics program, which began in 2015, with Stacy as project manager, and focused on careers for language and literature PhDs. Along with partnership programs at Georgetown, Arizona State, and the University of California Humanities Research Institute, Connected Academics sponsored a proseminar in the New York City area that brought together students from ten regional universities. Several years out, proseminar alumni have embarked and are embarking on a variety of exciting careers, both within and beyond the university. Proseminar alumni are currently working for universities in both faculty and administrative roles, as well as in cyber security; diversity, equity, and inclusion consulting; documentary film production; educational technology; government organizations (including the NEH); and much more.

Connected Academics and its sibling grant, Career Diversity, at the American Historical Association, were both very much focused on career pathways. However, a new wave of grants from the Mellon Foundation since 2018 or so, including a grant to the Obermann Center at the University of Iowa for the creation of an interdisciplinary doctoral program called Humanities for the Public Good and a grant to the Graduate Center, City University of New York (CUNY), called Transforming Doctoral Education for the Public Good, suggests a new emphasis. Although these grants are interested in helping students create viable career pathways, they are more focused on changing the purpose and structure of doctoral education—and even higher education more broadly—to make these more publicly engaged.

This is not simply a change in rhetoric but a change in philosophy. The new emphasis on "the public good" both acknowledges the ways in which academic disciplines, especially in the humanities, have insulated themselves from the wider world and identifies a unique contribution that our field can make beyond academia. A publicly engaged doctoral student is, by definition, a doctoral student who understands the impact of their work and can communicate its relevance. A publicly engaged doctoral student is better prepared for a career outside the academy but is also better prepared for a different kind of career *inside* the academy.

That necessity is the mother of invention is a cliché but is also, in this case, true. Had the academic job market not crashed, it is possible that neither of us would be where we are today: Stacy, first at the Graduate Center, CUNY, directing the Mellon-funded PublicsLab and fostering public-facing work in the next generation of PhDs, now a freelance scholar and consultant focusing on graduate education transformation; Jenny, first at the Georgia Institute of Technology in a hybrid role as the designer and associate director of two new professionally focused master's degrees in applied language and media studies, now at the Fletcher School, Tufts University, designing executive education programs in interdisciplinary global affairs. When we first entered our programs in 2010, neither of us had the ability to imagine these positions or what humanistic work outside the tenure track could look like. However, we both recognized the limits of our imagined futures at the time. Our recognition of an as-yet-unformed broader horizon pushed us to think differently about our own careers and our identities as humanities scholars, writers, teachers, and professionals. The careers we have had since—which are themselves still only in their early stages—have pushed us to think deeply about the purpose and value of our training and to redefine the ecosystem in which we view our work.

The Affirmative Humanities in Yet Another Crisis

The 2008 recession had far-reaching consequences, and the aftershocks are still being felt over a decade later. However, when historians look back, they will likely conclude that that event pales in comparison to the crisis of COVID-19, the effects of which will shape all our lives for decades to come. Some of those changes will be obvious: more people are likely to wear masks on public transit, to stay home (if they can afford to) when they're sick, and to work from home at least a few days a week. Other changes are less obvious but perhaps more profound. Among them are the sudden fissures that have erupted in the relationships between individuals and their institutions.

Lindsey Ellis, writing for *The Chronicle of Higher Education*, called it "The Great Disillusionment": "College employees are . . . re-evaluating how work fits into their lives — a striking development for a field that thinks of itself as a calling and has long been seen as a stable employer with solid benefits." Although Ellis does not go so far as to identify a lack of trust between individuals and their institutions as the issue at hand, it is clear that the inability—or unwillingness—of institutions of higher education to treat their employees with dignity, to respect their time and outside responsibilities, and to reward them in tangible ways has a great deal to do with the decision many are making to leave the field. Ellis identifies student affairs and other student-facing positions as being particularly at risk, since they tend to be low-paid positions that demand high levels of care. Many of those positions are more arduous now, Ellis notes, and students are returning to campus more anxious and depressed and less motivated than before the pandemic. Similarly, although many faculty members are eager to return to in-person instruction, the less-than-ideal circumstances under which they're doing so have caused many to ask whether it is truly worth the risk.

Although this is not a problem specific to the humanities, the fissures that have erupted between the institutions in which the humanities are embedded and nurtured and the people who work there are critical to thinking about the future of graduate education—not least because many humanities PhDs start their careers in teaching or administrative roles at universities. In short, no matter how much we may love our institutions, our institutions cannot love us back, nor can they always care for us in the ways we want and need.

COVID has also shown us the difference between doing the work of the humanities and upholding humanities institutions. It has become increasingly clear how often the two are conflated, particularly in moments of crisis. The crisis of the humanities—which was and is largely a crisis of the academic humanities—precipitated calls for saving humanities departments and preserving institutional spaces. But these are not the only spaces where the humanities exist. There is a much broader humanities ecosystem beyond academia, in which people continue to do the work of the humanities, often unacknowledged by academic humanists or even derided as "not really humanities." And it is those parts of the humanities ecosystem that are poised to help people deal with a crisis of meaning on the scale of this pandemic, perhaps far better than the academic humanities currently are. If we in the academic humanities want to be a part of that conversation, we must think beyond the preservation of our institutions. Moreover, we must be willing to be transformed by that work—and to allow our disciplines to also be transformed in service of making it possible. For those of us who are accustomed to operating within a single framework, this transformation can be uncomfortable but is also liberating.

One of the impediments to our field's engagement with the search for meaning is the academic humanities' culture of skepticism. The rhetoric of crisis and critique that has dominated the discourse on humanities-as-vocation reflects a broader tendency in the humanities of the latter half of the twentieth century. As a number of critics, including Rita Felski, Eve Sedgwick, and Bruno Latour, have argued, the academic humanities emerged from the last century with a powerful ethos of skepticism and critique but with few tools to articulate affirmation, purpose, and well-being. Felski points to Ricoeur's hermeneutics of suspicion as a style of reading that came to dominate humanistic research after the era of the world wars. In this framework, a literary critic's "self-appointed task is to draw out where a text fails—or willfully refuses—to see" (Felski 1). As a legacy of the Deconstruction era, the hermeneutics of suspicion is a "a style of interpretation that is driven by a spirit of disenchantment" that, according to Felski, pervades in our academic culture "across differences of field and discipline" (2). Indeed, grad students in a seminar are often asked to use terms like *fault lines*, *limitations*, and *breaking points* to describe an argument, emphasizing the failures and limitations of humanistic work. The hermeneutic of suspicion and their emotional effects on the overall field of literary studies are elaborated in Donald Moores's essay in this volume, "The Agony and the Ecstasy of Literary Study at the Graduate Level."

To be sure, a critical deconstructive stance has been an essential tool for dismantling hierarchies and recognizing the consequences of unconscious bias, privilege, and hegemony. Ethnic studies, gender studies, and queer studies have often given people—especially young people—language for describing themselves and their circumstances and for pushing back against oppressive social forces. Even the backlash against critical race theory that emerged on the far right in the summer of 2021 is itself a testament to the social impact of humanities research over the last half-century. We do not mean to undermine the importance of critique, both in the academic humanities and beyond, for envisioning a more just future. On the contrary, those of us who are engaged in this work must acknowledge and honor the work of Black feminist scholars and activists who have demonstrated the importance of pairing critique with vision. Scholars and activists such as bell hooks, Ruth Wilson Gilmore, Saidiya Hartman, Patricia Hill Collins, and Angela Davis, in their work on education, prison abolition, or the overlap between the two, employ rigorous critique in creating a radical re-envisioning of institutions and our relationship to them that is not only equitable but liberatory. However, the work of Black feminist scholars has often not been honored by the academy. Among many possible examples, the case of Lorgia García Peña's 2019 tenure denial at Harvard stands out for having burst into the mainstream. In the *New Yorker* article about García Peña's case, Graciela Mochkofsky writes, "Harvard does not disclose the reasons for its tenure decisions, but a few faculty members had expressed reservations about García Peña's work—most notably, that it was activism rather than scholarship, a criticism that is often levelled against scholars of ethnic studies." The assumption that activism is not and cannot be scholarly—that scholarship and activism in fact exist at opposite poles—remains pervasive, and it may account for the fact that in many graduate programs at predominantly white institutions, critique is not coupled with a radical sense of possibility or vision but rather with skepticism. Skepticism trains students in the essential ability to see a concept from all sides and entertain multiple points of view, but it also risks creating a culture of disenchantment and disassembly that perpetuates and empties out its own reality.

The humanities are not unique in their struggle to replant the razed fields of meaning left by the twentieth century's posttraumatic skepticism. The social sciences and natural sciences are also experiencing a paradigm shift that yearns for the restoration of affirmative meaning to our work. As Martin Seligman noted in his president's address to the American Psychological Association back in 1999, the field of psychology, like the humanities, spent the latter half of the twentieth century "healing damage" and learning "how people survive and endure under conditions of adversity" (560). This has yielded tremendous progress in the treatment of pathology, "[y]et we have scant knowledge of what makes life worth living" (560). Some progress has been made in this area in the last twenty years; scholars of well-being like Brené Brown and Arthur Brooks have become widely known in the public sphere, and their work on vulnerability and happiness is regularly featured in mainstream media.[3] Now, the humanities find themselves at a similar crossroads. Alongside the sharp eye of critique, we must imagine the humanistic tools of reconstruction, affirmation, and sustenance that can pierce the emptiness.

As academics and as humanists, we are faced with the task that follows *after* recognition—that messy, precarious challenge of imagining and creating a better future. We call upon our profession to not stop at clearing the rubble of human society's failures but also to take the risk of building meaning and value within that society. In this volume, we would like to propose an affirmative humanities—an approach to humanistic work that has the capacity to build. We take it as a given that a humanistic education has value beyond our disciplines and institutions and that professionals with humanistic training can—and already do—contribute significantly to all sectors of society and industry. But what would a hermeneutics of affirmation look like in the context of graduate education? What are the intellectual projects and pedagogical structures of an affirmative humanities? And what would the relationship of our institutions be to these projects?

To that end, this volume takes as its premise that the humanities do not exist solely in the academic space at all and that academia is rather one component of a much broader and highly dynamic ecosystem. The "humanities sector" or "humanities ecosystem," as it is sometimes called, comprises all the many places in which humanistic work gets done. Academic humanities departments operate in a space that includes museums and archives, public and academic libraries, humanities centers, public humanities councils, humanities-focused foundations, scholarly associations, cultural nonprofits, and K–12 education. Our ecosystem also includes think tanks, policy institutes, and for-profit companies in communications, media, consulting, cultural programming, and organizational change management. The humanities ecosystem imagines the humanities in the broadest sense, both as a set of questions or interests having to do with human relationships, language, and culture and as a set of tools that include qualitative methodologies, textual analysis, and historical and cultural contextualization.

One of the key contributions of this volume is that we embrace the full scope of the humanities ecosystem, and the majority of the essays in this volume describe work that engages in some form of dialogue with this sector. Understanding of and strong engagement with the humanities ecosystem are crucial for sustaining and reimagining our future. A lack of familiarity with the full scope of the humanities sector leads both faculty members and students to underestimate their professional worth and the myriad ways in which they can contribute to society, find meaningful work, and create value. It compounds the sense—pervasive in academia and, as we hope to show, counterproductive—of the humanities as a whole being in crisis. It elides the fact that humanities knowledge production and knowledge transmission (otherwise known as research and teaching) happen in a multitude of places, many of which are sites not of crisis but of thriving. And it obscures the opportunities that exist—especially now, when so many of us are searching for meaning and attempting to make sense of our lives—for expanding that ecosystem and carving out new spaces for ourselves and for others.

Expanding the Humanities Ecosystem: *Zora's Daughters* and Edge Effect

To illustrate what this might look like, we reached out to several current graduate students who are engaged in expanding the greater humanities ecosystem in ways that we find innovative and exciting. They are examples of what we might think of as humanities entrepreneurship: new ventures that are rooted in humanistic values and ways of thinking.[4]

Zora's Daughters

Alyssa A. L. James and Brendane Tynes, doctoral students in anthropology at Columbia University, created the *Zora's Daughters* podcast in 2020. Tynes and James describe the project as "a society and culture podcast that uses Black feminist anthropology to think about race, politics, and popular culture" ("About"). They consider the podcast to be "an unapologetic contribution to the movement for Black liberation" and hope that their listeners, "from many walks of life . . . will feel inspired to bring Black feminist principles to their families, friends, workplaces—wherever they gather" (E-mail interview). In its third season as of 2023, *Zora's Daughters* remains firmly rooted in the discipline of anthropology, as James and Tynes use their platform to amplify the work of Black feminist anthropologists in their ICONversations, discuss current events such as the death of Queen Elizabeth ("Death") and the fall of *Roe v. Wade* ("Looting"), provide support to fellow graduate students of color ("Notes" and "It's Not You"), and continue to lift up the contributions of Zora Neale Hurston, specifically in anthropology ("Practicing" and "We Call Her Zora").

The origins of the project lie with the little-known fact that Hurston herself was once a graduate student in anthropology at Columbia. It was that connection to Hurston, and its omission from most discussions of her biography, that prompted James to come up with the idea for the podcast in 2020. "As Black women graduate students at Columbia," James and Tynes write, "we see [Zora] as our forebear; we follow in her footsteps. We are 'daughters' of Zora. Alyssa created the name and the concept of the podcast by building on her skill in producing scholarship that centered her communities and communicat[ed] knowledge in relatable ways" (E-mail interview).

Centering communities, producing and communicating knowledge in ways that are accessible, reviving forgotten narratives and histories, and bringing people into conversations from which they have traditionally been excluded are all ideas central to the project of *Zora's Daughters*—and to how James and Tynes see the humanities at work in that project. In an e-mail conversation about the podcast, its creators emphasized that "[h]umanities scholarship traditionally invokes a universal definition of the 'human' that excludes Black women, Black queer and trans people, Black children, and others." In contrast, *Zora's Daughters* "critiques this universal understanding and brings forth viewpoints that are erased. We highlight Black women's, Black queer and trans people's agency, our right to determine our own meaning and to shaping our own lives." This work is a clear example of the sort of envisioning that Black feminist scholars have been doing for many years and that the academy has persistently undervalued (when it has recognized it at all).

Indeed, James and Tynes are clear that this project not only exists beyond the scope of their institution but also resists the culture of hierarchy, prestige, and exclusion that is endemic to the academic humanities (particularly at elite institutions like Columbia). They seek to "break apart parochial understandings of 'human' and challenge hierarchies of knowledge" while at the same time "bring[ing] those who are often excluded from scholarly conversations—despite being the subjects of those studies—into them by making that knowledge accessible." Furthermore, they say, "*Zora's Daughters* is a space where we assert and affirm that we are the authors and theorists of our own lives, regardless of whether we are authorized by the academy" (E-mail interview). In other words, the *Zora's Daughters* podcast seeks to repair the violence that has been perpetrated by the university itself, and in so doing, imagine better and more just possibilities for its creators, their peers, the academy, and the world.

Edge Effect

Jessica Applebaum and Nicolas Benacerraf are graduate students in theater and performance studies at the Graduate Center, CUNY, and fellows with the PublicsLab. They describe their organization, Edge Effect (edgeeffectmedia.org), as "a think-and-do tank that designs hybrid performances, across media, for the public good." Repurposing methods from theater practice, Edge Effect brings together "performers, designers, scholars, scientists, journalists, activists, technologists, funders, and organizers in the creation of works that resist and demystify the mechanisms of mass persuasion in contemporary corporate culture" (Applebaum and Benacerraf). What the resulting work looks like varies wildly, as it is responsive to the collaborators and communities involved. Applebaum and Benacerraf say that the possibilities include "live performances, online videos, psychosocial experiments, hoax storefronts, immersive installations, theatrical lectures, and white papers—all designed to live at the intersection of analysis, enigma, spectacle, and delight."

The origin story of Edge Effect goes back to 2013, when Benacerraf and Applebaum served together on the organizing committee of the Brooklyn Commune, an artist-driven and -directed study of the economic landscape of the performing arts in the United States. In 2014, they collaborated with other artists in producing *Happiness Machine*, "a mock storefront in midtown Manhattan that played mischievously with the family imagery that gets slapped onto all sorts of products during the holiday season." Applebaum and Benacerraf write:

> [*Happiness Machine*] was our first effort to play with the materiality of Public Relations as a covert genre of persuasive performance, which hides its underlying logic from the public(s) whose behavior it wishes to alter. Not only did our immersive storefront give people an uncanny experience of encountering an overload of Christmas imagery at the wrong time of year, but it became a place for community gathering—a truly *public* space for individuals to take refuge with no expectation of commercial exchange.

Happiness Machine opened the door to a number of subsequent collaborations and eventually led to Edge Effect, a project Applebaum and Benacerraf, who understand public relations (PR) as an industry "dedicated to widening existing power imbalances," describe as a "transdisciplinary critique of PR power." Indeed, the work of Edge Effect is predicated upon a complex analysis of power, both present-day and historical, and that analysis drives the principles of the work and of the organization.

The humanities are alive and well not only in the content of the work that Applebaum, Benacerraf, and their collaborators (who include other graduate students) have done but also in how they do it. They have built the organization slowly, in a way they hope will allow for its lasting sustainability. At its heart is a spirit of radical collaboration between and among people from many different disciplines. The name Edge Effect refers to unique natural phenomena that occur when ecosystems touch at their very edges. They have a practice of "gatherings," the first of which took place in November 2020, to bring new people into the community—what they call "collective onboarding"—while at the same time creating space to imagine collectively the future of their work together.

There is something decidedly utopian but far from naive about Edge Effect. Its founders hope "to intentionally rebuild culture, piece by piece, around the *human scale*" so as to create a system that "would give us all more time and resources for our collective nourishment" (Applebaum and Benacerraf). This is an enormous undertaking, but it is also very much in line with the situation described earlier in this introduction: the feeling that a culture of infinite aspiration, ambition, and acquisition (perpetuated, in Applebaum and Benacerraf's analysis, by PR culture) is failing us and has been for some time, leaving us drained of time and energy, isolated from those we love, and searching for meaning. Under these circumstances, an endeavor like Edge Effect seems especially timely. It demonstrates, furthermore, the ways in which the humanities could and should intervene in these conversations.

Edge Effect and *Zora's Daughters*, for all their differences, share particular attributes: they are collaborative, publicly engaged, and ambitious about effecting real change in the world. Unfortunately, the academy still does not always know what to do with projects like these. Applebaum and Benacerraf are quick to note that they have felt supported by their own program through independent studies, mentoring, and an openness to connecting research and practice. However, this remains the exception rather than the rule. Graduate students, especially in places like New York City, have always had side gigs, often in direct contravention of university policies about how much they should work while receiving a stipend from the university.[5] In the past, there has been more or less a policy of "don't ask, don't tell" around these side gigs, which has the consequence that many departments simply don't know what their graduate students are doing. They don't know that a student is doing translation and cross-cultural consulting for Netflix, for example, or that several students have come together to found a bilingual publishing company. They don't know that someone has started a nonprofit or a really stellar podcast or a *YouTube* channel based on their research.

On the one hand, this ignorance is preventive. No one wants the oppressive apparatus of the university to come down on moonlighting graduate students who are trying to make ends meet. On the other hand, none of the examples we just gave—all of which are pulled from real life—can really be reduced to "moonlighting." They are substantive intellectual projects that push at the boundaries of the humanities ecosystem and create new and fascinating possibilities for being a scholar in the world. Ignoring the work being done beyond the borders of the university by the next generation of scholars creates the illusion that that work doesn't exist. It makes it appear as though the humanities live and die with the university, when in fact that is not and has never been the case. Rather, the humanities challenge the policies, hierarchies, and economies of the university itself—and that might, in fact, be the true crux of the issue. Institutions have their own agendas, methods of self-protection, and ways of working in their own best interests. Those of us who are, for better or worse, institutionalists are ethically bound to confront the ways in which the interests of the institution and the interests of the people in them are not always one and the same. COVID has highlighted this more starkly than any other recent crisis.

This volume is about humanities graduate education. The humanities writ large, we are increasingly convinced, are not in crisis. Graduate education, however, is another story—a turbulent and unfinished story. The future of graduate studies in the humanities is still being written, and we are at an inflection point. This volume attempts to document that inflection point—to capture a system in flux and to share some of the innovations and reflections that have already taken place—while pointing toward a thriving future.

The Future of Graduate Education in the Humanities

This volume is not simply a response to the pragmatic need for new employment opportunities and broader professional pathways for those with humanities training. This volume offers an intellectual framework for thinking about graduate education in the humanities differently. We hope it provides you with the inspiration and resources you need, wherever you are in your career and in relation to the humanities ecosystem, to think about your work as a humanist in new ways. We have chosen to curate the collected essays in three sections that speak to what we believe are the pillars of affirmative graduate education in the humanities moving forward: an engaged curriculum that asks the hard questions and meets students where they are, a commitment to civic engagement and the power of the humanities to do good in the world, and a foundation of joy and well-being, the connective tissue of a meaningful life.

We believe we are in a transitional moment in graduate education that renders this volume of necessity incomplete. The essay by Marcia James, which explores the importance of humanities training far afield from academia, pushes the boundaries of the humanities ecosystem as we hope to see many more humanists do in the future. There is also much more to be said about how we might center social and racial justice in both graduate education and in our discussion of "the public good." The humanities ecosystem, broadly construed, should be deeply concerned with issues of equity and willing to turn its critical lens back on itself. In this volume, Todd Butler, Tabitha Espina, and Richard Snyder explore the challenges of a land grant institution, with all its history of colonialist expansion, in forging a reciprocal connection with the local Indigenous community, while Stacy Hartman and Bianca Williams consider the importance of joy and well-being for racial equity in graduate programs. Similarly, Will Fenton's essay provides an example of how to use humanities scholarship to challenge and rewrite hegemonic narratives, in this case in collaboration with Indigenous communities. Beyond the ways in which this volume's essays address issues of race and equity in graduate education, we hope and expect to see racial equity and social justice truly centered in current and future discussions about how to holistically transform graduate education.

Graduate students are often well ahead of their programs in advocating for such transformations. There are generational tensions in departments, manifesting in arguments over departmental core courses, reading lists, and dissertation formats and topics. Faculty members can see how far a field has come, while graduate students often see how far there still is to go. But the importance of the current generation of graduate students in manifesting a more just and equitable future for the humanities is visible in the essays in this volume that are contributed by such students. In particular, the concluding essay, "Radical Collegiality and Joy in Graduate Education," coauthored by six Rice University graduate students, articulates both the promise and the challenge of a new kind of graduate education—one that is collaborative and joyful, in which many kinds of people can succeed, and where many types of success are possible and celebrated. This type of graduate education reaches beyond the bounds of the department or the institution and contributes to a better society. It is a version of graduate education that represents a distinct shift into a new moment: a turn away from thinking about the PhD as an individual, private journey and toward an exploration of how we—meaning the broadest possible scholarly community within the humanities ecosystem—might contribute to an affirmative vision of the future in which many more of us can thrive and flourish.

The hypothetical university the six coauthors devised, "Ecalpon U" (which includes the words "no place" spelled backward), also reminds those of us who are engaged in graduate education as faculty members and administrators that the gravity of creating a better world does not lie solely in our students' promise of creative reimaginings and future goals. It also lies with us and our practices right now. What are we doing to create a "place" for them? What do we owe to the next generation of professional humanists? How do we hold ourselves accountable to them? We have serious and pressing responsibilities to those who are, right now, entrusting us with their lives and their futures as well as their education. We also have the tools and knowledge to do right by them.

Let's begin.

NOTES

1. David Laurence, writing for the Modern Language Association (MLA)'s office of research, noted in 2017 that even as the number of academic jobs in modern languages continued to drop, the number of PhDs earned continued to grow.

2. The "glut" of humanities PhDs and their nonacademic job prospects was the subject of a *New York Times* piece as long ago as 31 December 1980, during an MLA Annual Convention in New York City. The article, written by William K. Stevens, cites "a shift in the relationship of humanities scholars to the rest of society, and in many of the scholars' perceptions of their own roles." This shift was and remains incomplete.

3. Brené Brown is a scholar of empathy and courage at the University of Texas in Houston; her TED Talk on vulnerability and bravery is now a Netflix special and shaped the mainstream discourse on empathy in 2020. Arthur Brooks, of Harvard University, produces numerous podcasts and columns on "how to build a happy life" and is widely recognized as a public expert on happiness.

4. We are aware that some of our readers will consider "humanities entrepreneurship" a contradiction in terms. Having earned our degrees at Stanford, we understand the ways in which "entrepreneurship" as a concept has been co-opted by Silicon Valley, but that version of entrepreneurship need not be the only one. Entrepreneurship can mean simply creating something that hasn't previously existed or carving out spaces for people who haven't traditionally had spaces provided for them. We hope that our readers will sit with their initial reactions to putting "humanities" and "entrepreneurship" side by side and consider whether the friction that exists between the two concepts might be a generative one.

5. These policies, which often tell graduate students that they are not allowed to work more than eight to ten hours per week, both infantilize students and ignore the economic reality they inhabit.

WORKS CITED

Applebaum, Jessica, and Nicolas Benacerraf. E-mail interview, conducted by Stacy M. Hartman, 10 Sept. 2021.

Berlant, Lauren. *Cruel Optimism*. Duke UP, 2011.

Bivens-Tatum, Wayne. "The 'Crisis' in the Humanities." *Academic Librarian: On Libraries, Rhetoric, Poetry, History, and Moral Philosophy*, 5 Nov. 2010, blogs.princeton.edu/librarian/2010/11/the_crisis_in_the_humanities/.

Ellis, Lindsay. "The Great Disillusionment: College Workers Are Burning Out Just When They'll Be Needed Most." *The Chronicle of Higher Education*, 25 Aug. 2021, chronicle.com/article/the-great-disillusionment.

Felski, Rita. *The Limits of Critique*. U of Chicago P, 2015.

Grafton, Anthony T., and Jim Grossman. "No More Plan B." *The Chronicle of Higher Education*, 9 Oct. 2011, chronicle.com/article/no-more-plan-b.

James, Alyssa A. L., and Brendane Tynes. "About." *Zora's Daughters Podcast*, Zora's Daughters, 2021, zorasdaughters.com/about/.

———."The Death of Sovereignty." *Zora's Daughters Podcast*, season 3, episode 2, 21 Sept. 2022, zorasdaughters.com/episodes/the-death-of-sovereignty/.

———. E-mail interview. Conducted by Stacy M. Hartman, 10 Sept. 2021.

———."It's Not You, It's Them: Tips for Academic Conferences." *Zora's Daughters Podcast*, season 3, episode 5, 9 Nov. 2022, zorasdaughters.com/episodes/academic-conferences/.

———."Looting the Womb: Black Birthing People and Reproductive Unfreedom." *Zora's Daughters Podcast*, season 3, episode 3, 5 Oct. 2022, zorasdaughters.com/episodes/looting-the-womb-black-birthing-people-and-reproductive-unfreedom/.

———."Notes on the Field." *Zora's Daughters Podcast*, season 2, episode 11, 2 Mar. 2022, zorasdaughters.com/episodes/notes-on-the-field/.

———."Practicing Zora." *Zora's Daughters Podcast*, season 2, episode 16, 25 May 2022, zorasdaughters.com/episodes/practicing-zora/.

———."We Call Her Zora." *Zora's Daughters Podcast*, season 3, episode 7, 7 Dec. 2022, zorasdaughters.com/episodes/we-call-her-zora/.

Laurence, David. "The Upward Trend in Modern Language PhD Production: Findings from the 2015 Survey of Earned Doctorates." *The Trend: Research and Analysis from the MLA Office of Programs*, 6 Feb. 2017, mlaresearch.mla.hcommons.org/2017/02/06/the-upward-trend-in-modern-language-phd-production-findings-from-the-2015-survey-of-earned-doctorates.

Lusin, Natalia. *The MLA Job List, 2018–19*. Modern Language Association of America, Nov. 2020, www.mla.org/content/download/134145/2569649/Job%20List_2018-19_Linked.pdf.

Mochkofsky, Graciela. "Why Lorgia García Peña Was Denied Tenure at Harvard." *The New Yorker*, 27 July 2021, newyorker.com/news/annals-of-education/why-lorgia-garcia-pena-was-denied-tenure-at-harvard.

Report of the MLA Task Force on Doctoral Study in Modern Language and Literature. Modern Language Association of America, 2014, apps.mla.org/pdf/taskforcedocstudy2014.pdf.

Seligman, Martin. "The APA 1998 Annual Report: The President's Address." *American Psychologist*, vol. 54, no. 8, Aug. 1999, pp. 559–62.

Smith, Sidonie. *Manifesto for the Humanities: Transforming Doctoral Education in Good Enough Times*. U of Michigan P, 2016, https://doi.org/10.3998/dcbooks.13607059.0001.001.

Stevens, William K. "More Scholars Seeking Business Jobs." *The New York Times*, 31 Dec. 1980, nytimes.com/1980/12/31/archives/more-scholars-seeking-business-jobs-evidence-6000-scholars-the.html.

PART ONE

Engaged Curriculum

Introduction

Curriculum is the beating heart of graduate education. It is how a discipline collectively determines what is critical and what is not; it is how departments and programs decide what knowledge should be passed from one generation of scholars to the next, what "counts" within the discipline and what does not. It is a way of curating a vast body of knowledge for those who are new to it and, simultaneously, acculturating new members into the values, norms, and practices of the discipline. It is a process of disciplining and discipline, of inclusion and exclusion.

Because the curriculum is so central to the disciplines, we have chosen to examine it in the first part of this volume. Achieving consensus about curricular changes can be very difficult, and it can feel easier to revert to the disciplinary norms with which we are comfortable. Changing the content of a first-year core course, adding an internship course for credit, moving from a written model of examination to a portfolio model, keeping or altering language requirements, and allowing for digital or publicly engaged dissertations are all issues of curriculum about which members of the same department can feel both very strongly and very differently. And yet, if we hope to change the graduate school experience in ways that are lasting rather than ephemeral, those changes must take place within the curriculum.

However, even a department that has achieved philosophical consensus will face subsequent roadblocks to changing its curriculum. Readers who have tried to institute a new course, new minor, or new degree program will likely attest that the most material barrier to curricular change is the program development process itself. Turning an idea into a program that actually runs is often a matter of defending the discipline to outside stakeholders in other fields, who come into the conversation with their own goals and interests. It also requires designing a concrete, temporal, interpersonal structure that effectively teaches the intended values and content. Lastly, it always requires labor—time and energy dedicated by faculty members, staff members, and often students—that may or may not be rewarded, depending on the culture of the institution. Thus, discussions of an engaged curriculum need to also include discussions of strategy, models, ethics, and approaches to navigating the systemic barriers that keep the status quo in place. We need to acknowledge the higher education ecosystem in which we operate and the tools and strategies required to be successful in that system.

For both philosophical and strategic reasons, we therefore think expansively in this volume about what constitutes "curriculum." When we define *curriculum* as the acculturation of students to the discipline, coursework is only part of the process. Acculturation also includes advising, exams, internship opportunities, para-curricular events, community formation, and the values and expectations placed on student work, such as the boundaries of a traditional dissertation or public-facing project. All of these experiences shape how a student views the discipline and themselves within it, and all of them can be tools for implementing high-impact change that shapes the future of the field.

The essays in part 1 examine the challenge of creating a curriculum that is engaged with the world beyond the department and discipline and, in many cases, beyond the institution itself. Such engagement requires a program to be nimble, responsive, and open in ways that may be uncomfortable at first; it almost certainly requires all members of the academic community to think in ways that are transdisciplinary and collaborative. But these changes are, as many of our contributors argue here, necessary for creating a doctoral education that meets twenty-first-century challenges.

Part 1 opens with an essay by a former president of the Modern Language Association, Sidonie Smith. In "A Twenty-First-Century Doctoral

Curriculum: Praxis, Scholarly Communication, and Capacity Building," Smith follows on from her well-known *Manifesto for the Humanities: Transforming Doctoral Education in the Humanities in Good Enough Times*. Drawing on several decades of experience in doctoral education, Smith suggests a three-pronged approach to sustainability: a "praxis-based co-curriculum"; better grounding in new and evolving forms of scholarly communication; and the deliberate and expansive development of what Smith calls "capacities" rather than skills. Smith outlines concrete examples of each of these three elements and argues that this approach offers the flexibility necessary for sustainable graduate education in "good enough times."

The following two essays explore curricular models that prepare students to enter a broadly conceived humanities ecosystem that includes nonprofits and the private sector. Jenna Lay and Emily Shreve outline an approach to preparing PhD students for such roles in "Collaborative Ethics: Practicing Engagement in Our Academic Communities," which advocates for an ethos of collaboration that encourages students to "engage more thoroughly and professionally with multiple publics" and cultivate a framework of "collaborative, reciprocal, and ethical" professionalism. Drawing on a short essay by Lauren Berlant that considers the academy's ambivalence toward the concept of "professionalism," Lay and Shreve argue for strengthening the "pedagogical/collegial ethics" Berlant proposes and initiating graduate students into a professional community that spans the university and university-adjacent ecosystem. Shreve and Lay describe Lehigh University's graduate assistantship program, which positions doctoral students in a range of administrative assistantships that replace the traditional teaching assistantship with experiential opportunities that prepare participants for a range of careers.

Anna Westerstahl Stenport and Richard Utz's contribution, "Reforming and Revalidating the Humanities Master's Degree at a STEM-Driven University," focuses on the potential of master's education to reinvent the humanities in a STEM-driven economy, describing two new professionally oriented terminal master of science degrees in humanities. STEM-focused institutions such as Georgia Tech, Stenport and Utz argue, often allow humanities faculty members greater latitude in pursuing novel program ideas, "extending applied engineering, maker space, internships, co-ops, and design-thinking approaches to academic programming in ways that encourage experimentation and entrepreneurship." The result is a "purpose-driven" graduate curriculum that not only sustains itself in a context that might at first glance seem unwelcoming but also helps students learn to thrive in a variety of professional situations.

Introduction to Part One

The final two essays in part 1 look at programs and initiatives that can be undertaken within many different institutional contexts. David Pettersen's "Purpose and Vocation: Rethinking the First-Year Graduate Proseminar" provides a fresh interpretation of a staple departmental offering. Indeed, the reimagining of the departmental proseminar that Pettersen outlines is a possible first step toward a more engaged curriculum in nearly any graduate program. Pettersen's first-year proseminar, offered through the University of Pittsburgh's English department, is focused not on foundational theoretical texts but rather on "the macro- and micro-level skills they will need to develop a plan for graduate study." Further, Pettersen argues, "The shape of graduate education in the humanities needs to be as much about helping students discover their own sense of vocation as it is about optimizing work habits." The course that Pettersen lays out in detail would be helpful for most any student but especially for those who may need extra assistance navigating the often unspoken requirements of a program or a discipline. In this way, it provides both an engaged approach to graduate education for individual students and an engaged way forward for programs that wish to nurture equity and a diverse student body. For a student account of the difference such a seminar can make, we direct you to the last essay in this volume: "Radical Collegiality and Joy in Graduate Education."

In "Experiential Learning and the Humanities PhD," Tiffany Potter and Elizabeth Hodgson examine the co-op structure as a potential framework for breaking open the PhD curriculum and reimagining the PhD as an experiential training ground. Potter and Hodgson describe the co-op program at the University of British Columbia, which allows PhD students to complete three cumulative terms of employment at "government, arts, community, and private-sector organizations" as an institutionally sanctioned part of their degree curriculum. The co-op structure takes the reasonable—and yet rare—next step of integrating career preparation for diverse pathways as a rigorous component of graduate study. Potter and Hodgson emphasize the importance of creating a robust pedagogical structure that centers career preparation and professional engagement within the academic structure of the degree itself.

A Twenty-First-Century Doctoral Curriculum: Praxis, Scholarly Communication, and Capacity Building

Sidonie Smith

For over a decade, I've been conversing with faculty members and graduate students about a twenty-first-century vision of graduate education in the humanities. Until the publication of *Manifesto for the Humanities: Transforming Doctoral Education in Good Enough Times* in 2015, my focus, buoyed by conviction that the times were good enough to impel and sustain changes large and small, centered primarily on introducing more flexibility in the kinds of dissertations doctoral students might pursue. Expanding the options for humanities dissertations necessarily prompted a series of conversations about what a dissertation is, what it does, how it unfolds, what forms it takes, to whom it is addressed, and what values it promotes.

Seven years later, our colleagues and institutions are reeling from the effects of intensified assaults on the academy in general and on humanities programs, theories, and fields particularly, as in the frenzied attempts by state legislatures to prohibit teaching of critical race studies in public schools. Even more daunting are the predictable and unpredictable challenges that faculties and institutions confront in the wake of the COVID pandemic. With its disruptions of recruitment, teaching, learning, research, and outreach practices, the pandemic and its aftermath will continue to affect the built environments, academic ecologies, technological infrastructures, redefined missions, sociopolitical dynamics, and financial exigencies at colleges and universities across all sectors and divisions. These pressures will affect the recruitment of undergraduate and graduate students; proportion of contingent faculty to tenured and tenure-track faculty; programmatic goals of equity, accessibility, and inclusion; pace of career trajectories through faculty ranks; concentrated and distributed technologies of teaching and learning; financial models for funding departments and programs; and degree of intrusion by state legislators in what is taught and how it is taught. In this new reality, it is harder for me to trust my conviction about the times being good enough.

Yet that, I believe, is all the more reason to grab and run with the mantra. A time of turmoil can also be a time during which unexpected opportunity, experimentation, motivation, and openness to imagine things otherwise can energize initiatives for rethinking what we teach, how we teach, and to what end we establish curricular designs and benchmarks for doctoral education in the humanities. The success, the sustainability, of the humanities inside and outside the academy will depend upon how humanities administrators and faculty members respond to the turmoil of the times as they pursue the goals of recruiting more heterogeneous cohorts into doctoral degree programs and preparing them to contribute to the critical work of humanistic endeavors in the academy and the larger workforce when they graduate. To that end, in what follows I supplement earlier work on reimagining the doctoral dissertation by proposing a three-pronged approach to achieving greater curricular and cocurricular excitement and efficacy: a purposeful praxis curriculum, a more engaged attention to emergent modes and media of scholarly communication, and a more inviting environment in which students can build heterogeneous capacities that will serve them in a multiplicity of career trajectories.

A fluid, elastic, and flexible praxis-based cocurriculum seeks to address the psychic and economic pressures of graduate student life: the struggles to understand what students need to know to succeed; what cultural capital they need to accumulate; and what more agentic narrative they might tell about their future as humanists inside and outside the academy. In other words, this concept contributes to the psychic, intellectual, and social well-being, the flourishing, of students for the duration of their studies, and provides students a means to find usable sustenance, a means to self-sustainability.

Engaging, guiding, and supporting doctoral students in gaining knowledge of the new ecology of scholarly communication in the humanities will help them gain competency in communicating to multiple audiences. Rarely discussed directly inside or outside the classroom, the ecology of scholarly communication includes many communication modes for professional humanists beyond the academy. It is critical to prepare doctoral students for the complexity of media, platforms, and distributed options for communicating and advancing recognition of their work to scholarly peers and to publics. This goal has the potential to satisfy the desire for access to audiences, for continued professional development, for advancement through tenure and promotion, and for successful adjustment to the demands of nonacademic careers.

Invoking the term *capacities* rather than *skills* puts a different spin on the value and importance of assembling a robust repertoire of expertises and experiences in the course of attaining a graduate degree. The purposeful attention to developing or honing diverse capacities can help sustain careers in the professoriate and open doors for those who aspire to humanities-inflected careers beyond the academy. Given the diminishing probability that PhDs in humanities fields will readily find tenure-track academic jobs when they complete their degrees, curricular and cocurricular attention to capacity building will serve students well as they imagine multiple career paths. Ultimately, the successful careers of humanists in and beyond the academy are the lived forms of testimony and advocacy for the work of the humanities in the world.

Graduate deans, departmentally based directors of graduate studies, faculty advisors, and graduate student organizations can pursue one or more of such curricular and cocurricular engagements through a broad range of initiatives, from the comprehensive to the finely targeted. They can build a series of initiatives on projects already in place within and across humanities departments in their institutions. They can benefit from the work being done elsewhere by an expanding network of major funders, faculty members, doctoral students, programs, institutions, and professional organizations, such as the Modern Language Association (MLA) and the American Historical Association, that are making changes large and small in how we educate future humanists in the next decades of the twenty-first century. Calls for such curricular and cocurricular engagements are in the air. My aim here is to give them focus and urgency.

The Praxis-Based Cocurriculum

There are many challenges to restructuring the graduate curriculum with attention to praxis: the precariousness of faculty buy-in, the need to move students expeditiously through coursework and on to their dissertation research and writing, the bureaucratic barriers to altering credit hours attached to certain kinds of professional praxis. There may even be confusion around the concept of the praxis curriculum altogether. Most graduate courses are commonly understood to focus on "content": on theory, field methodologies, deep reading, textual analytics, and historical contextualization. After all, that's what doctoral students come to campus to study: a field or set of intersecting fields. However, we also need to attend to the culture of doctoral study. A praxis curriculum examines our expectations for students, including the features and dispositions of the scholarly persona and identity, the cultural capital requisite to success, the ecology of humanities inquiry and of academic institutions, the opportunities to try out various kinds of inquiry and modes of communication, and the encouragement to think imaginatively about multiple kinds of careers. There are ways to build a praxis-oriented curriculum purposefully, on a micro level and, for the organized and ambitious, at the macro level.

What might praxis look like at the macro and micro levels? Let's start on the micro level with the ubiquity of the seminar paper in the humanities, with its expected length of twenty to thirty pages and its goal that students demonstrate their individual scholarly aptitude, sophistication, and elegance of style. This course expectation is undoubtedly critical to graduate education: doctoral students need to gain confidence and enhance their capacities to deliver excellent work in the short form as a prelude to writing dissertation introductions and chapters. This is standard, normative praxis training in content courses. But I would argue that students are disadvantaged if they are only asked to write the normative twenty- to thirty-page paper. Here I think of the students I have had the privilege to work with as a dissertation advisor or committee member. They can often produce a chapter of a dissertation focused on a deep reading of one or a few texts. But they struggle to define the purpose of the deep reading, the larger argument they are trying to make, and the limitations of their theoretical framing. They would benefit from familiarity with, and expertise in, other kinds and forms of thinking and composing and shaping intellectual work.

That's why in *Manifesto* I called for professors to rethink what they ask of students and to explain on their syllabi the reasons behind the requirements they have set. Certainly, colleagues in humanities departments set requirements that are not the standard humanities paper; here are alternatives gleaned from my own experiments and from colleagues around North America: collaboratively written essays; collectively produced glossaries of terms and concepts; grant applications addressed to a real grant program; deep reading journals; creative portfolios; detailed lectures for an undergraduate survey course. Seminars might be organized around a double-format analytical project, with submission of scholarly objects in traditional print form and in a multimedia platform such as *WordPress* or *Scalar*; a visual mapping project; a curation of texts and objects; a term-long blog edited into a publishable piece; an ensemble of short pieces, some directed to scholars, some to a more general audience; explorations in audiovisual storytelling; and even forays into algorithmic literacy.

In my own graduate theory courses I have long asked students to collaborate in writing a short-form theoretical essay of some twelve pages and to reflect upon the process, its frustrations, and its benefits. In one of the last genre courses I taught in autobiography studies, I told students they could choose any kind of final project. Several wrote standard essays, one submitted a graphic memoir, and still others created a complex map of theoretical concepts and moves for a field argument or an annotated syllabus for a field course. The benefit for me was a more pleasurable experience at the end of the course because the final projects exhibited such diversity; the benefit for students was that they could go in new directions with their intellectual interests and produce new knowledge for themselves out of alternative modes of writing about the subject of life narrative. A more capacious set of options for completing course requirements would better serve students as they move through the stages of the doctorate and contemplate heterogeneous kinds of dissertation projects, however configured.

Experiments in course design will be of particular importance to combining content and praxis goals in field courses. I had the opportunity in winter 2019 to spend several hours in a graduate seminar taught by my English department colleague Hadji Bakara on literature and the new migration studies. Bakara had conceptualized his seminar around a bold challenge: to set the students' collective sights on producing an ensemble of essays with a collaboratively written introduction that could be submitted to a journal as a cluster on "the new migration studies." Collectively, class members had been exploring readings in this emergent field and had each proposed an idea for an individual essay on diverse texts across diverse historical periods and global locations.

When I visited the class to talk about collaborative writing in the humanities, the students were well along in the term. They had a collective sense of how they wanted to frame their theoretical approach to migration studies for what would become the introduction to the cluster. They were working on their individual textual analyses. They had hit the point in the term and the project, however, when the pressures of deadlines generated individual and collective anxiety around the challenges of thinking and writing collaboratively, negotiating the thorny details related to decisions about whose individual essays would be included in the cluster and how the work of those whose essays were not chosen would be recognized, staking out field parameters with greater and greater theoretical sophistication, and determining their precise interventions and contributions in the field. The fracturing approaches and imminent deadlines had begun to undermine their sense of enthusiasm for the pleasures of collective thinking.

Experiments in radical course design and collaborative writing such as Hadji's can be unpredictable in outcome; and indeed, my follow-up correspondence with Hadji indicates that the original goal of the course remained elusive. Students struggled to complete the ensemble of essays within a limited time frame and to navigate the tensions related to collaboration and "distributed authority," which revolved around who would determine in the end which essays would be included in the final cluster. Hadji's next step was to set up an extracurricular writing and reading group on migration studies with the goal of writing a collaborative review of the recently published *Penguin Book of Migration Literature*. This strikes me as a thoughtful follow-up in the form of an extracurricular praxis opportunity.

There is safety in staying with a course design that sets the normative seminar paper as its final product, but "failure" through risk, while disappointing, may offer success of another kind, modeling for students the difficulties and challenges of various modes of scholarly inquiry and communication, experimenting with new kinds of distributed scholarly authority, and gaining greater understanding of how to reimagine scholarly sociality. Risk and failure are productive experiences and are critical to achieving a mature understanding of humanistic knowledge-making and pedagogies.

So far, I have alluded to innovative reconceptualization of the kinds of work we ask students to do in their "traditional" courses, but the more I have engaged with departments and faculties that are trying to develop an alternative vision of doctoral studies in the humanities, the more I have come to recognize that a defined "praxis curriculum" of doctoral study will become centrally important. Here are several kinds of praxis courses that would serve students:

> The *introduction to doctoral study*, in which students have access to the department's philosophy of the dissertation or capstone project; where more advanced students are invited to talk

with new students about what those stages are like and how to negotiate the challenges; and where questions are set in motion that enlist students to think proleptically about what they will want to have done when they go on the job market.
- The *prospectus minicourse and colloquium* as an organized occasion for students to think about the content of the dissertation project together and to take stock of the repertoire of capacities they will require to successfully produce a dissertation.
- The *writing cohort workgroup*, informally or formally constituted, to add the element of ongoing sociality and collaborative thinking to the process of researching and writing the dissertation.
- The *advanced writing for publication* course, to give students the opportunity to turn part of the dissertation into a publishable piece and to gain knowledge of the ecology of scholarly communication.
- The *multiyear colloquium on preparing for academic and alternative job markets*, to encourage students to think agentially about the kind of professional and scholarly identity or identities they want to develop and project.
- The *self-narrative project*, a multiyear engagement with narrative self-presentation.

Given my scholarly work in autobiography studies broadly defined, I've recently added the last arena of praxis to my list. Applicants to doctoral programs submit a portfolio of life writing genres composed to present themselves as exciting candidates. These genres include a short autobiography of education; an intellectual self-narrative; increasingly, an ethical self-portrait, attesting to commitment to educational justice and the values of access, inclusion, and equity; and that most instrumental of self-portraits, the curriculum vitae. They bring self-narratives with them to their studies that may persist during the years of doctoral training and beyond: the narrative tied to imposter syndrome; the ignorance narrative regarding their sense of inadequately accumulated cultural capital; the betrayal narrative of those who worry that they are leaving communities, relationships, and political commitments too far behind. Once in programs, students absorb implicit narratives that program materials and mentors project on them: that there is only one profile for the successful student and that the valued work of humanities scholars is done in isolation, rarely in collaboration, among others. Students often internalize these model narratives as measures by which to judge themselves.

The self-narrative project aims to provide students opportunities for negotiating these kinds of stories—for discarding or reforming them. For instance, students might be asked to submit a CV every year to which they attach a metacommentary on the state of the profile in the CV, noting what has been achieved and what is on the list to achieve, including the skills and capacities they want to accumulate in the next year. At the end of coursework or in the final months before graduation, they might be asked to present their "ideal" CV by projecting what they would want to have achieved in three or five years' time.[1] In this way, the CV becomes a living, breathing document that imagines and plans forward rather than always being retrospectively cast. Another project might be a summative metanarrative of professional (applicant) identity written as students enter the job market. This late-stage narrative might consider what students have learned about themselves as humanists and scholars; what they've learned about the work of the humanities, the institution of higher education, and the vehicles and voices available for communicating their ideas and knowledge; how they see themselves as job applicants; and how they understand their relationship to publics. Or students might be asked to tell their stories of "delight" and "failure": both of which are critical to sustaining stamina and promoting intellectual and emotional flourishing. Stories of delight enliven, energize, and reaffirm imagination and intellectual passion; stories of failures and dead ends capture how the trajectory of a humanist's life swerves in ways that bring pain and loneliness but also new self-understanding and unexpected directions.

To be sure, I am not advocating for an expansion in course requirements for doctoral students. There is too much money and too much time already on the line. I am advocating for a more imaginative and purposeful staging of the praxis components of doctoral education: familiarization with what is required of a humanities scholar and teacher, with what a dissertation is and what it does; enlivening and emboldening opportunities to conceptualize, produce, and circulate scholarly work through diverse vehicles and for diverse audiences; opportunities for students to create learning and thinking communities, to think with and through the expertise of others; and welcoming environments in which students can become who they want to become and discover what career horizons rise up before them. These opportunities need not be packaged in the normative three-credit course; they might come in one- or two-credit units or in informal settings and activities. They might be distributed across different locations: in the library, in digital studies institutes, in centers for research on teaching, in onsite and offsite internships, and in student-organized interest groups run out of a department or graduate school.

A purposeful praxis preparation helps liberate students to work toward their meaningful vision of excellence, expertise, competency, and scholarly acumen. It is critical in energizing and facilitating greater student agency in preparing for, conceptualizing, and realizing a dissertation project of their own design. It better prepares students to imagine multiple career horizons before them and to ready themselves for entry into the job market, academic or otherwise. Attention to all aspects and stages of praxis ensures that the commitment of humanities departments to attracting diverse cohorts of students and supporting their aspirations for success is front and center in doctoral study. Whatever their personal circumstances and struggles, students can expect to achieve a shared level of cultural capital that will enable them to learn and enact what is expected of them in their doctoral studies. Such interventions join the values of excellence to the goals of sustaining diversity, inclusion, and equity.

The New Ecology of Scholarly Communication

Doctoral students come to their programs excited about pursuing their passions. They are promisingly adept in conceptualizing an interesting question and in poking around archives in search of materials that will motivate and energize an argument. And they are comfortable with the format, if anxious about the undertaking, of the normative seminar paper. Rarely are they exposed to or prepared for our twenty-first-century ecology of scholarly communication. I tried to offer students a glimpse of the changes in and complexities of this ecology in my Writing for Publication course by addressing, if only briefly, the shift in the imaginary of scholarly publishing to that of scholarly communication. We read targeted essays and blogs on the state of scholarly publishing in the humanities, the new modes and media of scholarly communication, the venues and politics of open access, and the role of scholars as curators of their own work.

As another means to mentor doctoral students with regard to scholarly communication, three years ago I hosted, as then director of the University of Michigan's Institute for the Humanities, a discussion focused on a Mellon-funded project involving the development of a prototype for a new model of publishing contract for book fields (see Macklin). Four faculty fellows at the institute that year and two humanities graduate students, current and former fellows at the institute, provided feedback on a proposed model contract to Charles Watkinson, director of the University of Michigan Press, and a legal librarian from Emory University. Michigan and Emory partnered with the Mellon Foundation in a funding initiative pertaining to the contractual basis upon which scholars and publishers agree to the conditions of communicating and disseminating their books.

According to the team charged with drafting the contract, the motivations were several-fold. The book contract used by the press at the time (and typical of that at many academic presses), had been drafted in the 1960s or 1970s, had changed little since then, and was now entirely out-of-date and inadequate to the new concepts of bookishness and scholarly communication in which humanities scholars had begun to work. In the legacy print system, humanistic scholarship took basically two forms: the essay and the long-form book. This system assumed the following: that the final work outcome is the printed form of the book in hardcover or paperbound editions; that when the final version of the book goes to the press, that is the end of changes to the book form; that the book is bought by individuals or libraries and sits on shelves (in people's offices or in the stacks); that the publisher holds the copyright; that there is some expectation of a remuneration for hard work in modest royalties. Book contracts addressed this set of assumptions. They were drafted in legalistic language that advantaged publishers rather than book authors. Humanists confronting contracts often had little knowledge of the publishing system or of the terms to be negotiated. In early career mode, authors were mostly grateful that the press issued a contract.

In the third decade of the twenty-first century, conditions, terms, expectations, and modes of scholarly communication cannot be addressed through old contractual relations. Humanities scholars accumulate online data and documents, which they often seek to make available to others. They experiment with established and new multimedia platforms to determine the best vehicle for their thinking and their answers to motivating questions. They are challenged to imagine scholarly communication that is distributed across offline and online sites and can be interactive, iterative, and open to re-versioning. They increasingly recognize the value of greater access to their work for the public good and thus seek to find means to unlock knowledge through opportunities for open access.

As Daniel J. Cohen, formerly of George Mason University's Roy Rosenzweig Center for History and New Media and now director of the Digital Public Library of America, pithily observed a decade ago, "*The largest hidden cost is the invisibility of what you publish.* When you publish somewhere that is behind gates, or in paper only, you are resigning all of that hard work to invisibility in the age of the open web. You may reach a few peers in your field, but you miss out on the broader dissemination of your work, including to potential other fans." For those seeking open access alternatives to the closed publishing system, issues arise related to the copyright infrastructure of Creative Commons, the reversion of copyright for earlier work, and the affordances of institutional repositories. Issues also arise related to the tenure and promotion processes and faculty attitudes toward open access venues.

On their side, academic presses have struggled to develop economic models that can sustain new forms of scholarly communication. They were assisted for many years with funding from the Mellon Foundation, which took the lead in building cyberinfrastructure for supporting and preserving new online modes and media platforms and in assessing and seeding new business models for sustaining book culture in a digital age. At Michigan alone, collaborative projects funded by Mellon contributed to the establishment of Lever Press, "leading the way in establishing best practices for born-digital, peer reviewed, open access monograph publishing" ("About"), and the development of Samvera/Fedora, "a platform that will enable the publication and preservation of digitally enriched humanities monographs" ("Mellon Grant Funds"). Yet it is important to note that major initiatives in the transformation of the ecology and vehicles of scholarly communication depend on significant external grant funding; and funders like to seed transformation but expect institutions or consortia to ensure sustainability. This is to say that the ecology of scholarly communication is at this time dynamic, shifting, exciting, and precarious as well as increasingly important for students' future career paths.

Our discussion at the Institute for the Humanities about a new model contract for academic presses encompassed issues of preservation, versioning, attribution of credit to all the sources of support, open access and reuse desires, and attention to roles and responsibilities of the different actors. Two advanced doctoral students, one in American culture and one in screen arts and culture, sat at the table with senior faculty members, the editor of the University of Michigan Press, and the legal librarian from Emory. Invoking Creative Commons licenses, reversion rights, preservation plans, versioning, and terms of accessibility in open access publishing, these scholars asked, What is "the author"? What is "the work"? How is contribution attributed, recognized, and remunerated? How will work last? What are the new terms of accessibility? How will readers of scholarly work be invited into an interactive mode with it?

How will readers "read" our work? The discussion became the occasion for pondering the intersecting issues of faculty generations, the economics of publishing, the struggle to ensure lastingness of contributions to knowledge, and the future of doctoral education.

Over the course of that hour and a half, students received an advanced tutorial on the future ahead for academic humanists. All humanities doctoral students would benefit from gaining this knowledge. It would serve those whose career paths go through the academy and those whose career paths take them in a myriad of other directions.

Capacity Building

The third project in the transformation of doctoral education in the humanities focuses on supporting students in expanding their repertoire of capacities requisite to careers inside and outside the academy. This work of capacity building is absolutely essential to the training of academic humanists now. These capacities are requisite for success in the academy—the goal of most doctoral students, though in today's difficult job market no longer the only goal. Capacity building is not a second order of knowledge acquisition or expertise, not a lesser kind of doctoral preparation, not an offshoot of corporate discourse. We wouldn't say that of the capacity to carry out deep reading, or the capacity to refine motivating questions, or the capacity to articulate the contradictions in theoretical frameworks, or the capacity to write with precision. The pursuit of a broader range of capacities is part and parcel of the intellectual and imaginative power constitutive of the scholarly life and necessary to the fullest achievement of thinking, conceptualization, realization, and communication of humanistic inquiry.

At the same time, capacity building is critical to preparing students for multiple career horizons and to breaking the hold of the one-model-of-success culture in many humanities departments. Those who, by virtue of the constrained job market or their career aspirations, seek positions outside the academy benefit from the capacity to translate for multiple audiences the values, practices, expertise, and inquiring dispositions earned through the hard work of doctoral training. This capacity itself is one of advocacy—talking with people outside the academy about the centrality of humanistic inquiry and knowledge production across worlds of labor, professions, social activism, creative cultures, and political fora. It is advocacy as well for the pleasures produced by the humanistic engagement with diverse cultural legacies, objects, relationships, histories, and words.

This large project—reorienting professional development of doctoral students—is now unfolding in programs across North America. Graduate directors, chairs, and faculty mentors are becoming advocates and agents of change in the culture of professional development: establishing new internship programs, identifying sources of training for students outside the department or program unit, locating graduates now in careers outside the academy and inviting them to come back to campus to share their career narratives, and providing funding for opportunities to gain further capacities at seminars and short courses offered at other universities.

As graduate faculty members engage in discussions of capacities and futures, they must pose and answer the following questions: What repertoire of capacities and expertise should students be developing? Where and how do they gain these capacities? How might the cataloging of capacities and expertise be made explicit at various points in their studies? In discussions of this changing mode of professional development, talk can turn to the way in which focus on skills demeans the notion of the humanities doctorate, introducing too much instrumentalism into the conversation. Fundamental to answering these questions is a reorientation of faculty attitudes toward talk of capacities training. We disadvantage our doctoral students if we persist in setting up intellectual inquiry and skills training in a binary opposition, the former the real work of the humanist and the latter debased as related to the market, to lesser forms of knowledge, and to the rise of the neoliberal university. We need to reframe our attitude to skills and our rhetoric about them, perhaps by choosing other terms and definitions, as I have attempted to do by referring to capacities and praxis.

Many professors express concern that their coverage of course material will suffer if they are also expected to help students learn new capacities or that they are unequipped to teach students capacities that were not a part of their own training. My response to these earnest concerns is to suggest that capacity building can be far more collaboratively orchestrated: that mentors can be tapped in various places in universities, such as libraries or centers for teaching and learning, and that students benefit from access to an assemblage of guides, mentors, and experts inside and outside the university. Individual faculty members can support doctoral students who aspire to careers in the academy by making explicit in syllabi and conversations the formidable set of skills the students are accumulating. The graduate program can support student preparation for multiple career horizons through the praxis component of doctoral training. Students can be encouraged to take agency as they move through the doctorate, purposefully naming the capacities they already have or seek to acquire: language proficiency; archival persistence; conference organization; innovative teaching; facility in engaged scholarship and the public humanities; and IT expertise. Those who increasingly use and create digital archives can pursue opportunities on their own campuses and at others to gain expertise in coding, visualization, design, or big data analytics. Because future faculty members in humanities disciplines will require flexible and improvisational habits of mind and collaborative skills to bring their scholarship to fruition, current faculty members could work with students to launch large-scale research projects and scholarly assemblages, helping students gain experience in program management and budget preparation. They could learn, too, the basics of social media outreach and scholarly network mobilization. Since so many students come into doctoral programs with diverse experiences in the workplace, graduate programs might assemble a group of peer mentors tasked with advising other students on ways to gain certain kinds of experiences or offering workshops on specific capacity building.

I think of capacity building as critical to the well-being of students and the sustainability of their creative, scholarly, and professional passions. When everything seems so intense, when pressures don't abate, when reserve energy flags, when stress wracks the body, far too many students struggle to contain their insecurities, suspicions of unbelonging, and anxieties about their futures and their debts. Hopefully, there are counseling services to support them through difficult times. But if programs have successfully incorporated capacity building into the formal and informal curriculum, they provide students with routes to self-empowerment and the confidence of their agency in forging their pathway through the program and toward multiple career horizons. Yes, graduate students are constrained by the requirements of their programs and by the interests, energy, and commitment of the faculty with whom they work. But they can and do take charge of their own learning, stewarding their intellectual passions, gaining knowledge and accumulating capacities with whatever help and guidance they can find, for the possible futures ahead. They recognize, gain, and hone a range of capacities increasingly necessary to doing scholarly work and teaching in the humanities. They seek knowledge about the state of scholarly publishing, the shifts in scholarly practices, the new kinds of relationships scholars will have to their work, and the opportunities and challenges of an open access ethos. They increasingly use and create digital archives and innovate digital modes of scholarly presentation and communication. They seek opportunities to engage in publicly oriented scholarship and to gain greater facility in acts of public engagement for the public good. They become comfortable in joining an ensemble of colleagues whose expertise animates their imagination, sense of opportunity, and purpose. They imagine multiple career options ahead of them.

The overriding goal for faculty members entrusted with educating future humanists is ensuring and sustaining excellence in doctoral education and passion about its pleasures, commitments, and efficacies. That excellence involves promoting students' intellectual excitement, analytical heft, depth of scholarly habits, imaginative elasticity, and capacity to flexibly craft their scholarly voice for multiple audiences. It involves attracting students with diverse lived experiences to programs and breaking apart a social and intellectual milieu that reproduces procrustean models of professionalization. And it involves valuing the potential diversity of the future careers toward which students may find their way. Successful doctoral education is key to addressing the higher education accessibility deficit here and abroad and to ensuring a culture of intellectual curiosity, scholarly boldness, and pedagogical innovation as cornerstones for evolving and building twenty-first-century knowledge institutions. For those institutions to flourish, for the humanities to flourish, the next generations of doctoral students will need to flourish through the guidance of faculty members who teach, advise, mentor, and themselves imagine new possibilities for the humanities doctorate.

I entered the doctoral program in English at Case Western Reserve University in September 1968. I am now retired. I've been thinking about doctoral education for fifty-five years—as a student, as a teacher, as a dissertation advisor and committee member, as a chair, as an associate and interim dean of arts and sciences, and as a president of the MLA. I remain optimistic about the future of humanities doctoral education, despite the times we live in. I remain optimistic because the students I have taught and talked with are always drawing me into new fields of study. They energize me with their enthusiasm, even as they worry me with their anxieties. They are the reason I am advocating for a more imaginative notion of the total doctoral curriculum: a praxis curriculum that meshes with the content-based curriculum, an advanced engagement with the current and shifting ecology of scholarly communication, an expanded repertoire of capacities, and a more capacious set of alternatives for the capstone dissertation.

Ever before us, then, is the prospect of becoming: what we want future humanists to become, what we want the humanities doctorate to become, and what we want our relationship to publics beyond the academy to become. I come back to my mantra. I persist in imagining the times as good enough to make change and to advance the work of the humanities in higher education and in the world. The best antidote to my own feelings of distress and despondency is ongoing conversation with faculty members and graduate students about new directions in graduate education and new modes and methods of scholarly inquiry as it takes place in the classroom, in the writing group, in the personal writing and thinking space, and in public exchange.

NOTE

1. I am grateful to Dana Murphy for introducing me to the concept of the ideal CV in a virtual meeting hosted by the University of Michigan, held on 20 November 2020. Dana indicated that she was encouraged to compose an ideal CV by her dissertation advisor at the University of California, Irvine.

WORKS CITED

"About Lever Press." *Lever Press*, 2023, leverpress.org/about/. Accessed 6 Mar. 2023.

Bakara, Hadji. E-mail to the author. 9 Dec. 2018.

Cohen, Daniel J. "Open Access Publishing and Scholarly Values." *Dan Cohen*, 27 May 2010, www.dancohen.org/2010/05/27/open-access-publishing-and-scholarly-values.

Macklin, Lisa, et al. "Model Publishing Contract for Digital Scholarship." *University of Michigan Library*, 18 Oct. 2017, deepblue.lib.umich.edu/handle/2027.42/138828.

"Mellon Grant Funds U-M Press Collaboration on Digital Scholarship." *Michigan Publishing*, 1 Apr. 2015, services.publishing.umich.edu/2015/04/01/mellon-grant-funds-u-m-press-collaboration-on-digital-scholarship/.

Smith, Sidonie. *Manifesto for the Humanities: Transforming Doctoral Education in Good Enough Times*. U of Michigan P, 2016, https://doi.org/10.3998/dcbooks.13607059.0001.001.

Collaborative Ethics: Practicing Engagement in Our Academic Communities

Jenna Lay and Emily Shreve

In 1995, David Damrosch offered an early argument for reforming graduate education, including a description of doctoral work as a process of antisocialization that still rings true today: "When people acculturate themselves to academic life by enhancing their tolerance for solitary work and diminishing their intellectual sociability, they reduce their ability to address problems that require collaborative solutions" (148). To mitigate isolation and its negative consequences, Damrosch focused primarily on the dissertation as protomonograph, arguing instead for "dissertations conceived as several articles written with a number of different sponsors" in order to "increase the student's active engagement with differing perspectives and points of view" (163). Yet, more than twenty-five years later, changes that would enhance public engagement, collaborative learning, and prosocial capacities—whether through the dissertation or through other curricular and cocurricular opportunities—remain limited to a relatively small number of graduate programs.

As labor inequities in academic life and stagnation in academic hiring have grown more acute, this isolating approach to humanities doctoral programs has become increasingly unsustainable. For a long time—far too long, given evidence of the varied careers pursued by humanities PhDs in recent decades—a narrowly focused faculty apprenticeship model was the assumption at the heart of graduate education in the humanities, and that model still motivates much pedagogical and advisory work at the doctoral level.[1] Students are asked to focus on coursework, teaching, and research, and they are too often welcomed into their academic communities with the admonition that they should, above all else, prioritize the latter. Such a narrow conception of graduate education does damage not only to students but also to the pedagogical mission, rigorous inquiry, intellectual freedom, and public significance of the humanities. Or, to put it another (perhaps more polemical) way, the conservative boundaries humanities disciplines have constructed around the training of future faculty members do little to preserve the core values of the humanities, unless one of those values is replication. Instead, these boundaries limit both individual and collective senses of the possible and constrain the forms of growth and change necessary to a thriving academic and public culture.

Thus, we advocate for a doctoral ethics of community and collaboration, one that creates opportunities for humanities PhDs to engage more thoroughly and professionally with multiple publics. Our essay builds on Lauren Berlant's conception of professionalism as "an explicit pedagogical/collegial ethics," an approach that demands robust collaboration "in discussion and across publics" (135, 132). We suggest that intra-university partnerships and programs offer a necessary first step in developing this pedagogical/collegial ethics and preparing for broader forms of public engagement, and we call for collaborative opportunities that allow humanities graduate students to work with students outside the classroom, with student affairs colleagues, and with humanities and nonhumanities professionals within and beyond the university. In this cowritten essay, we draw on our own history of collaborations—especially those associated with Emily's position as a graduate assistant in Lehigh University's Office of First-Year Experience, which we describe in detail—in order to emphasize how professional identities and habits develop through collaborative processes within and across various communities. By more fully engaging with professionals across the university, humanities graduate students are empowered to acculturate themselves to the broader community of which they are a part and to practice habits of professionalism that enable ethical engagement with multiple communities. In arguing for this sociable reorientation, we seek to resist a market-based professionalism that reinforces the current inequities of the academic labor market and instead propose a horizontal ethics that responds to our current structural and systemic challenges with professional optimism and intellectual sociability.

Professionalism

Transforming graduate education with professional and career development in mind, whether the career in question is within or beyond academe, can raise alarm bells for those who value the capacity of the humanities to transcend or trouble a market-based worldview that would subsume all activity to that which is practical and capital-generating. This concern often manifests in the claim that professional development activities encroach upon a valuable space in which scholars can question, learn, and explore without prioritizing only those outcomes recognized by markets.[2] Wendy Brown is one of the more incisive critics of this "formulation of education as primarily valuable to human capital development, where human capital is what the individual, the business world, and the state seek to enhance in order to maximize competitiveness" (176), and she mentions graduate education in the context of the academic job market:

> Faculty gain recognition and reward according to standing in fields whose methods and topics are increasingly remote from the world and the undergraduate classroom. Graduate students are professionalized through protocols and admonitions orienting them toward developing their own toeholds in such fields. This professionalization aims at making young scholars not into teachers and thinkers, but into human capitals who learn to attract investors by networking long before they "go on the market," who "workshop" their papers, "shop" their book manuscripts, game their Google Scholar counts and "impact factors," and above all, follow the money and the rankings. (195)

We share Brown's critique of universities and academic programs in which "*knowledge, thought, and training* are valued and desired almost exclusively for their contribution to capital enhancement" (177) and wish to expand on her brief suggestion that graduate education is caught in this trap through a focus on professionalization to support individual career advancement on the academic job market.[3]

While we would question whether a bucolic, market-free space has ever existed in academe, PhD students preparing to enter an oversaturated and highly competitive academic job market since 2008 have especially good reason to believe that they must focus on building their CVs through academic and professional accomplishments that will be legible to search committees. But this view of how to become a professional—individualistic, self-promoting, and outcome-oriented—does damage, as Brown suggests, to "forms of association, knowledge, and teaching that serve the public good" (195). Berlant offers an alternative formulation of an engaged and community-oriented professionalism in "Affect Is the New Trauma," a short essay that explores the market-based anxieties that bubble up at an academic conference. Berlant describes how participants fear their work on affect will be dismissed as trendy—as something they have pursued strategically for the capital enhancement Brown decries in her account of graduate student professionalization. For Berlant, professionalism is the solution to, rather than the cause of, anxieties fostered by the professionalization pressures of the academic job market. Berlant's understanding of *professionalism* as a consciously chosen mode of being-with-others is a necessary corrective to notions of *professionalization* as the rote accumulation of marketable skills and research areas to which job seekers feel they must passively succumb. Berlantian professionalism is instead an active and ethical choice that foregrounds engagement and collaboration and is thus akin to Kathleen Fitzpatrick's work on "generous thinking" as "a mode of engagement that emphasizes listening over speaking, community over individualism, collaboration over competition" (4).

What does it mean to be a professional in academe? In the essay from which our practice and this chapter take their inspiration, Berlant argues that professionalism is "pedagogical," elaborating:

> It's our job to show up and think, to show up and think with others, to collaborate using what we know and what we don't know to push concepts beyond where they were when we entered the room. . . . Doing this, focusing on building skills for thought, discussion, debate, expressivity, critique, and becoming different, regardless of how we feel at the moment, regardless of the noise of ambition that creates our own and our colleagues' nervous conditions, is the practice of professional obligation. (133–34)

Professionalism is the mindset that allows members of a community to work through and counter the forces that encourage antisocial individualism and competition.[4] Professionalism in an academic community is what opens the space for faculty, staff, and students to question, learn, and explore in partnership *with others*. Its pedagogical emphasis reorients faculty and staff members toward colleagues as fellow learners with whom it is valuable to think, just as it is with students. This vision of professionalism is robustly ethical. According to Berlant, "[T]he stories we so often tell ourselves about professionalism—it's what unimaginative people aspire to, a pedantic, rank-based bureaucratic formalism propped up against genuine conceptual richness—bar serious talk about the ethics of collegiality and pedagogy under conditions of aspiration" (134). In other words, professionalism enables a shared foundation for dialogue concerning how members of a community might learn and collaborate with one another. Rather than disrupt dreams of "collective worlds," professionalism's obligations make those worlds more possible while community members collaboratively build the intellectual competencies that are essential to the academic humanities and to the many forms of engagement the humanities can enable (134).

Berlant's account of professionalism offers a foundation for a more nuanced understanding of professional development in graduate education, whereby professional development activities are designed to expand students' horizons and enhance their capacity for both academic and public engagement rather than prioritizing market-based individualism. Yet professionalism also raises another, seemingly paradoxical, concern: that it removes *all* individuality, enforcing a homogenizing set of expectations that reconfigure students—with their particular interests, enthusiasms, and aspirations—into an undifferentiated mass of professionals. A. W. Strouse, for example, has argued that configuring "professionalism as a norm" opposes creative, affective, and queer ways of being and knowing, thereby creating an environment in which "a student's own aspirations and proclivities might be replaced, through doctoral education, with new goals and affective states" (122, 124). The paradox, of course, is that the individualized focus of market-based professionalism can lead to the pursuit of nearly identical markers of professional accomplishment: a set of boxes to be checked that succeed only in stripping away individuality. Thus, the twinned anxieties of professionalism—hyperindividual and anti-individual—end up meeting in the same, heavily circumscribed place. It is no wonder, then, that professional development is often treated as an amorphous enemy of the academic humanities rather than as a way for students to explore and develop their specific aspirations through thoughtful engagement with multiple mentors, colleagues, and intellectual trajectories. As Berlant describes it, professionalism demands that we work with others; through this encounter, faculty members, staff members, and students build skills not to enhance marketability but to enhance forms of democratic engagement that recognize and celebrate difference: "skills for thought, discussion, debate, expressivity, critique, and becoming different."[5] The pedagogical ethics of this form of professionalism allow for the development of the individual (graduate student, colleague, community partner) in specific ways that attend to difference without chasing market-based distinction.

Scholars who study and create programs in community engagement foreground this robustly ethical attention to difference, and their work informs our understanding of the actual and potential partnerships that might cultivate graduate students' skills of collaborative professionalism. In particular, we see John Saltmarsh, Matt Hartley, and Patti Clayton's emphasis on the importance of "collaborative knowledge construction" as essential to the practice of thoughtful and democratic partnerships in a university setting (Saltmarsh et al. 9). These authors' "Democratic Engagement White Paper" cautions against "engagement defined by activities connected to places outside the campus" that "does not focus attention on the processes involved in the activity—how it is done—or the purpose of connecting with places outside the campus—why it is done." Saltmarsh, Hartley, and Clayton are especially concerned about projects based in the community that are "pursued as ends in themselves" in order to benefit the university and its students. In such projects, engagement is "reduced to a public relations function of making known what the campus is doing for the community and providing opportunities for students to have experiences in the community" (6). In other words, community engagement, like professional development, can easily be co-opted into "capital enhancement" for the sake of the university and the individuals within it: a list of partnerships without true reciprocity or knowledge creation (Brown 177). Instead, Saltmarsh, Hartley, and Clayton propose "a focus on the processes and purposes of engagement" (6); that is, they highlight, as Berlant does, conversation with other professionals as the key to democratic engagement. We see this vision—ethical partnerships grounded in a professionalism that highlights process and purpose—as the foundation for transformative graduate professional development programs. These programs would recognize participants' unique aspirations and capacities, facilitate creativity and growth, and create careful scaffolding for responsible and reciprocal community engagement.

As part of the scaffolding designed to introduce students to the hows and whys of democratic engagement, we propose partnerships within the university community as a necessary first step whereby graduate students can practice collaborative, reciprocal, and ethical professionalism—since, as bell hooks reminds us in her work on democratic education, "[L]earning is never confined solely to an institutionalized classroom," nor is "the corporate university . . . set apart from real life" (41). We are particularly compelled by the case Thomas Keenan makes for ethically oriented engagement within university communities in *University Ethics*: he highlights the many ethical crises endemic to the modern university, from the adjunctification of labor to the status of student athletes, and suggests that academics have mistakenly assumed their own ethical practice to be universal or sufficient rather than working to create a professional ethics in conversation with one another (4, 9).[6] Using examples from other professions, Keenan demonstrates that professional ethics are the result of intensive community discussion and negotiation. He suggests that a collaboratively designed ethics for the contemporary university should be horizontal: while faculty members like himself have vertical accountability "to our chairs and deans," such academic professionals rarely cultivate robust standards of horizontal accountability to students, colleagues, and the broader university community (18). Keenan highlights, in an echo of Damrosch, the ways in which a lack of professional ethics encourages individualism rather than collaboration and allows nonpedagogical value systems, including those centered around the market, to take root in the academy (57, 205). He urges, "If we are really interested in running universities where students learn the collaborative work of critical thinking collectively and of attending to the needs of the common good, then we must take ownership of our universities and learn those lessons as well" (79).

Keenan is focused on the mission to educate undergraduates with the goal of preparing them to be engaged citizens, but his point is at least as relevant to graduate education—and arguably more so. If, as we have suggested above, graduate education in the humanities should prepare PhDs to practice professionalism grounded in active engagement—in academia, in other community settings, and in our democracy—and to cultivate democratic engagement in others, then it is essential to immerse students in collaborative training grounded in pedagogical/collegial ethics. And there is no better place—no more imperative place—than within the university itself. "We must," says Keenan, "find ways of knowing more about our own universities, their practices, and their policies" (78). A graduate education that prioritizes this knowledge opens space for discussions of university ethics that engage multiple members of the university and prepares all graduates, regardless of future careers, to engage collaboratively in the multiple communities of which they are and will be a part. In the following section, we trace one example of what this education can look like in practice.

Academic Partnerships

A graduate education in professionalism would provide opportunities for graduate students to actively engage with the multiple communities that make up the contemporary university. Depending on the institution, this engagement might take the form of interdisciplinary collaborations or shared governance through graduate student organizations. However, we argue that greater challenge and possibility arise from collaborations that bridge the academic and student affairs gap. At Lehigh University, where Jenna is a faculty member and Emily was a PhD student, the English department has pursued opportunities for graduate students to work directly with student affairs professionals through partnerships designed with a pedagogical emphasis and reciprocal benefit in mind. While English department graduate funding is primarily tied to teaching positions in the First-Year Writing Program, administrative support over a five-year period (2014–19) enabled the department to facilitate students' interest in contributing to other units on campus. In this collaborative model, students are offered the option of working in administrative positions instead of teaching: they retain their departmental stipend and hold positions outside the department for at least one academic year. The department's first partnership, which we will describe in more detail below, was with the Office of First-Year Experience; subsequent partnerships have included the Center for Gender Equity, the Pride Center, the Office of Multicultural Affairs, the Center for Community Engagement, and the Writing across the Curriculum Program.[7]

Emily's graduate assistantship with the Office of First-Year Experience (OFYE) was an early entrée into the collaborative and pedagogical possibilities of intra-university partnerships. Based on her experiences teaching in the First-Year Writing Program, Emily hoped to learn more about other offices on campus with a focus on first-year students. In conversations with Jenna, who served as the English department's job placement officer at the time, it became clear that the opportunity to work directly with Lehigh's OFYE would be invaluable for Emily—so we coordinated with the director of that office and with the director of graduate studies and the chair of the English department to partner in the creation of a position designed for Emily, in which she would gain an administrative learning experience and the OFYE would benefit from her skills as a trained teacher of first-year writing and a scholar of literature. Thus, Emily's initial interest in exploring the university's student affairs division was bolstered by relationships already in place between the English department and OFYE but the assistantship was nonetheless a more substantive partnership between units than had previously existed.[8] In order for the partnership to take shape, leaders in OFYE and the English department, including Jenna, worked together to navigate university policies, to bridge university silos, and to articulate how both the university and the students involved (including first-year undergraduate students) would benefit. There were thus pedagogical benefits of the partnership for faculty and staff as well as for Emily.

Working in OFYE allowed Emily to visualize the shared educational project that unites work in student and academic affairs and to see how theories of the humanities are distilled into praxis. Emily's experiences in the role could be challenging, whether these involved demystifying complicated university bureaucratic procedures for incoming students or selecting a book for a common reading experience that satisfied multiple stakeholders. But they were also generative, as she brought the methodological and theoretical training of her PhD coursework and exams to bear on these experiences. The position thus had a ripple effect through her work, not only shifting what she imagined as her future career but also opening up research questions that she had not previously considered or known were possible. As a result, Emily developed a new dissertation project—on the role of literature in introducing students to an academic community—that aligned her research interests, skill sets, and professional ambitions, and she asked Jenna to serve as her advisor. While not every student involved in such an on-campus partnership will incorporate the lessons learned directly into a dissertation project, Emily's research on the responsibilities higher education institutions have to incoming students, as well as the methods by which literature can contribute to an ethical and community-centered education for new undergraduates, demonstrates how transformative such an experience might be. Her daily practice in the OFYE enabled her to explore carefully the very process of entering into a community that scholars like Berlant, Keenan, and Saltmarsh emphasize and thereby to integrate the research, teaching, and administrative aspects of her graduate curriculum. At the same time, it transformed Emily and Jenna's collaborative relationship: from career-focused advising to mentorship grounded in research and writing and ultimately to a partnership as coauthors sharing an ongoing commitment to reforming graduate education and investigating university ethics.

Emily also noted the pragmatic benefits of gaining experience as an administrator facilitating the first-year transition beyond the college classroom. She particularly valued the exposure to daily practices of professional collaboration that differed from the committee model practiced in many academic departments: weekly full-office and one-on-one meetings to foster intentional implementation of programming and ensure accountability (to coworkers, to campus partners, and to students); expectations of consistent e-mail response windows to allow collaborations to maintain momentum; models of supervisory relationships that included regular and structured feedback from multiple members of the office; and the informal brainstorming and problem-solving that arise with regular use of a shared office space.[9] On a broader scale, the OFYE also brought Emily a stronger understanding of the structure of the university, from varied office and department funding models to a richer comprehension of the privileges, pressures, and goals of both faculty and staff roles. The position introduced her to mentors and colleagues with similar interests, at Lehigh and across the nation, by way of conferences dedicated to the support of first-year experience initiatives. Her reorientation to the university community as a staff member in OFYE thus enabled Emily to participate in broader conversations about what Berlant calls "the ethics of collegiality and pedagogy under conditions of aspiration" (134). Today, building on her knowledge of first-year students and continuing to integrate the administrative and research skills she developed through her graduate experiences, Emily continues these conversations in her position as associate director of academic transitions in the Academic Success Center at the University of Nevada, Las Vegas, where she coordinates, teaches, and researches the efficacy of the university's largest first-year seminar.

But the benefits were not to Emily alone: her experiences as a teacher of first-year writing and a scholar of literature enabled her to contribute to the OFYE's mission "to provide support and resources for the academic and social transition of new students and their families" ("First-Year Experience"). She led the Summer Reading Committee; developed, wrote, and edited materials that educated students on first-year expectations; and initiated programs and partnerships that helped bridge academic and student affairs (one of which we will describe in more detail below). In addition to benefiting from the skills developed through Emily's disciplinary training, hiring an advanced graduate student—whose doctoral studies allowed her to commit to more than the standard one-year assistantships typically held by MA students—gave the OFYE increased consistency and the capacity to build on the groundwork established in year one of the assistantship. As a result, this partnership not only offered Emily the opportunity to learn more about "universities, their practices, and their policies" (Keenan 78) but also enabled the English department and OFYE to develop a reciprocally beneficial collaboration grounded in the pedagogical project shared by both units.

Engagement within and across multiple units on campus offers graduate students an opportunity to practice collaborative professionalism and, simultaneously, to learn more about the wider publics with whom members of the institution interact. Student affairs offices are often more directly public-facing than academic departments; in many cases, entire administrative offices have a responsibility to respond to members of the community, while individual members of academic departments can choose whether or not to engage with the public—and may or may not collaborate with others on campus in doing so. In working for the OFYE, for example, Emily supported an office whose mission statement highlights new students' families as the second audience of the unit's work. Since the OFYE represents the university and higher education as a whole to this wider public, all materials produced by the office and all activities sponsored through it must be developed with public engagement in mind. Emily learned to consider how academic institutions can effectively communicate research and philosophies on student development and academic success in ways that build trust with worried parents and guardians. This was especially important when considering the families and networks of first-generation students, who may have limited or no firsthand knowledge of university structures or opportunities. In these outreach efforts, university staff members must consider how they might exemplify to parents and families the varied purposes and benefits of a university education. Graduate student work in university offices outside the department thus often requires translation of academic missions, procedures, and research developments to a public outside the university that may have very different investments.

This broadly conceived public—the parents and families of students—is only one of the outside communities with whom students in administrative positions might engage, since campus offices are often involved in various forms of community outreach and partnerships. Through her assistantship, Emily was able to create and run an immersive preorientation program that introduced students to the university and local communities through the local food system. In this program, students explored city restaurants beyond the boundaries of the campus, considered cultural traditions in the course of touring a nearby market, and met with a vegan activist in the community. The program highlighted the intersection of community and campus when participants received a behind-the-scenes tour of one of the university's dining halls and learned more about the mechanisms by which their food was purchased and prepared and the people who performed the labor. Through this program, Emily enacted what she had learned about the practices of ethical engagement through her work in OFYE. She integrated collaborative learning into a pedagogical experience for new undergraduate students that helped them consider the university's relationship to the local community through processes that made space for community organizations to share their professional expertise, knowledge, and insight with students whose ethical orientation to those organizations would form a foundation for their time at Lehigh.

As the list of subsequent partnerships mentioned earlier suggests, the OFYE is one of many possible administrative experiences that provide professionalism training to complement graduate education. In each case, graduate students gained substantive practice in engaging with various constituencies and ongoing community partnerships—far more than is typically possible in a single semester or a single course project—with the support of experienced administrators. The responsibilities and obligations of administrative positions held outside the department require a collaborative professionalism that necessitates rethinking boundaries between academic and student affairs, faculty and staff, university and publics, theory and practice, the intellectual and the professional. These positions thus equip graduate students with a repertoire of prosocial capacities that enable more robust contributions to their many communities, which may include future participation in academic service and shared governance as tenure-track faculty members, leadership responsibility for collective pedagogical efforts as staff members in academic or student affairs, or engagement with nonacademic communities as humanities professionals outside the university.

Graduate programs that seek to enhance their students' ability to engage with multiple publics and to develop intellectually engaging and meaningful future careers should therefore evaluate the collaborative opportunities possible within their own institutions. As with community engagement efforts, such experiences should be implemented with careful attention to purpose and process in order to cultivate ethical, active professionalism and thereby ease the pressures of market-based professionalization. By scaffolding these opportunities within graduate curricula that attend to issues of ethical engagement, these new visions of meaningful pedagogical and community-engaged work can make room for the challenges, joys, and achievements of collaborative and intellectually sociable work with other professionals and expand students' capacity for ethical engagement in multiple communities.

NOTES

1. For a brief overview of the varied career paths of humanities PhDs, see David Laurence's posts for *The Trend*, particularly "Where Are They Now? Occupations of 1996–2011 PhD Recipients in 2013." The Council of Graduate Schools has also pursued research in this area through its NSF- and Mellon-funded PhD Career Pathways project, as has the American Historical Association (AHA) through its Mellon-funded Career Diversity for Historians project and the database *Where Historians Work* (historians.org/wherehistorianswork).

2. See, for example, recent essays in *The Chronicle of Higher Education* that critique professional organizations such as the AHA and the Modern Language Association (MLA) for expanding professional development programs. In "Shamelessness and Hypocrisy at the MLA," Sharon O'Dair suggests that conference programming on the topic of "The Profession" threatens academics' central task: "to read a lot of books, think about them, write about them, and talk about them." O'Dair argues that reducing the number of PhDs is the only ethical option—with no acknowledgment of how a reduction in numbers of students or programs could adversely affect access for students in already underrepresented groups. See also Daniel Bessner and Michael Brenes, who suggest that attention to a broad range of careers is simply "a form of bootstrappism and market-Darwinism."

3. Using the evidence of book manuscripts, *Google Scholar* counts, and impact factors, Brown's critique makes visible graduate training's heavy reliance on a model of research productivity that molds students for a limited range of academic jobs—those akin to the research-intensive positions held by their professors at doctoral-granting institutions.

4. Fitzpatrick points out, "However much we as scholars might reject individualism as part and parcel of the humanist, positivist ways of the past, our working lives—on campus and off—are overdetermined by it" (26). We concur with her diagnosis of the costs of this competitive individualism, which she calls "astronomical, not only to each individual scholar in setting a course toward stress-related burnout, but to scholars collectively in undermining our ability to understand ourselves as a community, one capable of disagreeing profoundly and yet still coming together in solidarity to argue for our collective interests" (38).

5. Strouse, too, recognizes that professionalism might be approached with these skills in mind and concludes by suggesting that "we might see how the history of 'professionalism' gives us license to create doctoral programs in which students can 'make the most of themselves.' Rather than coercing students into unthinkingly taking up academia's norms, we might invite students to develop their own values and goals" (133). We see intra-university partnerships as one of the mechanisms by which such an invitation might be extended to graduate students.

6. Berlant identifies a similar assumption in their advising relationships: "I had so many students perform the presumption that to work together was a private, intimate relation separate from its institutional mediation; and I saw so many of us presume that if *we* were managing and producing distinction

we must be doing it in the right, anti-authoritarian, anti-bureaucratic, barely compromised way" (134).

7. Other models for these types of partnerships include the UGrow program at the University of Miami (ugrow.as.miami.edu) and the Fellowship in Higher Education Leadership at Fordham (fordham.edu/info/21272/gsas_funding/7058/fellowship_in_higher_education_leadership). For another summary of Lehigh's program, see Cassuto.

8. The previous relationship had involved the director of the First-Year Writing Program serving on the Summer Reading Committee for a number of years and sometimes incorporating a chosen book into the syllabus shared by first-time writing instructors.

9. The shift to fully remote work for many faculty members and staff during the COVID-19 pandemic revealed both the importance of these informal collaborative opportunities and the need for greater creativity and flexibility in labor configurations across the faculty-staff divide.

WORKS CITED

Berlant, Lauren. "Affect Is the New Trauma." *The Minnesota Review*, nos. 71–72, 2009, pp. 131–36.

Bessner, Daniel, and Michael Brenes. "A Moral Stain on the Profession." *The Chronicle of Higher Education*, 26 Apr. 2019, chronicle.com/article/a-moral-stain-on-the-profession/.

Brown, Wendy. *Undoing the Demos: Neoliberalism's Stealth Revolution*. Zone Books, 2015.

Cassuto, Leonard. "Outcomes-Based Graduate Education: The Humanities Edition." *The Chronicle of Higher Education*, 19 Jun. 2019, chronicle.com/article/outcomes-based-graduate-school-the-humanities-edition/.

Damrosch, David. *We Scholars: Changing the Culture of the University*. Harvard UP, 1995.

"First-Year Experience." *Lehigh University*, 2019, studentaffairs.lehigh.edu/content/first-year-experience.

Fitzpatrick, Kathleen. *Generous Thinking: A Radical Approach to Saving the University*. Johns Hopkins UP, 2019.

hooks, bell. *Teaching Community: A Pedagogy of Hope*. Routledge, 2003.

Keenan, Thomas. *University Ethics: How Colleges Can Build and Benefit from a Culture of Ethics*. Rowman and Littlefield, 2015.

Laurence, David. "Where Are They Now? Occupations of 1996–2011 PhD Recipients in 2013." *The Trend: Research and Analysis from the MLA Office of Programs*, 17 Feb. 2015, mlaresearch.mla.hcommons.org/2015/02/17/where-are-they-now-occupations-of-1996-2011-phd-recipients-in-2013-2/.

O'Dair, Sharon. "Shamelessness and Hypocrisy at the MLA." *The Chronicle of Higher Education*, 4 Feb. 2018, chronicle.com/article/shamelessness-and-hypocrisy-br-at-the-mla/.

Saltmarsh, John, et al. "Democratic Engagement White Paper." *New England Resource Center for Higher Education*, 2009. *Scholarly Commons*, repository.upenn.edu/gse_pubs/274.

Strouse, A. W. "Getting Medieval on Graduate Education: Queering Academic Professionalism." *Pedagogy*, vol. 15, no. 1, Jan. 2015, pp. 119–38. *Project Muse*, muse.jhu.edu/article/563212.

Reforming and Revalidating the Humanities Master's Degree at a STEM-Driven University

Anna Westerstahl Stenport and Richard Utz

Humanistic graduate education has long emphasized the PhD as its primary goal, with a professorship as the idealized profession of choice. This obviously must change, and the narrow assumptions underlying the PhD-to-professor calculus indeed are very much in the process of changing. In this essay, we specifically address the potential of the master's pathway for a positive and sustainable transformation of humanistic graduate education attractive to diverse student groups who seek a range of career outcomes, and joy and community-building purpose, as part of the process. We draw on our experience from STEM-oriented, research-intensive universities, but the observations and principles apply to any academic context. The thrust of this essay is a call for a change in academic culture through the career-oriented humanities master's, one that opens up more advanced degree opportunities to more students, integrates interdisciplinary approaches, foregrounds applied learning, and emphasizes multiple pathways to personal and professional success. This is also a civic duty: our society and communities need more humanities professionals with an advanced degree who work in a range of sectors, public and private. Now is the time for reform, revalidation, and, ultimately, celebration of the humanities master's degree.

The humanities master's degree has been overlooked for so long that its "rehabilitation may be difficult," as Leonard Cassuto and Robert

Weisbuch argue in *The New PhD: How to Build a Better Graduate Education* (3, 184). It is certainly true that most humanities master's degrees in the United States have had no clear curricular distinction, limited or nonexistent career preparation, and few discernible purposeful outcomes.[1] Students who care deeply about the humanities can hardly help observing that most master's degrees appear to offer few career options and are associated with low and insecure levels of compensation. Some students who intend at first to pursue a PhD leave with their "terminal" master's degrees because the programs they encountered do not articulate the value of graduate education to their careers or to society. In contrast, departments, often conservative and reluctant to change, present the story that students were successfully weeded out and deemed not to be "PhD material."

The absence of a range of robust master's degrees is a negative for all concerned. Students who enroll in a PhD that does not fit their career goals may lose valuable time and earning potential without gaining the skills they need. At the same time, the perception of the master's degree as a concessional or inadequate degree leaves little incentive for departments to integrate career-oriented and applied approaches or to change their curricula to create new forms of humanities training. A trickle-down consequence of this cycle is the decline of diversity in the traditional PhD, reinforcing the perception and experience of the PhD as elitist and disciplinarily narrow. Successful master's degrees display a variety of positive educational outcomes, including deepened subject-matter knowledge, communication and leadership expertise, and an emphasis on immediate and long-term career success in a range of areas. Departments that shy away from integrating these outcomes into their curriculum and creating new, more accessible degree programs do so to their and their students' detriment. Based on this synthesis of the current status, we believe, as Cassuto and Weisbuch do, that "the recovery of a viable master's degree [in the humanities] is a worthy goal" (185). A formidable book full of strategic, tangible, and practical recommendations for humanities graduate education reform, *The New PhD* is one of few publications to gesture toward the degree's potential, though we note that the rhetoric surrounding the master's degree discussion in this insightful assessment is one associated with illness and deficit rather than joy and sustainability.[2]

We argue throughout this essay that fostering and promoting strong master's degrees in the humanities is a critical social imperative. It also has the potential to proactively and positively resolve the so-called crisis of the humanities. If created ethically—with financial support for students and measurable return on investment—the master's provides opportunities for more students, and more diverse students, to earn an advanced degree in ways that will sustainably serve them.[3] This includes those who wish to pursue a PhD and an academic position, since "students from underrepresented groups are significantly more likely to enroll in a master's program on the way to a PhD compared to the graduate student population at large" (Cassuto and Weisbuch 165). In addition, as Julie R. Posselt notes, the master's degree has closed gender and racial gaps better than the PhD (3). The master's program can thus be an intersectional vehicle of social mobility and advanced educational equity and should be embraced as such by faculty members and administrators alike.

The humanities master's degree also provides opportunities for more organizations—private and public—to integrate the distinctive expertise of the humanities into their workforce. This should be seen as a civic priority by employers and academic institutions alike, since the humanities teach ethics, empathy, inclusive communication, cross-cultural competence, and social analysis. In contrast, the long and specialized PhD training distinctive of most humanities programs has shown to be less attractive to nonacademic employers. Rehabilitating the master's degree is also imperative as more institutions are shifting recruitment strategies toward emphasizing combined bachelor and master's programs (shorthanded as 4+1, 3+2, 3+3, etc.) in their pitches to high school students and their parents. This package deal often includes humanities programs that may not all be fully prepared to provide the diverse career preparation incoming students expect and deserve. Humanities programs seeking to better serve students and society face a challenging transition from an analysis/synthesis mode to an applied, experiential, and change-oriented mode in which students enjoy seeing their work leading to tangible results outside the classroom, both for their communities and their own careers.

There are some inspiring models of distinct, interdisciplinary, robust, and professionally oriented master's programs in the humanities, however. These include the MA in digital humanities at the City University of New York; the MA in translation at the University of Illinois; the MA in environment, culture, and media at the University of Miami; the MA in translation and localization management at the Middlebury Institute of International Studies; the MS in applied languages and intercultural studies at Georgia Institute of Technology; and the MS in communication at Rochester Institute of Technology.[4] Educators and program administrators can also learn from STEM-driven contexts and from technological universities with a focus on applied, entrepreneurial, interdisciplinary, and career-oriented education about successful master's programs that benefit a diverse group of students and contribute to a range of organizations.

In leading the development of a new interdisciplinary and career-oriented master's of science in global media and cultures (MS-GMC) at Georgia Institute of Technology in Atlanta, we set out with the ambition to design the kind of master's education needed in the humanities, in the region, and in the nation.[5] Georgia Tech is a large public institution recognized worldwide for its top-ranked engineering and computing programs. It is also a local anchor institution with extensive public and private partnerships in the greater Atlanta region, which is known for its vibrant media, international, and civic communities as well as its deep and long-standing racial and economic inequities. The faculty and student leaders we worked with to conceptualize and implement the degree made clear that these characteristics should inform the MS-GMC program. In addition, we drew substantially from the principles articulated in the National Academies of Sciences, Engineering, and Medicine's consensus study report on the state of US higher education *The Integration of the Humanities and Arts with Sciences, Engineering, and Medicine in Higher Education: Branches from the Same Tree* (Skorton and Bear). The report locates alternatives to the hyperspecialized and siloed nature of current academic degree programs in a more holistic model of education that would consciously integrate academic disciplines in order to better prepare students for work, life, and citizenship (see also Cassuto and Weisbuch; Hartley; Staley; Stross).

Approaches that consciously integrate the kinds of knowledge, modes of inquiry, and pedagogies found in the humanities, arts, sciences, engineering, technology, mathematics, and medicine increase students' written and oral communication skills, teamwork skills, ethical decision-making, critical thinking, and ability to apply knowledge in real-world settings, the Academies concluded. The report confirms that integrative approaches are correlated with outcomes such as higher-order thinking, content mastery of complex concepts, improved visuospatial reasoning, and enhanced communication and teamwork skills, along with increased motivation, empathy, resilience, and enjoyment of learning. Increased enjoyment of learning is mentioned as an observed outcome throughout the report, which was based on studies of diverse forms of integration (engineering and history, medicine and art observation, neuroscience and poetry), pedagogical approaches (project-based learning, lecture, living-learning community), and curricular inclusion (stand-alone course, cocurricular activity, fully integrated program).

The National Academies' endorsement of integrating arts and humanities into STEMM (the final *M* represents medicine) has particular potential for the conceptualization of new graduate programs, especially the humanities master's degree. It opens the way for curricular reforms that integrate the core human needs of meaningful interaction, communication, joy, and sustainability with long-term career success and civic contributions. In addition, private and public sector employers articulate the need to follow this recommendation to ensure domestic prosperity, social stability, and national competitiveness in global markets. A 2017 Pew Research Center report predicts that core humanities "capabilities and attributes such as emotional intelligence, curiosity, creativity, adaptability, resilience and critical thinking will be most highly valued" (Rainie and Anderson 13). At the same time, industry is expressing clear concerns that students are not being adequately trained to meet these needs. In 2019, the McKinsey Global Institute confirmed that "[w]orkforce skills have been a growing concern in the United States for many years. Now new and higher-level skills are in demand, including not only digital skills but also critical thinking, creativity, and socioemotional skills. The skills needed in fast-growing STEM roles, in particular, are continuously evolving" (Lund et al. 17; see also reports by the Bureau of Labor Statistics in Gehlhaus 4; Hart Research Associates; Commission on Language Learning).

Humanities Master's Education at an Institute of Technology

Committed to the principles articulated above, we also know from personal experience, benchmark analyses, and discussions at events such as HumanTech (see Pearson) that universities and colleges focused on technology and science play a crucial role in advancing the priorities outlined above. Moreover, as graduate and undergraduate enrollments in languages and literatures have declined over the last decade, and programs have downsized or closed (see Looney and Lusin; Hayot), the need for the capacities and expertise provided by the humanities has continued to grow. This is a paradox, tied to a demonstrated misalignment of resources, priorities, and policies on a national scale, that we believe STEM-driven institutions with strong humanities initiatives can help resolve. Reconceptualized and reformed humanities master's education writ large is another way to address this discrepancy.

Humanities departments at technological institutes inhabit differently defined intellectual and programmatic spaces than those of their sister units at other institutions of higher education. There are several reasons for this. At our current and recent institutions, Georgia Tech and Rochester Institute of Technology (RIT), in addition to sustaining relatively small or midsize undergraduate programs and providing relatively large portions of general education to STEM (and other) majors, educators in the humanities are usually vested in finding creative ways of balancing their humanistic perspectives and methodologies with their institution's science- and technology-driven visions and missions. This approach has transformative power for graduate education.

One of the effects of this increased importance of interdisciplinarity is that humanities faculty members at STEM-driven institutions often explore innovative educational paths, multidisciplinary work, and collaborative projects and degree programs. In our experience, institutions such as Georgia Tech or RIT operate differently with respect to curricular implementation, extending applied engineering, maker space, internships, co-ops, and design-thinking approaches to academic programming in ways that encourage experimentation and entrepreneurship. Acknowledging that complex social problems may not be solved in disciplinary isolation, faculty members and students in such units often find joy and fulfillment in experimenting with new structures of higher education (see Utz and Head; Stenport and Ozkan). For example, humanities faculty members at Georgia Tech, where most humanities majors concurrently major in STEM or business, often build integrative courses or for-credit labs running a student-led research project to combine their own disciplinary knowledge, methods, and skills with those prevalent in STEM-oriented fields of study. Many of these courses focus on global perspectives, cross-cultural communication, environmental and social sustainability, digital media cultures, justice and equity, and economics.

Conceptualizing the Master of Science in Global Media and Cultures

The Schools of Literature, Media, and Communication (LMC) and the School of Modern Languages (ML) have nearly one hundred PhD-holding faculty members combined and feature undergraduate degrees, such as a BS in digital media or in applied language and intercultural studies, that bridge science, technology, and the humanities. These degrees—which have attracted and retained a diverse student body—are distinguished by the integration of creative tools, information visualization, new models of media- and game-based learning, computational tools for scientific discovery, and competency in professionally oriented applied language learning and intercultural communication. These degrees, and twenty associated minors and more than twenty faculty-led study abroad programs, became the foundations of the MS-GMC curriculum. Specifically, we focused on exploring how digital media technologies, global perspectives, and applied language learning can enhance and reconfigure arts and entertainment in collaboration with private and public sector partners to advance community culture and civic life. Building on the cornerstones of the undergraduate programs, we addressed what Cassuto and Weisbuch have subsequently articulated as a key to success in graduate education. As they outline, a rigorous curriculum is not comprised of a scattered set of courses derived from (and serving) specialized faculty expertise, a disassociated set of exam requirements, and an independent thesis. Instead, it should consist of a cohesive course of study that extends beyond classroom learning, examination, and original research into experiential and applied learning and career education for a range of professions (203–14).

Specifically, we built the curriculum around threads in existing bachelor's programs in LMC, spanning literature, media, communication, design, social justice, and science, technology, and culture. The BS in computational media, collaboratively run with the College of Computing, foregrounds the computer as an expressive medium. Students learn about the hands-on, theoretical, and historical-critical aspects of computing as well as the principles and applications of visual design and the history of media. Threads in this degree also encourage students to choose a purpose, rather than a discipline or major, by selecting courses on intelligence and film, performance and media, and people and game studies. Through its mission-driven version of the Georgia Board of Regents' traditional "composition" requirement, LMC offerings in multimodal communication teach Georgia Tech students essential elements of written, oral, visual, electronic, and nonverbal (WOVEN) communication, an overall approach that became integrated into the MS-GMC.

ML has undergraduate majors in Chinese, French, German, Japanese, Korean, Russian, and Spanish as part of three interdisciplinary degrees: global economics and modern languages (GEML), international affairs and modern languages (IAML), and applied languages and intercultural studies (ALIS). The majors in these languages became the seven language tracks for the MS-GMC. The school's approach has been content-based and applied, speaking to the fact that seventy percent of advanced foreign language enrollment at Georgia Tech comes from STEM students, and nearly two-thirds of ALIS majors are double majors, most with STEM concentrations. Therefore, ML focuses more than half of its advanced language coursework on nontraditional content (that is, content other than language, literature, and linguistics), offering over eighty-five interdisciplinary courses addressing topics in business, economics, media, public policy, computing, engineering, and the sciences. Many of these are taught abroad in faculty-led programs with foci such as design, engineering, health care, and sustainability. Graduate versions of these courses were developed and integrated into the MS-GMC as well as into the school's stand-alone MS in applied languages and cultures.

In addition to international and foreign-language internships and service-learning courses, three ML initiatives were integrated as foundational components of the MS-GMC. A course and associated lab called Career Design for Global Citizenship is open to any student with intermediate knowledge of a foreign language. This course emphasizes the significance of twenty-first-century humanities and critical competence skills in a spectrum of professional arenas. Further, the lab-based and applied approaches distinctive of STEM institutions have been translated into for-credit project labs, where faculty members work closely with a group of undergraduate and graduate students on a multiyear research project, such as the Polivision media platform, which engages with Latin American artists in Atlanta. Finally, in collaboration with Georgia Tech's European campus in Metz, France, the school is now offering a start-up entrepreneurship course in French and semester-long on-site service-learning and internship programs.

The application and enrollment numbers for LMC and ML majors have been stable or increasing over the last seven years, in contrast to declining numbers in languages and literatures nationwide (see for example Looney and Lusin). We cannot claim causal connections between the two schools' interdisciplinary and applied undergraduate curricula and robust enrollments. However, the available quantitative, qualitative, and narrative evidence, along with anecdotal observation, has convinced us that the general institutional STEM context of our humanities programs and our focus on programmatic purpose and transdisciplinary integration are foundational elements of the schools' continued popularity.

Innovation in the Humanities and Professionally Oriented Master's Programs

At the outset of the development process, we asked faculty members, student liaisons, and ourselves, How do we expand, deepen, and transfer this integrative model to professionally oriented humanities graduate degrees? Similarly, we had to consider how we would go about articulating the value of a new humanities master's degree as a distinctive, marquee effort at our particular institution. A provost commission report from 2018, *Deliberate Innovation, Lifetime Education*, proposed that all Georgia Tech graduates should embody the characteristics of a "T-shaped" professional in terms of cognitive skills (problem solving, creativity, critical thinking), interpersonal skills (communication, teamwork, leadership), and intrapersonal skills (adaptability, initiative, discipline, ethics, persistence) (Georgia Tech Commission 34–35; Brooks). Similarly, Georgia Tech's strategic plans of 2010 and 2020 emphasized global connections, experimental learning, and interdisciplinarity (*Designing*; *Georgia Tech*). We took these reports as models in arguing for the integration of an interdisciplinary humanities master's program as core to the principles of a STEM-driven institution and in generating start-up as well as ongoing student support for the degree. Large-scale university strategic planning helped us move these programs forward; while the suspicion among faculty toward strategic planning is long-standing, in our experience, mobilizing the principles articulated as strategic priorities to strengthen the humanities can be successful.

In related ways, the National Academies' report outlines the role of "integration" in graduate medical education. Although graduate education tends to require a higher degree of disciplinary specialization, the study concludes that programs inclusive of the humanities, arts, and social sciences in medical training may "(1) ingrain aspects of professionalism, empathy, and altruism; (2) enhance clinical communication and observation skills; (3) increase interprofessionalism and collaboration; and (4) decrease burnout and compassion fatigue" (Skorton and Bear 142). Other recent studies similarly acknowledge the value of multidimensional, transdisciplinary, integrative, and mission- or purpose-driven elements in graduate education (see for example Cassuto and Weisbuch).

The "Atlanta Factor"

A critical motivation for the creation of the MS-GMC is Georgia Tech's location in Atlanta, whose current and future workforce—and civic society—stand to benefit from the kind of educational experience the MS-GMC promotes. The greater Atlanta region is the largest economy in the Southeast and one of the country's fastest-growing urban centers. An international, multicultural, and globally oriented city and region, Atlanta boasts 146 in-the-home languages (U.S. Department of Commerce);

seventy-three consular or trade offices ("Consular Offices"); headquarters of thirty-one Fortune 1000 companies, including seventeen in the Fortune 500 (Metro Atlanta Chamber); and the world's busiest passenger airport. Between 2000 and 2012, Atlanta's foreign-born population increased by twenty-two percent and immigrants accounted for nearly two-thirds of the region's expansion ("World"). The region is known for its media industries and for its global connectivity—all critical building pieces for the GMC. Atlanta has the fifth-largest agglomeration of higher education institutions in the country, providing an accessible recruitment base. Atlanta's multilayered social fabric, diverse social ecosystems, and wide range of civic, community, and educational institutions were taken into consideration during the conceptualization of the MS-GMC and influenced the partnerships we are building to serve our students and alumni. This also includes the recognition of deep social, political, and economic inequities and continuing racial inequalities, which many of the MS-GMC courses and projects address.

Considering that new graduate programs in the humanities face an inimical climate, we did not want to build our new programs upon traditional, faculty-driven paradigms based on narrow research interests. Instead, we wanted to design an educational experience that integrates faculty capacity more broadly conceived. We learned from interviews with representatives of other Georgia Tech graduate programs in STEM and business with strong educational and preprofessional ecosystems. The interest in a purpose-driven curriculum was expressed through extended surveys and focus group conversations we conducted with ML and LMC alumni and students. Career education, internships, hands-on learning in labs, developing a professional portfolio, working in interdisciplinary and cross-cultural teams, and becoming proficient in aspects of library science and data analysis were all factors identified as key to programmatic success and integrated into a range of courses.

Distinctive Characteristics of the Master of Science in Global Media and Cultures

The design of the MS-GMC reflects our belief that a professional-level humanities education does not lie solely in the space of academic research but rather comprises a range of activities that have a measurable impact on the world and society (see also Montlaur). The twelve-month (thirty credit hours) terminal graduate programs represent a competitive alternative to the traditional PhD in languages and literatures. A key element of these programs is widespread access to advanced-level humanities training for those who will become decision-makers in many sectors of society. This means that the MS-GMC foregrounds professional practice in the humanities, redefining what it means to have humanities expertise. Offered jointly by both schools and foundational to the MS-GMC is the rigorous study of foreign language, media, global cultures, and intercultural competence. Students complete coursework in one language concentration (Chinese, French, German, Japanese, Korean, Russian, or Spanish) at the intermediate to advanced level as well as courses in media studies with an emphasis on global and multicultural perspectives. These courses provide training in the analysis of cultural artifacts, the interpretation of arguments and narrative, text-based research, translation, aesthetic sensibility, historical and political contextualization, close analytical reading, verbal and aural communication competency, and the production of humanities texts and images. (A description of the program of study is included in the appendix.)

The professional orientation of students' learning is at the center of the program. Culminating in an individualized final project, the MS-GMC offers a student-centered core curriculum. Rather than a traditional master's thesis, the MS-GMC final project is a creative product or internship addressing a real-world challenge from a humanities and global perspective. The purpose is to leverage the final project as a career stepping stone. The Theory and Foundations course addresses global challenges such as diversity, migration, and the climate crisis through a science and technology perspective and examines how media and culture shape these inquiries. The required course in research methodology emphasizes communication, motivating students through the numerous positive ways in which their projects engage wider audiences and the public sphere. The third required course focuses on constructing a career portfolio through culture-oriented career development, foregrounding professional networks of cultural communities and identities. This course also emphasizes long-term individual career growth. A cornerstone of the program, internships abroad and in the culturally diverse Atlanta region advance cross-sector expertise. Internships are leveraged to promote industry-oriented, professional-level humanities expertise. The priorities of the three core courses of the MS-GMC are also engaged in parallel undergraduate and graduate courses such as Career Design for Global Citizenship. The applied aspects of the program, integrated into the core courses, are geared toward visible change—personal, professional, and societal. Students are encouraged to work in teams, building community. These priorities are different from those in most traditional academic programs and build on the principles of learned optimism and positive psychology, in which working together toward a greater good leads to joy (see for example Seligman).

The graduate program integrates the real-world relevance of humanities expertise by supporting MS-GMC students as research assistants who work in program management, marketing and communications, and organizational change management for other units at Georgia Tech. This funding model is different from a traditional TA- or RA-ship, which supports a professor's individual career goals. Students apply for their employment, which comes with an academic-year tuition waiver and stipend, as part of the admissions process, where their interests are matched with the needs of the sponsoring unit. An illustrative example is provided by the Global at Home Graduate Research Assistant (GRA) program, a partnership with the Georgia Tech Department of Housing and Residential Life. GRAs employed with Housing work on projects to enhance the multicultural inclusivity of the on-campus residential community. This partnership has generated intercultural training modules, enhanced campus-wide communications and events about global diversity, and augmented international student orientations. A related example is the partnership with Georgia Tech's Enterprise Innovation Institute, where GRAs work with international companies seeking to establish a presence in the greater Atlanta region. This hands-on experience guided by professionals is complemented by seminars on cultural management, diversity, and inclusivity. In this way, GRAs engage in a practical way the theoretical frameworks that underpin their studies, integrating tenets of cultural analysis, sociology, and organizational behavior. The goal is to integrate graduate students' study of language and culture with concrete professional experiences that have a tangible impact while rigorously articulating the form that humanities expertise can take in a professional industry context. These modes of employment speak to the interests of diverse students and position them as graduates for a range of career choices.

Building Culture, Community, Collaboration, and Partnerships

Funding for graduate education is a challenge at many institutions, and especially so in the humanities. At Georgia Tech, we benefited from the entrepreneurial ethos of faculty members who have created unique and innovative partnerships, such as the Global at Home program with Housing and Residence Life. Faculty members have also received grants that have in part been able to support MS-GMC students. These grants include an award from the Mellon Foundation to the Digital Integrative Liberal Arts Center (DILAC) in the Ivan Allen College of Liberal Arts, an award from the Halle Foundation, and a US Department of Education National Resource Center and Foreign Language and Area Studies (NRC-FLAS) grant, which offers fellowships for advanced language learning, especially in critical and less commonly taught languages. The schools of LMC and ML have also allocated philanthropy funding to support underrepresented and minority students. A program expansion allotment from the provost's office provided some complementary funding for GRAs in addition to the discretionary funding allocated by both schools. These GRA positions were tasked with building collaboration, community, and research interaction among faculty members, students, alumni, and partners of the two schools and with supporting recruitment and promoting the degree to internal and external constituents. Georgia Tech also allocates a small bonus for increased enrollments on the master's level, which the schools direct toward ongoing graduate student support.

Preliminary Outcomes

There is by now ample evidence that traditional graduate programs do not serve students, society, or perhaps even the professoriate well. Stemming from a late-nineteenth-century model, graduate education has for too long remained committed to a demarcation between an old-fashioned approach to liberal arts education and a professional and applied education (often championed at technological universities). Instead, the knowledge economy of the early twenty-first century recognizes the need for an active reintegration of the humanities and STEM approaches to resolve complex and globally connected problems. Reconceptualizing, reforming, and celebrating the distinct advantages of an interdisciplinary humanities master's degree can do precisely that. As we have argued throughout this chapter, Georgia Tech's MS-GMC provides a model for this new kind of professionally oriented, rigorous master's program where long-term student success and career outcomes are at the center.

These guiding principles have proven to be attractive. Enrolling fifteen students in the first class, the MS-GMC nearly doubled its application pool in its second year. When the third cohort graduated in 2022, the MS-GMC and its cohort sister program, the MS-ALIS, had graduated more than fifty students, with ninety percent of those on a fully funded academic-year package and a large majority having had an internship or applied career-oriented research experience. The ethnic, racial, and socioeconomic diversity of this group is particularly noteworthy. More than two-thirds come from groups traditionally underrepresented in the humanities. With alumni data being reported as we write this, we note that the large majority of graduates so far have embarked on a number of professions of choice, with employers ranging from foreign consulates to strategic consulting Fortune 500 firms.[6]

This data would indicate that students—with highly diverse backgrounds and career aspirations—are more than willing to join a graduate program that combines rigorous, human-centered graduate-level education with a clearly defined purpose outside the university. While our specific integration of technology, language learning, media and industry application, and global engagement had the advantage of the "Atlanta factor" and the context of a technological institute focused on innovation and entrepreneurial enthusiasm, there is no reason our model might not be replicated at traditional universities in numerous locations. In fact, alumni, current students, and applicants seem eager to embrace a graduate degree specifically built to provide an optimistic, creative, and joyful educational experience.

NOTES

An earlier version of the subsection "Distinctive Characteristics of the MS in Global Media and Cultures" was included in Stenport et al.

1. Serious calls for a rethinking of the humanities master's program in the United States date back to the late 1980s, when its status as "jack of all trades" began to be challenged (Green).

2. Gregory Colón Semenza's *Graduate Study for the Twenty-First Century* is typical of existing guides to graduate study. Its focus, declared in its subtitle, is "how to build an academic career in the humanities," and the master's degree is presented as merely a first step toward the PhD.

3. As Kevin Carey indicates in an article entitled "The Great Master's-Degree Swindle," academic institutions have damaged the overall reputation of the master's degree by "cashing in" through debt-financed programs: "Most master's programs are, for all intents and purposes, for-profit, regardless of who technically runs them." Especially in the arts and humanities, academic institutions should be aware of their "moral responsibility" for "a system that puts 100 percent of the financial risk on young people who may not be that financially oriented to begin with."

4. Some of these programs were presented in a session called "New Models for Master's Degrees in Languages, Cultures, Media, and Digital Humanities" at the 2020 Annual Convention of the Modern Language Association. The panel was cosponsored by the Association of Departments of Foreign Languages, indicating the association's interest in promoting career-oriented and applied approaches; Anna Westerstahl Stenport organized the session.

5. Georgia Tech does not award BA/MA degrees (only BS/MS degrees); at other institutions, a program like the MS-GMC would fit well also as an MA. Both coauthors led the formation of the degree during their times as school chairs—Anna for the School of Modern Languages (2016–21) and Richard for the School of Literature Media and Communication (2012–21).

6. We thank Yevgenya Strakovsky, formerly associate director of graduate studies and career education in the School of Modern Languages at Georgia Tech, for providing accurate information as of September 2021.

WORKS CITED

Brooks, Katherine. "Career Success Starts with a 'T.'" *Psychology Today*, 19 Apr. 2012, psychologytoday.com/us/blog/career-transitions/201204/career-success-starts-with-a-t.

Carey, Kevin. "The Great Master's-Degree Swindle." *The Chronicle of Higher Education*, 5 Aug. 2021, chronicle.com/article/the-great-masters-degree-swindle.

Cassuto, Leonard, and Robert Weisbuch. *The New PhD: How to Build a Better Graduate Education*. Johns Hopkins UP, 2021.

Commission on Language Learning. *America's Languages: Investing in Language Education for the Twenty-First Century*. American Academy of Arts and Sciences, 2017, www.amacad.org/publication/americas-languages.

"Consular Offices." Georgia Department of Economic Development, georgia.org/international/relations-protocol/consular-offices. Accessed 23 Mar. 2023.

Designing the Future: A Strategic Vision and Plan. Georgia Institute of Technology, 2010, hdl.handle.net/1853/36393.

Gehlhaus, Diana. "What Can I Do With My Liberal Arts Degree?" *Occupational Outlook Quarterly*, winter 2007–08, pp. 3–11, www.bls.gov/careeroutlook/2007/winter/art01.pdf.

Georgia Tech Commission on Creating the Next in Education. *Deliberate Innovation, Lifetime Education*. Georgia Institute of Technology, Apr. 2018, provost.gatech.edu/sites/default/files/documents/deliberate_innovation_lifetime_education.pdf.

Georgia Tech Strategic Plan 2020–2030. Georgia Institute of Technology, strategicplan.gatech.edu. Accessed 17 Sept. 2021.

Green, Joslyn L., editor. *The Master's Degree: Jack of All Trades*. SHEEO Association, 1987.

Hart Research Associates. *Fulfilling the American Dream: Liberal Education and the Future of Work*. American Association of Colleges and Universities, 2018, aacu.org/research/fulfilling-the-american-dream-liberal-education-and-the-future-of-work.

Hartley, Scott. *The Fuzzie and the Techie: Why the Liberal Arts Will Rule the Digital World*. Houghton Mifflin Harcourt, 2017.

Hayot, Eric. "The Humanities As We Know Them Are Doomed. Now What?" *Chronicle of Higher Education*, 1 July 2018, chronicle.com/article/The-Humanities-as-We-Know-Them/243769.

Looney, Dennis, and Natalia Lusin. *Enrollments in Languages Other Than English in United States Institutions of Higher Education, Summer 2016 and Fall 2016: Final Report.* Modern Language Association of America, 2019, mla.org/content/download/110154/2406932/2016-Enrollments-Final-Report.pdf.

Lund, Susan, et al. *The Future of Work in America: People and Places, Today and Tomorrow.* McKinsey Global Institute, 2019, mckinsey.com/featured-insights/future-of-work/the-future-of-work-in-america-people-and-places-today-and-tomorrow.

Metro Atlanta Chamber. "Fortune 500 Companies; Fortune 1000 Companies." metroatlantachamber.com/wp-content/uploads/2022/11/Metro-ATL-Fortune-500-1000-List-June-2022.pdf. Accessed March 23 2023.

Montlaur, Bénédicte de. "Do You Speak My Language? You Should." *The New York Times*, 26 Mar. 2019, nytimes.com/2019/03/26/opinion/learn-foreign-language.html.

New Models for Master's Degrees in Languages, Cultures, Media, and Digital Humanities. Organized by Anna Westerstahl Stenport, MLA Annual Convention, 10 Jan. 2020, Seattle. Panel discussion.

Pearson, Michael. "HumanTech Symposium Identifies Opportunities, Challenges for Humanities at Technological Universities." *News Center*, Georgia Institute of Technology, 2019, news.gatech.edu/2019/04/24/humantech-symposium-identifies-opportunities-challenges-humanities-technological.

Posselt, Julie R. *Inside Graduate Admissions: Merit, Diversity, and Faculty Gatekeeping.* Harvard UP, 2016.

Rainie, Lee, and Janna Anderson. *The Future of Jobs and Job Training.* Pew Research Center, 3 May 2017, pewresearch.org/internet/2017/05/03/the-future-of-jobs-and-jobs-training/. Accessed 17 Sept. 2021.

Seligman, Martin E. P. *Learned Optimism: How to Change Your Mind and Your Life.* Vintage Books, 2006.

Semenza, Gregory Colón. *Graduate Study for the Twenty-First Century: How to Build an Academic Career in the Humanities.* Palgrave Macmillan, 2010.

Skorton, David, and Ashley Bear, editors. *Branches from the Same Tree: The Integration of the Humanities and Arts with Sciences, Engineering, and Medicine in Higher Education.* The National Academies Press, 2018.

Staley, David J. *Alternative Universities: Speculative Design for Innovation in Higher Education.* Johns Hopkins UP, 2019.

Stenport, Anna Westerstahl, and Sebnem Ozkan. "COVID-19 Makes 'Think Globally, Act Locally' More than a Check-box Exercise." *The Saporta Report*, 24 May 2020, saportareport.com/covid-19-makes-think-globally-act-locally-more-than-a-check-box-exercise/.

Stenport, Anna Westerstahl, et al. "Radical Interdisciplinarity: Science, Technology, and the New Humanities of the Twenty-First Century." *ADFL*, vol. 46, no. 2, 2020, pp. 28–43.

Stross, Randall. *A Practical Education: Why Liberal Arts Majors Make Great Employees.* Stanford UP, 2017.

U.S. Department of Commerce. "Census Bureau Reports at Least 350 Languages Spoken in U.S. Homes." *U.S. Census Bureau News*, 3 Nov. 2015, content.govdelivery.com/accounts/USCENSUS/bulletins/122dd88.

Utz, Richard, and Karen Head, editors. *Humanistic Perspectives in a Technological World*. Georgia Institute of Technology School of Literature, Media, and Communication, 2021.

"The World in Atlanta: An Analysis of the Foreign-born Population in Metro Atlanta." Atlanta Regional Commission, Mar. 2013, documents.atlanta regional.com/arcBoard/march2013/dr_regional_snapshot_3_2013_foreign born.pdf.

APPENDIX: COURSE OF STUDY FOR MASTER OF SCIENCE IN GLOBAL MEDIA AND CULTURES

Each student's program of study includes a concentration in Chinese, French, German, Korean, Japanese, Russian, or Spanish and is designed to meet their individual career goals through electives, internship opportunities, and independent projects on campus and abroad. In the fall and spring terms, students complete twelve credits of coursework, including three credits of core courses shared across the cohort and nine credits of electives in either Modern Languages (ML; in the target language) or Literature, Media, and Communications (LMC; in English). The summer term asks students to choose a combination of options to complete the degree with a six-credit final project.

Fall

Global Media and Cultures (core course—three credits)
Approved LMC course (elective)
Approved course in the language of concentration (elective)
Approved course in either LMC or the language of concentration; alternatively, other courses by approval of graduate coordinators (elective)

Spring

Research Methodologies (core course—one credit)
Career Education and Professional Portfolio (core course—two credits)
Approved LMC course (elective)
Approved course in the language of concentration (elective)
Approved course in either LMC or the language of concentration; alternatively, other courses by approval of graduate coordinators (elective)

Summer

Independent project with substantive work in the language of concentration, in combination with an internship, practicum (teaching experience), or media production (six credits); or
Master's thesis with substantive research in the language of concentration (six credits)

Purpose and Vocation: Rethinking the First-Year Graduate Proseminar

David Pettersen

At a time when graduate student mental health concerns have reached a fever pitch, it behooves all of us who teach in graduate programs to help alleviate some of the pressures of graduate study (Wong; Puri; Perry). The reasons for the crisis are multiple, and many are effectively beyond faculty control. However, this is not an excuse to avoid intervention where it is possible. An important early opportunity for such intervention is the first-year graduate proseminar. Some students who attend graduate school may have received research opportunities as undergraduates and may already be equipped to navigate graduate study. Students without these affordances may not understand the expectations they now face and thus enter their program at a disadvantage. A first-year graduate proseminar is an excellent way to help new graduate students map the next several years of their lives and begin to prepare for their chosen career path.

    For some programs, a proseminar is a course that introduces new graduate students to the current state of a discipline. In the case of modern languages, this could be an introduction to cultural theory. My own department has such a course, as do most of the other language and culture departments at my university. These courses balance a history of the discipline with introductions to leading-edge subfields and research methods. Many of these courses focus on the "what" of graduate study without addressing the "how" and "why." They can include professionalization components, such as learning how to write conference paper abstracts, and can even culminate in a miniature seminar conference. However, attention to discrete skills does not obviate the need for a synoptic view of the arc of graduate study. Christopher Uggen and Heather Hlavka point out that such "methods" courses do not help new graduate students understand the process of graduate study and the competencies that they will be expected to develop. For this reason, they argue that a dedicated proseminar is necessary—one that does more than just discuss a graduate program's requirements; present university resources, like the library; and introduce students to professors through "an aimless parade of available faculty visitors to talk about their research interests, current projects, and, quite literally, whatever else they would like to discuss" (196). Uggen and Hlavka's description of the faculty parade corresponds to the proseminar I took in graduate school many years ago. While this model is easy to organize and requires little work for faculty members, it does not serve incoming students very well. Times have changed, and programs are increasingly offering one-credit proseminar introductions to graduate study, including overviews of conferences and publications alongside frank discussions of academic labor, career diversity, everyday bias, and structural inequalities. However, such courses often eschew talking about why one might go to graduate school in the humanities in the first place. The ideal proseminar should offer a space in which to reflect on the big questions of mission, purpose, and value in the life of each student and to connect these questions to the mundane details of graduate study.

The Rationale for Reading

Although faculty members are sometimes loath to assume teaching responsibility for a proseminar because it does not always count in one's teaching load, I agree with Uggen and Hlavka that it is essential for one faculty member to lead the proseminar. I disagree, however, with their prohibition against assigned reading (197–98, 200). While student discussion should be central to a proseminar, a reading list is also key. New students are not always aware of what the challenges of graduate study may be; to put it differently, they do not know what they do not know. A proseminar should introduce students not only to the discipline but also to the macro- and micro-level skills they will need to develop a plan for graduate study. By *macro*, I mean identifying one's interests and values and aligning these with a multiyear vision for scholarly inquiry. By *micro*, I mean the practical skills involved in working day to day in one's research, teaching, and service activities. Taken together, these skills can help new graduate students succeed not just in graduate school but in any professional context.

The readings I propose in this essay will introduce students to resources that they can revisit as they encounter the different milestones of a graduate program. In essence, the proseminar can help students identify a body of practical texts that can support them throughout their graduate careers and beyond. What to call this literature is an open question, but the texts I discuss below constitute something between a modern conduct tradition, a secular wisdom literature, and essays on personal development. For example, Eric Hayot's *The Elements of Academic Style* discusses the techniques as well as the psychology of academic writing. It is a book that one can reread at different points during graduate study, finding renewed inspiration during the panic of seminar papers or the doldrums of the dissertation. In addition to Hayot's work, students in the proseminar I am describing engage with the rich literature in the fields of positive psychology, resilience, creativity, the sociology of work, and executive coaching, areas that have productive applications for graduate study, as well as with pedagogy and learning science. Ideally, a proseminar can introduce students to ways of thinking about graduate education and about work in general.

I can envision two objections to this kind of proseminar. First, some might argue that positive psychology's pedagogy of resilience can have the dangerous effect of displacing responsibility for systemic problems in academia onto the individual (Denby; Chamorro-Premuzic and Lusk). Does helping students think about how to work more effectively simply provide cover for the work acceleration and increased precarity of neoliberal academia, at least for the lucky few who land full-time jobs? Should we not rather use the proseminar to give new students a sober picture of the profession they seek to enter? These options are not mutually exclusive, and I do not advise hiding the entrenched systemic labor problems of humanities departments in the United States. Indeed, any proseminar worth its salt will give new students a sense of where they will likely encounter challenges.

What I am advocating is that we not stop there. Yes, things are often bad, but given that students have decided to pursue a master's or doctoral degree, faculty members have a responsibility to indicate the skills, behaviors, and worldviews that can help them navigate dangerous waters with the least personal cost. Students need to know how to develop the skills and acquire the experiences that will position them for a variety of employment possibilities after graduation, including traditional faculty positions, administration, advocacy, grant writing, public humanities, and more. They also need to know how and when to exit gracefully from graduate study if they realize that it does not, in fact, fit with their personal goals. These messages can and should be communicated in an atmosphere of openness, without judgment for those who experience difficulty. At a time when many graduate students report significant stress and anxiety, faculty members should be working to bring out students' ability to thrive from the very first year. Furthermore, the faculty should not assume that it is the students' job to discover these skills on their own. Professors have had to develop the skills used in academic life, and the proseminar is an excellent place to share this knowledge.

The second potential objection concerns the use of self-help literature and the executive coaching genre in an academic setting. Some faculty members may feel reluctant to admit to colleagues that they have read such books, or they might consider them beneath the level of intellectual sophistication required of the academic. For this reason, I will offer brief summaries of the readings I assign first-year graduate students to give skeptical readers of this essay a sense of the kinds of wisdom that may be found there. I think it is well worth offering a curated list of such texts to provide students with quality resources. As Karen Kelsky points out in *The Professor Is In*, if professors are not giving good advice to their students, they will seek it out elsewhere (15–17). Even if faculty members are not reading such books, their students likely are. Much of the general guidance that can be readily found online is of dubious quality or so alarmist as to be unhelpful, and personalized advice from a caring professor can offer a realistic but humane look at the challenges students face. Second, graduate school does not have to be about misery, isolation, and disembodiment. One of the most moving experiences I have found in academic self-help literature was reading Hayot's description of his own insecurities and daily writing process (20–21). It gave me the sense that I was not the only one who struggles sometimes. Yes, graduate school is difficult, but faculty can also be vulnerable human beings who share their difficulties and failures; that is where wisdom and solidarity lie.

There is good reason to cross-check a professor's experience with academic self-help literature; any one perspective will be too limited to be of much help. One of the latent implications of self-help literature, including academic self-help literature, is that one can "do everything right" through cultivating proper behaviors. This is the biggest myth of the graduate school process—that there is one way to walk the path of graduate education and that one has to execute it perfectly at all moments. As

Marcus Buckingham and Ashley Goodall point out in their book *Nine Lies about Work*, excellence looks different from one person to the next (77–103). Moreover, success does not mean perfection. As Brené Brown argues in *Daring Greatly*, failure is a part of any life process, and the notion of "good enough" can be liberating for perfectionists, who are often the type of student that ends up in graduate programs (127–41). The texts that I will discuss below do not offer a single set of behaviors or techniques that will work for everyone. Rather, taken together, they offer a toolbox to use in a process of inquiry, self-study, and ultimately self-realization that will last throughout the years of graduate school and beyond.

The shape of graduate education in the humanities needs to be as much about helping students discover their own sense of vocation as it is about optimizing work habits. The first-year proseminar can become a place to present graduate education as an opportunity to learn how the humanities can help each student flourish as a human being. This mode of engaging the world can assist students in becoming good researchers, effective teachers, and caring mentors. Moreover, these skills give students the ability to move among different kinds of professional situations within and outside the academy.

In the second half of this essay, I will present an example of this proseminar model in modern languages that I piloted in fall 2019 at the University of Pittsburgh, where I work, and I will share some of the students' reactions toward the end of the article. I am not proposing the framework below as the best or only model for a graduate proseminar. Indeed, part of what I am arguing is that a graduate proseminar needs to be tailored to the discipline, the institution, a specific program's faculty members, and, ultimately, the graduate students themselves.

Graduate Program Cultures and Teaching

The first several weeks of the proseminar deal with the nuts and bolts of graduate education: program structure, department history, seminars, and teaching. The first two chapters of Gregory Semenza's book *Graduate Study for the Twenty-First Century* introduce students to the culture of a graduate program and the structure of a graduate career (18–53). I spend time early in the term talking about the graduate seminar, especially readings, discussion, presentations, and papers. Students read the fourth and fifth chapters of the Semenza book and the chapters on reading and speaking in Zachary Shore's *Grad School Essentials* (8–55, 78–96). Adapting to graduate seminars should not be assumed to be a natural progression for the student, and the quantity of reading is a major adjustment for most. This is especially the case for those undertaking a PhD in a language they did not grow up speaking, whether that is English or another modern language. For this reason, I ramp up the quantity of reading over time to train students to complete this workload.

Following this introduction, the proseminar turns to teaching and focuses on big-picture questions confronting instructors in the context of language teaching. Language departments at universities in the United States will have a mix of native English speakers, native speakers of the language of the program, and others whose native language is something else. It is helpful for everyone to reflect on what it means to teach modern languages and cultures from their positionality. Claire Kramsch and Lihua Zhang's recent book, *The Multilingual Instructor*, questions many common assumptions about native and non-native speakers (1–19), and it is worth talking about the expectations around language proficiency in modern languages departments. As Uggen and Hlavka point out, graduate students won't be comfortable teaching until they have some experience under their belt (202), and the same goes for language mastery. It is also worth considering what excellence in teaching means. Parker Palmer, in *The Courage to Teach*, and Ken Bain, in *What the Best College Teachers Do*, suggest that what matters most is not the latest pedagogical techniques but a personal connection to a discipline, and this simple idea calls into question any rigid separation between teaching and research (Palmer 26–34; Bain 15–20). Even though new graduate students typically will not have the chance to teach intermediate courses until later, these readings give them a framework to understand why there are breadth requirements and to pay attention to the ways their own teachers teach.

Many graduate students will have some teaching experience after the first few weeks, and this is the moment to discuss the practical aspects of teaching, including preparation, time management, and classroom management. Many of these same issues might be covered in a pedagogy seminar, but the proseminar offers a chance to discuss how to balance teaching with the other obligations students face. Robert Boice in *Advice for New Faculty Members* comes at the question of class preparation from the angle of mindfulness (19–54), and Norma López-Burton in *On Being a Language* shares a helpful typology of new graduate teaching assistants that will help students become aware of their own patterns in the classroom. Much of the discussion this week is about setting realistic expectations for class preparation and instructor performance. Not every class session need be at the level of the life-transforming teaching dramatized in a film like *Dead Poets Society*.

Research Skills

The next section of the proseminar helps students begin the process of conceptualizing a research agenda in the near and long terms, starting with effective work habits. Hayot makes the important point that all writing processes are individual and that ultimately students must experiment to find what works for them (17). Karl Ericsson and Robert Pool in their book *Peak: Secrets from the New Science of Expertise* challenge the stubborn idea that people have innate talents for certain occupations. They introduce the notion of deliberate practice, which seeks to push someone "to move just beyond the current skill level" (98). While Ericsson and Pool would likely not view graduate training as having a universal scale of excellence as in music, faculty members can nevertheless help students identify crucial skills that they must develop. Finally, Cal Newport in *Deep Work* argues for the importance of periods of distraction-free concentration on developing difficult skills like writing for excellence in any kind of profession (95–154). Although deep work may seem more appropriate to the dissertation stage, it is important to introduce the concept early because it can take years to implement.

Some students begin with a research specialization in mind and others need help or permission to explore. Newport makes the important argument in *So Good They Can't Ignore You* that passion is overrated and that one should adopt instead what he calls a "craftsman mindset" in which one focuses on what one can offer the world (37–38). One of the new graduate student's tasks is to identify what these areas and skills are. Newport's discussion of Peter Sims's notion of the "little bet" is crucial to this exploration (*So Good* 177–79). Adapted to academia, it involves undertaking a small project exploring some new direction of interest. Since it's a little bet, the energy and time required are relatively low and the feedback one receives from oneself and others can help a student determine whether this direction is worth continuing. Each little bet becomes a step toward choosing a specialty or a dissertation topic without forcing a student to commit too early. Ideally, this process of discovery will help students get in touch with their values as they encounter the areas of their discipline to which they have a positive response. Connecting expertise to values is essential for a long-term career in academia; proseminar students may get an early glimpse of how they will want to spend their time in a faculty or nonfaculty career.

When talking about research, it is worth openly discussing whether to pursue a PhD. For students in masters' programs, the decision to pursue a PhD can be difficult, and the discussion can also help students in a PhD program who may later decide not to continue. Graduate school is challenging for everyone, and if a student ultimately realizes that graduate school is not for them, faculty should celebrate their self-knowledge and help them transition to something else. Finally, it is important to talk about how to generate ideas for research. While many colleagues expect that graduate students will already have learned how to do this, I find that this is not always the case. Steven Johnson, in *Where Good Ideas Come From*, introduces the notion of the adjacent edge. For Johnson, "good ideas are not conjured out of thin air; they are built out of a collection of existing parts" (35). The edge is that place where one comes to the border between the known and the possible in a given disciplinary area. Well-constructed graduate seminars are designed to take students to this edge of possibility, and thinking about research in this way prepares students for their comprehensive exams and eventual dissertation prospectuses, in which they must seek their own adjacent edge.

How to Be Human Beings in Graduate School

The academy can seem so focused on the life of the mind that it is easy to forget that students also have lives, families, hobbies, nonwork needs, and dreams. Personally, I find the notion of work-life balance stifling. Approaches to solving the competing demands of work and life as a problem often encourage a level of micromanagement in one's personal life that is as impractical as it is inhumane. It is essential to have a life outside work, but the notion of "balance" is an ever-moving target, and pursuing it can create more anxiety than it alleviates (Buckingham and Goodall 181–205). Many, but not all, of the students who pursue graduate study tend toward the perfectionist, self-punishing mentality, and so I find it helpful to introduce students to Brown's work on shame, vulnerability, and letting go in *Daring Greatly* (18–56). Faculty members and students alike may shrink from discussing their own fears and failures with colleagues, and it is important in a proseminar to create a space of shared trust and vulnerability. Nothing increases stress like the feeling of isolation or the belief that graduate school comes easily to everyone else.

It is crucial in this part of the proseminar to talk about the challenges of belonging to an underrepresented group in graduate school. I refer here not just to the commonly cited axes of difference such as race, ethnicity, sexuality, or ability but also factors like class, culture, veteran status, and parenthood. Class is a particularly thorny issue and should be discussed directly. As Nancy Isenberg argues in *White Trash*, the United States does not generally talk openly about its class system (1–14). Leonard Cassuto in *The Graduate School Mess* locates the origins of the modern US university in the rise of the middle class. He describes how what he calls "research" and "liberal" culture contain unspoken assumptions about social class and the value of higher education (214–25). As a result, PhD students from working-class or first-generation college backgrounds may not be privy to certain implied rules of academia. Furthermore, some people in their families may not appreciate graduate school as a form of productive labor and valuable work. I find Dawn Rothe's essay "A Stranger to Paradise" especially helpful in framing these questions (49–59). Ultimately, a good proseminar can help all students catch up in terms of cultural capital and knowhow. While it reads as a bit dated now, the chapter "Swimming with the Mainstream" in Robert Peters's book *Getting What You Came For* (286–318) models a valuable organizational principle specifically addressing the experiences of women, underrepresented groups, and international students. Finally, I would say that this is one week in which I advise suspending my injunction on visitors, depending on the positionality of the instructor, so that those experiences can also be addressed for proseminar students in real time by people with a first-hand understanding of them.

Mentorship and Professionalization

Fierce competition for academic jobs pressures students to professionalize early and often. Gregory Semenza and Karen Kelsky offer helpful advice for attending conferences as a graduate student (Semenza 195–213; Kelsky 118–29). I have some personal reservations about the supposedly neutral, brutally "honest" orientation of Kelsky's book because its hypercompetitive view of academia risks complicity with the neoliberal direction of the academy. However, her advice columns are so visible that it is important to talk directly about these issues with students. In thinking about how to craft a professional trajectory, students can sometimes have a "more is always better" approach to building a CV, and it is vital to talk with them about how to prioritize those opportunities that will best help advance their professional agendas.

Even if it may be a couple of years before students begin to think about publishing, it is important to introduce them to the top journals in different subfields, and I encourage students to choose a few journals to follow regularly. Semenza's book and Wendy Belcher's guide to publishing journal articles are especially helpful for giving students an overview of the process (Semenza 214–37). Belcher, in *Writing Your Journal Article in Twelve Weeks*, has an excellent method for identifying the kinds of articles a journal publishes and for helping students discover the kinds of arguments they can publish successfully when they are still relatively unknown in the field. Furthermore, she offers a workable multiweek plan for revising a paper into an article (43–66).

Finally, it is crucial early in students' graduate careers to talk about mentorship, including how to work with professors and how to choose an adviser. My students have found the relevant chapters from *The Chicago Guide to Your Academic Career* and from Kelsky to be helpful (Goldsmith et al. 44–53; Kelsky 361–81). We also talk about how graduate students should relate to each other. Graduate students can bring a competitive mindset to graduate school in which they feel like they must compete with each other for attention, prestige, funding, and eventually jobs. While there may be a grain of truth to this, more often students from the same program do not compete directly with each other because excellence is idiosyncratic. One's graduate cohort is better understood as a peer group that can offer support, advice, and help. However, graduate students will not automatically treat each other as colleagues unless faculty help them to do so. It is not obvious to graduate students in the beginning that members of their peer group may well become recommenders and collaborators in the future. I ask students to read the chapters on writing groups from Joli Jensen's *Write No Matter What* as a way of making the case for cooperation rather than competition (131–41). Helen Sword in *Air and Light and Time and Space* has a good chapter about how to establish ground rules for a writing group (135–46). A well-designed graduate proseminar can prepare students to relate to their peers in a collaborative manner.

A Vision for the Future

In a time of desperation about the academic job market, students are eager to diversify the skills they present in their CVs, and they can benefit from acquiring professional experiences that are not a regular part of graduate study. Because emergent humanities fields like public and digital humanities cannot be absorbed in a weeklong workshop or a single semester-long class, it is important to introduce students to the different possibilities early in their graduate careers. My model here is the "little bet," which allows students to explore a new field without changing programs or disciplines. Rather, a student might take a class or a workshop or decide to make a presentation at a different kind of conference. If this little bet is successful, and the student feels energized by it, then that direction is worth continuing to explore. The same can be said for jobs beyond academia, and consequently students should begin planning early for various kinds of careers post-PhD.

My students examine as case studies two of the most successful new directions in the humanities: digital and public humanities. We read some short definitional essays, and we look at examples of online projects in each category. Because the storytelling and engagement skills of the public humanities and the coding and visualization skills of the digital humanities are not forms of expertise that come quickly or easily, students must engage with them early in their graduate careers if they think they may want to work in them later on.

The proseminar's final project is a personal vision and mission plan. It is based in part on the final project for Stanford University's Design School courses Design Your Life (undergraduate) and Designing the Professional (graduate), which are described in Bill Burnett and Dave Evans's book *Designing Your Life* and draw on the individual development plans used by the United States government ("Individual Development Plan"). The goal of the personal vision and mission plan is for students to start articulating their purpose for graduate study. The risk of not having a vision, or what Burnett and Evans call a compass, is that one ends up following someone else's compass without realizing it (Burnett and Evans 31). This risk is especially high in graduate school, which students, who are used to doing what is expected of them, can experience as an ever-unfolding set of hoops to jump through. Because one can stay occupied just with meeting expectations, it is easy to avoid the self-reflective work of planning one's career path. If a student arrives at the dissertation or job market stage with little understanding of what their beliefs, values, and goals are, it can be challenging to craft a profile that will result in an academic or nonacademic job. The goal of the personal vision statement is to begin a process of self-study that will continue over the next several years of graduate study. The self-reflection involved in drafting a personal vision statement allows for students to become cocreators of the arc of graduate study. Talking openly about personal vision and values allows everyone to make the best use of the programmatic structures and time afforded to students in graduate school.

At the end of the pilot course, I asked students to complete an anonymous survey asking what had helped them in the proseminar and whether other universities should consider adopting a similar proseminar model.

Their responses were largely positive, both about the issues discussed in the proseminar and about the feeling of mutual support they felt among their new graduate cohort. One student wrote that "the seminar allowed for an open communication to appear within the cohort, on issues that are often not being discussed, such as mental health, work-related insecurities, etc. This process allows the cohort to immediately share a bond and become an open and supportive group in a positive environment." They valued the course's effectiveness in helping them build "healthy work habits" and "plan ahead professionally." They also noted appreciatively that the proseminar "bears witness to the department's commitment to its students' well-being and concern with long-term personal and professional growth." This sense of departmental support is especially important in helping allay some of the fears among graduate students. Two different students spoke positively about the proseminar as an open forum for discussing sensitive issues: "This proseminar has answered questions about grad school and being a grad student that I didn't even know I had" and it answered questions that "I lacked information on" but was "too embarrassed to ask." Ultimately, as one student put it, the proseminar took "a very mysterious world, around which there are a lot of myths and poor information," and helped students "navigate [it] from the beginning, without recourse only to trial and error." Students enjoyed the self-reflection activities, and having read their vision plans, I can say that these plans will help me as director of graduate studies in advising them for the coming year.

During the coronavirus pandemic, I taught the proseminar remotely for a second time to a cohort of students that at the time of writing this essay I still have not met in person. It was stressful and unsettling for the new students to begin graduate study under such conditions, but I can say that they expressed gratitude for the proseminar as one of a limited number of opportunities for them to build the feeling of being a cohort. Because remote seminars and lectures did not offer the same chances for informal mentoring that in-person ones do, the proseminar was one of the rare places where such conversations could take place. In short, the new students found a proseminar to be more rather than less valuable during pandemic times.

As a final note, the personal vision and mission plan is not a contract. It is simply a snapshot of a moment in time, proposing concrete steps to try out in the next year that will be revised again and again over the course of graduate study. Like the proseminar as a whole, the plan seeks to model a process for approaching graduate study. Similarly, the readings for the proseminar I have described here are not set in stone. The structure needs to adapt as the concerns of graduate students change, institutional environments shift, and new resources become available. What should not change, however, is the ethical investment of faculty members in supporting graduate students as human beings through practical measures like a proseminar. Indeed, this ethical investment is crucial at a juncture when the humanities are undervalued within and outside the academy. Many faculty members justifiably feel anxiety about this state of affairs, as it impacts their own sense of identity and self-worth. However, the best response is not to retreat from engagement but rather to tackle the issues head-on. Such engagement requires vulnerability and a willingness to be present with difficult situations. There is thus some emotional risk, as uncomfortable feelings such as survivor's guilt will inevitably arise, but there is also a benefit: graduate students will feel the support of the faculty members who mentor them. The sense of being alone only amplifies feelings of mental distress. Experiencing a real sense of community can help students better navigate the landscape of contemporary graduate education, even knowing that ongoing structural issues will not be solved overnight. A first-year proseminar is one place to undertake this vitally important work.

WORKS CITED

Bain, Ken. *What the Best College Teachers Do*. Harvard UP, 2004.

Belcher, Wendy Laura. *Writing Your Journal Article in Twelve Weeks: A Guide to Academic Publishing Success*. Sage Publications, 2009.

Boice, Robert. *Advice for New Faculty Members*. Pearson, 2000.

Brown, Brené. *Daring Greatly: How the Courage to Be Vulnerable Transforms the Way We Live, Love, Parent, and Lead*. Gotham Books, 2015.

Buckingham, Marcus, and Ashley Goodall. *Nine Lies about Work: A Freethinking Leader's Guide to the Real World*. Harvard Business Review Press, 2019.

Burnett, William, and David J. Evans. *Designing Your Life: How to Build a Well-Lived, Joyful Life*. Alfred A. Knopf, 2016.

Cassuto, Leonard. *The Graduate School Mess: What Caused It and How We Can Fix It*. Harvard UP, 2015.

Chamorro-Premuzic, Tomas, and Derek Lusk. "The Dark Side of Resilience." *Harvard Business Review*, Aug. 2017, hbr.org/2017/08/the-dark-side-of-resilience.

Denby, David. "The Limits of 'Grit.'" *The New Yorker*, 21 June 2016, newyorker.com/culture/culture-desk/the-limits-of-grit.

Ericsson, Karl Anders, and Robert Pool. *Peak: Secrets from the New Science of Expertise*. Houghton Mifflin Harcourt, 2016.

Goldsmith, John A., et al. *The Chicago Guide to Your Academic Career: A Portable Mentor for Scholars from Graduate School through Tenure.* U of Chicago P, 2001.

Hayot, Eric. *The Elements of Academic Style: Writing for the Humanities.* Columbia UP, 2014.

"Individual Development Plan." *U.S. Office of Personnel Management*, opm.gov/WIKI/training/Individual-Development-Plans.ashx. Accessed 3 July 2019.

Isenberg, Nancy. *White Trash: The Four-Hundred-Year Untold History of Class in America.* Penguin Books, 2017.

Jensen, Joli. *Write No Matter What: Advice for Academics.* U of Chicago P, 2017.

Johnson, Steven. *Where Good Ideas Come From: The Natural History of Innovation.* Riverhead Books, 2011.

Kelsky, Karen. *The Professor Is In: The Essential Guide to Turning Your Ph.D. into a Job.* Three Rivers Press, 2015.

Kramsch, Claire, and Lihua Zhang. *The Multilingual Instructor.* Oxford UP, 2018.

López-Burton, Norma. "Types of Teachers; Dos and Don'ts." *On Being a Language Teacher: A Personal and Practical Guide to Success*, edited by López-Burton and Denise Earla Minor, Yale UP, 2014, pp. 141–77.

Newport, Cal. *Deep Work: Rules for Focused Success in a Distracted World.* Grand Central Publishing, 2016.

———. *So Good They Can't Ignore You: Why Skills Trump Passion in the Quest for Work You Love.* Grand Central Publishing, 2012.

Palmer, Parker J. *The Courage to Teach: Exploring the Inner Landscape of a Teacher's Life.* 20th anniversary ed., Jossey-Bass, 2017.

Perry, David M. "How to Make Grad School More Humane." *Pacific Standard*, 5 Feb. 2019, psmag.com/ideas/grad-school-continues-to-ignore-students-with-disabilities.

Peters, Robert L. *Getting What You Came for: The Smart Student's Guide to Earning a Master's or a Ph.D.* Farrar, Straus and Giroux, 1997.

Puri, Prateek. "The Emotional Toll of Graduate School." *Scientific American Blog Network*, 31 Jan. 2019, blogs.scientificamerican.com/observations/the-emotional-toll-of-graduate-school/.

Rothe, Dawn. "A Stranger to Paradise: Working-Class Graduate in the Culture of Academia." *Reflections from the Wrong Side of the Tracks: Class, Identity, and the Working Class Experience in Academe*, edited by C. Vincent Samarco and Stephen L. Muzzatti, Rowman and Littlefield, 2006, pp. 49–59.

Semenza, Gregory M. Colón. *Graduate Study for the Twenty-First Century: How to Build an Academic Career in the Humanities.* 2nd ed., Palgrave Macmillan, 2010.

Shore, Zachary. *Grad School Essentials: A Crash Course in Scholarly Skills.* U of California P, 2016.

Sword, Helen. *Air and Light and Time and Space: How Successful Academics Write*. Harvard UP, 2017.

Uggen, Christopher, and Heather Hlavka. "No More Lame Prosems: Professional Development Seminars in Sociology." *Academic Street Smarts: Informal Professionalization of Graduate Students in Sociology*, edited by Ira Silver and David Shulman, American Sociological Association, 2008, pp. 191–216.

Wong, Alia. "Graduate School Can Have Terrible Effects on People's Mental Health." *The Atlantic*, Nov. 2018, theatlantic.com/education/archive/2018/11/anxiety-depression-mental-health-graduate-school/576769/.

Experiential Learning and the Humanities PhD

Tiffany Potter and Elizabeth Hodgson

Around the world, doctoral programs in the humanities are being told we have a problem: we are graduating significantly more PhDs than will ever find stable, well-paying academic jobs. This criticism is the result of a narrative that is popular, though wrong, and often propagated by our own profession—that anything other than a tenured position at a Research I university represents failure for our doctoral students. So how do we change the narrative? Do we shut down our programs? Do we refuse students the chance to pursue intellectual brilliance and new insights that can inform our culture? Or can we create an academically and professionally engaged curriculum that changes the way that our students imagine what it means to have a PhD—an achievement that, rather than limiting one's choices to one kind of teaching or another, instead expands into a powerful range of potential professional identities.

In 2012, the Department of English Language and Literatures at the University of British Columbia (UBC)[1] initiated just such a culture change by creating a cooperative education PhD option. Our program recognizes that the excellence of our students is not limited to a classroom and that this group of exceptional thinkers, scholars, and communicators can rightfully envision themselves in positions of influence far beyond the university. This essay documents our institution's transformation of experiential professional learning from an activity relegated to the sides of desks and the backs of minds into a formalized graduate degree option that offers a new model of academic and professional engagement. We demonstrate how a graduate cooperative educational model can provide a path for meaningful intersection between graduate studies and professional or social communities.

Collaborating with other UBC programs, we developed an institutionally recognized degree option that invites our postcandidacy PhD students to complete three well-paid, professional, field-relevant work terms in government, arts, community, and private-sector organizations as a part of their degree. Our approach took advantage of existing, funded university infrastructure to expand the traditional professionalizations of research and teaching assistantships by creating new opportunities for our graduate students to professionalize both inside the academy and in the larger community through cooperative experiential education. The PhD co-op program has now been scaled to other humanities departments at UBC, fostering meaningful and profitable collaborations for our students, our graduates, and our communities. The particular option that we describe here is far from the only way that experientially engaged learning can be formalized and professionalized in a PhD program, but it demonstrates three things: that such a program is possible; that it does not have to involve large amounts of new money; and, most important, that it provides a significant benefit for the students who choose it. In a broader scope, such an option may, we think, have the potential to help wean our profession from its current dependence on precarious employment.

The Culture Challenge

In the last two decades, institutions, associations, and governments have been increasingly aware of the need to provide wider employment contexts (including administrative careers) for humanities PhDs, given the shrinkage in tenure-track hiring in North American universities and colleges. *The Economist* reported that by 2010, the ratio of PhDs awarded to full-time tenure-track positions was nearly two to one in Canada and eight to one in the United States in any given year,[2] an imbalance aggravated by each year's unhired candidates rolling over into the next year's pool of applicants alongside new graduates. In one study of scholars who received a PhD in the humanities in 2016, fifty-two percent reported some sort of academic job in the first year after graduation, though it is important to note that this number includes part-time and term-limited teaching positions, postdoctoral fellowships, and low-paid adjunct teaching positions ("Job Status"). On average, forty-two percent of students who begin a PhD in the humanities will complete it ("Attrition"), and those successful students will encounter a reduced number of opportunities to enter the tenured academic ranks: using the field of English language and literature as an example, in 2016–17, the most prominent job-advertising site in the field listed 552 tenurable positions internationally, down from 1221 in 2007–08 (MLA); the trend continued in 2018–19 with 442 tenurable positions (Lusin) before the pandemic interrupted most searches in 2020, and fiscal fallout impacted many more in 2021. Articles in *Inside Higher Ed* have reached similar conclusions, documenting that in 2015–16, nearly 1,400 PhDs were awarded in English language and literatures, and there were just under 1,000 job postings in total, including tenurable, term, adjunct, and postdoctoral positions (Jaschik, "Shrinking"). A few months later, the same publication reported that "the number of new Ph.D.s in history is routinely more than twice the number of positions being posted by the AHA" (Jaschik, "Another"). Data like these may account for part of the reason behind the evidence that nearly sixty percent of students never complete their doctoral program.

Katina Rogers, at the time a senior research fellow in the Scholarly Communication Institute at the University of Virginia, reflected upon the situation thus:

> It seems clear from the findings that the persistent myth that there is only a single academic job market available to graduates is damaging, and extricating graduate education from the expectation of tenure-track employment has the potential to benefit students, institutions, and the health of the humanities more broadly. However, as long as norms are reinforced within departments—by faculty and students both—it will be difficult for any change to be effective.

Rogers's research also points out the second part of the problem, one that faces not only new doctorates but all of us in the postsecondary system: that a culture change is needed around those reinforced norms. Given the core reality of supply and demand in our sector, as long as new PhD recipients see academia as their only natural habitat, they are more likely to continue to accept underpaid and exploitative adjunct or sessional contracts at universities and colleges. This work is not only damaging to those who do it: it is also significantly undermining the core principle of tenure at our institutions of higher education. Compared to other types of work, "[a]cademic employment is more precarious than [is] typical" in nearly any other industry (*Almanac*, sec. 3): in many industrialized countries, between forty and eighty percent of the academic workforce is contingent faculty ("Casualization"). Writing on data provided by the Modern Language Association's Office of Research, David Laurence made the case in 2014 in a two-part argument on the implications of casualization for graduate students and for the profession:

> There are too few tenure-track jobs for the PhD recipients who are qualified to compete for them. The problem is most commonly attributed to an overproduction of PhDs. But it can be understood and has been argued to be the result of an underproduction of tenure-track positions symptomatic of institutions' increasing reliance on non-tenure-track faculty appointments.
> ("Our PhD Employment Problem, Part 1")

Citing US Department of Education data, Laurence points out that "even in four-year colleges and universities, the percentage of faculty members holding full-time tenured or tenure-track appointments . . . dropped from 51.3% in 1995 to just 33.4% in 2011" ("Our PhD Employment Problem, Part 2"). We can reasonably blame our administrators for succumbing to the temptation to buy cheap, disposable teaching labor at a fraction of the cost of tenure-track faculty, but we can also recognize that our own monoculture training of PhDs is feeding the beast. Developing PhD programs that empower our students to trust their own worth in the wider world of work can help wean our academic administrators from their unsustainable dependence upon casualized faculty. In helping our doctoral students to develop a variety of viable future paths, we ironically protect the very institutions in which they may or may not choose not to work.

Of course, we at UBC are hardly the first to consider how to address these twin ethical demands to care for students and to shore up tenurable employment. The UK created its NewRoute or Integrated PhD program in the early 2000s (see Park), and in North America major universities like Stanford have been reinventing their PhD curricula to increase work-study and nonacademic professional training (see Jaschik, "Five-Year Humanities PhD"). *University Affairs, The Chronicle of Higher Education,* and *Inside Higher Ed* have all reported repeatedly and urgently on efforts like the Praxis Network[3] to broaden employment options for PhD students and graduates, particularly in the humanities.[4]

The PhD Co-op Program at the University of British Columbia

In the light of these pressures and realities, we in the UBC English department decided to act locally. We looked for a way to leverage existing university priorities and programs to create a fully accredited experiential professional component to our PhD program at almost no additional cost to our department's graduate budget but at great benefit to our students. We began by researching the many piecemeal internship, job training, and employment programs already in place at our university, nearly all of which targeted undergraduate students but had never actively engaged PhD students, especially at a curricular level. We discussed with Career Services their à-la-carte offerings and with the Faculty of Graduate and Postdoctoral Studies their various employment workshops. From our local research, and given our goals, we prioritized programs that offered professional work at full pay and created a partnership with the cooperative education office.

Because the UBC Arts Co-op Program had been providing master's students in the School of Information (offering graduate degrees in information science, library science, and archival studies) with a co-op option for some years, they were already engaged in training and placements for graduate students. Two other universities in Canada (Waterloo University and the University of Victoria) offered PhD co-op options, and they provided helpful advice. But developing a PhD-level arts co-op program at UBC was an experiment that English and arts co-op programs embarked on together. Before we launched the program, we surveyed students, faculty members, and potential employers and pitched the concept to the dean of arts, the dean of the Faculty of Graduate and Postdoctoral Studies, and the provost's office at UBC. These consultations demonstrated that administrators were enthusiastic, employers excited, faculty members relieved, and students both anxious and grateful. We felt that this was enough positive energy to proceed with, and so, supported by small start-up allocations from the deans and some modest financial underwriting from our department, we initiated the PhD co-op option as a pilot program in 2014, and the final version was approved by the UBC senate in 2016.

The arts co-op program at UBC (itself begun in the English department in the late 1990s) uses its relationships with three thousand employers across Canada to offer more than six hundred well-paid, degree-relevant, four-month placements each year to students accepted into the program. Students are offered formal professionalization and communications training and are required to complete critical reflections on each placement and its contribution to their degree and on their sense of their academic and professional futures.

Cooperative education is a model well known in Canada and in the United States, also thriving in Australia and parts of Europe. It provides students with career and employment coaching and then iterative short-term work placements with employers who have enlisted with the institution's co-op program. Most co-op programs have professional staff members who manage employer recruitment and relations, student recruitment and training, and program design. Co-op is considered virtually compulsory in some fields (engineering being a long-standing example), but humanities co-ops are growing rapidly (as here at UBC) as students realize the value of relevant, paid work experience framed by knowledgeable coaches and by reflections on the work experience itself. There is clear evidence that graduates of the co-op program tend to find work more quickly, earn more, and describe the work as more relevant to their educational programs (*Graduating*, sec. 3). The formal, internationally certified nature of the co-op system made it easier for us to create a version of our PhD degree that foregrounds the training of excellent scholars and future professors and also facilitates students' engagement with the full range of career options that value the innate talents and acquired skills of PhD students—and in many cases, the content of the degree itself.

The UBC English PhD co-op option requires graduate students who choose this path to complete three full-time work terms of four months each in their dissertation years, as a credited part of their degree program. The co-op office identifies appropriately senior professional placements, and graduate students' transitions are further facilitated by formal training on how to reframe academic skills using the rhetoric of professional communities outside the academy. The program actively guides PhD students through a defining conceptual shift: from thinking of themselves exclusively as academics to thinking of themselves as individuals highly skilled and credentialed in several translatable areas. By leveraging existing university resources to generate a pool of high-level professional job placements each year, we are able to give our students well-paid work experiences and a wider range of employment contacts, the better to try on different visions of post-PhD careers, in parallel with the way that their work as teaching assistants invites them to envision themselves as teaching professionals.

Students generally apply to the program at the end of their second year so that they can receive their coaching and training before starting work terms in their dissertation years. We generally require students to have achieved candidacy before we allow them to start work terms, but the system can be quite flexible. Students have completed both full-time and part-time work terms and have linked the co-op program with employers from their own personal networks.

Program Successes

About twenty to twenty-five percent of our PhD students in the English department at UBC opt to participate in the PhD co-op program. These students have taken on a broad range of jobs in government, health care, universities, publishing, communications, and arts and culture organizations. We provide here a few examples of the employers who are quite thrilled at the prospect of a highly educated, self-driven employee with exceptional research, analysis, and communication skills and a proven ability to manage complex projects. Within the university, the Faculty of Graduate and Professional Studies hired a student as a special projects officer to develop a Canadian version of the Responsible Conduct of Research course; to plan and facilitate a "Reimagining the PhD" symposium; to coordinate events such as Writing Week and graduate student orientation; and to develop database and online materials for a Doctoral Alumni Tracking Project. The local health authority hired a student as a communications officer to research, write, and publish research reports and outreach stories for one of its research institutes; to translate scientific research into public communications for media; and to manage several databases and the institute's public-facing media. A student working in Asian Canadian literatures was hired as lead researcher on a project to create a public memorial to historic abuses of Asian immigrants, and another was hired by a Vancouver museum as writer in residence to research archival materials and write the official history of the site (published as a coffee-table book) and then to create a marketing plan for the book. That student then moved into an editorial position with a local press and now has a full-time position as editor in chief. One history PhD student was hired by a local museum to organize and curate the exact body of union archives he needed for his dissertation research.

Jon Newell, one of the first entrants to the UBC PhD co-op program, continued working on his dissertation for an hour a day while on work terms. What Jon says he learned in his PhD was not just a lot about nineteenth-century speculative literatures but that his academic skill set and degree "are enormously marketable and genuinely useful in a wide variety of professional contexts, including, but *not limited to,* academia." Other students have reported a shift in their theoretical thinking; our student helping to memorialize the bitter experiences of Asian Canadian communities reports having to bracket her theoretically informed distrust of the reconciliation gestures made by local and provincial governments when she saw how meaningful these gestures were to the victims of oppressive policies. She reports that this made her own research questions more nuanced, more specific, and more generous. All of the students in the program report feeling more confident, more professional, more willing to trust themselves in new spheres, and less anxious about their futures. Our program is too young and too small for us to yet chart statistically significant outcomes for our PhD co-op students, but these kinds of reported shifts of perspective and self-perception alone are to us a major achievement.

Program Challenges

The difficulties we've faced in creating and sustaining this co-op option are definitely important to acknowledge and chart. The biggest challenge we face is, perhaps not surprisingly, in encouraging students to apply to the program. Students early in their PhDs tend not to feel urgency about acquiring alternative work experience; some students also come with alternative careers already well developed (such as web design, banking, or trade publishing). And some are in a desperate hurry to finish the degree and don't want to take the time for work terms. Many students are ambivalent about trying alternatives to the kind of work that they love and know the best; some have constraints that make work terms difficult; and a fortunate few have alternative financial means and can treat their PhD as an avocation. We have also sometimes perceived a hint of resentment of the program from students who don't avail themselves of it, as if either its opportunities or its assumptions are suspect. Opening the question and changing a culture will always provoke anxieties and concerns, including among those for whom it is designed, and this is a reality we have to accept.

The second difficulty we've faced is with some members of the graduate faculty. Many are extremely grateful for this option and endorse it, but the stigma attached to nonacademic endpoints for their students, an understandable interest in hurrying students along through their studies, and a lack of familiarity with the varied world of work, can sometimes feed a certain skepticism. A few colleagues assume that "corporate" or "for-profit" work is fundamentally limited or even corrupt, and we have had to take seriously these concerns. We have learned to engage regularly with departmental committees, graduate faculties, and graduate deans so that they will continue to understand the benefits of this option for UBC and for their students, and indeed for the wider world, even as we recognize that co-op and a broader working world will not suit everyone or every situation.

The third difficulty we've had to address is the lack of symmetry between undergraduate co-op programs, where students are happy to pay for the relevant training and supervision, and graduate programs, in which students generally (and rightly) expect to be paid rather than to pay for their training. We have had to improvise systems for covering the minor expenses attached to co-op training for our students; the fact that students on work terms in the program are making on average around $4000 per month helps reduce the need for this. And we have had to adjust to graduate students' generally less orderly path through both the degree program and the co-op program in comparison to undergraduates'. Because a PhD involves so much self-managed work, so few hard deadlines, and so much personal initiative, it tends to generate less linear routes through the degree than the traditional BA, and this has meant that we've had to be willing to adapt and pivot as students improvise, stall, accelerate, move, and pause.

Considerations for an Experiential Learning Program within the PhD

In imagining this sort of program, several considerations must be taken into account to ensure the fullest positive impact on students. In this era of unpaid internships and other ethically problematic systems of acquiring professional experience in tight job markets, we chose the co-op model because of its several strengths, but when examining institutional infrastructures, the following considerations seem essential:

How can we ensure that this new program gets off the ground at my school? The key is integration with existing infrastructure: UBC already had an undergraduate co-op program up and running, so infrastructure and implementation costs were very low, and when we went looking for the money we needed, the institution immediately recognized the model and benefits because they had already been using it for years. Leveraging an existing program or extending the duties of staff members with relevant experience makes this a much easier project. For universities without a staffed co-op program, there may be work-learn or career services programs or coordinated internship training offices that could be networked to provide similar support. Academic faculty members are generally not well equipped to provide the kinds of employer liaison, coaching, and employment mentorship needed for this kind of a program, and so it is productive to collaborate with the staff members who do have this expertise. Humanities administrators seem to be receptive to the need for programs like this, which may help.

How can we make sure that the co-op is an element of engaged curricula and not just a summer jobs program? As the Canadian Association for Co-operative Education documents, Co-operative Education is an educational model rather than a job placement strategy. Co-op Education promotes continuous learning through the integration of classroom and applied work-based learning. It has gained recognition within the employer and academic communities as having an increased educational value, providing the opportunity for students to develop both discipline specific and general education goals. (*Co-operative Education* 1). The important distinction between our program and summer job support is the structure within which our students complete their work terms. Co-op is intentionally designed as a curriculum program in which each work term is assigned a course number, framed with a student contract, and enriched with work-life assignments such as an informational interview, a report on a networking event, or a presentation to the student's academic department about their work term. Any similar program will distinguish itself from the jobs lottery by its ability to answer the following in the affirmative: Do the students get specific coaching and training? Do employers and program staff take their mentoring role seriously? Are there embedded reflection activities (like informational interviews or networking events)? Do the students get appropriate pay? And does the program explicitly encourage multiple work experiences, either experimenting across different work spheres or scaffolding to higher-level work within a particular sector?

Best practice in experiential learning comes through an iterative structure (Eames and Cates 44–45), and, like our PhD co-op, many existing programs designed for undergraduate students require completion of multiple work terms. Unlike one-off internships or summer job placements, UBC's co-op office allows students to get the work experience in their first term to qualify for higher-level professional jobs in each successive term—the repetition allows low-stakes sampling of different career paths as well as progressive skills development and résumé building. Training, iteration, reflection, and practice are key elements that make such a program higher-impact than a campus placement office.

How can we make sure our students are not exploited? Challenging job markets in recent decades have created an environment where students are at risk of economic exploitation in unpaid and desperately underpaid work where the value of their labor is assumed by certain employers to be compensated by a résumé line and networks. The leverage that professional programs like co-op have with employers is that they can guarantee a talented, trained, curated employee pool and low-risk limited-term employment contracts. By offering these guarantees, they can negotiate respectable wages for co-op students. They have also invested energy in relationships with employers, and both parties understand the value of that relationship. What is more, they understand the world of work and what is of value to employers; they—often more than we within the academy—are willing to insist on the kind of respect for talent, brains, and initiative that our students can take to the bank. This is a critical benefit of working with an existing program rather than arranging one-offs for our own grad students. The co-op staff generates a legal agreement between employer and institution, each worksite is visited by co-op office staff members, and salaries are formally offered through the co-op office. In our case, the work pays well, with salaries for graduate co-op students averaging between $3,500 and $4,500 per month. For institutions without a formal co-op program, starting up this sort of degree option will mean recruiting professional staff members with this kind of attitude toward, and investment in, employer relationships to protect all the parties involved.

Employer-based curricular programs are certainly subject to the vagaries of the wider job market, from industry change and the emergence of new kinds of work to economic recession or a pandemic. But our co-op office has also been diversifying for some years to expand our base of private-sector, government, and nonprofit employers to include positions funded by federal granting agencies and private donors, expanding the network of options available to students even when businesses are retrenching. These broader networks help to strengthen the program even in busy hiring years, and certainly will add to the range of placements and funding available in future periods of economic contraction.

How will doing co-op affect students' funding? Our experience suggests that the university is entirely aware that our humanities PhDs face financial challenges; the administration is therefore interested in ways to address the issues in publicly visible ways. Reducing tuition fees to a nominal registration fee in work terms, for example, seems an obvious option, as does allowing students to "pause" their internal university funding during a work term (so that a scholarship can be extended across five years instead of four, for example). NEH and other grants may also allow for work terms: our investigation revealed that existing government systems of graduate student funding could be integrated into our program. Canada's parallel to the NEH is the Social Sciences and Humanities Research Council (SSHRC). SSHRC allows PhD funding to be paused while students are on program-related work terms, so the formal nature of the PhD co-op option means that students can stretch their government and university funding to allow more time for dissertation completion.

In our example, the Canadian co-op curriculum works on a fee-for-service model approved by the university senate: participants pay an application and training fee up front and co-op fees during work terms to cover the program's administrative costs. Since our students receive tuition awards, and since they remain registered as students during their work terms, we continue to pay out their tuition awards but cover (through decanal or department funds) the small co-op fee during work terms. But over the life of our program, we and other departments and faculties have experimented with all of these options: pausing fellowships or other student funding during work terms so that the students have more resources in their final terms, allowing students to receive such awards during work terms so that they can bank and save, or offering to cover program costs while students are on work terms.

Can such a program affect recruitment to our PhD? Our program appears to be a useful recruiting tool: many of our applicants (both to the PhD program and to tenure-track positions in our department) mention the PhD co-op program, and about twenty-five percent of our PhD students take it up. Some of our most ambitious, best-published, best-funded students are also the most aware of the complexities of academic employment and of the transferability of their talents beyond the academy.

What about international students? Depending on location, a formal, degree-related employment program may allow international students to work where they would not otherwise be entitled. In Canada, for example, students who do not have legal permission to work other than on campus are eligible to work anywhere in the country if they are part of an official co-op program.

What about life satisfaction and mental health? Experiential learning gives our students the tools to answer the question of what they can do with their PhD and normalizes what best-practice career programs know: that a single-answer approach to life planning is rarely useful or productive—the myth of "the one" is no healthier in employment than in romance. Experiential learning and co-op experience counter the infantilization attendant upon graduate studies that debilitates so many of our smartest students; it facilitates completion confidence for some students and helps others realize that choosing from among a variety of career paths is a valid option. We believe that recognition of the wider relevance of our students' skills and experiences has the potential to contribute to program satisfaction and retention.

What about progress through the PhD? The co-op program as it functions for PhD students involves a year's worth of full-time work outside the dissertation during the PhD. This could mean that students take longer to finish; in fact, however, given that many PhD students spend time on projects outside the dissertation, such as additional teaching assistantships or other campus-based work, and many get conceptual or writers' blocks that slow down their progress, it has not been our experience that, as a group, students doing the co-op program take substantially longer, or withdraw from the program more often, than non-co-op students, though of course our sample size is still relatively small. Students in our PhD co-op cohort report returning from a work term refreshed and more attuned to the broader relevance of the work they are doing.

Our experience suggests that graduate students can and should be provided with program options that allow them to engage successfully with both academic and nonacademic career paths, and we have been happy so far with the results of the PhD co-op option as our strategy to leverage institutional resources to create those open doors for our students. The PhD co-op program started in English has now been scaled out to include several other humanities graduate programs at UBC, and an MA Arts co-op program is piloting in 2023. We hope that the PhD co-op can serve as a model that other universities can consider in the effort to provide students with a range of opportunities and paths into professional success.

NOTES

1. Located in Vancouver, the University of British Columbia is a 60,000-student Tier 1 Canadian research institution, ranked in the top 50 in the QS World University Rankings.

2. "America produced more than 100,000 doctoral degrees between 2005 and 2009. In the same period there were just 16,000 new professorships. . . . Even in Canada, where the output of PhD graduates has grown relatively

modestly, universities conferred 4,800 doctorate degrees in 2007 but hired just 2,616 new full-time professors" ("Disposable Academic").

3. See, for example, the report of the Scholarly Communication Institute, founder of the Praxis Network, on rethinking graduate education (Rumsey).

4. For an overview and assessment of such initiatives between 1990 and 2015, see Cassuto and Weisbuch.

WORKS CITED

Almanac of Post-secondary Education. Canadian Association of University Teachers, 2021, caut.ca/latest/publications/almanac.

"Attrition in Humanities Doctorate Programs." *Humanities Indicators*, American Academy of Arts and Sciences, 2011, humanitiesindicators.org/content/indicatordoc.aspx?i=51.

Cassuto, Leonard, and Robert Weisbuch. *The New PhD: How to Build a Better Graduate Education*. Johns Hopkins UP, 2021.

"Casualization Is Becoming a Global Trend in Higher Education." *CAUT Bulletin*, Oct. 2015, bulletin-archives.caut.ca/bulletin/articles/2015/10/casualization-is-becoming-a-global-trend-in-higher-education.

Co-operative Education Manual: A Guide to Planning and Implementing Co-operative Education Programs in Post-secondary Institutions. Canadian Association for Co-operative Education, 2005.

"The Disposable Academic." *The Economist*, 16 Dec. 2010, economist.com/christmas-specials/2010/12/16/the-disposable-academic.

Eames, Chris, and Cheryl Cates. "Theories of Learning in Cooperative and Work-Integrated Education." *International Handbook for Cooperative and Work-Integrated Education: International Perspectives of Theory, Research, and Practice*, edited by Richard K. Coll and Karsten E. Zegwaard, 2nd ed., World Association for Cooperative Education, 2011, pp. 41–52.

Graduating in Canada: Profile, Labour Market Outcomes and Student Debt of the Class of 2009–2010. Statistics Canada, www150.statcan.gc.ca/n1/pub/81-595-m/81-595-m2014101-eng.htm.

Jaschik, Scott. "Another Bad Year for History Jobs." *Inside Higher Ed*, 17 Nov. 2017insidehighered.com/news/2017/11/17/decrease-number-openings-history-faculty-jobs.

———. "The Five-Year Humanities PhD." *Inside Higher Ed*, 4 Dec. 2012, insidehighered.com/news/2012/12/04/stanford-moves-ahead-plans-radically-change-humanities-doctoral-education.

———. "The Shrinking Humanities Job Market." *Inside Higher Ed*, 28 Aug. 2017, insidehighered.com/news/2017/08/28/more-humanities-phds-are-awarded-job-openings-are-disappearing.

"Job Status of Humanities Ph.D.'s at Time of Graduation." *Humanities Indicators*, American Academy of Arts and Sciences, 2018, humanitiesindicators.org/content/indicatordoc.aspx?i=68.

Laurence, David. "Our PhD Employment Problem, Part 1." *The Trend: Research and Analysis from the MLA Office of Programs*, 26 Feb. 2014, mlaresearch.mla.hcommons.org/2014/02/26/our-phd-employment-problem/.

———. "Our PhD Employment Problem, Part 2." *The Trend: Research and Analysis from the MLA Office of Programs*, 11 Mar. 2014, mlaresearch.mla.hcommons.org/2014/03/11/our-phd-employment-problem-part-2/.

Lusin, Natalia. *The MLA Job List, 2018–19*. Modern Language Association of America, Nov. 2020, mla.org/content/download/134145/file/Job%20List_2018-19_Linked.pdf.

MLA Office of Research. *Report on the MLA Job Information List, 2016–17*. Modern Language Association of America, Dec. 2017, mla.org/content/download/78816/2172744/Report-MLA-JIL-2016-17.pdf.

Park, Chris. "The New Variant PhD: The Changing Nature of the Doctorate in the UK." *Journal of Higher Education, Policy and Management*, vol. 27, no. 2, 2005, pp. 189–207.

QS World University Rankings 2023: Top Global Universities. Quacquarelli Symonds, 2023, topuniversities.com/university-rankings/world-university-rankings/2023.

Rogers, Katina. "Humanities Unbound: Supporting Careers and Scholarship beyond the Tenure Track." *Digital Humanities Quarterly*, vol. 9, no. 1, 2015, digitalhumanities.org/dhq/vol/9/1/000198/000198.html.

Rumsey, Abby Smith. "Scholarly Communication Institute Reports on Rethinking Humanities Graduate Education." Scholarly Communication Institute, 2013, libraopen.lib.virginia.edu/public_view/kd17cs909.

PART TWO
Civic Engagement

Introduction

Much of traditional education is spent training students into a posture of disengagement. The ideas of objectivity and rationality have been central to Eurocentric scientific inquiry since the late eighteenth century, when Enlightenment thinkers—nearly all of them European, economically privileged, and male—argued that to attain knowledge that is objective and true, one must take a stance that is impersonal and disinterested. The research university popularized and spread this idea throughout the nineteenth and twentieth centuries. But objectivity is not and has never been truly objective. Objectivity is, in fact, a specific brand of subjectivity, one that is usually invisible because it is so often assumed. Its invisibility allowed it to escape accountability for longer than it should have—accountability for academic isolationism, for scientific racism and misogyny, and for the fraught relationship (or lack thereof) between the university and its publics.

Civic engagement, as we understand it, is not simply a format or a matter of translation; it takes context and community as a starting point for questioning and creativity and acknowledges the potential implications of a project for the public good throughout the process. This kind of engagement requires academics and the university writ large to acknowledge and take seriously other forms of expertise; to become much better listeners; and to relinquish control, which is not something that institutions tend to encourage. Finally but perhaps most importantly, it necessitates being open to the idea that the university, an institution to which many of us have devoted our lives, has done significant harm. The history of higher education in the United States is also a history of colonialism and slavery. There is no way forward without that recognition.

Indeed, if those of us at universities truly want to change our relationships with the communities we purport to serve, then we must recognize much more than that: we must understand the ways in which that historical and epistemic violence has embedded itself in the fabric of our institutions. A persistent dedication to Eurocentric notions of objectivity is one way this violence makes itself felt, especially to graduate students of color. Students' identities as humanists are intersectional. They are shaped by racial and cultural identity, gender identity, moral identity, and existential boundary conditions like family, health, finances, geography, and history. Processes of acculturation to the discipline lean heavily on disciplinary norms that students of color often find alienating, and work that students understand to be critically important is derided as "me-search." True civic engagement calls for an openness to students' diverse subjectivities and to the ways those subjectivities come to bear on scholarship, teaching, professional goals, and levels of access.

We won't deny that civic engagement can be a difficult endeavor for the university, fraught with the sort of risk that institutions seek to avoid. But if we want the humanities—and graduate students, both present and future—to thrive in and beyond our institutions, then we must take that risk. And we only need to look around in our own lives to understand what is possible if we do. Judith Butler's *Gender Trouble*, while often misunderstood, has fundamentally changed the ways people understand gender and the ways they view themselves and one another. Similarly, critical race theory has made its way from graduate school classrooms into the mainstream to such a degree that entire segments of right-wing cable news were dedicated to attempting to discredit it in the summer of 2021. Although discomfiting to watch, this was evidence of how great an impact humanities research can have and how crucial it is to be an active participant in the conversation.

The first two essays in part 2 provide something of a bridge to part 1 and begin to outline the theoretical and pedagogical framework that can underlie a more civically minded form of engagement. In "New Pathways for Access, Inclusion, and Public Engagement in the Land-Grant Humanities PhD," Todd Butler, Tabitha Espina, and Richard Snyder examine graduate education reform in the specific context of the rural land-grant university. Based on their experiences as fellows or faculty members with Washington State University's Publicly Engaged Fellows program, which grew out of an NEH grant, Butler, Espina, and Snyder "reaffirm that the land-grant framework . . . must be reimagined as less a matter of institutional type than a set of principled and outward-facing commitments, ones that insist we need to listen deeply and repeatedly to the students and communities we might serve prior to beginning any formal program of public scholarship and engagement." They emphasize the importance of listening and responding to a community's real needs, particularly when those communities have a historically troubled relationship with the institution in question.

In a similar vein, "Graduate Students and Their Communities: The Obermann Institute," by Teresa Mangum and Jennifer New, examines the challenge of initiating mutually beneficial community partnerships. Mangum and New describe a collaborative and interdisciplinary initiative that trains students to create sustainable community partnerships. In a weeklong institute that partners with one public organization per cohort, students develop a strong understanding of the organization's needs and propose a project that both draws on the research and skills of the student teams and directly supports the organization. In the process, students practice a multidisciplinary, collaborative, and engaged form of humanistic work that inherently widens this volume's concept of the humanities ecosystem.

The next two essays provide a glimpse of what this work looks like from outside the academic humanities. Will Fenton's "Generative Collaboration and the Digital Humanities" shares the story of a multimodal examination of the Paxton Massacre of 1763. In the author's quest to provide a more comprehensive account of the massacre and ensuing pamphlet war, his project transformed from a traditional early American studies dissertation to a public digital archive displaying an interconnected political discourse to a graphic novel that provides an alternative account of the events from the perspective of the Conestoga native people. Fenton's project demonstrates the generative exchange that can take place when humanities scholars join forces with creative artists and local communities to reflect carefully about the concepts, histories, and discourses that underlie our social reality—and highlights the agency and potential impact that graduate students can have early in their careers.

Marcia Halstead James provides us with a countervailing perspective on the role of the humanities outside academia. In "Working Knowledge: Narrative Theory in the Real World," James offers a close reading and theoretical reflection on her work as a development officer in nonprofit and philanthropy settings. James draws attention to the extensive narratological discourse in the nonprofit research sector as well as to the role of language, storytelling, and rhetoric in her work. She examines fundraising and development literature in terms of their genre conventions and demonstrates the critical importance of humanities training for both the success and the sustainability of responsible development work. James offers a humanistic account of philanthropy that reminds us of the very real and immediate power of narrative in professional contexts and of the critical contributions that a humanistic skill set can make in strategic high-impact roles.

The final two essays in this part both offer considerations for the future and models for what a civically or publicly engaged graduate education might entail. In "Sustainability and the Posthumanities," Alex Christie and Katie Dyson turn to the posthumanities as a way of considering a "nonreproductive future beyond the limited scope of the humanities and humanism." Christie and Dyson argue that our present is not sustainable and that imagining something else requires us to let go of much of what we have been taught to value in honoring "the impossibility and undecidability of what is to come. Against a model of sustainability predicated on the perpetual reproduction of the same or capitalist accumulation, nonreproductive futures allow us to think about the present as mutating beyond itself to become something other than itself, especially in this moment of crisis." They see the possibility of the humanities operating in a "wider public ecology," one that is "collective and relational."

As for the role that the academic humanities might play in such an ecology, the final essay offers some ideas. In "Humanities in Action: Centering the Human in Public Humanities Work," we listen in on a conversation between two colleagues, Veronica T. Watson, program director for graduate studies in literature and criticism at Indiana University of Pennsylvania, and Laurie Zierer, executive director of the Pennsylvania Humanities Council. Watson and Zierer negotiate definitions of humanistic work, of the public humanities, and of collaboration in the future of our field. They are particularly concerned with issues of equity and access, noting, "When the humanities are understood primarily as academic subjects that are delivered as part of a curriculum, that framing is always already exclusionary. . . ." Watson and Zierer use their essay not only to envision but also to model a mutually enriching, access-oriented form of humanistic dialogue—a road map to increased understanding and better relations between the academic and public humanities.

New Pathways for Access, Inclusion, and Public Engagement in the Land-Grant Humanities PhD

Todd Butler, Tabitha Espina, and Richard Snyder

In 1862 the United States Congress passed the Morrill Act, initiating thereby a radical transformation in American higher education. Drawing upon revenues generated by allocations of federalized land within or near their borders, the act charged states with establishing a national system of industrial colleges in order "to promote the liberal and practical education of the industrial classes in the several pursuits and professions in life" (United States Code). Combined with extensions of this program in 1890 to the former Confederacy and in 1994 to the establishment of similar colleges for American Indians, the land-grant system has over a century come to encompass more than a hundred colleges and universities, each charged with expanding the educational franchise and extending their research directly to the wider populace they are designed to serve.

As evidenced by this volume, this mission not only is timely but also speaks directly to the challenges faced by graduate students and faculty members in the humanities, the larger disciplines we study, and the multiple publics we engage. At the same time as observers are decrying political polarization and the need to reinvigorate our shared sense of purpose, for example, prospective and current doctoral students are increasingly indicating a desire to do work that matters within both their classrooms and their communities. A recent survey of publicly engaged graduate students and early-career scholars—the majority of whom were in the humanities—demonstrates that such individuals see little distinction between the contributions they might make to their discipline and those they might make to the "public" (Eastman 40). In particular, doctoral students from underrepresented groups are also more likely than nonminoritized students to pursue work also applicable outside higher education, a fact which suggests that enabling publicly engaged scholarship offers an underrecognized pathway to further diversifying the academy (Day et al. 165). As these studies suggest, commitments to public work inform careers, and with them the future of the humanities as a catalyst for positive social development. The professional and societal value of publicly responsive work has also been increasingly recognized by initiatives from national disciplinary associations such as the American Historical Association and the Modern Language Association, whose respective programs Career Diversity for Historians and Connected Academics have regularly linked public engagement and graduate career diversity. To these are joined broader initiatives in higher education such as Imagining America's Publicly Active Graduate Education network and Campus Compact, the latter of which in 2007 explicitly called upon research universities to develop community-engaged research programs as part of their graduate educational mission (Campus Compact 21).

Drawing upon our shared experience of learning and program building at Washington State University (WSU), this essay explores one possible pathway to answering this call. More importantly, it presents a program model designed specifically to engage the needs and expectations of rural and underserved communities. These populations are rarely served by even the most innovative programs in graduate career development, which more frequently draw upon and serve universities situated in more urban areas. This failure to engage with rural communities unduly limits the reach of the humanities and blinds many of its academic practitioners to the diversity of opinion and individuals that can characterize these regions. Given this diversity, what follows is less a specific playbook for "rural engagement" than a set of principles illustrated from experience and animated by our belief that, properly reconceived, the land-grant model offers a vital pathway toward understanding graduate professional development as more than just self-interest or self-promotion. At its core, this revised model relies upon and promotes an ethos of reciprocal generosity informed by the land-grant ideal that knowledge should be locally invested and shaped by public conversation.

Yet while our model rests upon this ideal, it also recognizes that historically, land-grant universities and their faculties—ourselves certainly included—have unevenly engaged with their origins and their surrounding communities. Our program takes this ignorance as its starting point, using a two-stage approach that encourages participating students and faculty members to first learn the complex history of the system in which they participate, including the continuing inability of land-grant universities to reckon fully with their genesis in the expropriation of Indigenous lands. We then seek to unlearn traditional academic presumptions regarding doctoral study, replacing epistemologies of individualized scholarship, analytical detachment, and historical and interpersonal distance with a values-based approach increasingly seen as vital to the success of public scholarship.[1] Only after that shared vision is in place do students pursue more concentrated training and community-building initiatives. Ultimately, we reaffirm that the land-grant framework—and any parallel program of graduate public engagement—must be reimagined as less a matter of institutional type than a set of principled and outward-facing commitments, ones that insist we need to listen deeply and repeatedly to the students and communities we might serve prior to beginning any formal program of public scholarship and engagement.

Land-Grant Universities and Graduate Education

When placed within their historical context, the establishment and mission of the US land-grant system feel hauntingly contemporary. In particular, the 1862 Morrill Act was the product of a nation divided over questions of race. The act's passage was ultimately enabled by the Civil War fracturing of the American polity that had elected Abraham Lincoln to the presidency and removed Southern senators from Congress, thereby blunting previous opposition that had been based on states' rights and a resistance to any federal measures that might pave the way for further intervention on matters of race and slavery (Sorber). Meanwhile, another of our country's pernicious blind spots—its shameful treatment of American Indians—endured largely unexamined. As Margaret Nash has argued, "Indian dispossession . . . was fundamental to the existence of these institutions" (439). More than ten million acres in the West were appropriated, a redistribution of land that, when paired with the contemporaneous Homestead Act land grants to railroad companies, provided a vital framework for America's westward expansion.[2] The aim of the act born from this troubled legacy was to enable the creation of colleges where students might pursue, in addition to scientific, classical, and military studies, what the act terms the "agriculture and the mechanic arts" (United States Code). Importantly, such education was not intended to be narrowly vocational or simply mechanical. Rather, it was designed to advance high-level research and applications that might lift both its students and its sponsoring nation into positions of leadership. Both the act and its political environment thus speak to concerns as operative in the twenty-first century as they were in the nineteenth: a need to reckon with racialized structures of higher education, an increasing interest in applied learning, a growing connection between individual educational attainment and collective social betterment, and an abiding worry over the potential dangers that arise when income and class inequality are magnified by disparate access to more established institutions of higher learning (Aoun; Fogel; *Forging Pathways*).[3] Though the original commitment to remedying these challenges should in no way be over-romanticized, at its core lies a compelling vision of education placed in service to disadvantaged populations and an external rather than simply internal understanding of a university's obligations.[4]

If for no other reason than sheer weight of numbers, this land-grant mission might reasonably be expected to exercise a formative influence on contemporary American graduate education. Land-grant universities, the majority of which are classified as institutions with "high" or "very high" research activity, currently train at least seventy percent of all graduate students at research-intensive institutions, and they similarly perform a majority of federally funded research in the United States (Gavazzi 29). Even so, awareness and implementation of the land-grant mission vary considerably across and within these institutions. Traditionally, this responsibility has most frequently fallen to universities' technical and agricultural components, the latter of which include statewide cooperative extension services originally established by the 1914 Smith-Lever Act.[5] Seemingly most isolated from this mission, by contrast, have been faculty and graduate programs in the arts and humanities. As one administrator recently put it, while agriculture and education faculty members at land-grant universities generally recognize the need to engage directly with communities, "the typical English professor . . . doesn't seem to be aware of the fact there is a world outside of his or her office" (Gavazzi 119). To be sure, statements of this kind disregard much recent humanities scholarship and in doing so perpetuate highly pernicious stereotypes about the irrelevance of the humanities to remedying the problems of contemporary life. Yet there is also more than a grain of truth to such statements, especially in the aggregate and especially when applied to research partnerships rather than classroom teaching. These limitations are particularly reflected in graduate curricula, for at present there is little that distinguishes a humanities PhD awarded by a land-grant university from those awarded by other American institutions. Despite the distinctive role envisioned for land-grant universities, for example, few graduate students in the humanities ever have formal occasion to reflect upon the history of their institutions and how that history—and its continuing challenges—might inform their studies. Even at land-grant institutions, humanities graduate students interested in community partnerships will also encounter few if any programmatic or institutional pathways along which these relationships might form. Moreover, the lack of conceptual links within humanities disciplines between the intellectual work of scholarship and direct engagement with local communities frequently makes it difficult to theorize such pathways, and few faculty members have been trained—much less professionally incentivized—in how to do so.

Reimagining Land-Grant Graduate Education in the Humanities

In August 2018 we set out to directly address these challenges with the hope of identifying how PhD training in the humanities can be informed by the historical commitment of the land-grant system to access, inclusivity, and reciprocal engagement, the latter of which includes a particular focus on underserved and rural populations. Funded by a National Endowment for the Humanities Next Generation Humanities PhD Planning grant and accompanying matching funds provided by private donors, we brought together a wide-ranging team of participants that included key faculty members and administrators, current graduate students, and alumni, the last of whom all resided in towns of fewer than thirty-five thousand individuals. This focus on broadening the conversation also carried over to both the participating graduate students, half of whom were students of color, and administrators, a group that included not only the head of WSU Extension but also faculty members from the university's newly created medical school, which was founded with the express mission of improving rural health-care outcomes. Especially when facing public skepticism regarding their contemporary relevance, faculty members and students in the humanities tend to think their allies are few and narrowly located, but we found quite the opposite—the humanities have allies across campus and in the community, and reframing our interests in literature, history, languages, and the arts as occasions for partnership helps bring those allies into conversation.

At the outset, our group immediately identified several challenges to pursuing publicly engaged work at the graduate level. Some of these challenges are common across disciplines, but the particular structure of graduate education in the humanities can amplify them. For example, while graduate students as a whole frequently face significant financial and programmatic pressures regarding time to degree, the emphasis in humanities graduate programs on in-classroom coursework and assistantships devoted to classroom teaching magnifies these limitations considerably. As a result, the very nature of advanced study in the humanities repeatedly turns students inward toward their campuses. Because of this pressure, as well as the complexity of finding and developing community relationships that speak to graduate students' specific interests, pathways to community engagement must be established in departments or programs well ahead of students' involvement. Even if such structures are in place, however, graduate students may still struggle to realize the relationship between community engagement and their professional development as scholars, especially if, like many students, they arrive in graduate school with the intent of someday joining the professoriate. This predisposition is often reinforced by well-meaning graduate faculty members who, worried over the highly competitive academic job market, foreground within their own courses and mentoring the traditional and presumptively universal priorities of modern academic work: publication, conference presentations, and professional networking (Krabill).[6] Despite recent calls for more locally responsive and place-based pedagogies, both the necessarily transient nature of graduate study and the collapse of tenure-track positions in the humanities also discourage doctoral students from investing in their immediate locales or prioritizing a particular form of institution or geographic region in their job search.[7] Together, all these considerations encourage a narrow focus on self-interest and individual career development, favoring a nascent version of the academic star system and militating against graduate programs' developing a distinctive focus on the land-grant mission and community-engaged scholarship in the humanities.

Addressing these concerns required establishing within our discussions a shared familiarity and outward-oriented purpose otherwise absent from our individual programs. Community building must first be emphasized *within* programs for public engagement precisely because humanities faculty members and students who are individually interested in public engagement frequently feel isolated in those commitments. Humanities programs seeking to develop graduate offerings in public engagement that neglect the initial cultivation of ethos, as well as an institutionally specific rationale, are likely to falter after graduating an initial cohort of early adopters, because there are simply too many institutional and disciplinary pressures that socialize students away from such work. During our program's development phase, participating graduate alumni who lived in rural areas similarly reminded us of how traditional hierarchies of academic authority have conditioned not only the experiences of graduate students but also the academy's interaction with the publics it has attempted to serve. In particular, rural and underserved communities have frequently endured one-sided or uneven relationships with interested academics, a history that includes general disregard for community expertise and agency as well as more practical problems such as inadequately trained or poorly supervised interns placed with local service providers. From the outset of our planning, we therefore prioritized deep and sustained listening as a primary pathway forward, albeit in an unusual fashion. After both graduate students and alumni talked about how their departments had *not* served them entirely well, and how academia frequently misunderstood the rich sociologies of small communities, the initiative leader (Todd) then required that the attending faculty members and administrators only ask questions rather than offer comments of their own. Situating our students and alumni as experts, and faculty members as learners, made the discussion a matter of divining and fully understanding the needs of the first two groups.[8] The design process thus embedded—and encouraged its participants to experience—the reciprocal generosity embodied in our land-grant mission. Focusing on needs, and taking the time to listen to those needs, became our guiding ethos. When reinforced in subsequent meetings, that ethos transformed us into a problem-solving operation that resulted in the establishment of WSU's first graduate Publicly Engaged Fellows (PEF) program.

Designing a Publicly Engaged Fellows Program

Begun formally in fall 2019, our year-long PEF takes a deliberately incremental approach to graduate student development, emphasizing education and conversation before action. It begins in the fall with the Land-Grant Seminar, a semester-long series of informal discussions and workshops designed to help students learn about the historical roots and contemporary mission of the land-grant university as well as the variety of practical ways those can be expressed. These weekly meetings re-create the educational and imaginative design initially experienced within our grant, situating each new cohort of students in an ethos of public engagement prior to their ever pursuing such work. In addition to introducing the land-grant framework, the seminar provides practice-based instruction in topics ranging from project management and public writing to interviewing and self-assessment in sessions cotaught by a humanities faculty member or university administrator and, ideally, a community partner. By inviting community members into the traditional space of the classroom, the program visibly asserts that expertise can indeed be defined widely, and that partners exist who can help students articulate a larger social purpose for their graduate work and explore the ways they might pursue it. Students also have an opportunity to share their nascent plans for community engagement through a session of "quick response" conversations with similarly mixed audiences. In this workshop, pairs of graduate students circulate among small groups of faculty members, administrators, and community leaders, repeatedly presenting three- to four-minute summaries of their ideas, making individual connections, and getting feedback. Throughout the semester-long series, discovery rather than mastery remains the primary mode of learning, introducing new kinds of problems while simultaneously valuing each student's potential solutions. Along with simply providing a refreshing change from the intellectually competitive if not combative environment of a humanities graduate seminar, this approach allows students to explore their limitations and identify the particular skills—academic, practical, even social—they need to be successful in this new approach to their studies.

Two skills—cultural humility and digital literacy—receive particular emphasis in the seminar, as they represent important components of not only our own scholarship but also any institutional or individual partnership with underserved communities. We favor the term *cultural humility* over the more familiar *cultural competency* because it embodies the fundamental values of deep listening and reflection that animated our initial project and resulted in its most important educational moments. Learning to engage justly with any outside community, and with underserved communities in particular, requires graduate students to consider positions and experiences outside their own before they attempt to navigate them. Within the PEF series graduate students are therefore quickly introduced to approaches that decenter authority and distribute responsibilities equitably. At a land-grant university, such training must begin with an acknowledgment that the land at the heart of their institution was originally held by Native communities and that even presumptively legal, treaty-based cessions of such land were secured within a larger history of compulsion and disregard for Native sovereignty (Martin and Hipp; Nash). At the same time as it acknowledges this history, however, the program also seeks to introduce Native ways of knowing as potentially productive reformulations of academic and public work. This conversation is led by faculty members from WSU's Center for Native American Research and Collaboration, part of our university's larger Native American Programs office, which help coordinate WSU's formal relationship with eleven federally recognized tribes. Drawing upon Shawn Wilson's centering of relationships within Indigenous research methods, we consider across several sessions how similar models of equitable reciprocity can ground our own collaborative work. Importantly, these discussions are not designed to enable the casual adoption of Indigenous research methodologies. Rather, introducing the richness of these methodologies becomes a way to decenter assumptions about the value and outcomes of more familiar ways of working. Participants thus test their capacity to treat such knowledge systems with respect to recognize their own scholarly limitations and to work equitably with other communities.

Building from this foundation, we then introduce other concepts vital to working with partners in diverse communities. Drawing from experts in WSU's Critical Literacies Access and Success Program (CLASP), which aims to enhance the success of first-generation, low-income, and otherwise underrepresented students, our seminar series turns its focus to stereotype threat, microaggressions, critical literacy, decolonial pedagogies, and collaborative dialogue.[9] The selection of these topics provides a bridge from typical graduate student learning, since students have encountered at least some of these approaches in their department's teaching assistant training. Here, however, we ask our students to extend their thinking beyond the classrooms they inhabit. To be successful in working with rural and underserved communities, graduate students must become more mindful of their own implicit biases and aware of the insidious ways that stereotypes can manifest in social interactions—including the ways that verbal, behavioral, and environmental interactions can communicate hostility or target persons or groups, whether intentionally or unintentionally. We also discuss how the standard paradigm of graduate research in the humanities may, however inadvertently, reinforce these behaviors. In particular, the emphasis on independently conceived and executed projects may render graduate students less immediately equipped to work in dialogue. It may also make students and faculty members more prone to present themselves, however inadvertently, as stereotypically abstract experts ready to deploy their expertise upon an unthinking, nonacademic public. The overarching approach of all these sessions is to resist defining public engagement within a deficit model, presenting engagement as mutually enriching rather than as remedying a fault or lack in an external community.

Within its introduction to practical skills, the series highlights in particular the potential of digital technologies to enable rural partnerships. Unlike urban engagement programs, those serving rural communities may find their potential partners to be distant and widely dispersed. This lack of immediate proximity can present significant practical challenges, especially since the classroom-based structure of graduate training in the humanities, as well as the financial and personal obligations of many graduate students, frequently prevent long- or even short-term field work. The COVID-19 pandemic has highlighted both the challenges posed by social and geographic distance and the capacity of many digital technologies to compensate for a lack of physical presence. Communications technologies can enable projects that might begin and end with a series of site visits or short-term residencies but then continue to develop through messaging services (e.g., *Slack*), live document editing, *Zoom*, social media, and other forms of digital collaboration. Especially as institutions grow their investments in online outreach or digital humanities, technological tools can also provide relatively inexpensive platforms for projects themselves. Online tools such as *ArcGIS*, *Twine*, and *Scalar*, for example, can help create richer, multimedia explorations of texts, issues, or community voices, and the availability of web-based archives can allow communities to access scholarly products more regularly and directly.[10]

New digital technologies in the twenty-first century can thus play the same role as new agricultural technologies did in the nineteenth century, with humanities graduate students—many of whom already incorporate digital humanities into their pedagogy and research—providing training and resources potentially unavailable to partner communities. Doing so ethically, however, also requires that students, and in particular those who might work with underserved, Native, or Indigenous communities, also critically consider the context, production, and impact of the technologies they choose to use. At WSU such critiques are most frequently generated by one of our seminar's partners, the Center for Digital Scholarship and Curation, which takes as its primary focus the advancement of both new scholarly technologies and Native, Indigenous, and First Nations leadership in the curation of their digital heritage.[11] Drawing from this expertise, the seminar introduces at the outset of its digital modules the need to reconsider notions of ownership that in Western and more traditional academic humanities are highly individualized. Similar discussions inform our review of other potential partnership technologies, such as digital archiving, audio and video capture, data sovereignty, and web hosting. In being introduced to such digital affordances, students ideally learn not only skills such as web design but also how to make their digital work an occasion for effective and genuinely equitable partnerships.

Throughout its design, the seminar presumes that students must wrestle with the idea of engaged scholarship and consider its audiences before being asked to consider pursuing such work. It also recognizes that our PEF exists within an institutional environment that socializes graduate students into more traditional models of scholarly and professional work. Offering foundational education in community engagement, by contrast, helps broaden the pool of potentially interested students, in part by lowering the initial barrier to entry.[12] A "course," or in this case a seminar series, is a familiar mode of learning for both students and faculty members. It thus represents a comparatively limited "ask" of students, one that both new graduate students (who find themselves needing to make multiple career-impacting choices) and individuals more advanced in their programs (who will have already formulated their course of study) can accommodate. In addition, by introducing and then interrogating the relevance of the land-grant mission, the seminar establishes a conceptual framework for its skills-based offerings, providing an academic and values-based rationale for its material that our graduate students described as more compelling than appeals to self-interest or the lack of academic jobs (variations on which they have likely heard since their undergraduate years). Just as importantly, this framework enjoins graduate students considering community partnerships to reflect deliberately and repeatedly on the real work that culturally and ethically sensitive engagement must entail. As such, at the end of the seminar the PEF also supports the choice of students to opt *out* of immediately pursuing engaged scholarship, recognizing both that students must be genuinely prepared for such work and that simply exposing students to the idea of community engagement should itself be considered a success.

For those students deemed by themselves and participating faculty members to be ready for further engagement, the PEF subsequently offers the opportunity to complete a summer project in collaboration with a community partner. Funded by awards equal to the teaching of a summer course, which is itself an important conceptual equivalency, the specifics of these projects are designed over the spring semester and supported by a three-pronged team of a faculty adviser, a university administrator, and a community partner who together will challenge students to understand the needs and resources of a community and then shape their work to support them.[13] The three-tier mentoring program simultaneously aims to support students and to reassure community partners, many of whose time and financial resources are already stressed, that students are adequately prepared and will not become solely theirs to manage. The program devotes an entire semester to individual planning precisely because creating a sustainable public engagement project demands that organizers account for the fact that partnerships can be slow to build and that the collaboration and design process is itself an educational opportunity. Students learn to negotiate the expectations of a community and how limitations on time, energy, and resources can define a project just as much as the ethos and enthusiasm that first animated it. Successfully navigating this design stage thus often means accepting stages of uncertainty that can often be remedied only incrementally, with each successive conversation between student and partner better defining the scope, occasions, and methods of any given project. For example, one graduate student planning a small downtown arts gathering found herself repeatedly scaling back her ambitions as she worked with participants and coordinated with multiple city agencies on permitting and access. In the middle of the process, she reported, "I'm not sure I'm accomplishing anything, but I'm learning so much!" However complicating and frustrating it can be, such give-and-take lies at the heart of reciprocal generosity. The program is also mindful, however, of the expectations that accompany traditional academic progress. In the PEF, we therefore require students not only to be a physical or digital presence in the community but also to produce written work for their partners, such as a white paper or needs assessment. This work extends students' skills in collaboration, analysis, and writing to a different genre and potentially provides a form of "publication" (and work) that can be listed on a CV. Offering such "translational" work is often key to establishing the merit of community outreach, as it renders what might otherwise seem a radical departure from academic career preparation in more familiar terms.[14]

Piloting Community Engagement in the Program

Pilot versions of these community engagement projects have already begun to show promise and reinforce the conclusions—and challenges—undergirding the PEF's design. Deep listening and dialogue, in which program faculty members at once listen for graduate students' core interests and consider how those might be articulated in a broader way, have been key to identifying these projects. In the case of work conducted by the coauthors of this essay, including collaborations with Humanities Washington, our state-level humanities council, aimed at improving outreach to immigrant communities (Tabitha) and with a small regional public library focused on leveraging digital technologies like virtual reality (VR) headsets to improve youth engagement (Richard), both initiatives began with multiple rounds of conversation designed to familiarize students with their external partner and to explore how a shared project could advance both their and the partner's goals and visions. Just as the conversations of our NEH grant began with listening for the needs and desires of the graduate students and then engaging in dialogue, Tabitha and Richard approached their partners not as benevolent saviors but as critically engaged, culturally conscious collaborators, ready to learn and to give.

Strikingly, in each case these initial conversations quickly centered on access, in particular the challenge these disparate organizations faced in securing engaged audiences for their own programming. While each organization was embedded in one or more communities, neither partner had encountered regular success in working with underserved elements of their local populations. The desire of local institutions like these to improve their own engagement actually offered an important starting point for partnership and academic outreach. For example, aiming to explore Humanities Washington's commitment to "live up to the equity values" that underlie the arts and humanities, Tabitha conducted a case study in how the state humanities council might better engage with members of the Filipino community, a group that despite being an essential part of the history of the region does not often figure in local or state-level arts programming. This is work that Tabitha, with her own dissertation work on the Filipino American diaspora, was well positioned to pursue and that Humanities Washington had neither the staff nor resources to accomplish. Her aim was to begin identifying particular obstacles to the involvement of regional Asian American and Pacific Islander groups in humanities programming and outreach, a key first step for any subsequent outreach efforts. An initial series of collaborative engagements took place at the Filipino community's hall in Wapato, culminating in an intergenerational roundtable, "Visions of the Past, Present, and Future with the Filipino American Community of Wapato," coordinated and moderated by Tabitha. Cosponsored by the Yakima Valley Community Foundation, Filipino American National Historical Society Seattle Chapter, Washington State Arts Commission, and Humanities Washington, the roundtable invited members of the Wapato community to take part in discussing the history and contributions of Filipino Americans to the region, while partaking of Filipino foods prepared by the hall's members. These engagements directly confronted two of the most significant needs expressed by the Filipino American community in Wapato: support and affirmation. These conversations have since initiated a network of financial and promotional support from state-level humanities organizations for the Filipino American community's programs, as well as a recent NEH-Humanities Washington CARES Act grant, authored by Tabitha in collaboration with the hall's leaders, to support humanities and arts-related community outreach during the coronavirus pandemic. Perhaps the most significant finding of this work, however, was that members of the community were moved by Tabitha's scholarly interest and Humanities Washington's willingness to collaborate and provide financial support, remarking that these partnerships attest to the value of their history and presence, both of which they had previously believed to have been "forgotten."

In like fashion, Richard drew upon both his own graduate work in digital humanities and his family's experiences in rural parts of Oregon and Washington, where some libraries are closing owing to lack of funding and lack of support from community members who see libraries as outdated and a potential waste of tax money in the digital age. Much as in Tabitha's case, Richard found that for the local library in Colfax, Washington (population 2,800), the challenge was not so much technical as human and relational. Though this library had enough funding to buy digital technologies like VR headsets and train staff members in their use, bringing new patrons into the library remained a major challenge, resulting in the headsets and other expensive equipment going unused. In response, Richard worked with a local librarian to inventory and suggest new uses for their technology and to plan for a local family fair a display and hands-on demos highlighting for new audiences some of the technologies now available at their library. In doing so, Richard helped create a model for thinking through the best use of technologies as community outreach, and for conducting similar events in the future.

Lessons Learned and Looking toward the Future

To be sure, neither of these projects (or similar efforts by subsequent PEF cohorts) completely resolved the challenges faced by publicly engaged graduate students and their community partners. Yet embracing the exploratory nature of such partnerships is perhaps the most fundamental requirement for engaging both graduate students and rural communities. Inherent in this process must be the willingness to embrace failure—or at least the possibility of failure—as a potential outcome. We observed in designing the PEF that experiences or mindsets on both sides may, at least at the outset, limit participants' ability or willingness to develop sustainable, long-term relationships. Addressing these concerns requires collaboration across the institution, a shared commitment to listening, and the willingness to learn (and value) the perspectives of the community prior to articulating those of the program. If done correctly, at times such work may paradoxically result in *not* establishing collaborative projects, or at least not doing so in any given year. In our case, that has meant a continuing reflection on how best to meet the burdens of our land-grant university's relationship with Native peoples. While WSU has formalized, long-standing relationships with twelve Native tribes, we quickly realized that respect for Native sovereignty, history, and governance structures meant that a great deal more conversation would be required before our program was appropriately prepared to offer graduate student engagement with these communities. Participating in dialogue with and maintaining respect for the sovereignty of these tribes, we hope, will make our engagement with these nations not only more equitable but also more sustainable. To do so, however, we first had to further educate ourselves, regardless of how genuinely felt our initial commitments were.

All this work takes time, which is another foundational element of engaging with rural and underserved communities. Though some elements of our program rely upon collaborator relationships that have themselves been painstakingly developed, other key features—dialogue, mindset growth, and meeting students and communities where they are—inherently demand a developmental approach that must be nurtured incrementally. By contrast, starting immediately upon the visible work of direct community engagement can unfortunately neglect much of the labor, both individual and institutional, that successful commitments actually require. To do so is to overlook the fact that learning to converse with, listen to, and learn from external audiences is itself engagement. As one experienced faculty presenter explained in a session entitled "Moving from Vision to Project Management," sustaining the relationship between a researcher and the underserved community is ultimately more important than the outcome of any particular project. Much of our program design, which emphasizes a full semester of training and another of individualized student-partner conversation, exemplifies these considerations.

So too does this essay. Like early-adopting graduate students, readers already committed to the core principles of equitable engagement and humanities outreach may have hoped our writing here would have more immediately focused on the projects being developed between our fellows and their community partners. By focusing instead upon the rationale for the PEF and its seminar design, however, we have sought to foreground the educational process we have pursued and that we believe others must pursue when seeking to engage underserved communities. From our experience, beginning as learners rather than experts, and approaching community partners as equals, inspires a reciprocal generosity unusual in graduate education in the humanities, which otherwise often favors critique as its primary mode of inquiry (Fitzpatrick). Nurturing such generosity in ourselves and then redirecting it into our traditional classrooms and work as faculty members and students thus presents yet another benefit to working with rural and underserved communities, one born from identifying a greater social potential for the work we do and the things we might learn. Instilling such a values-based and civic orientation also offers another pathway by which students, faculty members, and departments can move beyond the demands for vocational and economic utility that increasingly determine research in public higher education. Indeed, though the "job crisis" has been undeniably catalytic to reconsidering graduate professional development in the humanities, it is only a small part of what must be a larger conversation about the greater ends and audiences such professional development must serve.

NOTES

1. On traditional academic epistemology, see Schön; Peters 24–32. On the connection between values and public scholarship, see Fear and Sandmann; Peters et al.; Strand et al.

2. For an accessible, deeply researched examination of the particulars of this dispossession, including a database identifying these lands down to individual parcels, see Lee et al.

3. One of the long-standing responses to all these challenges has been the LEAP initiative by the American Association of Colleges and Universities (see Schneider).

4. This vision derives some of its power from its capacity to obscure for administrators, educators, and the general public the historical and continuing inequities that accompany both higher education and American society (Geiger and Sorber ix). As this essay details, our program wrestles with these challenges at the same time as it seeks to reintroduce the larger spirit of the land-grant mission into humanistic study. For a broader call to action along similar lines, see Goldstein et al.

5. The land-grant mission also manifests itself, especially in the view of the general public (and the legislative bodies that represent it), in the undergraduate teaching mission of such colleges and universities. In the case of research

universities such as WSU, however, demands for an increasing selectivity in admissions and the pursuit of elevated institutional rankings often supersede the historical obligation to educate a broad range of students.

6. Not surprisingly, faculty members often have similar concerns for their own careers, in particular the question of how publicly responsive work might count—if it is recognized at all—toward tenure and promotion, annual reviews, and individual research agendas.

7. On place-based pedagogy, see Ball and Lai.

8. We should note that the participating faculty members willingly accepted this role (however initially disorienting it may have been) and were eager to ask questions.

9. CLASP seeks both to help underrepresented students identify and navigate the "hidden curriculum" of our institution and to support faculty members in learning how their own actions can advance that goal. Over more than a decade CLASP has consistently driven measurable gains in student retention and persistence (see clasp.wsu.edu and Buyserie et al.). On the foundational links between colonialism and the creation of land-grant universities, see both Nash and Stein.

10. For an example project that highlights a rural community, see the website *Company Town Legacy* (companytownlegacy.github.io/). Coordinated by Diane Kelly-Riley, a professor at the University of Idaho and a PEF seminar presenter, this web archive focuses on the logging town of Potlatch, Idaho, located approximately twenty miles from WSU.

11. Among the CDSC's projects, for example, is an internationally accepted content management system called *Mukurtu*, which enables Native and Indigenous communities to digitize heritage items while maintaining control over their public display. More information can be found at cdsc.libraries.wsu.edu and mukurtu.org.

12. Two additional elements also act to increase initial student interest: at least some of the participating students are informed that they were nominated for the program by their director of graduate studies, and all participating students will receive a stipend of at least $300 for completing the seminar series. In the absence of course credit (which would have required more complex institutional negotiations to arrange), the stipend provides some compensation for graduate students adding these workshops to their schedule.

13. At present the funding for these awards is provided by a variety of university offices, some of which have designated their support to students interested in partnering with particular constituencies (such as extension or medical outreach). The readiness of these offices to offer such funding stemmed in large part from their sustained involvement in designing the PEF, a fact that demonstrates how collaboration within the university can support collaboration outside it.

14. In other disciplines, such as anthropology or public policy, white papers and other agency-related documents are more commonly recognized as academic work, a fact that further suggests the potential crossover value of such writing.

WORKS CITED

Aoun, Joseph. *Robot-Proof: Higher Education in the Age of Artificial Intelligence.* MIT Press, 2017.

Ball, Eric L., and Alice Lai. "Place-Based Pedagogy for the Arts and Humanities." *Pedagogy*, vol. 6, no. 2, 2006, pp. 261–87.

Buyserie, Beth, et al. "Retention, Critical Pedagogy, and Students as Agents: Eschewing the Deficit Model." *Retention, Persistence, and Writing Programs*, edited by Todd Ruecker et al., UP of Colorado / Utah State UP, 2017, pp. 151–66.

Campus Compact. "New Times Demand New Scholarship: Research Universities and Civic Engagement: Opportunities and Challenges." U of California, Los Angeles, 2007, www.compact.org/wp-content/uploads/initiatives/research_universities/Civic_Engagement.pdf. Accessed 12 July 2019.

Day, Kristen, et al. "New Ways of Learning, Knowing, and Working: Diversifying Graduate Student Career Options through Community Engagement." Gilvin et al., pp. 163–82.

Eastman, Timothy. "The Arc of the Academic Career Bends toward Publicly Engaged Scholarship." Gilvin et al., pp. 25–48.

Fear, Frank, and Lorilee Sandmann. "The 'New' Scholarship: Implications for Engagement and Extension." *Journal of Higher Education Outreach and Engagement*, vol. 7, nos. 1–2, fall 2001-winter 2002, pp. 29–39.

Fitzpatrick, Kathleen. *Generous Thinking: A Radical Approach to Saving the University.* Johns Hopkins UP, 2019.

Fogel, Daniel Mark. "Challenges to Equilibrium: The Place of the Arts and Humanities in Public Research Universities." *Precipice or Crossroads? Where America's Great Public Universities Stand and Where They Are Going Midway through Their Second Century*, edited by D. M. Fogel and E. Malson-Huddle, State U of New York P, 2012, pp. 241–57.

Forging Pathways to Purposeful Work: The Role of Higher Education. Gallup and Bates College, 2018, www.gallup.com/education/248222/gallup-bates-purposeful-work-2019.aspx#ite-248231. Accessed 31 Dec. 2019.

Gavazzi, Stephen, and E. Gordon Gee. *Land-Grant Universities for the Future: Higher Education for the Public Good.* Johns Hopkins UP, 2018.

Geiger, Roger, and Nathan Sorber. Preface. *The Land-Grant Colleges and the Reshaping of American Higher Education*, edited by Geiger and Sorber, Transaction Publishers, 2013, pp. ix–xiv.

Gilvin, Amanda, et al., editors. *Collaborative Futures: Critical Reflections on Publicly Active Graduate Education.* Syracuse UP, 2012.

Goldstein, Jenny, et al. "A Manifesto for a Progressive Land-Grant Mission in an Authoritarian Populist Era." *Annals of the American Association of Geographers*, vol. 109, no. 2, 2019, pp. 673–84.

Krabill, Ron. "Graduate Mentoring against Common Sense." Gilvin et al., pp. 285–300.

Lee, Robert, et al. "Land-Grab Universities." *High Country News*, 2019, landgrabu.org.

Martin, Michael V., and Janie Simms Hipp. "A Time for Substance: Confronting Funding Inequities at Land Grant Institutions." *Tribal College: Journal of American Indian Higher Education*, vol. 29, no. 3, spring 2018, www.tribalcollegejournal.org/a-time-for-substance-confronting-funding-inequities-at-land-grant-institutions.

Nash, Margaret A. "Entangled Pasts: Land-Grant Colleges and American Indian Dispossession." *History of Education Quarterly*, vol. 59, no. 4, 2019, pp. 437–67.

Peters, Scott. *Democracy and Higher Education: Traditions and Stories of Civic Engagement*. Michigan State UP, 2010.

Peters, Scott, et al. "The Craft of Public Scholarship in Land-Grant Education." *Journal of Higher Education Outreach and Engagement*, vol. 8, no. 1, fall 2002-winter 2003, pp. 75–86.

Schneider, Carol Geary. *Making Liberal Education Inclusive: The Roots and Reach of the LEAP Framework for College Learning*. American Association of Colleges and Universities, 2021.

Schön, Donald. "Knowing-in-Action: The New Scholarship Requires a New Epistemology." *Change: The Magazine of Higher Learning*, vol. 27, no. 6, Nov.-Dec. 1995, pp. 27–34.

Sorber, Nathan. *Land-Grant Colleges and Popular Revolt: The Origins of the Morrill Act and the Reform of Higher Education*. Cornell UP, 2018.

Stein, Sharon. "A Colonial History of the Higher Education Present: Rethinking Land-Grant Institutions through Processes of Accumulation and Relations of Conquest." *Critical Studies in Education*, vol. 61, no. 2, Dec. 2017, pp. 212–28.

Strand, Kerry, et al. *Community-Based Research and Higher Education Principles and Practices*. Jossey-Bass, 2003.

United States Code. Title 7, section 304, *Legal Information Institute*, Cornell U Law School, law.cornell.edu/uscode/text/7/304.

Wilson, Shawn. *Research Is Ceremony: Indigenous Research Methods*. Fernwood, 2008.

Graduate Students and Their Communities: The Obermann Institute

Teresa Mangum and Jennifer New

In what sounds like the beginning of a joke, a literature scholar, a political scientist, and a creative writer walked into the University of Iowa's Obermann Center for Advanced Studies in 2006 and proposed a program for graduate students longing to bring together their academic and activist commitments. The University of Iowa is a public university, we argued; it seemed only right to ask how the art, scholarship, and research produced on campus could contribute to local and global communities.

We had been inspired by a public humanities institute developed at the University of Washington's Simpson Center for the Humanities. This program invited graduate students to consider how their academic work might be enriched through contact with civic and cultural organizations in Seattle. Because the Obermann Center serves an entire university, our goal was to convince the director of the Obermann Center and the dean of the Graduate College that our reimagining of the Simpson Center's institute as a cross-disciplinary initiative with humanities methods and values at the heart of our training was at least worth a trial run.

Fourteen years later, more than two hundred graduate students have participated in the annual four-day interdisciplinary Obermann Graduate Institute on Engagement and the Academy, and the importance of training them in the principles of public engagement is increasingly clear. The simple question at the heart of the institute—"How can my work be made better through collaboration with community experts?"—often transforms how a student perceives a research project. When scholars commit to sharing their studies with a broader audience, while also being receptive to the needs of community partners, the value of intellectual labor becomes clearer not only to the public but to the scholar. Similarly, engaged teaching offers students rare hands-on experiences that enhance their studies and benefit their communities. However, to succeed in building these bridges, graduate students need grounding in the methods, practices, and ethics that community-based forms of experiential learning, project-based courses, and cross-disciplinary studies demand. With that training, institute participants have realized projects with partners locally and in other parts of the world; one, for example, collaborates with a transgender group in Guatemala and another has started a website for members of the Filipina diaspora. Students' work with communities can also expand their career options. Many report that familiarity with public engagement helped them secure job interviews, especially for hybrid positions that combine teaching, research, and administration. Many end up developing transformative programming on our campus and in the world beyond.

Most important, the institute heartens students vulnerable to the loneliness of graduate school. Focus on disciplinary excellence by graduate programs can have the unintended consequence of stifling cross-disciplinary and cross-sectoral collaboration. Students seeking those connections find a supportive cohort of like-minded colleagues and mentors in the institute. We are also gratified that the institute experience sends students back to their graduate studies with a renewed sense of purpose, passion, and hope. As Tala Al-Rousan, a participant from the College of Public Health, tells us, "The Institute reinforced the importance of collaborative work and the impact engagement can leave on whatever research I do during my career." After a postdoctoral fellowship at Harvard, Tala is now an assistant adjunct professor in family medicine and public health at the University of California, San Diego. The passion, commitment, and successes of Tala and other institute alumni argue that students would welcome programs like ours at every university. By sharing our experience—the daily operation of the institute, feedback from our students, and our hopes for the future—we hope to inspire colleagues across the country to create their own versions of the Obermann Graduate Institute.

Our Philosophy

Nicholas Lemann's 2019 article in the *Chronicle of Higher Education*, "Can a University Save the World?," asks whether project-based research can effectively address real-world problems. Our answer is, "Well, we have to try." Our goal is to provide students with skills, fellow travelers, hope, and inspiration as they adapt disciplinary knowledge to serve the small and large transformations we need to save the planet and the beings on it. More specifically, the conceptions of publicly engaged teaching and research guiding the Obermann Institute have been strongly influenced by the national organization Imagining America: Artists and Scholars in Public Life (IA).[1] IA encourages deep, codeveloped, mutually beneficial collaborations among campus artists, scholars, and "public" partners. Their Publicly Active Graduate Education (PAGE) program also informs our institute (see imaginingamerica.org/what-we-do/fellowships/page/). Since 1999, ten PAGE fellows have been selected to meet at the IA annual conference. That in-person meeting has evolved into a radical experiment in collective leadership and virtual networking in public arts and scholarship that continues throughout the year. The impact of PAGE is documented by Sylvia Gale in "Arcs, Checklists, and Charts: The Trajectory of a Public Scholar?" We are also influenced by theorists of public culture from Paulo Freire to Toni Morrison to Kathleen Fitzpatrick, whose recent book *Generous Thinking: A Radical Approach to Saving the University* reminds us that we are in a historical moment when those of us leading graduate programs have a moral obligation to balance critique and skepticism with an intellectual as well as moral and affective appeal to ethics, justice, and generosity.

The changing context of graduate school and students' self-awareness about what they need from their graduate studies, especially if they want to prepare for a range of careers, also shape the institute. Since the institute's inception, the number of students who participate knowing that they do not plan to stay in the academy has grown. Often with funding from the National Endowment for the Humanities or the Andrew W. Mellon Foundation, academics across North America are experimenting with new approaches to graduate education. Originally driven by a decline in tenure-track positions, these experiments—like the Obermann Institute—are increasingly fueled by the spirit of intellectual excitement and passion that pervades the essays in the spring 2019 issue of *Profession*, titled *Public Humanities* (Krebs). In fact, we see the public arts and humanities as a ballast against the dangers of short-term thinking in critical arenas—politics, the economy, the environment. We encourage students to explore public arts and scholarship as a method of investigating research questions through practice, develop skills for varied careers, bridge intellectual passions and public service, and become better citizens as well as scholars.

During the week of the institute, students develop a proposal for a publicly engaged project that both roots deeply into their scholarship and reaches outward to a public partner. Some students fine-tune projects that are already in motion; others will cultivate ideas for years before acting on them. In either case, the institute encourages graduate students to pause for serious self-examination. Do their research interests, personal commitments and constraints, and potential partners truly fit with the intentions of their projects? Will the collaboration genuinely help community partners meet one of their goals? Our students' partners have included the campus Office of Sustainability, a local arts nonprofit, the University Domestic Violence Prevention Office, private and public museums, a historical farm site undergoing renovation, a youth literacy program, public schools, Special Collections in the university library, and our community senior center.

The crux of our philosophy is that partnerships should be a win-win, leading to the creation of new knowledge for the student artists and scholars and a significant outcome for the partnering organization. In that spirit, we encourage students to learn what assets possible collaborators would bring to a project rather than solely focusing on the needs of a community as the first step in forging an equitable partnership. The institute also helps students see that academics bring their own needs and limitations to a project. We ask students to be sure they can make good progress in their graduate studies while developing a partnership and a project. We also want them to be responsible collaborators, so we point out that most will soon leave Iowa City. Will they extract time and resources from a partner, then disappear? We caution students to resist thinking of public scholarship and teaching in additive terms, which can lead to stress and unfinished projects. Engaged practice is a method, and we argue that individuals should only undertake an engaged project when it gives life, energy, and meaning to their education as opposed to creating a distraction from "real" academic work. However, we also recognize that some students are so revitalized by public projects that if their departments will not support public scholarship, the students will manage to make time for the collaboration as a means of surviving graduate school.

Both IA and the National Humanities Alliance have collected case studies that we share, along with examples from our own alumni, to show students how varied publicly engaged teaching, arts, and research projects can be.[2] These examples demonstrate the powerful educational benefits of tethering scholarship to applied practice and submitting the individual, autonomous habits and emphasis on content knowledge that most of us experience in graduate school to the proving ground of teamwork, cross-sectoral interaction, and proliferating expectations and outcomes.

How the Institute Works

Thanks to the continuing generosity of the Graduate College, we have provided a $500 stipend for up to fifteen students each year. The students are selected by an advisory board of institute alumni, faculty members, mentors, staff members, and community partners. While the institute is open to students from across campus, most are from graduate programs in the arts, education, the humanities, public health, and the social sciences; occasionally, students from professional programs and the health sciences also participate. For the first several years the founding directors (including both of us) led the institute with the help of a returning "senior" graduate fellow, but we soon realized that a sustainable program would need rotating leadership and began to recruit faculty codirectors who serve two-year, overlapping stints. Jennifer and Obermann Center staff members help with logistics and the structure and content of the institute. Our fifteen different directors and their disciplines—including engineering, dance, English, history, communication sciences and disorders, and business—have had a powerful impact on the program. When an engineer and a dancer or an urban planner and a visual artist codirect, we're all forced to rethink what we mean by engagement, collaboration, method, research, and pedagogy. An unanticipated benefit is that these faculty members share and celebrate their own publicly engaged accomplishments, which are not always valued in their home departments. As a result, they often forge deep connections with each other. Some have even developed ongoing collaborations. The faculty members also delight in mentoring students far outside their disciplines and report that being part of the institute was one of the most satisfying teaching experiences of their careers.

The institute meets for four consecutive days in January just before spring semester classes begin. On the first day, we focus on definitions and theories of engagement. On days two and three, we dig first into teaching and then into research. We read key essays and hear from panels of faculty and former institute participants, who discuss the nuts and bolts of their engaged art and scholarship and the ways their academic work has been strengthened through public collaborations. We also take a field trip to a community partner's space and provide time for the students to work on their project proposals with input from us and their fellow participants.

Aside from readings and presentations, however, our pedagogy differs significantly from that of a typical graduate seminar—at least a humanities seminar—in part because we invite students to move outside their usual academic comfort zones. For example, we've learned firsthand how valuable experiential, embodied learning is for graduate students who spend hours sitting—in classes and at their computers. Institute directors and colleagues working in dance and theater have taught us nonverbal exercises that get us all on our feet and challenge students to collaborate on a task without speaking. Simply moving to the space of a homeless shelter or afterschool program and meeting on a potential partner's turf instead of on ours can be mind-altering. We also ask graduate students to reflect actively on what they are learning, to share those reflections, and to respond to each other's perceptions both before and during the institute. They use various senses to gather insights and a range of media to disperse discoveries. For instance, we encourage graduate students to prepare for the institute by responding to prompts like these:

> Explain how you understand *community*—in words, images, or sound—and then introduce us to one of your communities by making a three-minute video to share with the group in advance.
>
> Write about the experience of visiting an unfamiliar space and explain what you saw and how it felt.

We also post "invitations" each evening that encourage students to surface what they're learning throughout the fast-moving week. The directors of the institute read and briefly respond to the comments of the students who participate; they also react to one another. Sense-making thus moves back and forth between an individual and a collective process.

The glue that holds the institute together is often a project, and we have experimented with the nature of that project over the years. We ask students to propose an actual or hypothetical project they want to develop. Over the course of the week, students consider where their projects sit on a continuum that stretches from outreach to public engagement as we help them define each of the two ways of working—and the many degrees in between. Put simply, we define outreach as a one-directional sharing of knowledge or resources (for example, giving a presentation at the local public library) and engagement as work that two or more experts design and implement together that produces outcomes that benefit all the partners involved.[3]

On the final day of the institute, students present their individual project ideas to members of the advisory board. We organize small groups that combine students and reviewers with aligned experience and interests, such as people who want to work with K–12 students or who are focused on environmental issues. Each participant is allotted half an hour: ten minutes to share their project ideas and pose questions, which can include how to hone the project and whom to ask for specific kinds of assistance, and twenty minutes to receive feedback and advice.

As effective as this individual project workshop is, we've also had good success with students working in small teams to design a project for that year's site partner. During the site visit, which often occurs on the second day of the institute, we ask students to imagine how they might work with this partner and to ask our hosts questions that will inform the students' design process. We ask the partner to share their needs with the students frankly. Ironically, those needs often differ significantly from the kinds of projects the students initially wish to provide. We also encourage the partner to be honest about when and why past partnerships with faculty members and other outside visitors have foundered—a key moment in the graduate students' education as well as in our own ongoing self-assessment both of our process and of the program.

To make the assignment more demanding and realistic, we as directors impose two requirements. First, the project must be anchored in the scholarship of at least one team member; second, the project must draw upon skills from all members of the team.[4] Our hope is that students will expand their sense of what a person can bring to a project. Therefore, whereas a student developing their own project can rely on personal knowledge and skill to write a single-authored essay, these groups are intentionally messy. Negotiating with student colleagues from drastically different disciplines simulates the give and take that serious cross--disciplinary team work requires and surfaces skills and abilities that students and their advisers often ignore or take for granted.

Each group of three to four students develops a one-page proposal for a project that must meet one of the needs the partner identifies. For example, one partner, a youth literacy organization, made clear that they had absolutely no need for more programming ideas. Rather, they struggled with the perpetual need to fundraise. They were also stymied by a growing need for Spanish-speaking materials and sought ways to better prepare their mainly white undergraduate student volunteers to work with diverse young students. These are typical parameters for the collaborative assignment. During the community partner's second visit, each group pitches a proposal and the community partners respond. Students receive honest feedback on what is compelling about their ideas and what misses the mark, prompting lively conversations between the partners and the students.

No one assumes, in this case, that the students are committed to doing those projects. Rather, to use design-thinking language, this is an ideation exercise. The mutual benefit is that students learn to listen carefully to possible partners, to develop ideas that draw on a range of their talents, to pitch an idea, and to absorb helpful criticism. The community partners walk away with a list of possible projects and a useful sense of how well they are communicating the mission, work, needs, assets, and constraints of their organizations. That said, occasionally an organization and a group find common ground. To our delight, these conversations have recruited volunteers, inspired teaching assistants to take their undergraduate classes for site visits, and even provided graduate students with short-term paid employment. In a few cases, our Office of Engagement has even provided funding to support a proposed project a community partner found especially compelling.

From the perspective of the institute more generally, this collaborative exercise fulfills two further goals: we want students to value all kinds of knowledge and to see how necessary different forms of expertise are to a successful collaboration. Graduate students tend to think that the only treasure they can barter is the content of their disciplinary knowledge. This is one of the most significant obstacles students (and faculty members) face when they try to reshape graduate studies to prepare students for careers outside academe. The central research question of a dissertation on Victorian novels probably won't help a community partner working on water quality or even on literacy. However, a group might realize that one team member's ability to record and edit audio is as pertinent to a project as another person's critical race scholarship. Through this collaborative proposal process students realize they have so, so much more to offer than content alone.

Supporting and Advising Students

The week of the institute is intense. Over the years, we have tweaked the schedule to give students greater opportunities to learn against the grain of their usual graduate studies. We have cut back on scholarly articles and added film, podcasts, and newspaper articles. We host social gatherings where students meet representatives from a number of community organizations in a congenial off-campus space. We have built in embodied, multisensory approaches to learning along with collaborative projects. Most recently, we've tried to de-escalate students' anxiety about their final projects by stressing that a project can be a thought experiment that looks ahead to a future time when students have graduated and are feeling more settled.

One concern that regularly surfaces among the students each year is about "what counts" during evaluation. As Miriam Bartha and Bruce Burgett observe in discussing the University of Washington's Certificate in Public Scholarship, which evolved from their initial institute, debates over definitions and practices of public scholarship can trap students in anxieties about how to assess outcomes meaningfully. We aim for transparency by asking faculty panelists to explain how their publicly engaged work has been regarded by their departments during tenure and promotion, how they cite their public scholarship on a CV, and how their work has evolved as they gained greater professional stature. We work against the fear that one can only do publicly engaged work after gaining tenure by reminding students, as Bartha and Burgett put it, to "ground their provisional definitions of public scholarship in their existing and emerging practices" (35).[5] In this way, public scholarship can be seen through a wider lens of possibility. An individual assignment in a class or an aspect of a dissertation can have a public component. "Go big or go home" is the antithesis of what we try to encourage in the students' attitudes about public scholarship. We'd much rather see students learn through projects sized to allow the failure and recovery that can lead to real learning.

Additionally, students can be paralyzed by the imperative to do no harm. If they enter a community to which they do not belong, how can they avoid creating unforeseen problems? This is a justifiable concern we address through extended conversations about the ethics of publicly engaged work and collaboration. We don't want students to talk themselves out of trying engaged practice—which clearly speaks to them—out of fear. Instead, we counterbalance their anxiety by encouraging them to learn about a community before proposing a partnership. Simply volunteering is an excellent first step toward gaining a better understanding of an organization or a social issue. Students can also join long-term projects that our faculty members already have in place or work together in pairs or trios on a small pilot project. Developing experience before plunging in is especially important for students who want to work in highly structured and complicated environments, like prisons or public schools, and for students who want to work with vulnerable communities, like immigrant groups. In addition, we offer guidance to alumni of the program who undertake projects after the institute, providing project critiques, helping them to find partners, and assisting with budgets and communication plans.

Responding to Changing Student Aspirations

Over time, we have seen fascinating changes in the kinds of students who apply to the institute. Initially, we had to search for participants who had prior experience as publicly engaged graduate students. Now, we often encounter applicants who are in the midst of impressive public projects. Originally, nearly every student in the institute wanted to be a professor. Now, many students come to us knowing they'll seek careers in the public sector. The institute continues to hold special appeal for women, LGBTQ students, older students, and people of color, who feel caught between their scholarly passions and their desire to work in, with, and on behalf of the communities with which they identify. These students especially benefit from meeting each other and forming connections across disciplines ("Taking It to the Streets"). Their varied perspectives and subject positions have helped us understand the ways higher education can fail students of color, first-generation graduate students, trans students, and students with disabilities. Their participation in and consistent appreciation for the institute give us hope that engaged, project-based practice can create an inclusive learning environment that might help graduate programs appeal to and retain students from a variety of backgrounds with myriad needs and expectations for graduate school. Both our partners and the projects students bring to the institute teach each cohort ways to address implicit biases, to approach collaborations with humility, and to gain insight into a community's dynamics without exploiting the members of that community. Graduate students thus come to their own recognition that whatever their disciplines, they can grow as teachers, scholars, and potential collaborators by learning skills and practices like thoughtful networking, active listening, greater self-awareness, and self-correction.

While some students discover in the institute that they will be happier working in communities than on campuses, most tell us they have gained skills that will serve them well both in publicly engaged work and in their graduate studies. Reaching outside their departments, students learn to connect with public audiences. They translate their research interests into accessible language through elevator pitches, memoranda of understanding (MOUs) with partners, and grant applications that knit together academic and public purposes. Then, seeking to validate the knowledge developed with public partners, the students discover they will need to review, revise, evaluate, and document their public scholarship just as rigorously as their more conventional academic work (see especially Doerneck et al.). In other words, we designed the program to prepare successful academics to work in public, only to realize that the institute has the added benefit of strengthening students' confidence and performance as scholars.

We have learned that if we are serious about supporting graduate students who want to be public scholars or who seek to adapt their advanced graduate work to careers outside the professoriate, then those students must have inspiring, supportive mentors. This means we also need to train faculty members to be publicly engaged artists, scholars, and researchers who can be informed, receptive advisers, role models, and dissertation directors. A decade ago we partnered with the university's Center for Teaching to host what was essentially a graduate institute for faculty members. That institute produced a cohort of faculty members who share a commitment to the principles of public engagement and understand the benefits and challenges of publicly engaged teaching and research. The faculty participants designed service-learning courses for undergraduates and continue to support each other. Many have since been codirectors of the graduate institute. In January 2020, we held a second institute for faculty and staff members involved in graduate education. We encouraged the participants to create courses, single assignments, or projects in which graduate students could enrich their studies by working with partners who would benefit from the students' expertise. The participants included not only tenured and tenure-track faculty members but also academic professionals from campus museums, a law clinic, and the library. Staff members from the Center for Teaching, the Office of Engagement, and the Office of Diversity Resources and Strategic Initiatives led sessions that built expertise and forged stronger connections among engaged graduate instructors and support units across campus. We look forward to seeing what new and exciting graduate courses this second institute will catalyze.

Changes on the Horizon

At this juncture, we are contemplating what the long-term and sustainable future of the Obermann Graduate Institute might be. A number of changes at the University of Iowa and in higher education suggest that we're now in a good position to take a more tiered approach to preparing graduate students interested in publicly engaged practice. First and foremost, we want to ensure that graduate students with little experience in working with their communities are supported. We are delighted that our campus Office for Community Engagement will take the baton of the institute. The institute will become a three-day orientation, completion of which will provide a student entrée into a growing array of workshops about specific aspects of public engagement work and funding opportunities.

This development will allow us to focus on a new project that was inspired by the institute and that would serve students who see engagement as part of a larger commitment to social justice. Spurred by a generous grant from the Andrew W. Mellon Foundation, we are working with departments and our digital librarians and museum curators on a new cohort-based, cross-disciplinary, experiential Humanities for the Public Good PhD. This new program will explore the ways humanities methods and mindsets can enrich a range of workplaces. The curriculum will ask students to collaborate with community partners in numerous ways. For example, several groups of faculty members, staff members, and graduate students are designing humanities labs courses in which they will work with community partners to weave the materials and methods of the humanities into cocreated community-based projects. In our future PhD program, graduate students will take courses like the Humanities for the Public Good labs along with their classes in humanities departments to learn professional skills that we hope will help them address challenging social issues.

We also see radical interdisciplinarity as a path to publicly engaged graduate education. While we have been leading the graduate institute, colleagues in the College of Engineering have launched master's and doctoral degrees that ask students to work with local communities to improve water quality. Faculty members in theater and the visual arts are planning a certificate in social practice art. Leaders of all these initiatives see fascinating commonalities in the theories and practices required for team-based, applied research rooted in problem-oriented, project-based graduate education, whatever the discipline. We're now considering the benefits of teaching fundamental theories and practices of public engagement in multidisciplinary courses where students in engineering, English, and printmaking might learn together and from one another. We still have questions. Most immediately, we're asking how we can leverage the insights of cross-disciplinary collaboration on the one hand while respecting both significant differences in the work each discipline values and graduate students' desire to learn skills embedded in rather than abstracted from their disciplinary studies and individual research projects on the other. These tensions between centralization and anatomization all too often obstruct publicly engaged graduate education, so working with them will be crucial.

Further, we see great potential for connecting the graduate institute with a summer graduate internship program we've developed as part of the Mellon grant. This program embeds ten graduate students in a community organization for two months. During that time, the ten interns meet regularly as a cohort to reflect on their work experience and how it illuminates their graduate studies—and vice versa.[6] Eventually, we hope to fund yearlong graduate internships where students can take the introductory skills they learn in the newly designed graduate institute or in a Humanities for the Public Good course into workplaces where they fully participate as humanities scholars of practice.[7]

The good news is that in all these approaches to teaching publicly engaged practice at the graduate level, universities have extraordinary opportunities to collaborate with nonprofits, public policy organizations, government, and the business sector. To move forward, we need leaders who promote and reward publicly engaged forms of collaboration and knowledge creation. Doing so would benefit not only graduate students but the knowledge enterprise and the communities in which we live and work. Perhaps that change will come from the ground up—that is, from engaged students and faculty members. We would love to see more faculty members work across their disciplinary differences to imagine the many ways graduate students could benefit from doing some of their graduate work out in public. If more faculty members and administrators advocate for engaged graduate education, we see great hope for transforming graduate education in the humanities and other disciplines into preparation for innumerable career paths rather than one increasingly narrow track.

To that end, we are trying yet another experiment in the near future with support from a different Mellon grant. Antoinette Burton, professor at the University of Illinois, Urbana, and leader of the Humanities without Walls consortium, to which the Obermann Center belongs, is advising the center on a new kind of faculty institute that will be codesigned with leaders from business and the nonprofit sector. Our goal for that institute will be to inspire faculty members to develop courses and internships in the humanities in collaboration with partners both in and beyond Iowa City.

Over the last fifteen years, the institute has had a major impact both on students in the program and on the faculty and staff members who have served as directors, panelists, and mentors to the students. For many participants, connecting with other students who share their interest in working with and for their communities—including in public sector and public service careers—gives them courage to share their wide-ranging career ambitions with their advisers and colleagues. Seeing students' passion for engaged work encourages faculty members to have more frank and open-ended conversations with their students about their career paths. Many of our alumni tell us that the institute remains one of the most rewarding experiences of their graduate careers. It provides them with relationships, tools, and—perhaps most valuable of all—permission to come to their work as whole people, joining academic passions with their desire to work in collaboration with communities beyond the academy. Some of our alumni have found careers outside the academy, applying community engagement principles to their work in libraries and museums. Kelly Grogg is a digital librarian at PBS; Peter Likarish is a software engineer at Google and board member of the Hoboken Shelter, in New Jersey; and Sylvea Hollis held a two-year postdoctoral fellowship for the National Park Service and is now circling back to higher education. She has just accepted a tenure-track position at Montgomery College, Maryland's premier community college, where she will serve both as a public historian and as an educator. In this role, she will join many of our alumni in seeding change through direct engagement and substantive collaboration with public organizations and local communities.

Other students have gone on to academic positions around the country, starting their own programs as a way to pursue their commitment to publicly engaged scholarship. Kirsten Beyer is the associate director of a doctoral program in public and community health at the Medical College of Wisconsin, Kira Pasquesi is program director of the leadership studies minor at the University of Colorado, stef shuster is an assistant professor of sociology and a mentor in one of the residential colleges at Michigan State University, and Jennifer Proctor is associate professor of journalism and screen studies at the University of Michigan-Dearborn. Bridget Draxler, who received her PhD in English, now directs the Writing Center at St. Olaf College. Her comments echo the sentiments we hear from many Institute alumni: "Being part of the Obermann Graduate Institute reenergized my excitement about the future of higher education and the humanities. It gave me a new sense of meaning and purpose in my own work as a scholar and a teacher. I don't know that I would have persisted in graduate school without the motivation and mentors I found in this experience." The institute shaped Bridget's dissertation topic; it also enhanced her scholarly work, as seen by the coedited volume she later published, *Engaging the Age of Jane Austen: Public Humanities in Practice*, about publicly engaged classes in literature departments. Perhaps most important, as several of these examples demonstrate, the institute set many of these and other students on the path to hybrid careers that combine teaching and research with administration or community engagement work. These students had decided early in their programs that they were not interested in careers at research-intensive universities. The institute gave them hope and confidence that they could find careers that spoke both to their pleasure in literature, history, the arts, sociology, and so forth, and to their hunger for collaborative, community-based work, often with an emphasis on social justice.

The students who are attracted to the institute often recognize that they will need every possible skill and award to crack the academic career nut. But that's not why most apply. These are people who are unable to ignore a world in turmoil, a precarious environmental and economic future, and human suffering. They are the people we want educating our children and leading our communities. They humble us and inspire us, and they have reminded us every January that graduate education should offer more opportunities, open more minds and doors, and listen much, much more carefully to who our graduate students are and what they want to do with their art, scholarship, research, and teaching.

NOTES

1. IA's philosophy and its impact on universities is now documented by a number of publications. See Jay for an excellent overview of how IA's theories can be put into practice; see also Ellison.

2. IA provides examples on their blog (imaginingamerica.org/category/blog/). The Obermann Institute maintains a blog featuring our alumni and their public-facing work at graduateinstitute.wordpress.com.

3. There is a substantial literature on publicly engaged research and teaching, although less is available on graduate education, especially for the humanities. The fall 2017 special issue of the *Michigan Journal of Community Service Learning* is therefore especially useful (see Doerneck et al.). For the continuum we use the IAP2 Spectrum of Public Participation and the Community Engagement Assessment Tool from Nexus Community Engagement Institute.

4. This assignment is based partly on a similar assignment from the Rackham Graduate School program at the University of Michigan (UM). UM's opportunities for graduate students have evolved over the years and continue to inspire us; see "Rackham Program."

5. Bartha and Burgett provide a strong rationale for this form of graduate education and offer a useful list of "lessons learned."

6. The website *Humanities for the Public Good* (uihumanitiesforthepublicgood.com) lists intern projects organized by year; the program is also featured in Cassuto.

7. We are also inspired by the American Studies PhD at Indiana University–Purdue University, Indianapolis, which is built around internships and led by Raymond Haberski, a history professor.

WORKS CITED

Bartha, Miriam, and Bruce Burgett. "Why Public Scholarship Matters for Graduate Education." *Pedagogy*, vol. 15, no. 1, Jan. 2015, pp. 31–43.

Cassuto, Leonard. "Doctoral Training Should Include an Internship." *The Chronicle of Higher Education*, 27 Aug. 2020, chronicle.com/article/doctoral-training-should-include-an-internship.

Community Engagement Assessment Tool. Nexus Community Engagement Institute, 2018, www.nexuscp.org/wp-content/uploads/2017/05/05-CE-Assessment-Tool.pdf.

Doerneck, Diane M., et al. "Community Engagement Competencies for Graduate and Professional Students: Michigan State University's Approach to Professional Development." *Michigan Journal of Community Service Learning*, vol. 24, no. 1, 2017, pp. 122–42.

Draxler, Bridget, and Danielle Spratt, editors. *Engaging the Age of Jane Austen: Public Humanities in Practice*. U of Iowa P, 2019.

Ellison, Julie. "The New Public Humanists." *PMLA*, vol. 128, no. 2, 2013, pp. 289–98.

Fitzpatrick, Kathleen. *Generous Thinking: A Radical Approach to Saving the University*. Johns Hopkins UP, 2018.

Gale, Sylvia. "Arcs, Checklists, and Charts: The Trajectory of a Public Scholar?" *Collaborative Futures: Critical Reflections on Publicly Active Graduate Education*, edited by Amanda Gilvin et al., Syracuse UP, 2012, pp. 315–27.

"Humanities for All." National Humanities Alliance, 2022, humanitiesforall.org.

IAP2 Spectrum of Public Participation. International Association for Public Participation, cdn.ymaws.com/www.iap2.org/resource/resmgr/pillars/Spectrum_8.5x11_Print.pdf.

Jay, Gregory. "The Engaged Humanities: Principles and Practices for Public Scholarship and Teaching," *Journal of Community Engagement and Scholarship*, vol. 3, no. 1. 2010, pp. 51–63.

Krebs, Paula M., editor. *Public Humanities*, special issue of *Profession*, spring 2019, profession.mla.org/issue/public-humanities/.

Lemann, Nicholas. "Can a University Save the World?" *The Chronicle of Higher Education*, 21 Nov. 2019, chronicle.com/article/can-a-university-save-the-world/.

"Rackham Program in Public Scholarship." U of Michigan, 2022, rackham.umich.edu/professional-development/program-in-public-scholarship.

"Taking It to the Streets: Ten Years of the Obermann Institute." *YouTube*, uploaded by ObermannCenter, 5 June 2018, youtube.com/watch?v=nNlGw-cStIU&t=5s.

Generative Collaboration and the Digital Humanities
Will Fenton

I wrote a stubbornly traditional dissertation. I conducted research at archives and special collections as a research fellow, assembled a dissertation committee of early American literary scholars, and presented work at various stages at the customary platforms of an early Americanist—the Society of Early Americanists, C19: The Society of Nineteenth-Century Americanists, and the McNeil Center for Early American Studies. At the time, I saw my work in the digital humanities as a complement to my "real" academic work.[1] Five years later, as that "real" academic work gathers dust under a ProQuest embargo, my digital scholarship and its afterlives sustain me intellectually, interpersonally, and professionally.

One way or another, PhDs must reimagine their dissertations for other publics, or, at the very least, for an audience beyond their committees. Often, it's an article or two and, eventually, a revised scholarly monograph. For me, that reimagining began alongside my dissertation and has continued through a graphic novel, a public art exhibition, and a series of public programs supported by a major grant from the Pew Center for Arts and Heritage. In this essay I discuss my work on *Digital Paxton* and its recent adaptation through *Ghost River: The Fall and Rise of the Conestoga* and consider how PhD students who choose to write traditional dissertations can use digital projects to reimagine their research with new partners for new audiences.

The Paxton Massacres and Pamphlet War

Imagine colonial Pennsylvania. After almost a decade of grisly war that exposed profound tensions between European empires, colonists, and Native peoples across North America, the Treaty of Paris, signed in February 1763, ended the Seven Years' War and brought a precarious peace to the colony. But across the trans-Appalachian West, the cease-fire collapsed almost as soon as it began. That spring, a group of disparate Native peoples united behind the Ottawa warrior Pontiac and staged a series of attacks on colonial forts in defiance of British military expansions across the Great Lakes. Those battles came to the Pennsylvania borderlands with the sieges of Fort Pitt and Fort Bedford later that summer.

A hundred miles west of those attacks, a group of former militiamen from the Paxtang township, just outside what today is Harrisburg, the capital of Pennsylvania, plotted their revenge. Their target was Conestoga Indiantown, a small group of unarmed Native peoples to their east.

There was no rational reason for the Paxtang militiamen's ire at this community. The Conestoga remained neutral throughout the Seven Years' War, and most of the twenty inhabitants at Conestoga Indiantown were "praying Indians"; they had Christian names, wore Christian dress, and spoke English. The parents traded woven baskets. The children played with the children of settlers (see Barber). The Conestoga and their neighbors shared a plot of land that had been set aside for them by their "brother Onas," William Penn, at the founding of the colony of Pennsylvania.

All that changed in December 1763. In two massacres—the first at Conestoga Indiantown and the second two weeks later at Lancaster—a mob of fifty so-called Paxton Boys eradicated the Conestoga people from the colony of Pennsylvania. Their attacks were intended for public consumption: the Paxton vigilantes burned Conestoga Indiantown to the ground and desecrated the bodies of victims in daylight. The Pennsylvania government responded with alarm, fearing renewed violence across the colony. Unable to shuttle 140 neighboring Moravian Indians (Lenape converted by Moravian missionaries) to New York, Governor Penn reluctantly took the group into Philadelphia.

A month later, a mob of several hundred Paxton Boys marched on Philadelphia to protest the refugees' protection by the Penn government. The marchers were stopped six miles north of Philadelphia by a militia and delegation led by Benjamin Franklin. They ultimately disbanded without violence. None of the leaders would face punishment for the murders they had committed in Conestoga and Lancaster. But before they left, they published their grievances in a pair of pamphlets that would reshape Pennsylvania settlement policy—away from treaty-making and accommodation and toward a more bellicose policy of Indigenous dispossession. The Paxton pamphlets, "Declaration" and "Remonstrance," sparked a new war, one that would be waged in print in the public sphere (see Smith and Gibson).

In many ways, the 1764 Paxton pamphlet war, Pennsylvania's first major pamphlet war, was not so different from today's social media squabbles. Cheap and quick to produce and disseminate, pamphlets were used to anonymously and pseudonymously assail political opponents, wage unfounded ad hominem attacks, and circulate misinformation. They were written as dialogues and epitaphs, poems and songs, satires and farces, embellished with evocations of "White Christian Savages," troops of "Dutch Butchers," and Quakers "thirsting for the Blood" of opponents (Franklin; Dawkins; Dove). Literary scholars such as Edward White, James Myers, and Scott Gordon ("Paxton Boys") have demonstrated how the diverse forms and idiosyncratic rhetorical techniques of these pamphlets present a largely untapped bounty for literary scholars. Such generic and literary features have sparked and kindled my interest, and I suspect they will continue to captivate scholars and readers for a long time to come.

For decades, John Raine Dunbar's print edition *The Paxton Papers* has delimited the corpus of Paxton pamphlets. Tallying some four hundred pages, *Paxton Papers* is a significant—and substantive—scholarly edition. But it is by no means complete or reflective of the materials that scholars have excavated over the past sixty years. As I dug deeper into the Paxton materials at the Library Company of Philadelphia and the Historical Society of Pennsylvania, I saw how much of the incident wasn't accessible in the de facto print edition and could not be evaluated within the narrow frame of the pamphlet war. Notably, the 1764 pamphlet war included a lot more than pamphlets, and a great deal of the public debate was not mediated through print. Alongside a wealth of printed materials, such as newsprint, books, broadsides, and political cartoons, I encountered dozens of diaries, letters, and treaty minutes that not only placed the massacre in a longer debate about colonial settlement, democratic representation, and racial identification but also unsettled the authority of colonial printed records.

The *Paxton Papers* is restricted by its form—a print edition. But what if an editor weren't bound by the constraints of the codex? What else might they choose to include in a twenty-first-century *Paxton Papers*? I developed *Digital Paxton* to engage with these questions. In the process of creating and expanding it, I realized that I had developed a digital project that unsettled the conventions of a scholarly edition and blurred the boundaries between an edition, a collection, and a teaching tool.

The Digital Humanities as Unbounding

Digital Paxton began as a companion to a dissertation chapter on Charles Brockden Brown, whose fiction I read against the backdrop of the 1764 Paxton pamphlet war. My argument was that this little-known incident had outsize importance because it unfolded in Philadelphia, a colonial print powerhouse and the original seat of the United States capitol. The Paxton incident compelled Philadelphians to reevaluate how they related to the Native peoples. The debate they waged in pamphlets, broadsheets, letters, and diaries unfolded in an election year, which ultimately empowered the Paxton vigilantes and their allies. Those allies assembled a white-supremacist coalition that sought an adversarial relationship to Native peoples, greater representation for backcountry settlers, squatter's rights in contested territories, and a goal of displacement, pushing Native peoples out from the Pennsylvania borderlands to resettle in the West. In short, I saw the Paxton incident as a harbinger of manifest destiny, and I wanted other readers—especially those without the privilege of university library subscriptions—to have access to the rich materials that I was using in my research.

I thought a lot about how those materials ought to be presented. After all, I wasn't only looking to digitize pamphlets; I wanted to add other types of materials as they became available. Those materials might be colonial (e.g., letters between colonial authorities), Native (letters and artworks from Native peoples to colonial authorities), or hybrid (treaty minutes and letters transcribed by Native trading partners). It was important to me that the structure of the digital platform not inadvertently elevate a colonial record over a Native or hybrid one. I wanted a platform that reinforced the philosophical goals articulated by the editors of the *Yale Indian Papers Project*: that a digital collection could serve as a common pot, as a "shared history, a kind of communal liminal space, neither solely Euro-American nor completely Native" (Grant-Costa et al. 2). I chose the online publishing platform *Scalar* because its flat ontology enables all digital assets to occupy the same hierarchy.

That terminology may sound technical, but it's incredibly important to the practical and ethical design of *Digital Paxton*. In practical terms, the flat ontology means that a reader encounters Governor Penn's letters in the same pathway as letters between Quaker leaders and Native partners, accounts of diplomatic conferences, and the writings of Delaware leaders. That flat ontology can also be used to interweave text and context. Consider how a transcription might accompany a particularly vexing piece of eighteenth-century handwriting. By defining that transcription as an "annotation," I could make it available as an overlay that appears when a reader cursors over a scanned page. As a literature scholar, this is crucially important to me: I want readers to think critically about the relation of content to a document's form and materiality, and this feature enables scanned pages and transcriptions to occupy the same space. Similarly, *Scalar*'s design supports dynamic relationships between fixed items. That is, a contextual essay and scanned page can play different roles at different times: the contextual essay might be "tagged" with the scanned page; elsewhere, it might serve as a "tag" to that digital asset.

My attention to platform design speaks to the how behind *Digital Paxton*, but it doesn't get at the most important component of a public project: the who. When I say "who," I address the individuals and institutions who helped create the project and those who use it. In many instances, they're one and the same. For example, many of the transcriptions that are available on the site were contributed by students who used the project in a high school or university course. Teachers have contributed lesson plans, students have helped me identify helpful contextual essays and materials, and colleagues inside and outside the academy have helped me provide those sources. For example, a local historian in Lancaster contributed a thoughtful essay on the history of Conestoga Indiantown, and a scholar from whom I originally solicited a keyword essay on the weaponization of the term *elites* in the 1764 Paxton pamphlet war later introduced me to a host of extraordinary missionary diaries at the Moravian Archives, which are now available on the site (see Martin; Gordon, "Elites"; Moravian Indian Diaries).

These bidirectional and iterative exchanges reflect the kind of "generative collaboration" to which I allude in the title of this essay. Collaboration comes in many forms and at many stages of a project's life cycle. Certainly, I've collaborated on articles that look a lot like single authorship except that they benefit from division of labor. In other instances, I've collaborated at the beginning (e.g., comparing notes during research) or end (e.g., signal boosting) of a research project. In the case of *Digital Paxton*, collaboration is necessarily woven into the fabric of the project. There's simply no way to create a digital collection that contains three thousand pages of material from more than two dozen different libraries, archives, and cultural institutions without the support of countless archivists, curators, and technicians. If I were the only author on the site, visitors would be deprived of ten historical overviews and conceptual keyword essays written by some of the brightest historians and literature scholars working in early American studies. And every one of the fifteen lesson plans on the site was offered out of the generosity of middle school, high school, and university educators. The project is bigger, messier, and more inclusive because of its collaborative design, and I wouldn't have it any other way.

The Graphic Novel as Reinterpretation

Digital Paxton is richer than what I set out to create when I wrote my dissertation because it expanded to accommodate new materials, voices, and perspectives. However, thoughtful design and generous context can only do so much to address archival silence. The tension I have continually struggled with is how to tell a story about a pair of colonial massacres, mediated through colonial documents, that doesn't simply reproduce colonial biases, assumptions, and erasures. *Digital Paxton* has nearly reached its limits as a digital collection, scholarly edition, and teaching platform. But what if we could imagine a perspective on the Paxton massacres that, given the loss of the Conestoga tribe, cannot be retrieved?[2] That is, what if, instead of telling a story about the Paxton vigilantes, we sought to tell a story about the Conestoga, their fortitude, and their formative role in the history of colonial Pennsylvania?

To critically and creatively engage with those questions, I wanted to create a graphic novel. Complemented by a national teachers' seminar, a public art exhibition, and a series of public programs, *Ghost River: The Fall and Rise of the Conestoga* (Francis) revisits and reimagines the primary and secondary source materials available in *Digital Paxton*. The impetus for the project is a deceptively simple one: What would happen if we moved out from under the shadow of the Paxton vigilantes and told the story of the Conestoga and their kin? Certainly, who does the telling is vitally important. Cognizant of my own biases and blind spots (and, frankly, weary of hearing my own voice), I stepped into the role of creative director and, later, editor, empowering my Native creative partners to lead the inquiry. To support them, I assembled an advisory board of specialists from the Gilder Lehrman Institute of American History, the Free Library of Philadelphia, and the University of Pennsylvania as well as leaders from the Delaware Tribe and local Native communities at the Circle Legacy Center.

The outcome was a graphic novel that was Native from concept to development to production. More pointedly, *Ghost River* was written, illustrated, published, and printed by Native American artists. Lee Francis IV, a member of the Laguna Pueblo, wrote the script; Weshoyot Alvitre, of the Tongva people, illustrated it; and the book was published by Red Planet Books and Comics and printed by Tribal Print Source. Francis, in particular, has been instrumental in incubating the field of Native American comics and graphic art: he's the author of numerous graphic novels; a trained scholar and educator who regularly teaches at the University of New Mexico; the owner of Red Planet Books and Comics, the only Native comic book store in the country; the founder of the now international Indigenous Comic Con; and the CEO of the publishing company Native Realities Press. In the context of Native pop art, Alvitre is one of the most prolific and respected artists. In addition to contributing to the Eisner Award–winning comics collections *Moonshot* and *Little Nemo: Dream Another Dream*, she has experience translating historical events into educational graphic art, including partnerships with the Smithsonian National Museum of the American Indian on a new national educational initiative, Native Knowledge 360°, and with Elizabeth LaPensée, assistant professor at Michigan State University, on an educational game, *When Rivers Were Trails*. I was drawn to Alvitre and Francis as partners not only because they are comfortable working with scholars to reinterpret historical materials but also because they have a professional history that enables them to easily traverse the creative processes of writing and illustration.

From the outset, we agreed that the graphic novel shouldn't simply eulogize the Conestoga people. Certainly, the Paxton attacks were massacres, but despite their transformative effects on Pennsylvania settlement policy, the erasure of Conestoga Indiantown is not the whole story. Nor was it the genocide of the Conestoga, though scholars have traditionally treated it as such. Set aside by William Penn at the founding of Pennsylvania, Conestoga Indiantown had long served as a hub of trade and commerce in the mid-Atlantic region, and its residents were necessarily a hybrid community of Lenape, Delaware, and Susquehannock peoples. The Paxton vigilantes may have succeeded in murdering the last of the Conestoga at Indiantown, but the victims' kin have endured. To that point, before Francis began writing the script, our entire creative team, including Alvitre, Francis, and our advisory board, traveled to Lancaster and broke bread with local Native peoples, who represented Susquehannock, Seneca, and Lenape ancestry. The message we heard again and again was, "We're still here." To acknowledge that truth is to reject the passivity of the eulogy and to reckon with one's own agency and obligation to right historical wrongs.

The title *Ghost River* pays homage to the river upon which Susquehannock peoples lived and took their name. We crossed the Susquehanna many times during our site visits to the Hans Herr house, the historical site of Conestoga Indiantown, and the collections at Lancaster History—the same river that the Conestoga would have fished and bathed in centuries ago. The Susquehanna endures where Conestoga Indiantown does not, and, as a recurring metaphor in the text, the river provides a sort of visual correlative to the journey the reader takes with the graphic novel, forward and backward in time, from the raising of the first longhouses in the early 1500s to our research trip in 2018, from Penn's treaty-making in the 1670s to the Paxton violence of 1763. The subtitle *The Fall and Rise of the Conestoga* gestures toward these tensions. Yes, this is a story of violence and betrayal, but it is also one of resilience and renewal.

Ghost River recenters this narrative on the Indigenous peoples who endured the mob violence. The Paxton vigilantes who have dominated scholarly debates are not only absent from the title but are also anonymized—both unnamed and silhouetted. When violence does unfold, we have made deliberate choices about what it looks like. For example, in the final massacre, which unfolds at the Lancaster workhouse, Francis took the liberty of depicting the Conestoga rising to face their murderers.[3] Alvitre abstracted scenes of violence in order to prevent Indian bloodshed from becoming a kind of spectacle. For example, she shows the murders at the Conestoga Indiantown as if they were rendered in a wampum, the traditional shell beads used to commemorate treaties (22–23).

While colonial figures such as Benjamin Franklin are referenced in the text, the narrative of *Ghost River* is driven by the Conestoga and Lenape peoples, whose Indian names we have recovered from contemporaneous sources (see Proud; Heckewelder; *Minutes*). Even the most famous of the Conestoga people, Will Sock, is identified by his given name, Tenseedaagua. Francis also embeds a scene from the 250th anniversary conference, the reading of the names of the murdered Conestoga (14–16). For her part, Alvitre, inspired by the Library Company's political cartoon collection, has chosen to reproduce the styles and color palettes of eighteenth-century engravings. She opted to work on Bristol board—as opposed to a digital canvas—and to use a nineteenth-century gold nib to create her detailed linework. Her earth-tone color palette draws from our field trips into Pennsylvania and her research into the pigments that would have been available to eighteenth-century colorists (see Carlson and Krill).

The other key reinterpretative act happens outside the graphic narrative through accompanying educational and contextual materials. Alongside my introduction to the text and artist statements from Francis and Alvitre, the volume includes contextual essays that attend to visual materials like political cartoons and engravings (Ridner); manuscript records, such as letters and diaries (Gordon, "Print"); and graphic novels as mediums for Native representation in popular culture (Sheyahshe). The back matter supports use in secondary education, providing middle school and high school teachers with everything they need to integrate the text into their classes. This begins with a multipart unit developed by educational specialists at the Gilder Lehrman Institute of American History, keyed to Common Core standards. The volume also includes reproductions of archival materials that are either implicitly or explicitly cited in the text (with an invitation to readers to explore the larger corpus of materials at *Digital Paxton*) as well as the complete script of *Ghost River*, annotated with our editorial exchanges. The annotated script is particularly important to me because it documents the development of the edition, including our decision-making process, our consultants' contributions, and the primary and secondary source materials that informed the narrative. In total, these educational and contextual materials constitute fully one-half of *Ghost River*.

We have distributed the volume as widely as possible, both in print and through various efforts toward public outreach. The Library Company of Philadelphia donated more than one hundred copies to the Free Library of Philadelphia, which now circulates *Ghost River* through all its neighborhood branches, and Red Planet Books and Comics has also distributed the graphic novel to the tribal libraries of all 573 federally recognized tribes. But availability isn't the same as discoverability. To increase awareness in Native communities, I conducted both local and national outreach efforts to coincide with publication. At a regional level, I presented the project at events in and around Philadelphia and Lancaster. At a national level, I have presented the volume at the American Library Association, the Digital Library Federation, the National Council for Social Studies, the Smithsonian National Museum of the American Indian, and numerous other venues.

To promote the widest possible access, the Library Company has developed an open access digital edition of the volume. Unlike *Digital Paxton*, the digital *Ghost River* (ghostriver.org) explicitly addresses middle and high school students and teachers. While I have continued to supplement *Digital Paxton* with new primary and secondary source materials, the *Ghost River* site is narrowly designed to support and extend the print edition of *Ghost River*. By "extend," I mean that while the digital version includes all the aforementioned back matter, it also includes a video about the project's development process; thirteen additional lessons developed by the teachers who participated in our national teacher seminar ("Native Peoples"); and documentary interviews with our Native partners in Lancaster.

Finally, the Library Company hosted a free public exhibition (November 2019–August 2020) that put Alvitre's artwork into conversation with the institution's collections. Whereas past Library Company exhibitions had been almost entirely devoted to the collection, the *Ghost River* exhibition foregrounded Alvitre's artwork throughout its developmental stages, from her earliest storyboards to her most intricate inked and hand-painted pages. Thanks to the contributions of the designer, Keith Ragone, this truly novel exhibition reimagined not only the library's gallery but also the building's façade. The occasion called for it. Founded by Benjamin Franklin in 1731, Library Company of Philadelphia is, unequivocally, one of the oldest colonial institutions in the nation. Hosting a Native art exhibition that decentered its collections and history in order to center the works of previously excluded or marginalized peoples was a crucial symbolical and political act—one that I hope will serve as a model for other colonial institutions considering "decolonization."

The Public Humanities as Coalition Building

Ghost River is a post hoc reimagining of my dissertation. I cannot imagine pursuing it through the mode of the dissertation, given the structures and expectations associated with the definitive credentialing mechanism of graduate education. Perhaps this is a lack of imagination on my part. However, I have found that reimagining a dissertation project as a public work, even post hoc, is a generative activity—not only for the work itself but for one's own sense of scholarly identity.

As a recent PhD, I know how difficult it is to write a dissertation, teach, publish, attend conferences, cultivate professional networks, and apply for jobs. Given the daunting list of things students are told that they need to succeed, there's little time or incentive to consider public engagement. Nevertheless, both *Digital Paxton* and *Ghost River* have enriched my research, broadened my professional networks, and enabled me to share my work with new audiences.

I understand that grant-writing is often considered an onerous task that distracts from the very kind of work scholars enter the profession to pursue. Certainly, I would much rather write about Charles Brockden

Brown than draft a memorandum of understanding. But let me be candid: without the support of both the Library Company of Philadelphia and the Pew Center for Arts and Heritage, who funded this multiyear project, *Ghost River* would be little more than an idea, and a vague one at that.

To that point, I've found grant-writing incalculably clarifying. Coauthoring the *Ghost River* grant with the Library Company challenged me to think specifically about my audiences, how I propose to reach them, and why I believe my research is urgent. Assigning a budget to a project has a way of illuminating priorities: budgeting for a multiyear grant helped me to determine what my project was about and to whom I wanted it to matter. This required me to think tactically rather than intuitively. I was accustomed to working on a labor of love that served a small but forgiving audience of like-minded early Americanists. The grant application for Pew posed a number of questions I hadn't fully considered with *Digital Paxton*: Who were my core audiences, what actions would I take to address them, and how would I evaluate whether those efforts succeeded? At first, I chafed against this kind of tactical thinking, but the more I did it, the more I realized I had resisted because I didn't have the answers and I wasn't accustomed to asking such questions of my scholarly research. A year into this project, I feel that I have a better sense of why I'm doing what I'm doing than I did at any point in the dissertation-writing process. I suspect that many current and recent PhDs would welcome such clarity.

There's no way I could have translated *Digital Paxton* from a labor of love into a new public project without the support of a network of interdisciplinary experts, including librarians, archivists, and technologists who have helped me digitize, catalog, and add records. Equally important has been the counsel of historians, whose aid I have solicited to revise *Ghost River*, whose scholarship I have edited for the project's critical apparatus, and whose collaboration I am seeking as we develop new teaching resources.

Also importantly, both projects have opened new opportunities for me to share my research—not only on traditional platforms, such as the journals *American Quarterly*, *Commonplace*, and the *Journal of Interactive Technology and Pedagogy*, as well as websites hosted by Omohundro Uncommon Sense, the Organization of American Historians, and the Society of Early Americanists, but also in public venues, including the Smithsonian's *American Indian* magazine; the National Endowment for the Humanities' magazine, *Humanities*; the National Public Radio (NPR) podcast *Code Switch*; *The Philadelphia Inquirer*; and my local NPR affiliate, WHYY.

In the context of anemic public funding, shrinking enrollments, and deep-seated skepticism of humanistic inquiry, I am convinced that pursuing new modes of engagement, such as digital or public art projects, can enable scholars to reimagine both the stakes and forms of work. The reward is the process: collaboration is necessarily coalitional, and with each new effort we enlist support from new stakeholders and engender goodwill with future allies. I hope that *Digital Paxton* and *Ghost River* advance our common cause in some small way.

NOTES

1. Unlike Nick Sousanis's riveting yet rigorous comic book, or Amanda Visconti's truly participatory digital edition, my digital humanities project was less a reconceptualization than an extension of my dissertation.

2. At the heart of the project, and documented in the project charter, is an act of "critical fabulation." I borrow the term from Saidiya Hartman, who presents critical fabulation as a means to creatively imagine what might have happened, "to imagine what cannot be verified . . . to reckon with the precarious lives which are visible only in the moment of their disappearance" (12).

3. There is no detailed historical account of that massacre from which to draw our depictions. I have shared drafts and solicited feedback on this scene from the scholar who has paid the closest attention to the workhouse massacre, Jack Brubaker.

WORKS CITED

Barber, Rhoda. "Journal of Settlement at Wright's Ferry on the Susquehanna River." 1830. Historical Society of Pennsylvania, Philadelphia, PA. Manuscript.

Brubaker, Jack. *Massacre of the Conestogas: On the Trail of the Paxton Boys in Lancaster County*. The History Press, 2010.

Carlson, Janice H., and John Krill. "Pigment Analysis of Early American Watercolors and Fraktur." *Journal of the American Institute of Conservation*, vol. 18, 1978, pp. 19–32.

Dawkins, Henry. *The Paxton Expedition*. 1764. Library Company of Philadelphia. Cartoon.

Dove, David James. *The Quaker Unmask'd; or, Plain Truth*. Andrew Steuart, 1764. Library Company of Philadelphia. Pamphlet.

Dunbar, John Raine, editor. *The Paxton Papers*. Springer, 1957.

Fenton, Will. *Digital Paxton*. 2016–23, digitalpaxton.org.

Francis, Lee, IV. *Ghost River: The Fall and Rise of the Conestoga*. Illustrated by Weshoyot Alvitre, edited by Will Fenton, Red Planet Books and Comics, 2019.

Franklin, Benjamin. *A Narrative of the Late Massacres, in Lancaster County*. Franklin and Hall, 1764. Historical Society of Pennsylvania, Philadelphia, PA.

Gordon, Scott Paul. "Elites." *Digital Paxton*, 2018, digitalpaxton.org/works/digital-paxton/elites.

———. "The Paxton Boys and Edward Shippen: Defiance and Deference on a Collapsing Frontier." *Early American Studies*, vol. 14, no. 2, spring 2016, pp. 319–47.

———. "Print and Place in the Paxton Crisis." *Ghost River*, 2019, ghostriver.org/essays/gordon.

Grant-Costa, Paul, et al. "The Common Pot: Editing Native American Materials." *Scholarly Editing*, vol. 33, 2012, scholarlyediting.org/2012/essays/essay.commonpot.html.

Hartman, Saidiya. "Venus in Two Acts." *Small Axe*, vol. 12, no. 2, 2008.

Heckewelder, John Gottlieb Ernestus. *Narrative of the Mission of the United Brethren*. Philadelphia, 1820.

Martin, Darvin L. "History of Conestoga Indiantown." *Digital Paxton*, 2017, digitalpaxton.org/works/digital-paxton/a-history-of-conestoga-indian town.

Minutes of the Provincial Council of Pennsylvania. J. Severns, 1852. Edited by Pennsylvania Historical and Museum Commission, Library Company of Philadelphia.

Moravian Indian Diaries. "December 1, 1763–April 3, 1765." Moravian Archives, Bethlehem, PA. Manuscript.

Myers, James P. *The Ordeal of Thomas Barton: Anglican Missionary in the Pennsylvania Backcountry, 1755–1780*. Lehigh UP, 2010.

"Native Peoples, Settlers, and European Empires in North America, 1600–1840." Gilder Lehrman Institute of American History. Seminar.

Proud, Robert. *The History of Pennsylvania, in North America*. Zachariah Poulson, 1797. Library Company of Philadelphia.

Ridner, Judith. "Passion, Politics, and Portrayal in the Paxton Debates." *Ghost River*, 2019, ghostriver.org/essays/ridner.

Sheyahshe, Michael. "Indigenous Representation in Comics and Graphic Novels." *Ghost River*, 2019, ghostriver.org/essays/sheyahshe.

Smith, Matthew, and James Gibson. *A Declaration and Remonstrance of the Distressed and Bleeding Frontier Inhabitants of the Province*. William Bradford, 1764. Library Company of Philadelphia. Pamphlet.

Sousanis, Nick. *Unflattening*. Harvard UP, 2015.

Visconti, Amanda. *Infinite Ulysses*. U of Maryland, College Park, 2015, infiniteulysses.com.

White, Edward. *The Backcountry and the City: Colonization and Conflict in Early America*. U of Minnesota P, 2005.

Working Knowledge: Narrative Theory in the Real World

Marcia Halstead James

In a recent essay for the Modern Language Association's *Profession*, Lissette Lopez Szwydky makes a bold proposal. "Humanities departments," she argues, "need a professoriat composed of faculty members with diverse professional experiences who can actively mentor and train students for a range of careers." While a sweeping redefinition of humanities expertise in the academy is likely to generate as much passion as the so-called canon wars, increasing numbers of professionals are already teaching part-time while working full-time outside the academy. Moreover, many humanities departments have begun widening their scope to prepare students for jobs outside academe in response to decreasing enrollments and academic job opportunities; indeed, the many contributions in this volume exemplify this turn. While humanities educators have participated in good faith in the tradition of "reproductive" education (Rogers 23), training to do what their professors have done and training others to continue this work, they now recognize its limits.

Here I consider the intellectual value of humanistic work outside traditional academia. Over the past century, humanities departments have shown their capacity to grow and change by admitting, albeit not without struggle, new texts and new points of view. These are the same challenges that the nonacademic market presents. Having faced and been enriched by such challenges before, humanities departments ought not resist venturing out again. To be sure, even after what this volume calls the career diversity turn, there remains a systemic prejudice within academic culture against work outside the academy (see, e.g., Winter; Tannen). It is this prejudice that I wish to help mitigate.

Below I discuss the use of narrative devices in writing for fundraising,[1] a marriage of my academic study of English literature and my full-time work in the nonprofit sector.[2] After a brief literature review, I describe three occasions on which I successfully used narrative devices—specific, concrete language; narratorial character; and surprise and suspense—to contravene fundraising conventions. Using my own writing to develop and illustrate my argument allows me to discuss intentions, circumstances, and results with greater assurance than I could claim if discussing another writer's work. To provide context, I outline relevant areas of the fundraising field and include some of the beliefs and practices of fundraising experts.

While my subject is the use of narrative in fundraising, its purposes are broader. I hope to do what I wish someone had done for me as a graduate student: give a sense of the connections possible between what I was learning about literature and its use in the world outside the academy. I hope, too, to persuade humanities faculty members that what the poet James Merrill calls "[c]ommodity's black hole" is neither vacant nor ravenous nor alarming. At the very least I hope that faculty members will examine their own points of resistance to my argument, the better to question possible blind spots in their stance. Finally, I hope to suggest to university administrators that a system that encourages faculty members "to train and mentor humanities majors in a way that reframes the conversation around career diversity" can be intellectually rewarding, professionally dignified, and financially profitable (Szwydky). Katina L. Rogers asks humanities educators to "imagine what could happen if doctoral students were invited to apply a similar approach of inquiry, creativity, and exploration to their potential professional lives beyond the university's gates" (2). I hope that this essay will encourage such imagining.

The Current Conversation in Practice and in Scholarship

Much of the work on the use of narrative in nonprofit fundraising has been done by practitioners for practitioners. "How-to" instruction that draws on traditional literary theory, such as the rise and fall of a story arc and the conflicts between archetypal heroes and villains (Lombardi;

Kavanagh), is offered through storytelling workshops for nonprofits, storytelling templates, and even an annual nonprofit storytelling conference. Fundraisers are also approaching narrative from the standpoint of the social sciences, viewing it through an ideological lens as a way to understand or explain events and thus lay the foundation for change. In its December 2018 issue, for example, *Nonprofit Quarterly* ran "a cluster of articles on how narratives are used to form and sustain social structures" (Price). One article discusses "repatriating narratives," another "leveraging philanthropy to decolonize wealth" ("When"; Villanueva).

Scholarly research on fundraising is much rarer than works like those just described. The most pertinent inquiries for my purposes are two studies that take the linguist Douglas Biber's corpus-based approach to textual variation. In the first, Ulla Connor and Thomas Upton used Biber's multidimensional method to analyze a corpus of 316 nonprofit fundraising letters. They conclude that direct mail letters

> are more like academic expository texts than like personal letters; they have a strong informational focus as opposed to the involved, interpersonal features we expected to see; they are mostly expository in structure, only sprinkled with narrative tales; and they tend to be highly polished, closely edited texts, which is counter to the impression they attempt to give as quickly penned, chatty letters. (84)

In fact, direct mail letters were revealed to be more strongly "non-narrative" than academic prose (80).

In the second study, *Writing the Voice of Philanthropy: How to Raise Money with Words*, Frank C. Dickerson repeated Connor and Upton's analysis with what he believed to be an improved corpus, expecting to get results that scored higher in the narrative dimension and other dimensions associated with interpersonal engagement. Instead, his results were similar to those of Connor and Upton. His corpus of online and paper-based fundraising texts from a more inclusive and monetarily successful array of nonprofit organizations was still much closer to academic prose and official documents than to personal letters and fiction when scored on Biber's "narrative versus non-narrative" dimension (229).

An especially interesting component of Dickerson's study was his survey of those who "produce or cause . . . to be produced" the fundraising literature he studied (110). Asked to rate the importance of various features to a direct mail appeal, respondents ranked "using a human-interest (narrative) writing style" at the top and "using an argument-centric (expository) writing style" at the bottom (273). In short, these practitioners expressed certain beliefs about what fundraising letters should be—beliefs common in the fundraising field—but the fundraising letters actually used by their organizations took a very different approach.

The scholarly research discussed above was done by rhetoricians and linguists, and they agree that not all questions about the effects of fundraising literature can be answered within their disciplines. Connor and Upton, for example, conclude that "an important feature of promotional discourse, namely its persuasiveness, is not fully explored by [Biber's] type of analysis" (84). Dickerson asserts that "examining texts for levels of narrative is more an exercise in narratology . . . than linguistics." Citing a discussion in which Biber acknowledged that his software "is unable to detect and judge the effectiveness of narrative texts," Dickerson writes, "Corpus analysis is a vital first step that must be augmented with additional traditions of textual evaluation" (155). Clearly there is ample room in this conversation for other voices, including voices from the field of narrative theory.

Cases, Narratives, and "Narrative Worlds"

Historically, fundraisers have believed in appeals to reason. So entrenched is this belief that the term we use for such efforts is *making the case* for support. Mal Warwick, one of the nonprofit sector's leading voices in direct mail appeals for decades, writes, "[D]onors regard the letters they receive from charities as a source of special knowledge. I believe that this helps explain why long letters containing hard facts . . . often out-pull more emotional appeals" (15). More recent writers, however, emphasize the role of emotion (e.g., Brooks; Ahern). "Emotion . . . prompts action" (Sargeant and Shattuck 347), and it is this igniting spark that fundraisers are striving for when we insert a story into the case for support that we make in a brochure, an e-mail, or a letter.

I would argue, however, that we can incorporate narrative devices into our argument without actually telling a story and still trigger emotions likely to lead to financial support. Narrative theorists maintain that we are storytellers by nature, creating, for example, a narrative to go with the still photograph of a ship run aground (Abbott 6). It is my contention that just as a photograph can prompt storytelling, narrative devices can prompt story-listening. If we believe that we are about to hear a story, in other words, we pay attention, at least at first, and getting a prospective donor's attention is the first step toward getting a gift. The experiences I recount here support this idea and therefore the value of narrative theory to fundraising.

It may take very little to persuade us that a story is on its way. The psychologist Richard J. Gerrig claims that the single word *Texas*, for example, mentally transports the reader to the narrative world of Texas and argues that "no a priori limits can be put on the types of language structures that might prompt the construction [by the reader] of narrative worlds" (4). Marie-Laure Ryan suggests that we think in terms of "a text's degree of narrativity" rather than trying to distinguish narratives from nonnarratives (30), recognizing that even a hint of narrative functions as narrative. I would add that in texts that either exhibit low degrees of narrativity themselves or represent genres in which readers expect to find low degrees of narrativity, such as grant proposals, the hint of narrative and thus the invitation to create or anticipate the creation of a narrative world can be achieved simply through the use of specific and concrete language, as in the following example.

Specific, Concrete Language

Some years ago, the nonprofit organization I worked for received a corporate grant to offer an environmental education program to one of Arizona's tribal communities. After the formal check presentation, the corporate representative asked to meet me, the writer of the grant proposal. "That's the best grant I've ever read," he said, shaking my hand. "It was just like reading a novel." The unexpected comparison of my proposal to a novel was unsettling: in fundraising, a field that relies on its practitioners' credibility, evoking fiction seemed risky. When I got back to the office, I reread the proposal to see what he might have meant.

Asked by the application form to "describe the needs and objectives to be addressed," the proposal begins: "Our environmental education programs address two central objectives: to foster a culture of conservation in today's youth and to diversify the environmental movement." The whole first paragraph is written in the same bland expository language typical of grant proposals. The second paragraph, however, veers noticeably off the prescribed course:

> For many of today's children, the outdoor experiences we adults enjoyed daily growing up, and the knowledge we gained from them, are a rarity. Wherever they live, even in rural areas, children are now more likely to take lessons, join teams, or spend hours in front of a

television or a computer than they are to go into their own backyards and play. Wading in a stream, studying the behavior of an ant or a dove, climbing a tree, jumping from one rock to another—these are simple pleasures that many of our children don't know.

The move from typical grant-writing to novelistic narrative begins with "take lessons, join teams, or spend hours in front of a television or a computer" and continues with "wading in a stream, studying the behavior or an ant or a dove, climbing a tree, jumping from one rock to another." In Ryan's terms, I opted for a narrative mode of writing rather than an argumentative one by choosing "the particular versus the general, the temporal versus the timeless" (27).

I followed up on the narrative promise of the opening by returning occasionally to specific, concrete language, naming objects that could serve as entries into a narrative world. Citing marketing research, for example, I stated that "linking a product to the natural world, be it a shampoo made with herbs or a hotel with an atrium lobby, increases sales because . . . we are drawn instinctively to nature." The shampoo and the atrium lobby came directly from the marketing research; it was my choice to retain them, however, when omitting them would have yielded a sentence more like what is expected from grant proposals. Reading the sentence quoted above with and without those details demonstrates, if only to a small extent, the power to engage the reader that specific, concrete language offers.

There are good reasons for writing grants in general and abstract terms. The belief, now easily and unshakably enforced through the word limits of online grant applications, is that proposals need to be as brief as possible while still addressing the topics of interest to the funder. "An ant or a dove" uses five precious words; "wildlife" uses only one. General terms also encompass more possibilities. It is not only an ant or a dove that children can study in their own backyards, and there are those who believe that if we list some objects of study, we should list all, an impossible task. Finally and perhaps most importantly, abstraction heightens our authority and gives us credibility and influence. Of course we will continue to use abstractions. However, in a field where much of what we say we know is experiential, even anecdotal, rather than research-based, abstractions can be misleading. They can also be unhelpful when our object is to engage the reader's emotions.

In many respects my proposal was conventional, studded with statistics and scientific theories, reliant on generalizations and abstractions. However, its ant and dove; its tree, stream, and rock; even its herbal shampoo and hotel atrium were meant to nudge readers into creating worlds, or at least scenes, in their minds. With the creation of those scenes, I believed, would come an engagement with the proposal and, ideally, an emotional reaction, thereby helping to persuade readers of the value of the project. The granting of our request for support as well as the corporate representative's words to me suggest that this approach worked, and this initial success led to many years of continued support from a source usually difficult to access.

Narratorial Character

If the choice of solicitor is crucial to the result of a face-to-face solicitation, as fundraisers believe, then it is reasonable to suppose that this rule should apply to written solicitations as well. In theory, the response that a fundraising letter or e-mail receives will be different depending on who is thought to have sent it. Experts in direct mail, however, believe that the narrator of the letter should always be a person of authority because "people tend to obey authority figures" (Ahern 82). Following convention, then, we would choose our nonprofit's executive director, president, or CEO to speak on its behalf. In addition to their putative ability to command obedience, these narrators are prestigious figures, people we believe our donors will feel flattered to hear from. In positions of power, furthermore, they are presumed to know everything worth knowing about their organizations; readers will believe that these leaders possess any facts and figures that we wish to present in making our case for support. In most fundraising literature, in fact, the CEO and similar figures seem to possess the infallibility of an omniscient narrator of fiction.

Yet even in fiction, Jonathan Culler asserts, despite "the basic convention . . . that sentences not produced by characters are true" (190), there is no such thing as a truly omniscient narrator. Of the narratorial powers that Culler identifies in fictional narrators, the nonprofit CEO narrating a fundraising appeal often assumes the power of speaking with "the general consciousness of a community, a collective mind" and at other times, in more human form, seems like "a sharp operator who gets around and knows a lot" (200–01). This Dickensian-sounding sharp operator serves as a reminder that even a so-called omniscient narrator has character, character that is revealed by what is said (or not said) and how it is said, by content and form, in other words. Our sense of narratorial character is heightened and complicated in fundraising letters when we feel that we know the actual person over whose signature the letter appears and when we are aware at some level that this person is both created by and performing in language for our benefit. Complications like these rival those found in fiction and respond as readily, I believe, to narrative analysis, even though the purpose of such an analysis, like the letter itself, is ultimately pragmatic.

It is not only the conventional narrator's omniscience that should be called into question. Since Stanley Milgram's experiments on obedience to authority in the 1960s, researchers have been confirming that, as the direct mail experts say, most people obey authority.[3] However, we now question what constitutes authority. The dictum that fundraising appeals should be written by a nonprofit's leader because people obey authority accepts, apparently without question, that authority stems exclusively from the power to make decisions about the organization's direction and its finances. (This in itself is a misconception since decisions of any magnitude are made in consultation with staff members and with oversight and approval from the board.) Authority, however, can stem from personal experience and the knowledge that comes with it, and that type of authority can be more persuasive than a high position on an organizational chart.

One example of a narrator with experiential rather than titular authority was the production stage manager over whose name I wrote a fundraising letter for the theater company then employing me. His position was squarely in middle management, which made him an unconventional choice for a letter that would typically come from someone higher in an organization's structure. My reasoning was that those who would receive the letter had just seen our popular and favorably reviewed production of Becky Mode's *Fully Committed*, a one-actor play about a reservations clerk at a trendy Manhattan restaurant. The phone on stage rings incessantly, and in the hands of our production stage manager, it became a character in its own right, to such an extent, in fact, that it got its own laughs and was praised by reviewers.

I believed that our stage manager, on this occasion, could speak to our target audience in a way that no one else could. Like them, he was offstage; like them, he nevertheless had a role that was essential to the success of the production and to the future of the company. Furthermore, sending a letter from him tapped into the pleasure given by a particular production, a particular experience of theater that the recipients of the letter would remember and relive. Rather than taking the advice of direct mail experts to use a sixth-grade vocabulary, clichés, italics, and bold type (e.g., Brooks 36–40), I wrote in the voice and style of the stage manager. With his permission and a sample of his handwriting, I hand-signed the letters, added postscripts, and wrote his initials above the return address on the envelope. The letter looked personal, and it led to more than double the responses that the organization typically received from such a mailing.

The choice of who tells the story of a nonprofit organization determines what the story will be and thus how the nonprofit will be viewed in its community. In considering thoughtfully who will narrate our fundraising letters and e-mails, and when, and why, we can learn something about our predilections and those of our donors. Including new voices gives fundraisers the opportunity to explore rhetorical persuasiveness rather than reinforce hierarchies of prestige and power.

Suspense and Surprise

When we tell the story of a nonprofit's past, present, or future, we conventionally present the organization in its best light. The reasoning is that people, whether acting as individuals or as decision-makers for funding institutions, will not waste money on "losers." (There are exceptions, of course. A reputable nonprofit that has suddenly fallen on hard times may be rescued, provided it has a strong plan for recovery and long-term stability.) Rather than write about our organizations' needs, therefore, we write about what our organizations can do, if funded, to better meet the needs of our beneficiaries. Widely accepted, time-honored conventions like this make the perfect setting for surprise and, through it, the emotional engagement of the reader.

According to H. Porter Abbott, surprise in narrative is the violation of expectations based on coded narrative formulas. In terms of narrative theory, these formulas are masterplots; for my argument, they are the conventions of nonprofit fundraising. Abbot believes that suspense precedes surprise: "Certainly the key to suspense is the possibility, at least, that things could turn out differently. And surprise, which is such a common feature of successful narrative, is what happens when, to a degree, things do turn out differently" (54–55). In fundraising, however, the conventions are so well established that the surprise of overturning them can, in itself, create suspense.

A grant proposal I wrote for what I will call the XYZ Museum, which showcases the works of artists of color, began with a simple but devastating sentence: "The XYZ is a white man's museum." In admitting this, I was not just failing in the task of portraying the organization as a success, as convention dictates. I was pointing out a serious weakness at best and accusing the museum of racism at worst. In a reversal of the pattern that Abbott discerns, my opening created surprise for the reader followed by suspense. Could the proposal redeem the museum after such a damaging admission?

Owning up to the museum's shortcomings risked alienating the funder, but it was a risk that the museum was willing to take in an effort to remedy the historical inequity that still separated it from those whose heritage was represented by the collections. To my relief, the proposal resulted in the largest grant that the museum had ever received for operating expenses. The proposal had redeemed the museum in the eyes of the funder, it seemed, by acknowledging the need to address ingrained racial bias and asking for help in doing so, and the grant provided a new level of accountability as the museum worked toward racial equity.

While there is still work to be done, the XYZ Museum now has more people of color in administrative positions, increased racial diversity on its board, and a racially diverse standing committee dedicated to the inclusion of the peoples represented by the museum's collections. The proposal described above was funded because the plan was thoughtful and the goal was worthy, not because it had a surprising first line that created suspense. However, I believe that the first line and the emotional response that it elicited did the important work of engaging the reader from the outset, and neuroscience supports this claim.

In his experiments with narrative, the neuro-economist Paul J. Zak measured cortisol, the so-called stress hormone, and adrenocorticotropic hormone (ACTH), which triggers the release of cortisol in response to stressors. According to Zak, both cortisol and ACTH are hormones that focus our attention and "[correlate] with a sense of distress" ("Empathy" and "Why"). Surprise and suspense are clearly stressors. Even when the surprise is a good one or the suspense is happily resolved, our initial reaction, Zak's work tells us, is to become attentive to the stressor, whatever it is. If we can create surprise or suspense when we write for fundraising purposes—for example, by saying, "The XYZ is a white man's museum"—we have used a narrative device the effects of which are documented by neuroscientific research. We do not need to tell the whole story; we just need to give a narrative cue, and our readers will engage.

The neurologist Robert Burton adds another neurochemical to the mix: dopamine, "the feel-good hormone." Burton argues that, "because we are compelled to make stories, we are often compelled to take incomplete stories and run with them." He explains, "With a half-story . . . in our minds, we earn a dopamine 'reward' every time it helps us understand something in our world—even if that explanation is incomplete or wrong." But how incomplete can a narrative be and still be recognized by our story-making brains as story? My hypothesis, supported by the examples above, is that familiar narrative devices such as the ones discussed here are enough to trigger our appetite for story, capturing our attention by neurochemical means and leading us to expect or at least hope for more.

Values, Change, and Responsibility in the Humanities

At the beginning of this essay, I spoke of a systemic prejudice in academic culture against nonacademic work. That prejudice may be founded on the belief that nonacademic work does not instantiate the high values that humanities departments believe they protect and preserve. Yet the three examples I have presented here demonstrate the application not only of narrative devices but also of humanist values such as free thought, creativity, and social responsibility. Moreover, knowledge of the humanities and the values underlying it surely deserve to be tested outside the academy, to inform action and to be considered and reconsidered against the results of that action.

Of course, the idea of a "real world" separate from the academy is a fantasy, as any educator who has dealt with such issues as productivity and promotion can attest. Like the image of the "ivory tower," however, it is a fantasy that expresses the barrier nonacademicians feel between their work and that of scholars, particularly in the humanities. It is the responsibility of humanities educators, therefore, to supplant the image of a barrier with that of a border, a porous border through which the learning of the classroom and its application outside can travel. In this way, the humanities can come to be widely recognized as catalysts for growth in nonacademic areas and thus as a vital part of that "real world."

A wise man of my acquaintance sometimes says, "I don't have problems I can't solve; I have solutions I don't like." So it is in the humanities, where those presenting graduate programs may be reluctant to educate students for jobs outside academe despite knowing that these are precisely the jobs that most of their graduates will have. If this essay has done its work, however, it will have conveyed the usefulness, challenge, and downright fun that I have found in using what I learned in graduate school, and the confidence I developed there, to work in fundraising. Humanities educators must *want* to explore how their knowledge intersects with the world outside academe before proposals like Lissette Lopez Szwydky's can find traction. Perhaps my experiences will tempt them to try.

NOTES

1. Throughout this essay, I have used the terms *fundraising* and *fundraiser* in deference to readers who may be unfamiliar with the language of nonprofits. In the nonprofit sector, we often use *development* and *development officer*. Although we are casual in our choice of terms, there is a difference. Development is relational; development officers build relationships between donors and nonprofit organizations, expecting that increased engagement will lead to increased giving. Fundraising is transactional; fundraisers ask for contributions.

2. Many colleges and universities are, of course, nonprofits. I use the term here, however, to mean noneducational nonprofits such as those dedicated to human services, the arts, or environmental conservation.

3. In Milgram's experiments, volunteer "teachers" were instructed to administer electric shocks to "learners" who answered incorrectly. The volunteers did not know that the learners were, in fact, actors and that the shocks they appeared to suffer were not real. Although questions have been raised about the validity of the study's conclusions (Perry), Milgram's work is still believed to show "the ease with which ordinary people can be induced by a legitimate authority to act with extraordinary cruelty against an innocent victim" (Blass).

WORKS CITED

Abbott, H. Porter. *The Cambridge Introduction to Narrative*. Cambridge UP, 2002.

Ahern, Tom. *What Your Donors Want . . . And Why! The Ultimate Guide to Fundraising Communications*. Emerson and Church, 2017.

Blass, Thomas, editor. *Obedience to Authority: Current Perspectives on the Milgram Paradigm*. Lawrence Erlbaum, 2000.

Brooks, Jeff. *How to Turn Your Words into Money: The Master Fundraiser's Guide to Persuasive Writing*. Emerson and Church, 2015.

Burton, Robert. "Where Science and Story Meet." *Nautilus*, 22 Apr. 2013, nautil.us/where-science-and-story-meet-234302/.

Connor, Ulla, and Thomas Upton. "Linguistic Dimensions of Direct Mail Letters." *Corpus Analysis: Language Structure and Language Use*, edited by Pepi Leistyna and Charles F. Meyer, Rodopi, 2003, pp. 71–86.

Culler, Jonathan. *The Literary in Theory*. Stanford UP, 2007.

Dickerson, Frank C. *Writing the Voice of Philanthropy: How to Raise Money with Words*. 2009. Claremont Graduate U, PhD dissertation. *ProQuest*, proquest.com.

Gerrig, Richard J. *Experiencing Narrative Worlds: On the Psychological Activities of Reading*. Yale UP, 1993.

Kavanagh, Meredith. "Infographic: A Nonprofit Storytelling How-To." *Classy*, 29 Mar. 2019, www.classy.org/blog/infographic-nonprofit-storytelling.

Lombardi, Linda. "How to Tell Your Nonprofit's Story." *Network for Good*, 31 July 2018, www.networkforgood.com/nonprofitblog/how-to-tell-your-nonprofits-story.

Merrill, James. "If U Cn Rd Ths." *The New York Review of Books*, 3 Mar. 1983, www.nybooks.com/articles/1983/03/03/if-u-cn-rd-ths/.

Perry, Gina. "The Shocking Truth of the Notorious Milgram Obedience Experiments." *Discover Magazine*, 2 Oct. 2013, www.discovermagazine.com/mind/the-shocking-truth-of-the-notorious-milgram-obedience-experiments.

Price, Mackenzie. "Reframing Narratives, Resetting Reality: A Conversation with Mackenzie Price of the FrameWorks Institute." *Nonprofit Quarterly*, 28 Jan. 2019, nonprofitquarterly.org/2019/01/28/reframing-narratives-resetting-reality-a-conversation-with-mackenzie-price-of-the-frameworks-institute.

Rogers, Katina L. *Putting the Humanities PhD to Work: Thriving in and beyond the Classroom*. Duke UP, 2020.

Ryan, Marie-Laure. "Toward a Definition of Narrative." *The Cambridge Companion to Narrative*, edited by David Herman, Cambridge UP, 2007, pp. 22–35.

Sargeant, Adrian, and Steven Shattuck. "Digital Fundraising." *Fundraising Principles and Practice*, edited by Adrian Sargeant et al., 2nd ed., Wiley, 2017, pp. 318–59.

Szwydky, Lissette Lopez. "From Alt-Ac to Tenure-Track: The Need for Diversifying Faculty Experience." *Profession*, summer 2020, profession.mla.org/from-alt-ac-to-tenure-track-the-need-for-diversifying-faculty-experience.

Tannen, Deborah. "Crossing Over: Writing (and Talking) for General (as Compared to Academic) Audiences." *Professional Development in Applied Linguistics: A Guide to Success for Graduate Students and Early Career Faculty*, edited by Luke Plonsky, John Benjamins, 2020, pp. 165–80.

Villanueva, Edgar. "Money as Medicine: Leveraging Philanthropy to Decolonize Wealth." *Nonprofit Quarterly*, 29 Jan. 2019, nonprofitquarterly.org/2019/01/29/money-as-medicine-leveraging-philanthropy-to-decolonize-wealth.

Warwick, Mal. *How to Write Successful Fundraising Appeals*. 3rd ed., Jossey-Bass, 2013.

"When Someone Steals Your Soul: Repatriating Narratives in the Nonprofit Sector." *Nonprofit Quarterly*, 23 Jan. 2019, nonprofitquarterly.org/2019/01/23/when-someone-steals-your-soul-repatriating-narratives-in-the-nonprofit-sector.

Winter, Frederick A. "Plus C'est la Même Chose." *Inside Higher Ed*, 9 Feb. 2021, www.insidehighered.com/advice/2021/02/09/new-reality-humanities-phds-transformation-not-crisis-moment-opinion.

Zak, Paul J. "Empathy, Neurochemistry and the Dramatic Arc." *Future of StoryTelling*, 2022, futureofstorytelling.org/video/paul-zak-empathy-neurochemistry-and-the-dramatic-arc.

———. "Why Inspiring Stories Make Us React: The Neuroscience of Narrative." *Cerebrum: The Dana Forum on Brain Science*, 2 Feb. 2015, www.dana.org/Cerebrum/2015/Why_Inspiring_Stories_Make_Us_React__The_Neuroscience_of_Narrative.

Sustainability and the Posthumanities
Alex Christie and Katie Dyson

It's unclear whether the crisis facing recent humanities PhD students will ever reach a peak. Writing from the vantage of 2021, in which a global pandemic has both decimated an already downward-trending market in tenured and tenure-track jobs and further exposed the systemic cruelties of university labor practices, we (i.e., those trained or working in or adjacent to the humanities) find ourselves wading through a crisis that seems to constantly exceed itself.

As recent graduates of PhD programs, our scholarship and our current jobs have attuned us differently to this crisis; one of us has turned toward the public humanities and the media sector and the other toward posthuman knowledge practices outside the academy. However, in discussing the murky waters we swim in on a daily basis, we have collectively come to see a link between the limits of sustainability, the limits of the humanities as a discipline, and the limits of graduate student training.

Sustainability, for all its resonance with environmentalism, is more often than not intrinsically human-centered. Sustainability figures human-environmental relationality as ecological resource management, rendering the natural ecology as a (primarily economic) resource and rewriting capitalist gain as flourishing and futurity. Futurity, counterintuitively, requires continuously reproducing the present. In graduate programs, sustainability is related to remaking graduate students in the image of the scholar as they retrace the path of their adviser and of others who came before them. But we question the efficacy of this training in the light of the continual decline in tenured positions and intensified production of a contingent labor force. What are these programs sustaining other than the adjunctification of higher education and increasing precarity? Can there be a nonreproductive future for the university?

To talk about nonreproductive futures opens the impossibility and undecidability of what is to come. Against a model of sustainability predicated on the perpetual reproduction of the same or capitalist accumulation, nonreproductive futures allow us to think about the present as mutating beyond itself to become something other than itself, especially in this moment of crisis.[1] In "The Sky Is Falling," Eric Hayot both outlines the desperate situation of graduate training and offers a warning to his colleagues that bears repeating here:

> [U]nless you are placing most of your students in the professorial jobs for which you are training them, you need to rethink what you are doing. We cannot go on like this—we cannot go on treating people like this, cannot go on allowing ourselves to accept students who believe that they will be the ones to make it, when we see so clearly that the job market is a matter not of individual talent but of structural violence, a matter not of desert or hard work but of pattern and system whose primary ideological function is to absolve the individuals who participate in it from any moral responsibility for its effects.

In Hayot's insistence that "[w]e cannot go on like this," we see the possibility for transformation, but only after professional reckoning. Indeed, Hayot's later claim that enacting this change "is a task for the institutional and moral imagination" situates us squarely in the territory of professionalized negligence and its reproduction.[2] We write, therefore, not to advocate a top-down approach or refiguring or even to preserve graduate education as a set of relations that could be sustained in the humanist sense. Rather, we write to imagine a graduate education that explicitly works against imperatives to professionalize. The future of graduate education is undecidable, but we cannot go on like this.

We turn to posthumanism for a critique and reconfiguration of sustainability and the humanities and posthumanities. Implicit in this argument is the need to reimagine the humanities by divesting from the exclusionary and violent legacies of the Enlightenment and liberal humanism and to confront the idea that there can be no systemic solution implemented from above. Following an outline of posthumanism that critiques a collective intellectual entrenchment in the human and the humanities, we consider different approaches to refiguring the university by redirecting our labor and thinking toward deprivatization and broader publics. To conclude, we gesture toward alternative possible horizons for graduate education by utilizing posthumanism to rethink education as such and attempt to think about a nonreproductive future beyond the limited scope of the humanities and humanism. These gestures remain a provisional invitation to think beyond the limits of the human, humanities, and higher education.

Posthuman Sustainability

Posthumanism confronts sustainability in terms of futurity. Writing about the climate crisis in the wake of the Cold War and possible nuclear annihilation, Rosi Braidotti asks, "Has Man a future indeed? Does the choice between sustainability and extinction frame the horizon of our shared future, or are there other options?" (7). Woven into these questions is the suggestion that what limits the possible horizons of the future to either sustainability or extinction is the rational, humanist subject. Posed from this vantage, sustainability becomes predicated on the perpetual reproduction of a present and the staving off of humanity's eventual extinction. Thinking about sustainability in terms of reproductive futurism links what might otherwise be an environmental and ecologically progressive mode of posthuman relationality with the undercurrents of neoliberal capitalism.[3] Put succinctly by Tim Morton, "[T]he common name for managing and regulating flows is sustainability. But what exactly is being sustained? . . . Capital must keep on producing more of itself in order to be itself" (111). This is precisely why capitalism, sustainability, and humanism constitute a Gordian knot for thinking about the future beyond a sustainability/extinction dyad. Posthumanism offers alternative modes for imagining and enacting the future by foregrounding the interwoven nature of these discourses and suggesting the need to reimagine our attachment to these terms and ideas. Humanity needs a model of sustainability uncoupled from the logics of reproductive futurity.

Divestment requires understanding sustainability as something other than continuity for humanity alone. Discussing various terminology associated with environmentalism, Claire Colebrook foregrounds the problem of understanding sustainability as continuity:

> Sustainability assumes the value of continuity: if one changes it is only insofar as is required in order for human life to continue, an implication that is less subtly contained in the strategy of mitigation. Not only do all these terms accept that humanity exists as something that has the right to continue, and that it must do so now only in the mode of damage limitation; they also have a primarily calculative conceptual base (where the calculations are arithmetical, concerning more and less, rather than differential). (54–55)

Resonating in a similar frequency as Braidotti and Morton, Colebrook here shifts the emphasis to "humanity" rather than capitalism and, importantly, argues that continuity is often understood as an implicit human right—a sovereign and self-given authority.[4] If continuity, and specifically the continuation of the liberal human subject, is understood as a human right, futurity as sustainability is not actually about the future. Rather, it is about maintaining the present until there is nothing left—"an eventual, barely lived petering out" (58). Colebrook suggests that sustainability needs to be reimagined from a posthumanist or nonhuman perspective in which the "we" that constitutes humanity might mutate into something (else) sustainable even as—and especially because—"we" humans will disappear. That is, Colebrook begins from the end. That humanity will not exist at some point in the future is not some possibility to avoid but an unactualized potentiality lying in wait. Rather than continuing to stave off the eventuality of extinction, Colebrook suggests we explore modes of theory that contend with this eventuality: "What ways of speaking would fragment, disturb and destroy the logics of self-maintenance that have always sustained humanity as an animal that cannot question its existence?" (58). Colebrook's intervention suggests that reimagining sustainability would require affirming the end of humanity and grappling with the ethical consequences of the human presence in larger and diverse ecologies.

Posthumanism challenges everyone to think about sustainability in ecological and relational, rather than humanist or individualist, terms by considering our situatedness within a longer and larger spatiotemporal register—a radically impersonal life that we are just passing through. Braidotti, for example, reads death as an enabling concept: "This proximity to death is a close and intimate friendship that calls for endurance, in the double sense of temporal duration or continuity and spatial suffering or sustainability. Making friends with the impersonal necessity of death is an ethical way of installing oneself in life as a transient, slightly wounded visitor" (132). In Karen Barad's work, which refigures relationality—rather than the individual—as the smallest unit of measure, sustainability similarly becomes unlinked from the individual and attached to a shared and inherited responsibility: "Responsibility—the ability to respond to the other—cannot be restricted to human-human encounters when the very boundaries and constitution of the 'human' are continually being reconfigured and 'our' role in these and other reconfigurings is precisely what 'we' have to face" (392). In each case, we give up individualist, human-centered ethics in favor of a different mode and speed of sustainability of which "we" are not the only participants. An ecological view of sustainability reconfigures who and (more radically) what counts as worthy of participation and recognition. This antianthropocentric and antihumanist orientation undergirds our own interest in the relation between sustainability and the humanities, especially as it relates to the reproductive logics of the humanities.

Understanding humanism as a fundamental problem for conceptualizing futurity also requires understanding the university as a central site of liberal humanism's reproduction. We're not posing this as a radical claim but rather as foundational for understanding how the university functions within both the liberal and the neoliberal economy. Consider that the response to the crisis facing the humanities is one of preservation—an injunction that the humanities must continue despite the economic imperatives that privilege a soft vocational training in science, technology, engineering, and math. Yet, as so many arguments for the humanities circulate around critical thinking and close reading,[5] it's difficult to see these departments as offering something other than the instrumental reasoning STEM is criticized as peddling. From this vantage, STEM and the humanities are not antipodes but allies in sustaining the university as a site for reproducing the present. Much in the way that Colebrook describes humanity, the humanities are understood to exist as "something that has the right to continue," entrenching itself in the present rather than mutating toward a future.[6] In this way, the logic of sustaining the humanities is similar to the logic of sustaining humanity and likewise often unthinkingly enables the logics of racism, colonialism, ableism, and anthropocentrism that subtend both.

We suggest that posthumanism charts a potential alternative trajectory for the humanities: to become other in order to endure in some form, even as—and especially because—the humanities will disappear. This trajectory requires modulations, modifications, and mutations that might render the humanities unrecognizable but also decouple it from many of its violent and foundational logics. The goal is not to sustain the humanities as they have been but to follow Braidotti's suggestion that "the humanities need to embrace the multiple opportunities offered by the posthuman condition" (172) by becoming something different.

The Posthumanities, the Undercommons, and Generous Thinking

We might call the humanities as mutated by posthumanist critique the *posthumanities*, utilizing *post-* to signify a response to, a critique of, and a grappling with the continued force of the humanities (and of the human). Braidotti uses this terminology to emphasize the interdisciplinary work already taking place in humanities departments in an effort to move beyond the limiting scope of the human and humanism (in fields such as ecocriticism or digital humanities, for example). Her provocation that "the 'proper' subject of the humanities is not 'man'" (169) foregrounds a subject in excess of the autonomous and bounded scope of liberal humanism, not so much shifting the object of study as making space for the nonhuman participants entangled in the act of studying. We also utilize the term *posthumanities* to name a disciplinary capaciousness, making space for the discourses, terms, and people that have often been denied access to the humanities. The term additionally borrows from posthumanism the presupposition that relationalities, rather than individuals, are the smallest unit of measurement, attuning us to collectivities and connectivity. However, we want to break with Braidotti's provocation by thinking beyond the academic humanities as a privileged form and space of study. The posthumanities require a rupture or reconfiguration that transforms the relation between the academy and the broader public it coinhabits and coconstitutes.[7]

In shifting focus from the academy to its relation with a larger and longer public ecology, we necessarily reframe the outcomes of humanities education as collective rather than merely individual. In describing the use value of the humanities, we often turn toward student outcomes and integration into the labor market to justify our research, teaching, and position within the university.[8] This is ultimately an argument for sustaining the humanities in their current configuration. However, these arguments present problems for those who see the value of the humanities as critical of current sociopolitical and economic configurations. Helping students integrate into the labor market makes the humanities practically (read: economically) valuable but says nothing for the less immediate values that humanities students and education provide the broader public, including new and different ways of thinking and knowing. The question becomes how the posthumanities can foreground these other values while also insisting on a disruptive criticality rather than instrumentalization. That is, whereas the humanities seem to perpetually make arguments for why they fit into current economic and academic structures, we see the potential function of the posthumanities as interrogating the structures the humanities already inhabit and forging alternative alliances. The posthumanities would proffer a revaluation of terms by which we can illustrate the value of the work already being done.

Kathleen Fitzpatrick's *Generous Thinking* has been invaluable in articulating how we might reimagine the university as a site of public engagement rather than mere career training and privatized knowledge production. For Fitzpatrick, *generous thinking* names a model of thinking predicated on connection and community building and underscores the possibility (and necessity) of laboring with and for a public that stretches beyond the university. By allying itself with critical thinking and humanities research beyond the academy, generous thinking as described by Fitzpatrick foregrounds the public/private divide and frames this binary as the undergirding assumption that sustains the contemporary university. All too often, education and knowledge are understood as private and individual rather than a public or social good. Fitzpatrick writes, "As long as a university education is assumed to have a predominantly personal rather than social benefit, it will be argued that making such an education possible is a private rather than a public responsibility. And that economistic mindset will of necessity lead to the devaluation of fields whose benefits are less immediately tangible, less material, less individual" (22). We see this when the value of the humanities is coded after the fact, only when it attains market value. Yet value need not be tied to scarcity: generosity can become a powerful and sustaining force, even as other material and financial resources are scarce.[9] The value of education and the university must be reframed as primarily directed not simply toward sustaining a public within which these well-trained individuals might be integrated but instead toward cultivating a different kind of public altogether.

While Fitzpatrick's reconfiguration of the university in service of a public good remains optimistic, Stefano Harney and Fred Moten are hesitant, if not pessimistic, about the university's relation to the public. In *The Undercommons: Fugitive Planning and Black Study*, Harney and Moten sketch out the strange double bind of the contemporary scholar: "[T]o be a critical academic in the university is to be against the university, and to be against the university is always to recognize it and be recognized by it, and to institute the negligence of that internal outside, that unassimilated underground, a negligence of it that is precisely, we must insist, the basis of the professions" (31). What reproduces the university is neither mastery nor expertise but a negligence of what falls beyond the university's scope, which ultimately shapes both the grounds and limits of knowledge—what and how something can be knowable. Harney and Moten position studying against the intellectual production of the university as a way to "mark that the incessant and irreversible intellectuality of these activities is already present . . . To do these things is to be involved in a kind of common intellectual practice" (110). An intellectual practice divested from the privatization of knowledge and the circular logic of professionalization, studying becomes an engine of collective sociality and shifts knowledge production toward becoming wholly social and public. In a different key than Fitzpatrick's generous thinking, studying refigures the public/private distinction of the university by cultivating ways of knowing against the university's foundational negligence and the discipline's imperative to professionalize—one works within and against the university but does so generatively by rerouting labor to the activity of studying with and for others or to a collective project: "the reason we move into more autonomous situations is that it grows, and we spend less time in the antagonism of within and against" (148). This concept of generative knowledge might be understood as an ethics of nonprofit against profit-focused austerity measures at work within the university. To pose the concept as a question, how might working within the university, understood as an insular and often monolithic entity, generate knowledge practices that cannot be immediately recaptured and re-assimilated into the university? Or, phrased perhaps more crassly, how can those working in the university exploit the privilege of the university? Community and public engagement, collective activism, rerouting university resources for non- and antiuniversity purposes, and writing for a broad public all name ways of extracting and redistributing resources from the university. Finding a relationship to the university that isn't directly antagonistic can free us from the circular logic of professionalization and negligence, allowing us to divest from institutions that privatize and circumscribe study.

Divestment and professionalization are key concepts separating Harney and Moten's work from Fitzpatrick's, a contrast that asks us to think about the role of the university in a wider public ecology. In thinking about the posthumanities, we find resonances with the importance of working generatively toward new conceptions of a public, especially by way of generous thinking and, or as, a mode of study. The key difference seems to be where and how that studying takes place, and whereas Fitzpatrick sees the need to shift professionalization toward an arguably more humane and compassionate form, Harney and Moten help us see professionalization as the very mode of negligence that reproduces the university and its logics. Because of this difference, the university, as a place, a concept, and a kind of "factory," takes shape as a different problematic. We take these interventions as a cue for thinking through what the posthumanities might look like and how this act of imagination is limited by the costs of imagining the posthumanities within the university itself. Deprivatizing knowledge and its production potentially denatures the university and offers alternative, subversive intellectual practices that smuggle in publics, collectives, and communities that the university might otherwise discount or refuse. The university cannot go on like this, but something else could take its place.

We see the posthumanities as a possible future. As a set of emerging methodologies and practices, the posthumanities allow us to rethink our proximity to, and our investment in our proximity to, the university. The posthumanities locate the work of the humanities on scales that exceed the traditional professional bounds of the university, extending into spaces beyond classroom walls or the university campus and futures unimaginable in the present. A central site of the university's reproduction, graduate education becomes critical and contested territory for the posthumanities. Because it is bound up in professionalization and a critical negligence, graduate education in its current form sustains the perpetuation of the humanities rather than its possible futures. The posthumanities task us to conceptualize education beyond professionalization as a singular end and, instead, toward a world-generating activity.

Graduate Education and Nonreproductive Futures beyond the University

If sustainability, as the reproductive logic of privatized accumulation, undergirds how the university is understood, what kind of sustainability is entailed in a nonreproductive or a posthumanist future for graduate education? We want to consider graduate education beyond the narrow rails of academia—where it serves as a principal motor for the university, providing cheap labor and potential replacements for the exiting professoriate[10]—and professionalized negligence. In doing so, we reject the reframing of graduate education as geared toward "alt-ac," or the alternative professionalization programming offered to graduate students in lieu of actual resources or the possibility of stable academic futures. Investing in alt-ac becomes a way for those otherwise barred from the university to remain proximate, not just institutionally, but also to the university's problems and the impossibility of its solutions. "Alt-ac" is the cruel optimism that undergirds and sustains graduate education (see Macharia), ultimately inhibiting radical change. We also see the nonresponses to the precariatization of graduate education as a direct pipeline to the precariatization of adjunct labor and refusals to recognize graduate student unions across the country as willfully sustaining a fantasy for students, trustees, and the broader public at the expense of those who can least afford the cost. We see both "alt-ac" and the increased precariatization of graduate labor as undercurrents in the university's reproduction through cheap labor in the guise of graduate education. How do we imagine a nonreproductive future for graduate education?

In asking this question, we are bumping up against the perceived limits of what we in the academy have come to understand as graduate education, especially in terms of professionalization. We're taught to value scholarly individualism in the form of single-authored chapters, articles, and manuscripts, which ultimately frames knowledge production as a solo endeavor and reifies the theory that great individuals are the main producers and reproducers of knowledge. We are also taught to value mastery of subject matter, which ultimately delimits the forms that knowledge can take. In *Unthinking Mastery*, Julietta Singh frames mastery as the subtending logic of both humanism and colonialism, advocating for a

> dehumanist education through which "subject matter" comes not merely to describe a topic of study but to signal the physical matter that makes study possible. Coming to "know" ourselves through education must also be a radical renarration and reorientation of what it is that we are aspiring to know. A dehumanist education would insist that knowledge production itself become unpredictable, unanticipatable, and unmasterful. (67)

While mastery becomes the impossible (and misguided) telos of literary studies that must be unthought, Singh's articulation of the unpredictability of knowledge production also asks us to move beyond a position of negligence associated with professionalism by finally admitting that the questions we ask and the analysis we provide cannot be known in advance. Rather than mastering our subject matter, we abandon ourselves to knowledge practices and forms of study that denature the binary between knower and known, subject and object. This abandonment is radically incompatible with prescriptives to professionalize—"dehumanist" and posthumanist knowledge practices don't fit neatly into established forms, publications, and pathways but instead generate new forms. Graduate education becomes fertile ground for this work only if it can escape the circumscribed and limited notions of knowledge production available in the university.

Understanding the posthumanities as participating in, engaging with, and helping cultivate a broader public ecology fundamentally shifts how we think about preparing those who will inhabit and co-constitute that public. We know that preparation will require increased generous thinking, combined with a more capacious conception of study without explicit disciplinary or content boundaries, but cannot know in advance what the form and content should be. In their article about the possibility of a posthuman studies curriculum, Nathan Snaza and colleagues make a distinction between meaning and knowing: "Meaning would replace knowing for education since meaning, understood as the interactions among patterns of information creation and the randomness of unperceived patterns, has implications for action, choice, and social/cultural life in physical environments that are transformed by human 'knowing'" (51). The idea that education is aimed at tracing and participating in the relational forces of world making is one that is useful for describing both what we (posthumanists) can do but also how we are attuned to the world. We're moving from knowing something—capturing the object of knowledge—toward crafting and engaging with meaning and meaning-making.

The posthumanities highlight graduate education as a set of social relations tied to social (re)production. Rather than continuing to reproduce the private and privatized university, we might reconceive graduate education in service of the public and reconfiguring the public as such. As a site of "dehumanist" education, the posthumanities understand the university as an active participant in a wider public ecology. Unlike an economy tied to the competition among individuals, ecological thinking frames flourishing and futurity as collective and relational. While universities are part of broader academic ecologies—like the Humanities without Walls consortium, which links universities in the Midwest and beyond—a public ecology would include para-academic nodes, or "allied knowledge and cultural heritage institutions such as museums, libraries, academic presses, historical societies, and governmental humanities organizations" ("#Alt-ac in Context"). *The Los Angeles Review of Books* and *Public Books* are similar sites of public engagement, but we might add literary and cultural magazines like *n+1*, *Jacobin*, or online outlets like *The New Inquiry* and *Real Life Mag* to this list. These later publications, often inhabited by graduate students, early-career academics, and culture writers more generally, also cultivate an engaged public ecology in the circulation of their work on *Twitter* and other social media.[11] However, despite the promise of public engagement, workers in this broader humanities ecosystem nonetheless face similarly precarious labor conditions—inadequate compensation, limited or gig employment, and the general devaluing of knowledge work. Still, thinking beyond the public/private binary of higher education allows us to acknowledge the broader humanities ecosystems we already inhabit and participate in and gestures toward the non- or antiprofessionalizing work graduate education might help flourish.

In offering this analysis, we must admit that posthumanism offers few explicit correctives, solutions, or prescriptives. Instead, it offers alternative modes of attunement that allow us to reimagine the humanist logic underlying the present. The posthumanities take capaciousness as a central ethos in an effort to make room and respond to all that we encounter and all that we're entangled with and within. In this way, the posthumanities offer a revolution in thinking that better reflects the contemporary state of affairs we float in, but they also shift our concepts of sustainability away from education as mere market integration and task us with reimagining the university from within or below. Against instrumentalizing claims about the practical value of the humanities, we imagine the posthumanities as a mode of study predicated on capaciousness as nonprofit—a set of generative practices that make room for previously unimaginable forms of knowledge and knowledge practices rather than the cultivation of mastery in service of or parallel to capitalist accumulation. Such an ethos potentially reframes sustainability in terms of the perpetuation of a broader ecology rather than in terms of accretive reproduction. It doesn't tell us where to go but offers some ways of getting there.

In attempting to unthink this logic, we leave open the parameters through which the posthumanities are thought and practiced. We see this analytic as provisional rather than authoritative. We conclude by offering a series of questions, posed to generate, rather than limit, possible horizons of theory and praxis.

> What if the humanities or the posthumanities were enabled and practiced elsewhere? in the open? in public? toward refiguring the public for a wider polis that includes human and nonhuman forces? How can this work be supported?

What does studying in public look like, and how is it similar to or different from studying in the university? What resources are made available by the university that could be rerouted to the public? How does a shift toward the posthumanities offer novel and generative responses to these questions?

What does it mean to practice a new commons or new public as a graduate student within the neoliberal university? What set or sets of social relations sustain graduate studies without reproducing the university? What practices might be sustaining?

How might we study in service of another world, especially if we think this other world lurks in this world, awaiting the mutation or extension that will bring it into view?

These questions are invitations to the ongoing studying that might help us unthink the humanities and the university.

NOTES

1. See also Lauren Berlant's discussion of nonreproductive futures emerging from crises.

2. We borrow this idea of professionalized negligence from Stefano Harney and Fred Moten.

3. We borrow the term *reproductive futurism* from Lee Edelman's *No Future* but are thinking here in terms of capitalist reproduction in addition to heterosexuality.

4. Here, we see resonances with Jacques Derrida's work on the human subject as the autobiographical animal in *The Animal That Therefore I Am*.

5. Even the financial services corporation Deloitte sees this as a viable argument and published a report titled "The Value of the Humanities" in 2018.

6. We see this in the turn toward the digital humanities in literature departments. Daniel Allington, Sarah Brouillette, and David Golumbia describe the issue this way: "Neoliberal policies and institutions value academic work that produces findings immediately usable by industry and that produces graduates trained for the current requirements of the commercial workplace. In pursuit of these goals, the 21st-century university has restructured itself on the model of the corporate world, paying consultants lavish fees, employing miserably paid casual laborers, and constructing a vast new apparatus of bureaucratic control."

7. In this way, the posthumanities should be understood not as a "proper" field housed within the university but perhaps as a set of disparate but connected modes and methods for thinking antianthropocentrically.

8. Tellingly, articles in *The Chronicle of Higher Education* and *Inside Higher Ed* often turn immediately to job placement as an indicator of the humanities' worth.

9. This is not an argument that affect and generosity are remotely adequate substitutes for material resources.

10. That graduate education is a pipeline into the professoriate is a pernicious fiction—tenured and tenure-track positions are actively being replaced (or not renewed) in favor of contingent labor. Yet this fiction actively enables graduate study to continue in its current form. See Bousquet and Nelson: "We are not overproducing PhDs; we are underproducing jobs. There is plenty of work in higher education for everyone who wants to do it. The problem is that this enormous quantity of work no longer comes in the bundle of tenure, dignity, scholarship, and a living wage we call a 'job'" (40–41).

11. One example of an interest in engaging and cultivating an engaged public can be found in *The New Inquiry*'s supplement "Rent Strike 2020," which provides instructions and state-by-state resources for forming a tenants' union and holding a rent strike (Yaa).

WORKS CITED

Allington, Daniel, et al. "Neoliberal Tools (and Archives): A Political History of Digital Humanities." *Los Angeles Review of Books*, 1 May 2016, lareviewofbooks.org/article/neoliberal-tools-archives-political-history-digital-humanities/.

"#Alt-ac in Context." *#Alt-academy*, Media Commons, mediacommons.org/alt-ac/alt-ac-context.

Barad, Karen. *Meeting the Universe Halfway*. Duke UP, 2007.

Berlant, Lauren. "The Commons: Infrastructure for Troubling Times." *Society and Space*, vol. 34, no. 3, 2016, pp. 393–419.

Bousquet, Marc, and Cary Nelson. *How the University Works: Higher Education and the Low-Wage Nation*. New York UP, 2008.

Braidotti, Rosi. *The Posthuman*. Polity Press, 2013.

Colebrook, Claire. *Death of the Posthuman: Essays on Extinction Vol. 1*. Open Humanities Press, 2014.

Derrida, Jacques. *The Animal That Therefore I Am*. Fordham UP, 2008.

Edelman, Lee. *No Future*. Duke UP, 2004.

Fitzpatrick, Kathleen. *Generous Thinking*. Johns Hopkins UP, 2019.

Harney, Stefano, and Fred Moten. *The Undercommons*. Minor Compositions, 2013.

Hayot, Eric. "The Sky Is Falling." *Profession*, May 2018, profession.mla.org/the-sky-is-falling/.

Macharia, Keguro. "On Quitting." *The New Inquiry*, 19 Sept. 2018, thenewinquiry.com/on-quitting/.

Morton, Timothy. *Hyperobjects*. U of Minnesota P, 2013.

Singh, Julietta. *Unthinking Mastery*. Duke UP, 2017.

Snaza, Nathan, et al. "Towards a Posthumanist Education." *Journal of Curriculum Theorizing*, vol. 30, no. 2, 2014, 39–55.

"The Value of the Humanities." Deloitte Access Economics, 2018, www2.deloitte.com/content/dam/Deloitte/au/Documents/Economics/deloitte-au-economics-value-humanities-111018.pdf. PDF download.

Yaa, Nana. "Rent Strike 2020." *The New Inquiry*, 26 Mar. 2020, thenewinquiry.com/rent-strike-2020/.

Humanities in Action: Centering the Human in Public Humanities Work

Veronica T. Watson and Laurie Zierer

This essay draws upon a wide-ranging conversation that took place over the course of a year with the goal of exploring the alignments and places of disconnect between two significant contributors to the humanities ecosystem: graduate programs in the humanities and state humanities councils. As program director of graduate studies in literature and criticism at Indiana University of Pennsylvania (Veronica) and executive director of PA Humanities (Laurie), we speak not only from our positions within these organizations but also from our shared experience of working in the public humanities. Our paths first crossed in 2008, when Veronica was selected to be a humanities scholar for the Pennsylvania Quest for Freedom Live and Learn series. Live and Learn featured a common reading that was selected by PA Humanities (of which Laurie was assistant director), scholars to open and guide public discussions, and historical reenactors who brought the stories to life through the portrayal of historical figures. The series, which was free of charge, was available across Pennsylvania and was hosted by community organizations like museums, libraries, community centers, and churches. Subsequently, Veronica was voted to the PA Humanities board, where she served for five years. During that time Laurie, as executive director, guided the organization to put "the humanities in action" in Pennsylvania communities. As a result, PA Humanities developed Teen Reading Lounge, a youth reading and community engagement program, and expanded its capacity to support community reconciliation, racial justice, and economic revitalization.

Our conversation unearthed several themes that seem central to understanding the histories of how graduate programs and humanities councils have intersected and suggested possibilities for building fruitful collaborations. We concluded that the ways in which academic study "disciplines" students to focus on ever more specialized slices of knowledge often works against their transition into the work of public humanities organizations. An exploration of how humanities are taught in the academy also led to a greater understanding of differences in the ways the public humanities have been understood by those working from these two sides of the humanities ecosystem. Central to this tension are the fundamental questions of how the humanities are defined and who they are believed to serve, and central to those considerations are questions of equity. When the humanities are understood primarily as academic subjects that are delivered as part of a curriculum, that framing is always already exclusionary, limited to those who can afford, and have interest in pursuing, college-level education. Efforts to expand training in the public humanities has raised yet other equity-related questions and has left many emerging professionals underequipped to navigate the power differentials that often exist when community-based and academic humanities workers try to partner.

In times like these, when we as a society are grappling with how to address structural inequities and systemic racism that marginalizes so many citizens, the humanities can provide the tool kit that can keep us all continually learning and making change together. As we consider how to heal some deeply rooted schisms that exist between humanities organizations serving the public and humanities graduate programs, we consider possibilities for generative collaboration across the humanities ecosystem that will contribute to civic rejuvenation in the United States.

Defining the Public Humanities

Laurie

I loved the way the National Endowment for the Humanities (NEH) described us in 2016 when they were conducting a site visit to learn about our new directions: PA Humanities "isn't your grandmother's humanities council anymore." PA Humanities wants to have a social impact in a different way—for the humanities to make a difference in the lives of people who might not ordinarily go to a discussion with a scholar or to places like museums. These days, you are more likely to see us sitting at an artist gallery in downtown Chester plotting our next move on the block or at a table in a small town or city like Carlisle, Williamsport, Emporium, Ambridge, or Meadville with a mayor, community activists, artists, entrepreneurs, and everyday people, talking about their stories, values, and plans for the future.

Many times, the humanities are defined as a list of academic subjects—like philosophy, literature, religion, art, music, history, and languages—that we have used to document and understand our world. The humanities are fueled by these subjects and by acts of reading, reflection, and dialogue. Those have always been our bread and butter, and because my background is in English, rhetoric, and communications, I see what we at PA Humanities are doing in those terms also, but we are also bringing back the classical perspective of the liberal arts as civic arts—those indispensable skills needed for leadership in the new democracies of classical Greece. Classical Athenians like Aristotle saw the humanities as cultivating good habits of mind that anyone—not only an elite class—could apply to any issue, no matter how complicated, for the sake of acting for the common good (Knott et al). We at PA Humanities see ourselves as "lighting [people's] minds for civic action" (8)—not just for the benefit of the individual but for the benefit of the community as a whole.

I've always liked a definition the author and folklorist Zora Neale Hurston formulated: "Research is formalized curiosity. It is poking and prying with a purpose. It is a seeking" for all of us who wish to "know the cosmic secrets of the world" (91). Our experience at PA Humanities in the last few years is that people do want to poke and pry with a purpose, to ask big questions about what they value, and to make real change in their lives and their communities. And they want to be part of leading that change and creating places where everyone can belong and thrive. They are tired of simply talking about change. They want to see action—less crime, a new grocery store, or help for young people, seniors, or families struggling to pay the bills.

You can see this in action in our Williamsport's Second Street Community Garden project. First, people came together for a storytelling session in a low-income housing community as part of our PA Heart and Soul initiative to discuss and discover what they valued most in their community.[1] What surfaced repeatedly was their appreciation of the small-town feel of their community. Participants treasured the scale of the community because of its easy access to local attractions and because of the character, friendliness, and compassion of the residents. The session laid the groundwork for action in response to the news that a local grocery was closing and residents without cars would have no easy access to fresh vegetables: people took action together to create a community garden.

We are trying with our work in Pennsylvania communities to be national leaders in shifting perceptions about why the humanities are relevant to us today. We see ourselves finding the human connection in the humanities, taking the books off the shelves and putting them in people's hands. A theory of change fuels our vision and mission. We believe the humanities inspire people to grow their potential and shape an equitable society. We put the humanities in action to create positive change by making the tools and methods of our trade—like storytelling, historical perspectives, interpretation, creativity, and deliberative civic dialogue—available, whether for documenting culture, developing today's leaders, creating vibrant local economies, or celebrating community diversity and homegrown talent.

We have found success by pairing humanities skills and approaches with the knowledge and perspectives of sectors like education and community development. This framing of the humanities has required us to step out of our comfort zone and listen and learn with the people we serve and with scholars in other disciplines. The first step in this journey was to shift our focus from delivering humanities programming to asking where the humanities could have the deepest impact in areas of need in our state. Education was one clear place. Then we took our book programs, which back then were more like classes at a university, typically guided by an expert facilitator schooled in the humanities, and asked, What would happen if we put teenagers themselves at the helm with the support of caring educators, and they selected books based on their interests, explored activities to develop their learning, and took action on issues important to them? We've now worked with more than one hundred libraries and out-of-school time centers and with thousands of teenagers to develop our Teen Reading Lounge and Youth-Led Humanities programs.

We also worked with educators and human development psychologists to explore how the humanities build identity, learning, and social and emotional skills. This intentional, prosocial approach engages young people by recognizing their strengths and interests and building confidence, character, and leadership. That's where we have discovered that the public humanities are productive and constructive—not only for the individual but also for the community. We build on our talents and use the everyday theory and practice of the humanities to make positive change, practicing what Laurie Grobman and E. Michele Ramsey call "mind training" for the common good (54).

Veronica

I'm very interested in the turn toward "public humanities" and "public-facing scholarship" that many of us in university-centered humanities programs have made. In large part, this shift has been spurred by changing employment prospects brought on by the increasing adjunctification of higher education. But in my program, it has also been catalyzed by the students entering our graduate programs who are already actively engaged in social and educational reform efforts, community organizing, and social change movements and are already doing the work of community reconciliation and healing. They are teachers, community college faculty members, creative writers and poets, community leaders . . . and they are seekers. By that I mean they are open to and interested in a range of career paths and leadership opportunities that are supported by the training and professionalization they develop while pursuing their doctoral and master's degrees.

The National Humanities Alliance has, for a number of years, been building a database of "publicly engaged humanities work in U.S. higher education." That organization has identified five key types of engagement that characterize publicly engaged humanities that are connected to institutions of higher education:

1. Outreach: scholarly programming and media for a general audience, including public lectures, op-eds, and podcasts;
2. Engaged research: research initiatives in which higher education faculty and students partner with community members, including community-based research;
3. Engaged teaching: higher education coursework involving community engagement, including service learning and project-based learning beyond the university;
4. Engaged public programming: public programming in which the primary objective is not the transfer of knowledge but the creation of an experience, such as community conversation programming; and
5. The infrastructure of engagement: institutional structures that support engaged scholarship, including degree programs, centers, funding opportunities, digital technologies, and curriculum reorientation initiatives.   ("About")

The diversity of that work is impressive, and it is also telling of how many of us in higher education have come to the "public humanities" and of what we "teach" graduate students about the significance and the work of the public humanities.

When we in the academy talk about public humanities, we are often, fundamentally, talking about how to retool our esoteric interest for a nonacademic audience who may lack experience, training, or interest in the very focused thing that we have chosen as our life's work. We may not have thought very much about why someone outside the academy might be interested in our work or how we might connect that work to existing public dialogues in ways that would bring new people to our interests. So the term *public humanities* becomes a shorthand for reaching beyond our captive audiences—in the classroom, in our departments and universities, and in the publication outlets academics have tended to frequent for tenure and promotion—to connect to those who are not, in one way or another, predisposed to value our work.

The term *public humanities* also signals a second, related shift in thinking. The terminology often is used as a shorthand to encourage scholars to consider and articulate the *public good* our work serves. In our contemporary moment, those of us in academic humanities spaces are called upon to say why it matters that we study literature, history, cultures, languages, and ideas. Thus, when we are asked to frame our work in ways that answer the questions, "So what; why should we care?," or "What difference does X make to how we understand our lives?," we consider that thinking as "public humanities" work or "publicly engaged research." These terms signify a particular type of intellectual work undertaken to surface and articulate the ways our scholarship can and should be seen as related to the grand questions about how we live our lives.

Finally, *public humanities* is the term that is used when academics and scholars engage projects developed in community organizations and spaces. In this way, any of us can do public humanities work; and in some fields, we even create public humanities projects. This is the work that grows out of community need or interest, efforts to capture, preserve, and share stories that record our past and shape our future.

Many of us, especially when we first start thinking about bringing a public humanities framework into our graduate programs, begin by helping students make their work more accessible and get their scholarship and research outside of classrooms and into spaces they had not really thought of as epicenters of the humanities. However, these fairly modest shifts still happen within the context of academic institutions that often do not have reward systems, or prestige, tied to public humanities work. Thus, individual research remains at the center of the academic endeavor. Because that center is not really challenged, our graduate programs continue to do little to encourage, train, or support collaborative, team-based research or work that is centered with and in community settings.

The omission of these skills and experiences from the menu of things we cultivate in humanities graduate education likely means we are missing an opportunity to attract students from the institutions where there has been a consistent growth in humanities majors since 1987: community colleges ("Humanities Degrees"). At a time when so many are once again committed to making gains in diversity and equity in higher education, a more specific commitment to preparing students to contribute to public humanities organizations might be an important piece in the puzzle.

Framing and Equity

Veronica

Over the last two to three decades or so, study of the humanities has been significantly sidelined as the national conversation and focus have shifted strongly to workforce preparation and job readiness. The civic values and public benefits of the humanities are often not a central consideration for students and parents paying for a university education today. Seeing this decline and anticipating that many of the critical literacy and communication skills that are needed for democratic participation were also being de-emphasized, several humanities foundations, most notably the Mellon Foundation, provided support to programs and universities to reenvision graduate education in the humanities for the twenty-first century. What emerged from those conversations was a focus on public humanities and a greater commitment to preparing humanities graduate students for a variety of career paths. This has really been nothing but good for humanities graduate students and the broader humanities sector.

However, a large percentage of that money went to institutions that were already well funded and probably could have done this work without additional foundation support. Those are the institutions that also tend to serve students who already have certain class and educational advantages and to have less diverse student populations in their programs. Yet there are a significant number of smaller, less well-funded regional institutions with doctoral programs in the humanities that tend to serve students with a wider variety of identities and experiences—students of color, working-class students, first-generation doctoral students, and working professionals. These are institutions that were already preparing students for community college teaching or were working with students who had already shown long-standing dedication to their communities through a history of substantial engagement. These institutions and their students—save for the commitment of faculty members—have largely been left out of the conversations—and funding—meant to transform doctoral education in the humanities.

Another equity-related consideration that the two of us have uncovered during our conversations is a difference in the framing practiced by community organizers and that practiced by scholars and educators. Community organizations who use humanities tool kits are reluctant to think of their work as "humanities work," even when that label seems quite fitting.

Laurie

Academic institutions use a different kind of language, and their cultures are often very different from the communities they serve. When resources are brought to the table by a university, for instance, there are often questions about who the resources are meant to benefit or who controls them. It is not always clear in what spirit those resources are being made available to the community, because "the humanities" are often entangled with the ways in which local knowledge and expertise get marginalized, repressed, and even erased. For community organizations, the term *humanities* often has deep associations with class privilege and historic structures that have kept some people from being able to go to college, tell their own stories, or solve problems in their communities. Fundamentally, that is an equity issue.

PA Humanities has sought to understand itself within a larger group of organizations using humanities tools to cultivate social change for a more equitable future. In research conducted by Penn Praxis (a division of the University of Pennsylvania) that examines grassroots organizations from across the United States, most organizations simply did not define their work as "the humanities." Nearly all the interviewees, except for the ones working with PA Humanities on projects, viewed the term as alienating for the audiences with whom they work and at odds with their inclusive practices in the community (Donofrio et al.). Clearly, there is work to be done to rehabilitate "the humanities" outside the academy.

As a grant-maker and partner in resident-led community development, PA Humanities takes an asset-based approach that recognizes community expertise. Mauricio L. Miller argues in *The Alternative: Most of What You Believe about Poverty Is Wrong* that "if we recognize and invest in the talents and initiatives low-income families demonstrate every day—if we look for those traits rather than their deficits—we can create an investment system that helps those efforts grow" (4). PA Humanities has adapted this perspective in its work with communities by focusing on the assets that the community already has in place. When you believe people already have the know-how and talent to make a difference in their communities, your role is to listen, learn, and to provide a humanities tool kit that builds relationships, skills, and motivation to make a positive change. Our role is to amplify the voices of talented partners and individuals, and lead a movement to champion, research, and redefine the role the humanities play in their lives.

Preparing Graduate Students for Community-Based Collaboration

Laurie

One of the questions we always ask ourselves at PA Humanities is, How do we show up when we partner with a community, and how do we share power in obvious and deliberate ways so that the community's knowledge and power remains central to the work? Another of the central questions that community organizations and community-based researchers care about is the *why*: What is the "why" for you doing this work? We want partners from academia who understand they are not there to solve the problem and that the community is not the problem to be solved. We want collaborators who see themselves as part of the community and who respect that the community is perfectly capable of defining their own needs and figuring out the best way forward on any particular issue. These principles have guided our best practices, pushing us to design projects together with community members, to trust community and organizational leaders, and to support the journey of learning. To do so, it is crucial to work with (rather than work for) local residents, acknowledging and honoring their assets and expertise, creating spaces where we feel we all belong, and helping to build our mutual capacity to thrive and sustain positive change.

Veronica

In many humanities programs, community-based collaboration is not an easy training to provide. For disciplines like history, English, philosophy, and the like, students work largely independently. They research the artifacts that they have committed themselves to understanding, they write in solitude with a fairly limited audience in mind, they present to like-minded folk, and they often publish in journals and books that have a narrow reach. So, in the absence of experiences that require students to apply their training in professional relationships, questions of power-sharing and creating effective collaborations often remain theoretical. It will take some effort to figure out how to build that proficiency through doctoral training in the humanities.

Further, the willingness to learn from the community takes a certain kind of humility—and doctoral education doesn't do much to cultivate humility. For instance, when I take a class to our local historical society, my students encounter many volunteers who have not studied history as an academic pursuit. Many express surprise at how knowledgeable the staff members are about historical research and the materials they curate. They seemed shocked to learn that the collection and preservation of knowledge and artifacts could be pursued in institutions other than universities and museums.

In short, there is a certain investment that even working-class students have in the fantasy of intellectual work being exclusive to highly trained "experts" in particular "disciplines." And their work (perhaps their desire) as graduate students is to join that elite and rarefied strata of professionalization—to become experts who are able to enter the room with authority and who can expect a certain deference as a result of their training. In "There Is No Case for the Humanities," Justin Stover talks about this expectation as an unspoken foundation of the humanities, what he terms "courtoisie, a constellation of interests, tastes, and prejudices that marks one as a member of a particular class" (219). This sense that the doctoral degree makes one recognizable as a member of a certain class—which is not at all limited to one's economic status but instead is more closely tied to "knowledge as capital" or to the "personal empowerment that comes with esoteric knowledge"—may be part of the culture of the academy that community leaders and organizations find so alienating (Carnevale 26, 29).

It will take a certain creativity and intentionality to build humility into the skill set that students emerge with. We should probably call that a "character set," because we'd want it to be more than something people can put on in a certain context. We want students' approach to be authentic—a deep respect for the knowledge of people outside the academy with vastly different experiences and levels of education that equip them to confront the problems in their lives and communities.

Relationship Building and Interdisciplinarity

Laurie

In addition to having a greater respect for community expertise, and with the PA Humanities' work in mind, there are a few other skills that I would identify as necessary for a career in the public humanities. We look for people who have learned to build relationships across difference; who understand the importance of listening and fostering trust, mutual respect, and a sense of belonging; and who are ready to share power and embrace collaborative, participatory research and community-led action. Graduate school experiences can help many people get these desirable skills. When students learn the mutual benefit of authentic collaboration, they see that new strategies and tools are possible that neither they nor the residents they work with had individually, leading to powerful outcomes for community-centered work and providing what different people need in order to thrive.

Veronica

The idea that we have to be open to a radically different approach to the humanities when working with the community leads me to reflect on the fact that so many of the reward systems within the academy are designed with disciplinary expertise in mind. The disciplinary boxes we have inherited, and in some cases created, often work against our best efforts at interdisciplinary inquiry. But preparing graduate students to enter the public humanities work that is going on in community and cultural organizations as partners requires us to rethink our commitment to creating content experts who study a clearly defined artifact or contribute to a single discipline. As our colleague Stacy Hartman suggested in an e-mail exchange, "The type of work that you're describing is not only interdisciplinary, it's somehow antidisciplinary. . . . Much of the humanities work that has had impact beyond the academy in the last few years has also resisted disciplinary classification, or it's had to have a whole new discipline invented around it."

It is difficult to envision an immediate or wholesale reworking of how higher education is organized, but it is encouraging to recognize that disciplines in the academy do, in fact, change over time. They become more or less specialized, merge with or split off from other discrete areas of study, generate new lines of inquiry, borrow and blend methodologies from other disciplines, and, in general, evolve to reflect growth in knowledge and to respond to the new and pressing challenges of their contemporary world. For instance, we now recognize some work as being "transdisciplinary," a term that an academic search engine will reveal did not have much scholarly cachet before the start of the twenty-first century. So perhaps the question is not so much how to break out of our disciplinary thinking but more how to train ourselves and our students to hold those orientations lightly, to be ready and willing to cross borders and to build collaborations that advance knowledge and make a difference in the lives of people, both inside and outside the academy.

A good place to start building this particular mindset or skill set, I think, is with interdisciplinary work within the university, across programs, with faculty and students at different levels and from different fields of study. That, at least, provides a small experience where what is valued is not individual expertise but the ability to collaborate to build knowledge and to create something new that couldn't exist except for the work of the team.

For instance, in response to the murder of George Floyd and other unarmed Black people killed by police in the last decade, and the related national dialogue during the COVID-19 global pandemic, I launched a project called Humanities Training for Law Enforcement (HTLE). The HTLE is a training protocol that uses Black detective fiction and humanities methodologies to cultivate professional behaviors and habits of mind that work against implicit bias, anti-Black racism, and racial indifference in aspiring and active-duty law enforcement personnel. But the expertise I bring as an African American literature scholar and professor is only part of the picture. The HTLE team also includes criminologists, sociologists, and law enforcement professionals, as well as colleagues with different literary expertises, to develop curriculum, train officers, and evaluate the project. When graduate students join the HTLE, they have to adjust their stance; they are emerging scholars of literature, but the context we are working in—providing training to law enforcement officers—necessitates that they engage a range of disciplinary knowledge and learn along with the team as we all expand our specialized research or professional areas. Using African American literature to identify and unsettle racial bias in officers is an untried approach, and every member of the team is critical if we are to support police departments looking to expand community policing and repair frayed relations with communities of color.

Amplifying Humanities Skills

Laurie

With the additional preparation suggested here, humanities students can be even more valuable in community-based research and organizing and effective in all kinds of professional spaces. But the skills we already cultivate in the humanities are equally important in public humanities work because very often grassroots and public humanities organizations are doing reconciliation work, trying to repair deep, long-standing inequities and injustices in their communities. They are connecting groups who have been separated, fostering conversations that have been suppressed, and forging new ways for communities to work through the pressing issues they face with more voices and interests at the table.

For instance, our research with PennPraxis finds that storytelling is a consistent and vital element in grassroots social change organizations nationwide (Donofrio 16–17). Story-finding, -telling, and -sharing are essential for building inclusive, equitable relationships; they are the foundation on which the humanities have been built and are ways we can share and build power in our communities. Storytelling is more than a method of recording; it provides validation, empowers communities, sparks dialogue, nurtures empathy, and propels projects. While there is an inclination to search for commonalities that unite people, storytelling can also help raise valuable and important differences between groups that all participants need to understand before a path forward can be found. Storytelling is the sweet spot for the humanities inside and outside the academy; it is a tangible example of how and why our work is relevant to the lives of citizens and communities.

Veronica

The ability to foster dialogue and empathy is something that most humanities graduate programs could easily amplify in the existing curriculum. Conversations, role play, case studies, and the like can be used (and often are) to explore how to create inclusive spaces, encourage broad participation from the group, and facilitate power-sharing in fruitful and authentic ways. I'd like to think of this piece as low-hanging fruit in the curriculum we already deliver. And when the resources are available to provide externships for practical experience, we definitely should be asking students to be thoughtful and attentive about how dialogue and storytelling of all sorts are used to build community, negotiate difference, and facilitate change. But the learning cannot begin when the graduate student leaves campus. The ethics of relationship and community building require that the university foster the ability to collaborate and to support difficult discussions as a way of thinking and working that students are putting into practice when they leave the university.

Creating Partnerships for the Future of the Humanities
Laurie

If we really want our work to start with a commitment to the community, we need to discover what the public humanities mean to residents and ask why the work matters to them. When we embarked on this path at PA Humanities, it was a controversial shift in direction for us. My board was heavy with academics, and quite a few were wringing their hands about it, although they understood the value of positioning ourselves to address education and civic engagement, where we could make the most difference in Pennsylvania. But everyone wanted to spend time defining what we meant by the public humanities in these spheres. I said, "Let's stop this navel-gazing and show what the humanities *can do* and explore why it's relevant to Pennsylvanians with them." That set the stage for us to become what Amy Edmondson calls "the fearless organization" in her book of the same name: we got comfortable with taking risks and focusing on what we learn as we do our work with communities.

We now know that when everyone participates in the life of their community to improve and shape their future, civic engagement happens and its impact is felt. But when the deeper connections and relationships aren't there, it's difficult to work through challenges that arise because the community is divided and people do not feel equally empowered to speak or have an actual influence.

This is long-term work that we must commit to—and we must accept that what we do at a particular moment may not be enough to right all the wrongs in our communities. Rather, we must commit to the longer process of change, which, according to the participatory researchers Elizabeth Myrick and Rachel Williams, who have conducted research on our PA Heart and Soul collaboration, is something the humanities can help us with. The humanities, they found, help create resilience when communities face setbacks and resistance in pursuing equity. Community members also reported feeling the humanities became "better defined" and "more meaningful" because of their engagement. One declared, "Humanities play a huge role if you are going to work in the community. I never would have thought so before. . . . Through H&S, I've seen how the humanities are relevant to my work, with reconciling the past, race and racial justice[;] humanities give us ways to talk about and process difference, process trauma" (Myrick and Williams 10). Another said, "Because [the humanities] named the elephant in the room, we could begin to address the marginalization of African Americans and new communities" (13). These testimonials point to the ways that the humanities can give us a framework for sharing experiences to reenvision the communities we want to nurture into being.

Veronica

In the academy, our challenge is to make the public humanities, or public-facing research, more than just a way to teach our passions in a different context. We should want the public humanities to be rooted in a commitment to community: "There's some work in progress already, or that the community believes needs to be done, to which I can contribute my skills and interests." We need to do more than provide a professional experience with a humanities or grassroots organization for graduate students. We should be striving to create a graduate school experience that leads those emerging professionals to civic engagement and community-building opportunities that are amplified by the training and values they have cultivated and refined in our programs.

Neal Lester, the founder of Project Humanities at Arizona State University, offered a useful insight during an interview. He said, "While I can appreciate a disciplinary approach, that works for people who are inside the academy. So much of trying to bring people together and get people to support what we do is to step outside of those sometimes rigid and artificial boundaries" (Pettit). Like Lester, I've always thought that simply reserving the humanities to those who have the fortune of academic pursuit was a loss, which is why I love the approach of PA Humanities. PA Humanities models how to put the humanities to work to create more power-sharing, to open up more avenues for participation in community building, and to amplify the knowledge and grassroots strategies for democratic participation in all levels of our society.

In our contemporary moment, we need a study of humanities that is big, far-reaching, and centered in the lives of human beings. We can and should do more than just "study" the humanities. We can and should *use* the humanities to disrupt privilege and injustice, to build bridges among people and communities, and to bring more people into the project of participatory democracy. If we can redesign graduate program offerings to center ways of creating, sharing, and participating in the collaborative coconstruction of humanistic knowledge in both the classroom and the community, then we will have really released the potential of the humanities for all people.

NOTE

1. PA Heart and Soul, in partnership with the Orton Family Foundation, was piloted in Pennsylvania by PA Humanities and centers story-collecting and critical analysis to build relationships and shared understanding for the common good. Its collaborations now support community development and civic activism in twelve Pennsylvania communities. Some outcomes of the ongoing Williamsport PA Heart and Soul storytelling project are available on the Heart of Williamsport website (heartofwilliamsport.org).

WORKS CITED

"About." *Humanities for All*, National Humanities Alliance, 2023, humanitiesforall.org/about.

Carnevale, Anthony P. "Graduate Education and the Knowledge Economy." *Graduate Education in 2020: What Does the Future Hold?*, Council of Graduate Schools, 2009, pp. 26–59.

Donofrio, J. T., et al. *Humanities in Action: A National Perspective*. PA Humanities, 2022, pahumanities.org/uploads/files/Humanities-in-Action-A-National-Perspective-PA-HUMANITIES-2022-compressed.pdf.

Edmondson, Amy. *The Fearless Organization: Creating Psychological Safety in the Workplace for Learning, Innovation, and Growth*. Wiley, 2018.

Grobman, Laurie, and E. Michele Ramsey. *Major Decisions: College, Career, and the Case for the Humanities*. U of Pennsylvania P, 2020.

Hartman, Stacy. E-mail to Veronica Watson and Laurie Zierer. 10 June 2020.

"Humanities Degrees Declining Worldwide Except at Community Colleges." *American Academy of Arts and Sciences*, 14 June 2021, amacad.org/news/humanities-degrees-declining-worldwide-except-community-colleges.

Hurston, Zora Neale. *Dust Tracks on the Road: A Memoir*. Lippincott, 1942.

Knott, Robert, et al. *Lighting the Mind for Action: A Call to Trustees and Leaders of America's Liberal Arts Colleges*. 2017, static1.squarespace.com/static/5409fd72e4b08734f6c05b4c/t/5aa196c7e4966b3fcfa987b9/1520539342398/Lighting+The+Mind+Essay+2017.pdf.

Miller, Mauricio L. *The Alternative: Most of What You Believe about Poverty Is Wrong*. Lulu Publishing Services, 2017.

Myrick, E., and R. Mosher-Williams. *Humanities-Based Community Development in Pennsylvania: Insights from PHC's Heart and Soul Learning*

Project. PA Humanities Council, 2021, pahumanities.org/uploads/files/Humanities-Based-Community-Development-PA-Humanities-2022.pdf.

Pettit, Emma. "Are the Humanities Really in Crisis?" *The Chronicle of Higher Education*, 9 Feb. 2020, chronicle.com/article/are-the-humanities-really-in-crisis/.

Stover, Justin. "There Is No Case for the Humanities." *American Affairs*, vol. 1, no. 4, winter 2017, pp. 210–24.

PART THREE
Joy and Well-Being

Introduction

Of the three organizing principles in this volume, joy and well-being are both the most surprising and the most obvious. To speak of curriculum and engagement is expected, but the most common response we got to the statement that we wanted to frame the future of humanities graduate education around joy was bemused laughter.

Joy may be found in many places in humanities education: in a text, in the classroom, with colleagues, and in writing, to name only a few. Given that these joyful experiences often inspire people to undertake graduate study, we found the presumption that graduate education excludes or precludes joy puzzling. Did our colleagues feel a professional discomfort with joy as a goal of humanistic inquiry, given the deeply ingrained skepticism that undergirds contemporary critique? Had we in academe become inured to the idea that a certain amount of misery must be baked into the graduate experience in order to make it an authentic one, a legacy of Western individualism and the shame-oriented pietist pedagogy of the post-Enlightenment? Or had we come to simplify joy as a superficial sensory experience, more akin to fun? Were academics simply too distracted to reflect on the other layers that shape human flourishing, such as connection, purpose, impact, and beauty?

We have chosen in this volume to speak of "joy and well-being" as a duality, acknowledging that these experiences are intertwined and insisting that they are integral to the future of the humanities. Neither joy or well-being, as we imagine them, is necessarily about feelings of happiness or even fun, though both of these qualities are perhaps underrated and even essential. Rather, well-being is about the sense of safety and security that makes all other work possible, while joy is an experience of a sustaining contentment that stems from the opportunity to nurture relationships with others while doing meaningful and fulfilling work that has a larger purpose.

Cultivating a discourse that emphasizes well-being, agency, and fulfillment in humanistic work is essential, not only for the immediate goal of supporting students but also for the long-term hope of creating a sustainable profession. Today, about forty percent of doctoral students in the United States report moderate-to-severe depression, anxiety, or both (Flaherty). This speaks to a structural problem, and indeed, there are visible conditions that institutionalize the baked-in misery we mention above. There is the material deprivation of stipends that rarely offer a living wage, much less a household income. There is also a level of institutionalized neglect and, sometimes, abuse of power that leads to extreme vulnerabilities: unrealistic workloads, very little guidance and support, and, at the end, an uncertain and precarious future.

Certainly, some of these material conditions may feel beyond departmental control. But beyond the issue of subsistence, we contend that basic well-being is a necessary precursor to genuine creativity and innovation. The academic humanities have long fostered a culture of scarcity and threat ("publish or perish"). They have leaned too heavily on fear and insecurity as the primary motivators for productivity. This is where departments have immense control: faculty members can encourage student success in a number of ways. We can choose to create communities of practice that are either supportive or neglectful, inclusive or competitive, risk-averse or curious, hierarchical or empathetic. If faculty and administrators commit to advising and mentorship practices that deliberately promote creativity, collaboration, exploration, and holistic approaches to education, this will lead to more joy overall in graduate education as well as better student outcomes.

In part 3, we seek to amplify and center the spaces and structures that can foster well-being in and after graduate study. The essays in this part all make the case for joy in their own ways. A number of recurring themes emerge from these essays: the role of the body and physicality in graduate education; mental health; the importance of relationships, race, and gender; and the role of critique in an affirmative practice of the humanities.

The first essay interrogates the role of mental health in graduate education and advocates for a stronger attention to students' well-being. Katina L. Rogers, in "Cultivating a Joyful Workplace through Trust, Support, and a Shared Mission," focuses on the Futures Initiative, the center that Rogers coadministered with graduate fellows at the Graduate Center, City University of New York. Rogers underscores the relationship between sustainability and joy: "The ability to push through unsupportive environments is not what a PhD is designed to measure, but battling obstacles wholly unrelated to a student's intelligence, creativity, or research skills can push that student to the breaking point and prevent them from reaching their goal." Conversely, Rogers goes on to say, "Changing the structures that erode mental health for members of the university community is difficult but worthwhile and creates the possibility of sustaining scholars and enabling them to do their best work." Rogers treats her experiences with the Futures Initiative as a case study that allows her to imagine ways departments might adopt similar practices to help sustain their students and their doctoral programs.

The next two essays reflect on the role of joy in the humanities and examine how joy is found in both academic and professional pursuits. In his essay, "The Agony and Ecstasy of Literary Study at the Graduate Level," Donald Moores considers the discipline of literary studies itself and the reasons joy is considered a problem at all. "The problem of joy in literary studies, then," Moores writes, "is not that it is an emotion but rather that it is an affect not in keeping with the emotional atmosphere, or the collective mood, that informs the discipline." The reasons for this, Moores continues, are rooted in the hermeneutics of suspicion that grew out of critical theory in the 1970s and 1980s to become the dominant paradigm in literary studies. However, Moores suggests, this is now changing; we are seeing a return to joy, which opens the door to a more affirmative spirit in graduate education and literary studies more broadly.

Then, in "Finding Joy in the Graduate Internship," John Lennon takes on a topic of increasing importance from a perspective that differs from some of the others presented in this volume; he mourns the loss of a type of graduate education that allowed students to "read books, argue politics, and hang out with smart, passionate people interested in doing the same" without much thought about careers or life after graduate school. But he acknowledges that that world does not exist for his students and that under current circumstances, internships "can be a tool for entrepreneurial students" to pair "the creativity of a humanities graduate experience with the practical experience of a job in a different field to create unforged new paths." Lennon sets out to reclaim terms such as "creative" and "entrepreneurial" for graduate students. For him, "The goal of the internship is to find joy outside the academy, tapping into the desires that bring students to graduate school in the first place." In helping students who are willing to make this leap for themselves, Lennon increases the sustainability of graduate education overall, ensuring that future generations of students will continue to read, argue, and hang out.

Joy and well-being are fundamentally embodied experiences, and the following two essays grapple with the fraught legacy of mind-body dualism in the professional culture of our field. In "Bodies of Knowledge: Toward an Embodied Humanistic Practice," Manoah Avram Finston begins with a discussion of academia's famed "two-body problem"—that is, the plight of those scholars in committed relationships with other scholars, who must either find not one but two suitable positions in a geographic area or else live apart for an ill-defined length of time. He states provocatively that "the profession is not so much afflicted by a two-body problem as by a one-body problem—or, more bluntly, a having-a-body-at-all problem. . . . With its relentless focus on the life of the mind—as a lifestyle, a means to an end, and a series of interwoven professional and personal expectations—does the academy know how to adequately respond to the needs of actual bodies?" The answer to Finston's rhetorical question is *no*—somewhat ironically, he points out, given how interested in "the body" humanistic research often is: "Bodies, it seems, can stand as fascinating objects of inquiry, provided that they belong to someone else. When confronted with the stubborn demands and sheer material facts of a student's own body, however, the profession is largely, confoundingly silent."

The subsequent essay, "Humanities under Quarantine: A Reflection on Isolation and Connectivity in Graduate Education," by Yevgenya Strakovsky, draws on experiences of the COVID-19 pandemic to reexamine the role of the body in the humanities. Like Finston, Strakovsky calls out the humanities' strained relationship with physicality: "Despite a long history of grappling with the most profound of human emotions and experiences, the humanities as a profession—particularly in traditional graduate education—has a meager relationship to closeness in its real-world forms: physical proximity, teamwork, and intimacy." As the administrator for a graduate program that was specifically designed to counter this "meager relationship" in myriad ways, Strakovsky writes about the challenges—and opportunities—engendered by the pandemic. This leads her to "reexamine the role of physical closeness in the humanities, particularly in our traditional approaches to graduate education," rooted as they are in Cartesian dualism and the denial of the body as articulated by Finston.

Part 3 ends with two essays that look at joy as an issue of equity, justice, and sociality. In "Joy and the Politics of the Public Good," Stacy M. Hartman and Bianca C. Williams reflect upon the nature of the work they have undertaken together in the PublicsLab at the Graduate Center, City University of New York. The PublicsLab's mission is to support doctoral students and faculty members in creating scholarship "for the public good"—and yet "the public good" as a phrase elides more than it reveals: "'[T]he public good' as a phrase hides the fact that so much of what we do in the PublicsLab is about addressing systems of power. Work that addresses systems of power is not politically neutral. It is justice work, and it is deeply, unapologetically political." Drawing on Sara Ahmed's work on diversity, equity, and inclusion, as well as Stefano Harney and Fred Moten's concept of the undercommons, Hartman and Williams use their essay to publicly re-envision and rewrite the mission statement of the PublicsLab to more accurately reflect a commitment to doctoral education that is joyful, just, generous, and equitable.

The final word in the volume belongs to six current graduate students. In "Radical Collegiality and Joy in Graduate Education," Paul W. Burch, Brooke Clark, Sonia Del Hierro, Meredith McCullough, Kelly McKisson, and S. J. Stout of the Rice University English department "argue for a form of relationality that has the potential to reimagine graduate student well-being." As graduate students, Burch, Clark, Del Hierro, McCullough, McKisson, and Stout are able to imagine possibilities that may seem foreclosed to those who are already embedded in the system. "[O]urs is an argument for necessarily precarious joy," they write, "embracing a radical collegiality that we propose would open possibilities for the future of graduate education in the humanities." Although it is not dismissive of the work that has already been done, this final essay is determinedly and necessarily forward-thinking, looking toward the future of humanities graduate education and inviting the reader to coimagine and cocreate such a future together.

The final essay drives home a point that is made implicitly by the other essays in this part: If humanities graduate education is to have a future, it must be one that embraces joy. In imagining this future and working toward it together, we can create an affirmative vision for the humanities. In this vision, the humanities encompass critique but make room for other ways of reading. They acknowledge the body as essential to humanistic inquiry and incorporate wellness of all kinds. They speak truth to power and prioritize equity and justice. This is a vision of the humanities for the twenty-first century.

WORK CITED

Flaherty, Colleen. "New Study Says Graduate Students' Mental Health Is a 'Crisis.'" *Inside Higher Ed*, 6 Mar. 2018, insidehighered.com/news/2018/03/06/new-study-says-graduate-students-mental-health-crisis.

Cultivating a Joyful Workplace through Trust, Support, and a Shared Mission

Katina L. Rogers

A two-hour weekly meeting sounds like a chore. And yet, week after week, through all seven years of my work with the Futures Initiative, our team would walk (or click) out of our weekly meetings feeling a little more grounded, a little more joyful, and a little more connected than when we had entered two hours earlier. Gathering weekly was the glue that connected our team; the time we set aside gave us time to work, to connect, to get to know one another, and to support one another.

The Futures Initiative team works hard. During my tenure there, the weekly meetings for this program based at the Graduate Center, City University of New York (CUNY), included a sometimes daunting agenda, yet the various responsibilities on it became a source of sustenance for all involved. This sustenance was especially important since March 2020, when COVID-19 first tore through New York City and then the nation. While the Futures Initiative may be unique in many respects, it includes elements that could be applied to any graduate education context—whether in a department, a workplace, or an extracurricular group. These translatable elements include *trust, material support,* and a *shared mission*. I am convinced that every program can take steps to grow in these areas and thereby make a significant difference in the well-being of their students, the members of their faculty, and the members of their staff.

For many graduate students on the Futures Initiative team, these elements of support and the resulting joy of this community were a welcome counterbalance to the toll of graduate school, which—in its current manifestation—causes many students to experience significant emotional, psychological, and physical challenges that have nothing to do with their studies. For each moment of inspiration as a student works toward their degree, there may be dozens of moments of demoralization, too often building to severe anxiety and depression. Inadequate funding leaves many students and scholars reliant on food stamps and unable to afford health insurance. Anxiety and depression produce physical manifestations, decreasing health and making it all the more challenging for people to persist in their chosen pathways. The first years of professorship are little better: pressures increase while support from mentors and peers vanishes.

For scholars who are women, are people of color, have disabilities, identify as LGBTQ+, or identify with other groups underrepresented in the academy, the burden on mental and physical health can be particularly heavy, leading many to opt out before having a chance to truly shine. The ability to push through unsupportive environments is not what a PhD is designed to measure, but battling obstacles wholly unrelated to a student's intelligence, creativity, or research skills can push that student to the breaking point and prevent them from reaching their goal.

Suffering should not be a prerequisite to entering "the profession," and yet it is commonly accepted as the way things are through every layer of academia, leaving difficult navigation work to students who often feel unequipped for it. As Melissa Phruksachart asks, "[I]n light of these non-life-sustaining conditions, what would it take, and what would it look like, for minoritized subjects like women and queers of color to flourish in the academy?" (117). For Phruksachart, mentorship and the development of intentional community were key to weathering the depleting environment of graduate school and its unequal power dynamics. Changing the structures that erode mental health for members of the university community is difficult but worthwhile and creates the possibility of sustaining scholars and enabling them to do their best work.

This essay considers the Futures Initiative, located at CUNY's Graduate Center, as a model of how a program can better support the varied needs of its students, faculty, and staff. The Futures Initiative has built a supportive network of students and faculty members who also generate highly creative teaching, research, and programming. The program accomplished this by using collaborative methods, by fostering communities of practice that include faculty and staff members as well as graduate students, and by acknowledging and providing for participants' physical and human needs whenever possible. This is how our business meetings—which featured collaborative, participatory agenda setting and other practices that ensured all voices were heard—became a joy and a source of energy rather than a chore. Although the program is unique to a particular institution and context, the Futures Initiative's structures and practices can serve as models for other programs wishing to create lasting change.

A major challenge in creating holistic and sustaining programs is that higher education operates on an economy of prestige. In this economy, the so-called life of the mind takes center stage, leaving little room for attention to physical and emotional well-being. A different orientation— one that prioritizes people over prestige—is essential to creating supportive and sustainable structures. This shift in orientation is central to my argument and proposed models for graduate education in *Putting the Humanities PhD to Work*, and it is at the heart of the Futures Initiative. For instance, as a program, we focus partly on innovation, as do many digital humanities and digitally oriented centers and institutes. For the Futures Initiative, though, innovation alone is insufficient; to be meaningful, new technologies or methodologies must be used in service of equity in higher education, a positioning that upends the question of prestige and the usual gloss of educational technology to instead center equity and the public good. We strive to create an organizational structure that embodies this goal as well—in our meetings as elsewhere.

During my time as codirector of this program (together with Cathy N. Davidson, the founding director), I saw that giving people the space to work differently produced inspiring results. The undergraduates, graduate students, and faculty members who worked with the Futures Initiative did so outside the structures of their departments. They had freedom to explore ways that their work and ideas connect with other disciplines and to consider how to apply those ideas to big societal questions. Graduate students in the program ran a series called *The University Worth Fighting For* that tackled a wide range of issues related to higher education and gave students a way to think expansively about their work and how it can have an impact in the world. The program also incorporated a number of peer and near-peer mentoring relationships so that people were constantly teaching and learning from one another, formally and informally.

Programs in interstitial spaces often have greater flexibility than those with long-standing institutional mandates. The challenge, then, is how to build lasting change by incorporating similar methods into academic departments, where students and faculty members put down intellectual and professional roots. I do not pretend to be able to answer that question, but using the Futures Initiative as a case study, I will explore why it is so challenging for similarly structured programs to exist within academic departments. The case study focuses specifically on graduate students, but the matters of climate and support are also crucial to faculty and staff members, who face very similar emotional, psychological, and physical challenges. I then offer suggestions for reform and argue for their value to individuals, the quality of scholarship and teaching, and the public good.

Case Study: Futures Initiative Graduate Fellows

Graduate fellows are at the core of the Futures Initiative's structure. Each year, the program selects a cohort of doctoral students for specific roles. They work together as a team while also having distinct areas of responsibility, such as web development, communications, program management, and more. Fellows are typically doctoral students working in humanities and social sciences fields, such as English, sociology, psychology, geography, anthropology, linguistics, theater, and others. They are selected through a comprehensive process including applications, recommendations, and interviews. Current fellows are invited to participate in certain aspects of the selection process (being mindful of the challenges involved in peer evaluation), thus gaining a valuable opportunity to participate in a search process on the selection side. In selecting new fellows, we are especially attentive to how different skills, backgrounds, and personalities in the group will complement each other.

Once a cohort is in place, the fundamental starting point for our work together is a recognition that we, as humans, bring many things into the room—not only knowledge and skills but also anxieties, hardships, pain that, whether or not they are related to our studies, inevitably affect our approach and our presence. The leadership team invites group members to bring their whole selves into the meeting. We would do this not only by saying so but also by structuring meetings accordingly, typically using one hour for project-oriented agenda items and one hour for more free-form discussion on matters of importance to the graduate fellows. The discussion topics might include general aspects of doctoral work—navigating Institutional Review Board processes, developing strategies for time management and dissertation writing, addressing job search concerns, and so on. Or someone might request feedback on a specific piece of their work—a presentation or conference proposal, perhaps. Or the discussion might be a broader personal check-in. We would rotate the responsibility of meeting leadership, so each person has an opportunity to develop a meeting structure and discussion topic. In 2020–21, because the realities of the COVID pandemic meant an endless parade of *Zoom* meetings, sometimes fatigue would set in; in these moments, we supported one another by shortening our meeting time or shifting to quiet coworking in one another's company (something the team came to call the "*Zoom* café"). In short, adaptability and listening for cues were key.

Even the business-focused part of the meeting centers the students' voices and concerns. We would typically develop our agendas collaboratively during the first few minutes of the meeting.[1] Rather than rote status updates, the meetings focused on the key concerns and sticking points that are on people's minds, ensuring that our time together is maximally useful. Group meetings were complemented by one-on-one or small-group meetings with me, where details can be addressed as needed. Through this structure, we modeled a kind of academic leadership that did not try to exert control but instead recognized that our program's strength is in its people. The graduate fellows developed strong leadership, administrative, and project management skills—sometimes without realizing it.

The fellows run the bulk of the program; their role is akin to an internship in academic administration combined with a supportive peer mentoring cohort. They learn a tremendous amount about academic leadership, professional norms and expectations, and general workplace skills through their involvement in the program. Some of these skills include meeting leadership, collaborative project management, prioritization, time management, and creative workarounds and problem solving. Perhaps more importantly, they learn essential information about academic administration and structures that is often invisible to students. Underlying all this, they learn how to support one another and ask for help. All these skills prepare them for career pathways both within and beyond the classroom.

By making space and time in meetings for student concerns and distributed leadership, we brought many tacit elements of graduate school—the "hidden agenda" that can be especially tricky for first-generation and underrepresented students—into the light. We helped students realize that their experience can really benefit their peers and that norms across departments can vary widely. Most importantly, we built a trusting environment so that everyone was able to voice opinions, concerns, questions, and so on, without the oppressive performance anxiety that imbues many graduate seminars. Past fellows have taken to baking for one another, supporting teammates running the New York City Marathon, grieving loss, and celebrating success—and even coined the hashtags #TuesdaysTogether and #FellowsBackstage in order to share their experiences more broadly.

Creating this kind of environment also requires material and social resources. For graduate students working as fellows in the program, the Futures Initiative offered the maximum material support that is institutionally possible, flexible work arrangements, and space for reflection. We used student-centered and collaborative methods to cultivate a trusting and supportive community of students, faculty members, and staff members. In the undergraduate programs that we supported, we went one step further and, when possible, offered stipends, meals, and Metro-Cards to make it easier for students to take time off work, arrange for a babysitter, and make the trip to midtown Manhattan for in-person meetings. For faculty members involved in our program, we offered research funds—not common for most CUNY faculty—as well as an interdisciplinary cohort of peers who could provide mentorship and community. At each of these levels, we maintained high standards for the quality of research, programming, and other work generated through the program. Students, faculty members, and staff members worked hard in support of a clear mission.

Ours was not a perfect program. Joy does not necessarily mean happiness or even ease. As individuals and as a program we went through challenging periods and times of stress. There were tensions, both professional and personal. The graduate fellows pushed our group to advance our thinking and live our mission, and sometimes those efforts revealed blind spots that were painful to discover. We received our share of bad news—grant rejections, challenging critiques, difficult personal news. I sometimes cried in meetings. But because we invested significant time and energy in building trust with one another, we were able to weather these challenges and support one another. To me, joy was an undercurrent that persisted in spite of these ups and downs. Because we built up trust and community with one another, we could see the joy of the program even during moments of tension or grief.

Speaking personally, my tenure at the Graduate Center coincided with new parenthood; I started my position when my daughter was about six months old and had a second baby about three years into my work. When I returned from parental leave after giving birth to my younger child, I was dealing with postpartum depression. In addition to the support I received from my colleagues, it was astonishing and humbling to see the ways in which the students I had worked so hard to support stepped in to support me during my own difficult time. As I gained experience as a parent, I also grew in my leadership. I have no doubt that the two were related; navigating a new and complicated phase of life while also guiding and working alongside a group of colleagues—many of whom were also facing major life decisions—helped me develop a sense of perspective that I did not have earlier in my career. The support of our team was crucial in that evolution.

As I write this, I am preparing for a new transition, in which I will carry ideas and structures from our work at the Futures Initiative to institutions nationwide as an educational consultant. By taking this step, my goal is to help programs everywhere better support their students, their faculty, and their staff by designing and implementing creative, sustainable, and equitable structures. This is a significant step for me—one that represents a great deal of growth over the past decade. That our program creates space to foster such growth is essential—not just for me but for everyone in our program, from undergraduates to senior faculty members. As I have developed my own leadership skills, I have also helped the Futures Initiative graduate fellows see the spark of leadership in their own work—the ways in which their accomplishments are extraordinary, their paths meaningful, their voices powerful. Graduate fellows have a high level of responsibility, visibility, and ownership of nearly all aspects of the Futures Initiative's work, which involves both risk and reward. At the same time, they have safety nets and support so that they do not feel overly vulnerable. As the program's codirectors, Cathy Davidson and I scaffolded the students' leadership with the program in much the same way that a faculty member would scaffold learning in a course.

One fellow described the team collectively as being "like a therapist, academic adviser, relative, and life and work coach all at once." While our work was not therapy—and we actively and frequently encouraged students to seek mental health support from trained professionals—the sentiment is indicative of how hungry many graduate students are for a feeling of support and community. Overall, the program pulls back the curtain to reveal tacit knowledge about how a university works and offers strategies that prove helpful as students work toward achieving their goals. At the same time, the leadership team constantly works to make that tacit knowledge explicit so that fellows reflect on and realize how much they're learning and why their work and perspectives matter.

Finding Joy within an Economy of Prestige

The Futures Initiative has the advantage of being a flexible program that is neither an academic program nor a student services center. That institutional context made it possible to shift priorities relatively fluidly according to what we perceive as the needs of our participants. In many cases, the most robust support for students and emerging scholars is growing from interstitial spaces like the Futures Initiative.

One question we hear from our own students and faculty is, How can similar systems and methods be incorporated into academic departments? It is a difficult question; while elements of what we did at the Futures Initiative can absolutely be used in both academic and extra- or cocurricular programs, other elements may simply not be possible in a core academic department. Academic departments tend to be competitive spaces, with a limited amount of resources that are unevenly distributed. This is fundamentally different from a space like the Futures Initiative. There was no weeding out or formal evaluation, as we were not gatekeepers to degrees or careers. Students were not vying for resources or faculty time, nor were they jockeying for position. Perhaps the inherently competitive and evaluative nature of academic programs means that work like that of the Futures Initiative can only exist in interstitial spaces.

The question of the role that evaluation plays in creating a program of this nature relates to the overarching question of prestige—one of the most fundamental (and underdiscussed) issues in thinking about the future of the university. The prestige economy of higher education acts as a tacit undercurrent that propels and silently shapes both personal and structural decisions. From selecting a research topic to student and faculty recruitment to broader questions of institutional investment in particular programs or fields, there is nearly always an awareness of how such decisions will affect the relative prestige of the scholar, department, or university. The dominance of prestige is certainly at play in faculty life as well—for instance, in the tenure and promotion process. All this is understood as part of "the way things are" and may seem impossible to change. But because the pursuit and glorification of prestige have a deep impact on the way scholars work, all who are invested in higher education must be willing to look directly at the role of prestige in academia and to think critically about what constitutes scholarly or academic success. Until academics are able to think more expansively about that, it will be very difficult to make headway on meaningful reform efforts, whether those efforts are centered on diversity and inclusion, labor issues, reinvesting in teaching, broader career pathways, or anything else.

The university largely operates within a scarcity model, with limited resources (financial, intellectual, social) and a keen awareness of that limitation. That scarcity is often used as a motivating factor to urge students to work harder in order to secure more resources for themselves. Students competing for travel grants, an adviser's time, or other essential but limited resources may not see generosity as a safe posture. As Kathleen Fitzpatrick explores in *Generous Thinking*, institutional reward structures are not set up to support generosity. The kind of scholarship that is formally recognized and celebrated tends to be individual rather than community-oriented, reinforcing the model of scarcity and competition. This also makes it difficult to take risks, since outcomes that appear to be failures—an experiment that yields a negative result, a risky article that is not published in a peer-reviewed journal, a new teaching method that does not work as well as hoped, an unsuccessful grant proposal—are not eligible for formal recognition of any kind. In this model, it only makes sense for scholars to take on projects that are very likely to succeed in ways that have been traditionally accepted.

Typical modes of working and of assessing scholarly success revolve around what is valued as prestigious. This includes a pronounced dominance of research at the expense of teaching, service, leadership, and even collaborative projects (at least in the humanities). Teaching is undersupported, and faculty members may rely on course releases to accomplish the work that is valued for tenure and promotion, creating an educational system in which *not teaching* is seen as a reward. Service is totally undervalued, and people (usually women, and especially women of color) who take on higher service loads may be implicitly (or even explicitly) penalized for not making enough "progress" on the kinds of work that are formally rewarded. This devaluation occurs because teaching and service are often not incentivized within prestige economies, contributing to an increased reliance on adjunct faculty members who are not adequately supported or compensated for their work. The ways that teaching, research, and service can be mutually beneficial are largely erased as faculty members scramble to do more with less support. As long as prestige is the dominant currency in higher education, real change is very difficult.

Broadening the sense of what matters must include a critical consideration of the academy's formal structures of evaluation (promotion, tenure, admissions). This structural component is essential in order to make it possible for people to work creatively and thoughtfully. Otherwise, the status quo will continue to perpetuate investment in a conservative understanding of success that hinges on a very traditional prestige framework. This leads to training students to succeed in the same ways as their predecessors, and generally repeating what has come before, in a professionalization process that is reproductive rather than generative.

Changing the Paradigm

Opportunities like those afforded by the Futures Initiative are rare in academe—but they don't have to be. The collaborative nature of the program has proven to be intellectually generative and has sparked new scholarly insights. Graduate fellows in the program say they were waiting for this kind of opportunity; they find that it brings their work to life in a new way. This, to me, suggests there is an alternative to the more dominant, prestige-oriented model of graduate education. I look to Fitzpatrick's exhortation in *Generous Thinking* to replace the default scholarly position of competition with one of generosity. I look to bell hooks's earlier recognition in *Teaching Community* that "[e]ducating is always a vocation rooted in hopefulness" (xiv). Hope and joy are not a way of sugarcoating reality; on the contrary, hope is at its most powerful when the circumstances seem bleak. I think of Toni Cade Bambara's reflection on what she perceived as her responsibility: "As a culture worker who belongs to an oppressed people my job is to make revolution irresistible" (35). To extend Bambara's framework for arts and culture, I would argue that the beauty, joy, and hope of education are predicated on the possibility of change. To go a step further, perhaps graduate education can be a source of joy if it is also a lever of social justice.

As these examples suggest, generosity, abundance, hope, and joy can form a foundation on which our educational principles are grounded. Feminist scholarship by Black women, Indigenous women, and other women of color offers especially rich perspectives on the praxis of hope and joy, even (and especially) in difficult times. Scholarly work is all about creating new knowledge, new ways of being, new possibilities. Such goals could establish a mindset of curiosity and abundance, but higher education has come to be dominated by a sense of scarcity and competition. And yet a sense of scarcity is necessary to the university's value when that value is predicated on prestige. Shifting from a prestige-oriented system to one that is fundamentally rooted in abundance and generosity would require a massive change not only in values but also in the structures that have been developed on the basis of those values.

Such a shift is not impossible. It already happens at the program level, at least in certain extracurricular programs. Generosity and collaboration certainly animate the Futures Initiative, where students, faculty members, and staff members build on and support one another's work with enthusiasm. Working in this way reminds our group that scholarship is not a zero-sum game; one student's brilliant dissertation in no way diminishes a peer's. However, the fact remains that programs like ours are not part of higher education's gatekeeping mechanisms. Our fellowship selection process was competitive, but we did not evaluate our fellows' dissertations or teaching. We did not decide on tenure cases or perform other types of scholarly assessment. While our work was not easy, it was nonetheless easier than trying to implement new admissions criteria, curricula, or tenure requirements. Reform that gets to the heart of the question of prestige is nearly always met with resistance. If we want to imagine and create graduate programs that enable students to work with joy, it is critical to examine and challenge that underlying value structure of prestige.

Even considering the pervasiveness of higher education's prestige economy, there are ideas from the Futures Initiative's playbook that departments and individuals can adopt right now to help foster joy and stability among graduate students. Taking the first step away from a model of graduate education that replicates itself means considering *why* we do our work. For instance, a more holistic and grounded educational value structure might celebrate creative and critical thinking, versatility, meaningful teaching, many sources of knowledge, and connection with communities both within and beyond the university. Such a system would not need to turn away from complexity, rigor, or methodological expertise—but it would likely result in a much broader array of scholarly work while also working against the current model of scarcity and competition.

How can we help bring academia to a place where joy is a value that is supported structurally? Part of the answer involves material support for the full range of scholarly work (not just prestigious research), and part involves a fundamental shift in priorities. I think we see a glimpse into this through the Futures Initiative, but I would challenge all who are invested in higher education to think about how we can bring joy from the margins into the core of universities.

Working toward a new framework of abundance and joy also means developing and supporting fully inclusive, accessible, welcoming institutions. That is difficult, slow work and involves many interrelated reform efforts in order to fully support students and faculty members. Several recommendations follow:

> *Reinvest in teaching.* Advocate for a shift away from exploitative adjunct labor and toward well-resourced full-time positions. In addition to material support, consider ways your program might support faculty members' intellectual, emotional, and professional needs by providing opportunities for peer observation, working groups, support for experimental methods, and more.
>
> *Strengthen academic labor structures.* If you are part of a union, get involved. Examine policies that may have unintended consequences for students, faculty members, or staff members. If you can't change anything within your program, consider advocating at the level of the university or even more broadly.
>
> *Foster and celebrate work that has a significant public impact.* Revise formal reward structures (such as tenure and promotion guidelines) so that scholars whose work reaches a broad audience receive credit for that work. Share and celebrate colleagues' projects.
>
> *Examine and reimagine unstated expectations.* Consider hiring and recruitment practices and tacit assumptions about success and merit. Work toward bringing people into the field in new ways—for instance, by explicitly considering public impact and diversity in the admissions process. Most importantly, develop structural ways to meaningfully support that work so that students and faculty members on the leading edge do not feel isolated.
>
> *Support students and faculty members through mentorship— especially peer mentorship.* Develop formal and informal networks that make it possible for individuals to learn and grow by supporting one another through writing groups, syllabus sharing, peer observation, or other modes of mentorship.
>
> *Offer material and social support for all students, faculty members, and staff members, including benefits such as health insurance.* Provide food at meetings when possible. Talk about other commitments, like child care or elder care, that may be silent stressors in people's lives. Ask people how they are doing and allow their answers to be a factor in how you approach setting goals and timelines.

These are major, fundamental issues, and on some days the idea of tackling such reform seems frankly impossible. On other days, I see glimmers of hope through the efforts of individuals and programs that aim to operate differently. It will undoubtedly be slow work, but it is work that can begin even in small steps.

Reimagining scholarly structures can begin simultaneously in grassroots and top-down ways, and the Futures Initiative offers one possible model of what that can look like in practice. When students and recent graduates take steps toward their own professional fulfillment, and when prospective students increasingly seek programs that foster not only depth but breadth of thinking, programs have a stronger impetus to adopt new approaches and structures. And when students entering new programs are immediately encouraged to attend not only to academic rigor but to application, engagement, accessibility, relevance, and translation as well, their work will take on tremendous potential for impact beyond the academy. When scholars are seen first as humans—with lives, bodies, needs, and emotions—trust and collaboration can naturally grow together with research and teaching. Perhaps in such conditions, joy within the academy may become a delightful and sustaining possibility.

NOTE

1. For more details about this process, see the description by the Futures Initiative fellow Christina Katopodis in Jones.

WORKS CITED

Bambara, Toni Cade. "An Interview with Toni Cade Bambara." Conducted by Kay Bonetti. *Conversations with Toni Cade Bambara*, edited by Thabiti Lewis, UP of Mississippi, 2012, pp. 30–48.

Fitzpatrick, Kathleen. *Generous Thinking: A Radical Approach to Saving the University*. Johns Hopkins UP, 2019.

hooks, bell. *Teaching Community: A Pedagogy of Hope*. Routledge, 2003.

Jones, Jason B. "Better Meetings through Pedagogy." *The Chronicle of Higher Education Blogs: ProfHacker*, 24 May 2018, chronicle.com/blogs/profhacker/better-meetings-through-pedagogy/65545.

Phruksachart, Melissa. "On Mentoring Future Faculty of Color." *Feminist Teacher*, vol. 27, no. 2, 2017, pp. 117–32.

Rogers, Katina. *Putting the Humanities PhD to Work: Thriving in and beyond the Classroom*. Duke UP, 2020.

The Agony and the Ecstasy of Literary Study at the Graduate Level

Donald Moores

> "O the joy of my spirit—it is uncaged—it darts like lightning!"
> —Walt Whitman, "A Song of Joys"

In a recent article on *The Innocent Traveller*, a novel by the Canadian author Ethel Wilson, Misao Dean makes a statement that many beginning graduate students of literature might find rather curious:

> Braz and Sedgwick give me the license to say that I love Wilson's writing; I love her description of the British Columbian landscape and her wisely aphoristic statements about community, about death and the passage of time, but also I am simply in awe of her sentences—their rhythm, their balance, their variety, and their sound. Wilson's sentences please me, for they call up an involuntary laugh, demand to be said over and over, to be felt on the pulses and sung through the veins. (66–67)

Why, one might wonder, does a literary scholar need "license" to say that she loves a writer and finds herself awed by that author's sentences because their wisdom brings her great pleasure and because they continue to resonate in her imagination after she reads them? What is wrong, students might further ask, with being made joyful by art? Why does Dean seem almost apologetic about her joy when aesthetic pleasure has long been considered one of the primary end points of engaging in artistic appreciation? Why is joy a problem, an embarrassment, for serious scholars at the graduate and professional levels of literary studies? The answers to these questions are the subject of this brief essay, and it is impossible to respond specifically to them here other than to say that joy, both as a subject of and a response to sophisticated texts, is a knotty problem in the various disciplines of literary study at the graduate level and beyond. And yet recent critical developments have made discussions of joy once again possible, opening pathways previously stymied by tacit ideas and assumptions about this important emotion. Joy is on the rebound in the humanities.

Dean's curious statement, in effect, serves as a barometer of the discipline's mood, indicating the problematic reception joy has received in much critical discourse. Academic disciplines, despite the long-standing Western tradition of so-called dispassionate reasoning and its myth of objectivity, have underlying moods and are characterized by tacit emotional states. Where there are humans, there are limbic systems and inevitable emotional responses. In his insightful book *The Vehement Passions*, Philip Fisher compellingly shows that such emotions, while marginalized and even repressed in Western culture, nonetheless play a pivotal role in critical thinking, informing our decisions, judgments, values, beliefs, and "objective" analyses. And Fisher's claims are independently supported by neurology: people who suffer damage to the orbitofrontal cortex, the part of the brain responsible for bringing emotions into conscious awareness, have an extremely difficult time making decisions because they do not know how they feel about them in their thought processes (Haidt 12). Such individuals can see a myriad of possibilities but lack the emotional guidance necessary to determine which is the most preferable choice. The problem of joy in literary studies, then, is not that it is an emotion but rather that it is an affect not in keeping with the emotional atmosphere, or the collective mood, that informs the discipline.

The problematic reception of joy in literary studies is itself problematic, since there is an enormous, global tradition of celebrated, serious writers whose subject is joy itself. Because I offer a representation of this corpus in two anthologies—*Wild Poets of Ecstasy: An Anthology of Ecstatic Verse* and *On Human Flourishing: A Poetry Anthology*—I refer the reader to those works for a better understanding of how central joy is to many of the most important writers not only across the globe but across time. Suffice it to say here that joy is a common subject, sometimes even a preoccupation, among the best writers in the history of literature. For all its centrality in the literary tradition, however, the emotion often meets with a less than joyous response in critical studies. For instance, Emily Dickinson's poems about joy, which amount to a sizable percentage of her oeuvre, were completely overlooked by modernist-era critics who saw not the hundreds of lyrics she wrote about glee, rapture, delight, happiness, ecstasy, and other lexical cousins of joy but only "the half-understood, the obscure, and the chaotic everywhere in her poems" (Wilson 401). Even today, barring a few exceptions, Dickinson is often misrepresented in anthologies suggesting that she merely broods on death in morbid verse. Rabindranath Tagore, the first non-Westerner to win the Nobel Prize in Literature, has received a similar reception in some quarters. Although Tagore's verse is a paean to joy, especially his English volume *Gitanjali*, which served as a tipping point for the Nobel Committee, early detractors sometimes faulted his treatment of the subject as being "preposterously optimistic," as Thomas Sturgis Moore did when he first heard the poet read (qtd. in Dutta and Robinson 170). Such ideas persist. While contemporary scholars do not find fault with Tagore on aesthetic grounds, they often do argue that his enthusiastic endorsement of joy, which he called *ananda*, the Sanskrit term for bliss, is an example of how he "often lived happily beyond the bounds of common sense" (Haq 28). Such views are not only reductive but miss the mark if one is attempting to analyze a centrality in the poetics and aesthetics of the legions of writers who write affirmatively and enthusiastically about joy.

What is more, a sizable body of recent research attests to the psychological importance and value of joy and other positive emotions such as gratitude, love, hilarity, elevation, awe, wonder, inspiration, and the like. The field of positive psychology, catalyzed by Martin Seligman's tenure as president of the American Psychological Association in 1998 and the work of several other influential psychologists, has in the last twenty years generated a mountain of studies that attest to the extreme importance of positive emotion in human life (for an overview, see Peterson). One of the tipping points in Seligman's own positive transformation from a researcher who administered electroshocks to dogs in order to study learned helplessness to one of learned optimism and other sunnier subjects was the pioneering work of Barbara Fredrickson, a fellow research psychologist at the University of North Carolina, Chapel Hill, who has compellingly debunked antiquated ideas about the triviality of positive emotion. Whereas researchers previously saw positive affect as a mere epiphenomenon, or a useless secondary effect, Fredrickson clearly showed its value as a causal agent that plays a significant role in human well-being. Differing from negative emotions, which prompt an immediate response—fear makes us run; anger makes us fight; disgust makes us spit, etc.—positive emotions such as joy generally exert their benefits downstream. Such affects, according to Fredrickson, serve to "broaden our abiding intellectual, physical, and social resources" and help to build up "reserves we can draw upon when a threat or opportunity presents itself" (146). Joy and other positive emotions effectively counterbalance the harmful effects of negative emotions; they serve as healthy, mature defenses against unhappiness and the potentially hazardous internalization of the world's many sorrows; and they also function as a creative resource that broadens our perspectives and builds our emotional repertoires. According to this broaden-and-build perspective, experiencing joy and other positive emotions is inherently valuable because to do so makes us more complex, resilient beings.

Yet graduate students in literary studies quickly learn that one needs something of a license, as the quotation from Dean's essay shows, to be made joyous by reading a literary text. Of course, there is really no such license, and scholarly inquiry and the affective responses it provokes should (in theory at least) have no bounds whatsoever. Academic research in the humanities should enable scholars to explore all aspects of human life and all forms of affect, from misery to ecstasy and everything in between. But in literary studies, joy is too often dismissed as a light and thus unworthy subject, or it is reduced to a symptom of political oppression, or it is pathologized as an indicator of psychological disease. Because graduate programs are informed by such a critical orientation toward joy and other positive emotions, they typically do not offer courses on ecstatic lyric poetry or the literature of happiness. In graduate school there are also barriers to waxing rhapsodic over an exquisite image in a poem as the character John Keating does in the film *Dead Poets Society*. The kind of affirmative response to literature that Keating's ideas represent—he clearly loves literature and is profoundly stirred by its power and beauty, exhibiting a joyful response he tries to inspire in his students—is precisely what Dean is slightly embarrassed about but feeling licensed to express in her reading of Wilson's novel. Encouraging students to stand on desks in graduate school might get a professor fired (also the fate of Keating in *Dead Poets*).

Where does such a position originate in literary studies? The impressive rise of critical theory in the early seventies is the most immediate source. Critical theory carried with it a smorgasbord of sophisticated reading strategies that opened productive discussions not possible in the aesthetically focused discourse of New Criticism, leading to such groundbreaking theoretical approaches as deconstruction, postcolonial studies, feminist theory, gender studies, and new historicism. But all this impressive rigor also carried with it new forms of interpretation known collectively as "critique," the key elements of which, according to Rita Felski, include "a spirit of skeptical questioning or outright condemnation, and emphasis on [the text's] precarious position vis-à-vis overbearing and oppressive social forces, the claim to be engaged in some kind of radical intellectual and/or political work, and the assumption that whatever is not critical must therefore be uncritical" (2). Critique entirely changed the affective atmosphere of literary studies because underlying it is a hermeneutic of suspicion, or a refusal to accept textual elements at face value and an insistence that what is important in a text is always hidden, undisclosed, and often ideologically sinister—that is, oppressive, or psychologically diseased in some way. As both mood and method, suspicious critique redefined the critical landscape and fostered a spirit of distrust and disenchantment among literary scholars. Such a hermeneutic is partly the reason students sometimes feel uneasy in graduate seminars when they are moved to rapture by beautiful writing.

After the rise of suspicion, the celebratory spirit ended in the humanities, at which point graduate students and professors would no longer stand on desks, joyfully quoting inspirational phrases, but sit back down, their enthusiasm thoroughly curbed, and adopt an antagonistic stance toward the texts that once brought them so much joy. Fundamentally negative, as Felski shows, critique is "driven by a gnawing dissatisfaction that comes within striking distance of a full-blown pessimism" (122). The suspicion that accompanies it too often stymies any kind of joyous response, and to use it as a method is almost always "to make a judgment of a less than favorable kind" (127). So much for joy.

And so much for the zeal of graduate students who love literature and seek a degree that enables them to foster such love in their students. It is no wonder, Felski wryly quips, that "even the most chipper and cheerful of graduate students, on entering a field in which critique is held to be the most rigorous method, will eventually master the protocols of professional pessimism" (127). Students enrolling in programs in such a critical climate need to check their joy at the door, for the dangers of waxing rhapsodic in a graduate seminar come at the price of being labeled "insufficiently critical" (127), a surefire ticket to ostracism in the field.

Critical theory and its hermeneutic of suspicion are complicit in such attitudes toward joy, but this antagonism did not arise in an intellectual vacuum, a point Adam Potkay discusses in his groundbreaking, award-winning literary history *The Story of Joy: From the Bible through Late*

Romanticism. In his discussion of the academic reception of joy in the aftermath of World War I, Potkay traces the politicized dismissals of the emotion, showing that they often resulted in interpretations of joy as a form of naive denial and submissive quietism. "To experience and/or express joy in twentieth century academic discourse," he observes, "was a sign that you're not paying attention" (226). Such disaffirming thoughts, to an arguable extent, still permeate critical theory and literary studies at the graduate level. If students are mesmerized by the beauty of language; if they soar on the wings of imagery and skillfully crafted figures of speech; if they are profoundly stirred by imaginative genius; if they revel in the states of flow that reading an absorbing narrative puts them into; if they are deeply compelled to transform their lives and refashion their sense of self because of some fictional character who charms them or some play that roils their minds and stirs them to positive action; then, according to the canons of suspicious critique that took root in the twentieth century and are essentially still with us today, they are operating under grossly dangerous illusions that it is the professor's task to shatter. But there must be more to joy than this.

Jacques Derrida, for example, weighed in on the issue, taking an affirmative position toward the great books tradition: "As soon as one examines my texts," he says in an interview, "not only mine but the texts of many people close to me, one sees that respect for the great texts, for the texts of the Greeks and others, too, is the condition of our work" (qtd. in Caputo 9). Likely because he disapproved of many of the crude reductions and dismissals in the politicized form of the deconstruction he inspired, Derrida implicitly condemned extreme forms of textual antagonism, calling for a position that adopts a more affirmative approach to canonical texts.

For all this antagonism toward joy, the climate in literary studies is changing: just as young rebels like Derrida, Michel Foucault, Julia Kristeva, and others challenged the assumptions and methodologies of the literary establishment in the early seventies, almost entirely supplanting them with the critique of power and a hermeneutic of suspicion, so are many younger scholars today beginning to question the pessimistic ideas that permeate scholarship in the humanities. This "generational turn," as Jeffrey Williams calls it (B6), is inevitable in every age, and, after nearly fifty years of suspicion and critique, young scholars and others (like Felski) sandwiched in between the two generations have begun to question the jargon and automatic thinking that sometimes masquerades as professional literary scholarship. These scholars have grown tired of "textual harassment," as Peter Barry comically calls the politicized form of deconstruction (73), and they see the reduction of the rhapsodic response down to bourgeois aestheticism and false consciousness as a way of missing the point altogether.

This critical turn began in critical theory itself with an important essay by Eve Sedgwick, a brilliant scholar whose works *Between Men: English Literature and Male Homosocial Desire* and *Epistemology of the Closet* helped create the field of queer theory. Sedgwick challenged the heteronormativity of much critical discourse and insightfully opened numerous queer dimensions of texts that scholars had previously overlooked. To queer a text today is to pay homage to Sedgwick's valuable work. Before her death in 2009, nevertheless, Sedgwick had begun to write about the limitations of adopting an antagonistic response to texts as a blindly accepted, critically unexamined starting point in literary scholarship, seeing such a stance as a kind of fundamentalism not befitting the complexities of critical study. In what has become an oft-cited essay, "Paranoid Reading and Reparative Reading: or, You're so Paranoid, You Probably Think This Introduction Is about You," she challenged the extremes of suspicious critique and called for repairing the strained relationship between text and scholar.

The reparative turn Sedgwick called for in the essay eventually provoked an affirmative response. In 2009 Stephen Best and Sharon Marcus, editors of the influential journal *Representations*, devoted an entire issue to what they call "surface reading" as a means of challenging the surface/depth metaphor that underpins suspicion and critique. Questioning the dominant interpretive strategy that takes "meaning to be hidden, repressed, deep, and in need of detection and disclosure by an interpreter," Best, Marcus, and several contributors to the *Representations* issue particularly challenged the ideas of Frederic Jameson as he articulated them in his enormously influential work *The Political Unconscious*, which trivializes surface elements of a text as mere symptoms of underlying but undisclosed ideology that the critic, doing the work of the political activist, must expose (Best and Marcus 1). "The moments that arrest us in texts," they argue, "need not be considered symptoms, whose true cause exists on another plane of reality, but can themselves indicate important and overlooked truths. As Edgar Allan Poe's story 'The Purloined Letter' continues to teach us, what lies in plain sight is worthy of attention but often eludes observation" (18). In surface reading one can attend to such elements as a character's joy or a speaker's ecstasy without pathologizing them as indications of an obscured psychological or political disease, and one can respond joyously to such surfaces without being professionally ostracized for doing so.

"Surface" in this context does not function in the way it does in common use. Of course, scholars must see beyond the obvious in critical analyses, and the call here is by no means to attend exclusively to aesthetic concerns such as imagery and irony and thus return to the New Criticism or aestheticism of the twentieth century. Best and Marcus simply recognize, in effect, that the literary baby has been thrown out with the bathwater and that the tender one needs better care. Here, "surface" is whatever "is evident, perceptible, apprehensible in texts; what is neither hidden nor hiding; what, in the geometrical sense, has length and breadth but no thickness, and therefore covers no depth. A surface is what insists on being looked *at* rather than what we must train ourselves to see *through* . . ." (9). Trying to move the critical community beyond an excessive and now almost clichéd emphasis on ideological demystification and jaundiced psychodynamics, Best and Marcus recognize the limitations of critique and extol the value of a return to affirmative responses.

Having become one of the most frequently cited works in the last decade, the introduction to the highly influential *Representations* issue has sparked quite a significant response, raising the hackles of many scholars now considered to be the literary establishment, provoking considerable debate at the Modern Language Association's annual conventions, and fostering affirmative discussions in numerous journals and monographs. Best and Marcus recognize the considerable value in attending to textual elements (like the joys of Dickinson and Tagore) that are often dismissed as mere symptoms of ideological complicity or psychological disease. Of course, surface elements can be symptoms of oppression, and there are diseased forms of joy. Carolyn Burnham, the wife of the protagonist in the film *American Beauty*, is a prime example of both. Her constant smiling represents a faux joy that belies a profound unhappiness stemming from a jaundiced internalization of an overly materialistic and shallow version of the American dream. But perhaps literary scholars are too quick to equate all forms of joy with that of characters like Carolyn Burnham. A reasonable person must concede that there are other, healthier varieties of the emotion. Joy can be a symptom of psychological pathology in some individuals, but to dismiss it crudely and almost entirely as a symptom of disease or a form of political quietism that tacitly endorses problematic ideologies is to miss its enduring value and psychological importance. Not everyone who smiles is truly joyous, but many are. The affirmative turn in literary studies has taught us this important truth and offers the potential to rescue the discipline from the fundamentalism of extreme views and practices. It also has underscored the irony of unthinkingly adopting suspicion and antagonism as given starting points in a field of study that prides itself on bringing to consciousness unexamined values, assumptions, biases, and beliefs.

Graduate students entering the humanities and literary studies now have the kind of license Dean expresses in the quotation I started this essay with. But before professors encourage them to stand on their desk howling in rapturous delight over a passage from the ecstatic Whitman in a graduate seminar, a note of caution is in order: suspicion and critique are firmly entrenched in the critical landscape and will be for many years to come. A parallel can be seen in the influence of New Criticism. Although it is widely considered to be passé, New Criticism fostered a close reading strategy that outlived its historical moment and persists in the present day in nearly all critical methodologies (except distant reading and perhaps a few others). New Criticism, like the heavy metal music of the seventies and eighties, is still alive. Critique, too, is here to stay in the post-theory era and has earned its important place in literary studies. The affirmative turn does not represent the end of critical theory; that would be disastrous and take us to another ridiculous extreme.

Still, younger scholars today are increasingly seeing the limitations and excesses of the hermeneutic of suspicion as the only way of reading, adopting more affirmative stances to texts and cultural artifacts while exploring interpretive strategies that do not rely upon the heavy obligation of critique, which they see as but one of many hermeneutic possibilities. They are also beginning to recognize that to absolutize critique is to engage in a kind of narrowness of thought unbefitting of the humanities' mission of engaging with a multiplicity of ideas. While the hermeneutic of suspicion has proven effective in many contexts, scholars are now recognizing that it is but one of many possible reading strategies and often proves lacking in discussions of joy, happiness, and other aspects of well-being, a point several colleagues and I make in *The Eudaimonic Turn: Well-Being in Literary Studies* (see Pawelski and Moores). In the light of comments by Dean and numerous others, it seems safe to say that the related disciplines of literary studies are beginning to recognize the ethical, psychological, and social value of the joys readers find in sophisticated texts.

In 1974, precisely when suspicion and critique were budding and about to fully blossom in literary studies, Leslie Fiedler delivered an important address at the annual convention of the College English Association that was subsequently published in *The College English Association Critic*. Fiedler claimed that the endpoint of reading literature is the emotional response of ecstasy it arouses in readers. Presciently anticipating the rise of reader-response criticism, Fiedler saw considerable value in "the temporary release from the limits of rationality, the boundaries of the ego, the burden of consciousness" that one can experience as a result of affirmatively engaging with texts (11). Fiedler's idea never bore fruit, however, because the widespread adoption of critique as mood and method rendered it suspect. Today's affirmative turn, nevertheless, is slowly freeing scholars from the embarrassment of responding to literature in such a manner and even sanctioning readers' joys in ways that Fiedler might have applauded.

To be a graduate student in literary studies today, then, is to begin formal study of a discipline in the throes of positive transformation, for it is once again becoming acceptable to attend to joy as a complex subject worthy of sophisticated methodologies and also argue for the value of joyfully responding to literary works in ways that will not necessarily earn one the label of "apolitical bliss ninny." Joy is still standing and has even won the fight, thanks to some forward-thinking scholars who recognize that a hermeneutic of affirmation, one in which the joyous response is central, can be just as complex, perhaps even more so, as the hermeneutic of suspicion has been. The humanities have much to learn from joy as a subject of and response to literature, and the new generation of graduate students, freed from the jaundiced ideas that the ecstasy of reading literature is a disease and that suspicious critique is the only legitimate form of textual engagement, represent the vanguard of this promising development in literary studies.

WORKS CITED

American Beauty. Directed by Sam Mendes, Dreamworks Pictures, 1999.

Barry, Peter. *Beginning Theory: An Introduction to Literary and Cultural Theory.* 4th ed., Manchester UP, 2017.

Best, Stephen, and Sharon Marcus. "Surface Reading: An Introduction." *Representations*, vol. 108, no. 2, 2009, pp. 1–21.

Caputo, John D. *Deconstruction in a Nutshell: A Conversation with Jacques Derrida.* Fordham UP, 1997.

Dead Poets Society. Directed by Peter Weir, Touchstone Pictures, 1998.

Dean, Misao. "I Just Love Ethel Wilson: A Reparative Reading of *The Innocent Traveller*." *English Studies in Canada*, vol. 40, nos. 2–3, 2014, pp. 65–81.

Dutta, Krishna, and Andrew Robinson. *Rabindranath Tagore: The Myriad-Minded Man.* Bloomsbury, 2009.

Felski, Rita. *The Limits of Critique.* U of Chicago P, 2015.

Fiedler, Leslie. "Is There a Majority Literature?" *The College English Association Critic*, vol. 36, 1974, pp. 13–27.

Fisher, Philip. *The Vehement Passions*. Princeton UP, 2003.

Fredrickson, Barbara. "Gratitude, like Other Positive Emotions, Broadens and Builds." *The Psychology of Gratitude*, edited by Robert Emmons and Michael McCullough, Oxford UP, 2004, pp. 145–66.

Haidt, Jonathan. *The Happiness Hypothesis: Finding Modern Truth in Ancient Wisdom*. Basic Books, 2006.

Haq, Kaiser. "The Philosophy of Rabindranth Tagore." *Asiatic*, vol. 4, no. 1, 2010, pp. 27–40.

Jameson, Fredric. *The Political Unconscious: Narrative as a Socially Symbolic Act*. Cornell UP, 1982.

Moores, D. J., editor. *On Human Flourishing: A Poetry Anthology*. McFarland, 2015.

———, editor. *Wild Poets of Ecstasy: An Anthology of Ecstatic Verse*. Pelican Pond, 2011.

Pawelski, James, and D. J. Moores, editors. *The Eudaimonic Turn: Well-Being in Literary Studies*, Fairleigh Dickinson UP, 2013.

Peterson, Christopher. *A Primer in Positive Psychology*. Oxford UP, 2006.

Potkay, Adam. *The Story of Joy: From the Bible to Late Romanticism*. Cambridge UP, 2007.

Sedgwick, Eve Kosofsky. *Between Men: English Literature and Homosocial Desire*. 13th ed., Columbia UP, 2015.

———. *Epistemology of the Closet*. 2nd ed., U of California P, 2008.

———. "Paranoid Reading and Reparative Reading; or, You're So Paranoid, You Probably Think This Introduction Is about You." *Novel Gazing: Queer Readings in Fiction*, edited by Sedgwick, Duke UP, pp. 1–37.

Williams, Jeffrey J. "The New Modesty in Literary Criticism." *The Chronicle of Higher Education*, vol. 61, no. 17, 9 Jan. 2015, pp. B6–B9.

Wilson, James Matthew. "Representing the Limits of Judgment: Yvor Winters, Emily Dickinson, and Religious Experience." *Christianity and Literature*, vol. 56, no. 3, 2007, pp. 397–422.

Finding Joy in the Graduate Internship

John Lennon

I went to graduate school because I wanted to read books, argue politics, and hang out with smart, passionate people interested in doing the same. While in graduate school, I realized how little I knew about either books or politics, and I felt a real joy in that I could spend my days and nights learning from professors, fellow students, and, of course, the many books I collected throughout my years. I inhabited a world of ideas that were stretching me in ways that were both uncomfortable and thrilling; it was a world built on creative thinking and communal interaction that required an intensity of focus and deliberation. I had found a niche in university life that, I felt, was not connected to corporate America and where, sitting in a back booth of Yr Welcome Inn, I could rail against the injustices of capitalism and argue for a new world in the shell of the old.

Ah, those halcyon days. Now, as someone who (barely) survived years on the academic job market to land a tenure-track position in a research university, I realize how naïve I was in graduate school. We are in the age of the neoliberal university, a time where fiscal competition among departments stands in place of interdisciplinary collaboration, where arbitrary metrics have replaced shared governance, and where professors, students, and administrators are trying to accomplish more with diminishing resources. Listening to deans and provosts describe their hamstrung financial budgets as "the new normal," I yearn for those days when Dave, my favorite bartender, would slide me a free beer when I was short on cash. He got it: everyone needs a place to talk, argue, and think regardless of tight budgets.

While in graduate school, I did not think about jobs outside academia; truthfully, I did not think too much about jobs at all. When I graduated, I held, in turn, a postdoc position in interdisciplinary studies at the University of Miami, a full-time position in writing studies at St. John's University, a tenure-track position in English at St. Francis College, and a tenure-track position in the humanities at a regional campus at the University of South Florida (USF) before becoming tenured in the English department at USF's main Tampa research campus where I am now the graduate director. I left graduate school desiring a research position, and it's been a long, winding road to attain it, but at least there was a road for me to go down: as the numbers tell us, tenure-track jobs are down while applications for those positions are up (see Krammick; Pettit; Schmidt; Wanna). As universities double down on hiring adjuncts, building university education on the (breaking) backs of contingent labor, the future of academia is murky at best. Christopher Newfield painstakingly captures this demise of university ideals in *Unmaking the Public University: The Forty-Year Assault on the Middle Class*, and the volumes of "quit lit" found each year in *The Chronicle of Higher Education* viscerally and personally tell us this same story (see "'This Was a Hell'"; Pryal; Hall). Herb Childress in *The Adjunct Underclass: How America's Colleges Betrayed Their Faculty, Their Students, and Their Mission* describes the financial and emotional toll of continuing in the profession after graduation. Each year as graduate director, I wonder if we will have a class of MA, MFA, and PhD students who will want to apply to our program. And every year, people enter our program and want to read books, argue politics, and hang out with other creative people.

I choose this word *creative* purposely because creativity, to me, has always belonged in the realm of scholars. They are the ones who, through training, see the world slightly askew and can translate what they see to others. This allows for a felt interaction with our environments that we might not have experienced otherwise and thus can lead to a dramatic change within us and in our impact on the world. Or at least that's the romantic view. In *Against Creativity*, Oli Mould argues, "Creativity is a distinctly neoliberal trait [in the present age] because it feeds the notion that the world and everything in it can be monetized. The language of creativity has been subsumed by capitalism" (12). Anyone forced to sit through a provost lecture about "getting creative" because austerity measures give "the opportunity" for departments to figure out how to do more with less probably agrees with Mould more than with my romantic notion.

So how do we in humanities departments reclaim this term and balance the desire to give space and resources to students to be creative, wandering and wondering through texts and discussions in graduate programs, with the fact that this creativity is being fostered (and will bloom) in a capitalistic society that values skills over ideas and the practical over the theoretical? While internships are not the ideal solution to what graduate students are facing, they can be a tool for entrepreneurial students to bridge that gap, twinning the creativity of a humanities graduate experience with the practical experience of a job in a different field to create unforged new paths. While *entrepreneur* is a term that for me conjures up images of either slick salesmen peddling snake oil at county fairs or Silicon Valley hipsters selling half-baked ideas in Google boardrooms, it is a term I discuss with all my internship students. I want my students not to embody those stock characters but to tap into the entrepreneurial spirit that places creativity—that ability to see the world in a new light—in worlds they have not yet inhabited. The goal of the internship is to find joy outside the academy, tapping into the desires that bring students to graduate school in the first place. It is for this reason that I created an internship program focused around three types of positions: traditional, educational, and entrepreneurial.

Internship Case Study: The University of South Florida

What follows is an exploration of a program that I have developed over the past four years at the University of South Florida, a large public Research I university that serves over 50,000 students. Our graduate program has, on average, between 90 and 110 graduate students in three concentrations: the MA or PhD in literature, the MFA in creative writing (CW), and the MA or PhD in rhetoric and composition (RC). All our students have the opportunity to take an internship course for credit within their program of study, and we have encouraged students to do so by including the elective course as part of their degree.

When I became director of graduate studies, there was a vibrant undergraduate internship program for English majors created by Dr. Michael Shuman, who, over the course of a number of years, developed internship opportunities between 413 students and 144 community partners in the area. In our department, then, internships were part of our undergraduate culture. I wanted to contribute to that culture by creating a graduate-specific type of internship. It has been a steep learning curve. Although there is a general acceptance of internships in our department, there is no money or dedicated assignment devoted to the running of the program, so I have subsumed the responsibilities into my overall graduate director work. The program has developed incrementally through trial and error as key reliable internship partners have emerged and our graduate students have embraced the resulting opportunities.

Traditionally, undergraduate internship programs are seen as a way to give students valuable work experience. Our graduate students, though, often enter the program with substantial work experience and may have given up jobs that would pay the bills to obtain an MA, an MFA, or a PhD in English. My goal for the graduate internship program is to give students the space and opportunities to find the type of career outside the classroom that will excite them as much as their experiences within it.

Preparing Students for the Internship

Graduate students start thinking about internship possibilities as soon as they begin their program at USF. In their orientation, I talk to them about internships, including the application process, and invite graduate students who have completed internships to share their experiences (see "Internships"). It's important that during these first days, students not only learn the location of the library and the food courts but come to understand that their time on campus is finite and that they need to begin thinking about the future even as they get grounded in the present. As we are working through students' nerves about teaching their first class and introducing them to departmental faculty members, we are also prioritizing internships and signaling their value.

In their first semester, all MA and MFA students take an Introduction to Graduate Studies course.[1] It's a course that, as graduate director, I teach in order to ensure that I get to know program participants as people and students. This relationship helps me work with them throughout their time in the program. Because we have a mixture of literature, rhetoric and composition, and creative writing students in the class, it is a very different course than the one discussed in Gregory Semenza's widely used *Graduate Study for the Twenty-First Century*. We do not spend much time on bibliographic formatting; rather, we analyze the systems of power within a university, mental health issues among graduate students, and basic first-year survival skills.

Even in this first course of their graduate program, these students and I begin talking about career possibilities—both inside and outside the university. For example, while we discuss how students can prepare to apply to PhD programs, all students must also complete an informational interview with someone who is not a member of the professoriate. The parameters are completely open—it is the students' job to find someone in a career that they would like to explore. After they have completed these interviews, they present their experience and research to the class so that all the students can hear the myriad of job opportunities that are out there. As we encourage students to lose themselves in texts and ideas in their other courses, through this assignment, we create connections to nonacademic fields. While this is a practical way to get students thinking about internships, it is also a statement from the department that jobs outside the academy are no less important than jobs within the academy.

Complementing this introductory class, I hold optional weekly Friday meetings with all the graduate students in the department. Every other Friday, we also hold open meetings in order to discuss as a community issues that graduate students are facing (stresses related to the academic job market come up regularly). On the Fridays we are not holding open meetings, we are conducting workshops led by members of our faculty and staff and by alumni. At least three of these workshops—on internships, nonacademic jobs, and nonteaching positions within universities—are specifically focused on jobs after graduating.

Every semester, I send e-mails and, more important, stop by students' offices to discuss internship possibilities (at least, I do when there isn't a pandemic raging). Some are interested; many are not. Some poets want only to read and write poetry; some Milton scholars only want to spend time in the archives. I admire their dedication and leave these students to embrace their passions. To those who show interest, I offer a number of possibilities that they can explore and also invite students to find their own internships. Thus, every internship is prefaced by active encouragement, from the beginning of a student's time in the department, to seek one out.

Components of the Internship

The internship comprises a hybrid online course with me and a ten-hour-per-week internship. The course has six requirements:

> Students write weekly reflections on their internship tasks to help them translate these into concrete skills applicable to jobs.
> Students create a résumé and cover letter for the job they wish to have in the future.

- With their mentor serving as the point of introduction, students begin networking by conducting an informational interview with someone in their internship field.
- Students visit the career center and speak with a counselor or, where applicable, create an alternative assignment that fits their needs. Our CW students, for example, often create professional web pages to display their publications.
- Students combine all of their weekly reports into a practical essay that they can then consult when they apply for positions.

I meet with the interns as a group three times during the semester (at the beginning, in the middle, and at the end) to talk about their internships and collaborate to find opportunistic ways to get the most out of the experiences.

The internship itself can be face-to-face, hybrid, or completely remote. While we do have the advantages of being in a midsize city, we work with companies located throughout the United States and have expanded the program to Canada and Europe. To set up the internship, I have a conversation with each mentor where I explain the idea of the internship and its parameters. Crucially, I stress the need for actual mentorship—this is not an internship where mentors can "dump" work on our students. After establishing with the mentor the requirements of the position and their preferred intern profile, I introduce both parties over e-mail. The student then conducts a formal interview with the mentor. If they both agree, the internship begins the next semester.

Types of Internships

I categorize our internships as "traditional," "educational," and "entrepreneurial." While these are not hard borders, they help define the types of positions and the intended outcome of each.

TRADITIONAL

When most people think of professional internships, they think of this type of internship: Large corporations identify potential new hires and bring them into the company on a trial basis; then, over the course of an extended period, both parties see if they are a good fit for each other. For many English graduate students (and directors of graduate studies in English), these types of internships are somewhat hard to imagine, let alone acquire. There are possibilities, however, and ways to connect the graduate program with these companies.

An example of this type of internship is one I initiated with the financial company Raymond James. After meeting with a recruiter from the company and discussing their need for employees with strong writing and research skills, she asked if I knew a student interested in a potential professional and technical writing position at the company. I found a student whose experience was so successful that she was immediately hired at Raymond James. The recruiter wanted more students for various positions. Unfortunately, however, we did not have students who either wanted or had the skills to participate in the internship. Our students are trained in theories of professional and technical writing for purposes of scholarship. From a practical standpoint, however, our classes are not teaching graduate students how to *become* professional and technical writers.

Working with the head of the RC track, we discussed the benefits of these types of positions and focused on how to transform our professional and technical writing certificate program to allow for practical applications within each of the five courses required for the certificate. We then created a partnership with Raymond James and held meetings with the RC faculty to discuss how changes to the curriculum would affect their day-to-day teaching. This potential significant identity change within the certificate program highlights the importance of nestling internship programs into the curriculum of the department. Such changes can involve extra labor on the part of faculty members, and how best to adapt courses has been a subject of some debate within the track. Adoption of changes is slow, and the internship program has been evolving at the pace of these changes.

Another partnership we have set up is with Wittenberg Weiner Consulting, LLC, a federally focused consulting firm that principally works on grant proposals. After speaking with the president of the firm and the vice president of business development, we have established a partnership where one student per semester will be mentored in the art of becoming a project manager, connecting their research, writing, and time management skills with the detail-oriented and pressure-filled world of governmental deadlines. This is a growing field that has applications in both the private and academic sectors.[2]

For many of our RC students, this is a fantastic and logical opportunity. I envision these internships, though, as also a great opportunity for literature and MFA students. I tell students who entered the program to become academics and full-time creative writers that they should spend these years working on being their best version of themselves. If their dream is to be a tenured professor in a research university, then they can work toward that goal during their time at USF. However, if they are unable to land the tenure-track job they desire and are faced with the prospect of starvation wages while adjuncting in three universities, this internship offers an alternative path. The internships mentioned above have the very real potential to turn into actual jobs with advancement opportunities within large US corporations. Through the creation of these internship partnerships (and others like them), students have an actual realized and doable alternative path forward.

EDUCATIONAL

Many of our students love being in an academic setting, and while they wish to be professors and in front of the classroom, they also enjoy being part of the campus community. Numerous positions have opened up in recent years. As Rachel Arteaga and Kathleen Woodward point out, some universities are creating internships in administrative offices to equip students for related work in the future. Arizona State University Humanities Doctoral Internship Program and the University of Miami's Graduate Opportunities at Work both offer paid internships with various university offices ("Project Humanities"; "Welcome"). Lacking committed funding to develop such programs, I have been more opportunistic, relying on existing relationships to find places on campus where we can place interested students.

At USF, we have placed students in the provost's office working with a mentor on creating publishable stories about successes around campus. Other students have internships with university advising, as larger universities are moving away from faculty advisers and instead have professional full-time advisers. Still others we have placed with mentors in the graduate office. (At our university, this internship is not administered through the program: the office hiring the student pays the portion of their graduate assistantship that would otherwise have been connected with teaching duties, and the internship takes the place of teaching assignments). While students have been placed in campus positions, I have also arranged for students who wish to work in a community college to intern in various administrative capacities at our local community college. This experience—combined with teaching experience in a two-year institution—will hopefully lead my students to be more fully cognizant of the community college system and to future positions when they graduate.

ENTREPRENEURIAL

Many of my students have no clear goals for after graduation. They are in graduate school because they want to read, write and converse; they do not want a corporate job. There is a real joy in going to graduate school, and this desire burns hot; the risk of scorch marks is one they willingly assume when signing up for a graduate program. It is these students whom I encourage to be entrepreneurial. I want their graduate school experience to allow them to focus directly on who they are and then find opportunities that will help them grow in their identity. For too long, we have been telling undergraduate and now graduate students in English that they "can do anything" with a degree without telling them that they are responsible for creating their own spaces while giving them tools and opportunities to learn how to do so. An entrepreneurial internship can potentially be this bridge.

One example of this type of internship was developed by a student who wanted to engage creatively with feminism. I connected her with Elisa Kreisinger, a feminist podcaster and videocaster who, among many other things, created the series *Strong Opinions Loosely Held* for *Refinery 29* and worked for *Full Frontal with Samantha Bee*. My student gained practical skills for designing and shooting a feminist podcast and, in weekly *Zoom* meetings, learned how Kreisinger had created her own position and career path after graduating with a BA in communication and women's studies, navigating the gig economy to land full-time lucrative positions. While my student acquired numerous skills, it was the mentoring that I think is most valuable.

Another student is a lawyer who quit his job to become a creative writer. For his internship, he decided to combine his two passions and start a creative writing course in a local prison. I thought it was a great idea but that there would be an enormous amount of red tape for him to negotiate. I was correct on both counts. Logistically, my student needed to patiently go through background checks, interviews, and orientations as well as develop a knowledge of the prison hierarchy and a mental Rolodex of whom to contact when e-mails weren't returned. After nine months of coordination, he was able to teach a summer course at Zephyrhills Correctional Facility. Reading the course evaluations from his students showed how much an internship could mean on a variety of levels. From his hard work, we have continued this relationship with the prison, placing interns every semester and expanding the range of courses offered.[3]

This type of internship supports underresourced students and provides interns with an opportunity to devise a program or course for a challenging institutional environment. While most English graduate students have taught a freshman composition course, not many have created their own course within a prison. The internship sutured my student's lawyer background and his creative writing interests to produce a tangible and multilayered experience.

Companies may not advertise positions for a podcast creator or a writing teacher for incarcerated students. But, just as internships at Raymond James offer opportunities to learn the skills needed to gain permanent employment in the company, the internships just described cultivate the entrepreneurial drive necessary to forge a path in a career that has no set maps. For many of my students, conversations with mentors who have forged their own path by creating a position from scratch characterize the type of internship that they are seeking.

Considerations for Departments

Internships are a practical way to help students (and faculty members) break free from the mindset that students who do not go into professorships have somehow "failed." However, internships are certainly not the solution to the current crisis of higher education (see Schmidt; Stover; McWilliams; Hayot), and there are issues facing departments that wish to implement internships into their programs.

Paid and Unpaid Internships

Some of our internships are paid; some are not. There has been much discussion about the ethics of unpaid internships, which effectively exclude students who cannot afford to work for free (see Hoyt; "Fact Sheet"; Crain; Burke and Carton; Guarise and Kosenblatt). While I agree (especially regarding full-time internships, which we do not offer), there are three main reasons why I tolerate unpaid internships: First, students get academic credit for the internship and may only work ten hours a week, the same number of official hours per week they would spend in a course. Second, there is an actual mentorship component to all the internships—vetting and constant checking in ensures that this job is not grunt work but an educational experience. Third, students with fellowships or assistantships (that is, most of our graduate students) are technically not allowed to work outside the university. Being paid adds a layer of complication, especially in terms of financial aid. For our international students, paid internships could also be a violation of their visas.

Student Interest and Expectations

Many students do not want to do an internship. A literature PhD student may want to spend all their time reading and writing on a subject they care deeply about—often they do not want to be distracted by nonacademic responsibilities. An RC master's student wants to take as many interesting classes as they can—and does not want to sacrifice an elective for an internship. I understand both of these mindsets, and I do not think that internships should be mandatory. They are a choice on the student's part. This means that in any year, we have around ten students participating in an internship. Since we bring between fifteen and twenty full-time graduate students into the department per year, our averages are starting to reflect a growing interest.

Students' expectations for their internship also need to be handled. Students have specialized content knowledge that many will have spent two to seven years delving into. While some of the skills they have learned during this process will certainly help in their internships, many of their abilities as a Pynchon scholar or an experimental poet will go unused. We do a disservice to our students if we promote English graduate degrees as something inherently useful and practical. They are not. Students should be in a degree program because it brings them joy and fulfills a desire. Internships give them a pathway to a different field that is tangential to their expertise and often does not require the content knowledge that they are acquiring in graduate school. Students (and their faculty advisers) need to understand this when applying to jobs and thinking of careers outside of the academy. The degree holds some cachet in some fields, but students must be willing to acknowledge that their specialized knowledge is often not needed.

Faculty Time and Energy

To create a robust program, two things are needed: departmental buy-in and faculty time and energy. When I became graduate director and wanted to rework the internship on the graduate level, luckily, faculty members mostly thought it was a good idea. The internship coordinator, however, must spend a tremendous amount of time making contacts with potential mentors and setting up relationships with people outside academia. In my department, this activity was subsumed in my role as graduate director. It has been a passion project of mine that I have had to fit in around other responsibilities. The ideal situation would have a faculty member's labor counted specifically for the establishment, maintenance, and growth of the internship program. Without that commitment, the program will rise and fall on the energy of whomever is in the position. There is an obvious danger to this setup as it is implemented in my department, and I am currently trying to connect the program to university funding streams and outside grants (an additional investment of time). Faculty members who are interested in setting up an internship program would be well advised to seek a financial and time commitment from their department and their university. When working in universities that are severely underfunded by state legislatures, however, this is a very hard thing to do.

The Joy of an Internship

Graduate education in the humanities is in the process of transition. And while the rise of the digital humanities, medical humanities, and other "adjective" humanities are meant to justify the value of the graduate degree, it is my opinion that humanities departments are not going to get much traction among politicians who control the budget. In fact, I believe that we need to embrace what we do really well: read books, argue politics, and spend time with smart people, fashioning departments that allow folks to be the creative selves they want to be—regardless of how that manifests itself. This is why people turn to humanities graduate programs, and we do society a disservice if we become only skills-obsessed departments. As we bring students into the department, though, we need to give them options for when they leave. By talking with our students about internships as soon as they enter the program and offering an array of choices—traditional, educational, and entrepreneurial—to satisfy different career trajectories, we can hopefully tap into the creative desires that lead them to a graduate program in the first place and show them other spaces where those desires can be fulfilled.

NOTES

I would like to thank Elizabeth Ricketts, a PhD student at the University of South Florida and my research assistant, for copyediting this article.

1. PhD students do not take the Introduction to Graduate Studies course. Instead, they take a one-credit course with the graduate director, where I introduce them to the PhD portfolio, answer questions, and ease their transition into the department. We also discuss the value of internships in this course.

2. As someone who has written about the willful ignorance that many US English departments maintained during the Cold War in order to reap financial gains from unsavory government and corporate collaborations (Nilsson and Lennon), I am aware that corporate partnerships may be fraught with unintended consequences. While this type of relationship needs to be monitored, it is clearly beneficial for our students to have hands-on experience in a corporate environment.

3. The COVID-19 pandemic has put a hold on this relationship, but plans are set to continue it in spring 2024.

WORKS CITED

Arteaga, Rachel, and Kathleen Woodward. "Mentors, Projects, Deliverables: Internships and Fellowships for Doctoral Students in the Humanities." *Profession*, May 2017, profession.mla.org/mentors-projects-deliverables-internships-and-fellowships-for-doctoral-students-in-the-humanities/.

Burke, Debra D., and Robert Carton. "The Pedagogical, Legal, and Ethical Implications of Unpaid Internships." *Journal of Legal Studies Education*, vol. 30, no. 1, winter-spring 2013, pp. 99–130.

Childress, Herb. *The Adjunct Underclass: How America's Colleges Betrayed Their Faculty, Their Students, and Their Mission*. U of Chicago P, 2019.

Crain, Andrew. "Exploring the Implications of Unpaid Internships." *NACE Journal*, vol. 77, no. 2, 2016, pp. 26–31.

"Fact Sheet #71: Internship Programs under the Fair Labor Standards Act." U.S. Department of Labor, 2018, dol.gov/whd/regs/compliance/whdfs71.htm.

Guarise, Desalina, and James Kostenblatt. "Unpaid Internships and the Career Success of Liberal Arts Graduates." *NACE Journal*, vol. 78, no. 3, Feb. 2018, pp. 37–42.

Hall, Richard. "On the Alienation of Academic Labour and the Possibilities for Mass Intellectuality." *Triple C: Communication, Capitalism, and Critique*, vol. 16, no. 1, 2018, triple-c.at/index.php/tripleC/article/view/873.

Hayot, Eric. "The Humanities As We Know Them Are Doomed. Now What?" *The Chronicle of Higher Education*, 1 July 2018, chronicle.com/article/The-Humanities-as-We-Know-Them/243769.

Hoyt, Elizabeth. "Let's Get Legal. Guidelines for Paid vs. Unpaid Internships." *Fastweb*, 29 July 2022, fastweb.com/career-planning/articles/let-s-get-legal-guidelines-for-paid-or-unpaid-internships.

"Internships." *Department of English, College of Arts and Sciences*, usf.edu/arts-sciences/departments/english/opportunities/internships/graduate.aspx. Accessed 19 Sept. 2019.

Krammick, Jonathan. "What We Hire in Now: English by the Grim Numbers." *The Chronicle of Higher Education*, 9 Dec. 2018, chronicle.com/article/What-We-Hire-in-Now-English/245255.

McWilliams, James. "The Humanities Are Dead. Long Live the Humanities." *Pacific Standard Magazine*, 13 Mar. 2018, psmag.com/education/long-live-the-humanities.

Mould, Oli. *Against Creativity.* Verso, 2018.

Newfield, Christopher. *Unmaking the Public University: The Forty-Year Assault on the Middle Class.* Harvard UP, 2008.

Nilsson, Magnus, and John Lennon. "Defining Working-Class Literature(s): A Comparative Approach between U.S. Working-Class Studies and Swedish Literary History." *New Proposals: Journal of Marxism and Interdisciplinary Inquiry*, vol. 8, no. 2, Apr. 2016, pp. 39–61.

Pettit, Emma. "What the Numbers Can Tell Us about Humanities PhD Careers." *The Chronicle of Higher Education*, 6 Jan. 2019, chronicle.com/article/what-the-numbers-can-tell-us-about-humanities-ph-d-careers/.

"Project Humanities." *Arizona State University*, projecthumanities.asu.edu. Accessed 3 Apr. 2019.

Pryal, Katie Rose Guest. "Quit Lit Is about Labor Conditions." *Women in Higher Education*, vol. 27, no. 6, June 2018, pp. 1–2.

Schmidt, Benjamin. "The Humanities Are in Crisis." *The Atlantic*, 23 Aug. 2018, theatlantic.com/ideas/archive/2018/08/the-humanities-face-a-crisis-of-confidence/567565/.

Semenza, Gregory M. Colón. *Graduate Study for the Twenty-First Century: How to Build an Academic Career in the Humanities.* Palgrave Macmillan, 2005.

Stover, Justin. "There Is No Case for the Humanities." *The Chronicle of Higher Education*, 4 Mar. 2018, chronicle.com/article/there-is-no-case-for-the-humanities.

"'This Was a Hell Not Unlike Anything Dante Conjured.' Readers Share Their Stories of Fraught Academic Careers." *The Chronicle of Higher Education*, 29 Mar. 2019, chronicle.com/article/this-was-a-hell-not-unlike-anything-dante-conjured-readers-share-their-stories-of-fraught-academic-careers.

Wanna, Carly. "Grad Students Scramble as Humanities Jobs in Academia Dwindle." *Yale Daily News*, 2 Mar. 2018, yaledailynews.com/blog/2018/03/02/humanities-academia-jobs-dwindle/.

"Welcome to the UGROW Program!" *University of Miami College of Arts and Sciences*, ugrow.as.miami.edu/. Accessed 3 Apr. 2019.

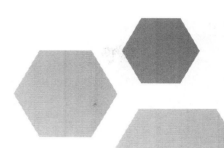

Bodies of Knowledge: Toward an Embodied Humanistic Praxis
Manoah Avram Finston

Anyone even passingly familiar with the academic job market has undoubtedly encountered one of the most enduring and infamous conundrums in higher education—the two-body problem. Derived from the supposition that a faculty job offer will rarely include or accommodate an equally sound job opportunity for an academic's partner, the two-body problem poses a tortuous question: How may partners find two distinct positions that are simultaneously geographically favorable and professionally advantageous? Historically, there have been no easy answers, and, as the recent literature suggests, deliverance from such anxieties about quality of life remains far off for younger members of the profession.

Conventional wisdom has long held that much self-abnegation is required over the course of a doctoral program and, indeed, even in the span of a career in the professoriate. Hours are long, salaries are low, and the relentless pace and focus of research output can strain relationships and shrink social opportunities. Historically, aspiring academics have accordingly been conditioned during graduate training to subjugate material concerns to the greater good of the research enterprise. Certain traditional hallmarks of adult success—career stability, family expansion, home ownership—are all but expected to arrive later than desired if at all. And troublingly, the willingness to defer certain comforts or deny certain forms of agency is often presented to students as a sine qua non of scholarship, simply a condition of entry into the field: One either accepts the rules or is deemed "not cut out for this."

Writing in 2013, first in *Inside Higher Ed* and then in *Slate*, Matt Reed explained the worrisome nexus of these beliefs within the two-body problem this way:

> In grad school, I remember absorbing by osmosis the lesson that if you were truly "serious," you wouldn't think twice about applying nationally. Acting on some sort of preference for place, or even region, was considered selfish, and reaching above one's station. At 22, I didn't think much about it; I was young and single, and the sheer brutality of the market hadn't hit me yet. At this point, though, I would not—and do not—advise my kids to follow in my career path. Life is too short for nomadic monasticism, and wanting a family you actually see doesn't make you less intelligent or less capable. The core of the two-body problem isn't the second body; it's the missing job. I hadn't figured that out yet at 22. I hope someone tells this generation before it does anything stupid.   ("Two Bodies")

Five years later, Reed had occasion to revisit the column, which had generated substantial interest since its initial publication. In a fresh article for *Inside Higher Ed*, Reed reviewed his prior pronouncements on faculty recruitment and opined, woefully, "This is not healthy. It is not reasonable. People who object to it are right to object. . . . It would have been nice to reread that piece from 2013 and chuckle at how ephemeral the issues were. Instead, it held up better than it should have" ("Two-Body Problem").

Three years later and well into the COVID age, the problem has assumed even more frightening dimensions, as the pandemic has so disrupted the fiscal health of universities and colleges that the sheer continued existence of many doctoral programs, academic departments, and faculty recruitments—or even entire institutions—is an open question.

It is important to note that Reed's original piece came to life partly as a response to a post by Rebecca Schuman, writing on her popular (now retired) personal blog *Pan Kisses Kafka*. Schuman, a Germanist by training, had assigned each job listing posted in her field on the 2013 MLA *Job Information List* a letter grade, with commentary. Thousands of page views later, Schuman sought to clarify her remarks in a follow-up post, explaining why she had particularly pilloried the language of one job listing from a prominent institution in the American South.

Writing critically about the illusion of "fit" as an objective criterion in campus job searches, Schuman offers a somewhat dark observation:

> If [the institution] has, from what I can tell, no or next to no faculty of color, and next to no students of color, and is located in a state . . . whose government refused to expand Medicaid under the Affordable Care Act, largely to spite our Black President for attempting to provide health insurance for the poor, who in this particular region are disproportionately Black, and you are a person of color . . . I'm going to go out on a limb and assume it will be a similarly bad "fit," no matter how allegedly "open-minded" your legions of White colleagues and students are, and no matter how vehemently some of them believe institutional and regional racism to be a "closet monster." And if you're a woman of color? See above. A single woman of color? I hope you like the Life of the Mind, because it will be the only thing you have.

For both Schuman and Reed, the academic job market is exigent to the point of cruelty. It presents too many awful, impossible choices. In Reed's telling, potentially damaging existing relationships or foreclosing the possibility of new partnerships should not be fixed as an accepted prerequisite for career advancement. Schuman goes even further, forcefully noting that there is more at stake in a relocation than changing friend groups and dating pools. For female-identifying scholars, LGBTQ+ scholars, international scholars, scholars from underrepresented minority groups, and anyone intersectionally identified, life within and proximate to certain campus environments can be fraught, isolating, or even downright dangerous. But what happens when entering such an environment is the only option for continued, steady employment in the field?

At the time of this writing, the ongoing global pandemic has added an entirely new set of complications and concerns to campus life. After a year of mostly or fully remote instruction, many institutions are welcoming students, faculty members, and staff members back to campus and heralding a return to almost-normalcy. Yet, with widely varying institutional postures on vaccine and masking mandates, and as the virus continues to spread across the country and the world (leading, in some recent cases, to localized campus outbreaks), students and faculty members alike are confronting the uncomfortable possibility that sustained participation in academic life might be a hazard to one's health. How then should a young scholar proceed, in reconciling already limited job opportunities with professional responsibilities that, when executed, may make people sick?

Our current moment alarmingly illuminates the germ animating the two-body problem: Must doctoral candidates be willing at times to not only endanger their relationships but even risk their physical, emotional, and mental well-being in order to remain in the profession?

Viewing the two-body problem through the lens of actual risk abruptly thrusts into focus one of the most easily overlooked (or consciously elided) truths of the industry: actual bodies are involved in academic labor, and, moreover, academic labor cannot be performed fairly and equitably without taking actual bodies into account. What this taking into account has historically looked like for the profession, and what it might look like in the future, is the principal concern of this essay. I posit that the profession is not so much afflicted by a two-body problem as by a one-body problem—or, more bluntly, a having-a-body-at-all problem.

In the midst of a global health crisis, the urgency and relevance of this question cannot be overstated: With its relentless focus on the life of the mind—as a lifestyle, a means to an end, and a series of interwoven professional and personal expectations—does the academy know how to adequately respond to the needs of actual bodies?

I argue here that the humanistic research disciplines have not gone far enough in making space for the body within the work of scholarship, teaching, and service. And, further, that the current insufficiencies in this regard have long been perpetuated by a doctoral training model that repeatedly denies a view of the scholar as a holistic self even as scholars are taught to examine and chronicle the intricacies of the self in their own research. While humanistic scholarship ostensibly strives toward a greater understanding of the mind and body as codependent and coincident entities, humanities doctoral training itself ironically pushes the body toward the margins in valorizing and overdetermining intellectual exertion as purely a product of mind.

A perusal of almost any program's graduate course catalog followed by a few minutes of frank conversation with that program's current students will reveal an almost frightening reality: PhD programs in the humanities traffic in the strange paradox of training students to become scholars highly sensitive to the problematics of personhood, the precarity of self-determination, and the stakes of inhabiting and navigating a body through time and space, even as they simultaneously demand the flattening or outright denial of these notions on the part of scholars themselves. Bodies, it seems, can stand as fascinating objects of inquiry, provided that they belong to someone else. When confronted with the stubborn demands and sheer material facts of a student's own body, however, the profession is largely, confoundingly silent.

What is the origin of this disjuncture, and how did humanistic doctoral training come to rely so heavily on narratives of sacrifice, abnegation, and refusal as the currency of scholastic production? I venture casually that the heritage of the modern Western research university in the monastic and cathedral schools of the early Middle Ages plays a not insignificant part in the transfiguration mythology of the scholar as martyr. Yet it seems absurd to believe that a millennium of knowledge-making has not moved the humanities further toward a recognition, if not a full-bodied embrace, of the total (embodied) personhood of its own practitioners.

I hold that the modern-day outcome of this monastic tradition is the promulgation of a set of increasingly pernicious expectations surrounding how, when, and where academic labor should be performed, anchored by an underquestioned apparatus of privilege residing at the very heart of higher education. The work of humanistic scholarship and teaching ostensibly requires a body of a certain kind, even as the profession outwardly ascribes value almost exclusively to attributes of mind—depth of analysis, probity of argument, breadth of knowledge, clarity of language, and so forth. In failing to acknowledge that bodies play a role in making good scholars and teachers, the profession reinforces the flawed notion that all bodies are equally equipped—or at least equal in their unimportance—for the field. Yet this amounts to a critical erasure of essential nuance, a denial of what individual bodies bring to the work.

The unfortunate result is that many bodies are quietly (or loudly) failing to clear the thresholds of acceptance into the field—thresholds that continue to be constructed with implicit bias. The one-body problem thus finds its clearest expression in the humanities' semipermanent crisis of professionalization, in which the very structures designed to afford entry into the humanities workforce are instead operating as an apparatus of privilege and exclusion.

Indeed, the COVID-19 pandemic has thrown into relief just how much the entire American educational system is built on certain assumptions about access and inclusion—regarding factors from the number of households that can support Wi-Fi-delivered remote instruction to the number of families that are willing and able to relocate to achieve better academic (and health) outcomes for their children. The clash between business needs and institutional missions at colleges and universities is at the nexus of these questions, prompting campuses and their surrounding communities to consider what, precisely, different bodies can afford to bear in order to keep schools in session.

A serious intervention is required to reverse this damage, to do better. A first step involves acknowledging the sheer diversity of bodies one is bound to encounter in academe. Now, there are so many different types of bodies, each bearing a history and an identity, that elaborating an adequate inventory or taxonomy would far exceed the scope of this essay. Instead, in a very preliminary way, I can simply signal some of the bodies most at risk in the academy, bodies subject to a certain form of exposure or even disclosure, bodies that reveal or announce features of themselves in a way that heightens their presence—and thus their vulnerability—within academic spaces that have historically been ill-equipped to accommodate difference. Indeed, I argue that the superstructure of the academy is comprised of spaces whose configuration has heretofore been informed by the *idée reçue* that bodies are indistinct if not invisible—and that the invisibility of bodies derives from their superfluity to the demands of scholastic production. When certain bodies, alive with vibrant differentiation, actually arrive in these maladapted academic spaces, the result can be a kind of involuntary hypervisibility, eliciting surprise, scrutiny, suspicion, or occasionally something even more sinister.[1]

Here are a few examples of such bodies at risk of exposure and disclosure: the female body, the queer body, the trans body, the nonbinary body, the Black body, the Indigenous body, the body of color, the pregnant body, the body recovering from trauma, the body living with chronic illness or chronic pain, the immunocompromised body, the disabled body, the fat body. The poverty of this list should be obvious. I have offered a nonexhaustive selection of rather broad categories but have presented them as individuated states, whereas the realities of identity and intersectionality are much denser. Truly, having a body is a unique and complicated enterprise.

Recognizing the primacy, dignity, and distinctiveness of bodies requires both questioning whether every space where bodies can go is safe and equal for everyone and acknowledging the ways in which a given space may perpetuate bias and inequity, even unintentionally. In a university context, we can take the bedrock example of the first training ground for PhD students—the seminar room—to test the exercise.

An instructor ready to engage with such concerns might begin with purely structural questions: Is the room accessible for disabled persons and ADA compliant? Would the chairs and table comfortably accommodate a variety of body types? Is it easy to move around in the room? They could then move on to consider the very framework of a doctoral seminar.

Is the classic format (multiple consecutive hours with a short break in the middle) fair to all students? Can everyone in the course sit that long without pain? Is the format equitable to students with focus problems, anxiety, or other learning issues? And then there are the nuts and bolts of classroom management to consider. How can the instructor ensure that students are always referred to by their preferred names and pronouns in the classroom, even if that information does not match the course roster? How can they ensure that the same respect toward names and pronouns is also extended to the authors of texts engaged in the course? Is there a no-computer or no-device policy in force? If so, is it fair to all students? Is there a lateness policy in the syllabus? If so, precisely what purpose does it serve? Is the grading policy for the course fair and equitable to everyone? Is the course format hospitable to adaptive technologies and to students attending remotely? Naturally, all these questions take on additional valences in the strange new world of hybrid and asynchronous instruction ushered in by the coronavirus pandemic.

These questions help illuminate the potentially numerous assumptions that pass without due consideration through an instructor's thinking. How often does the casual and unexamined belief that all bodies are equal—that is, equally invisible or equally indistinct —around the seminar table actually perpetuate inequality or cause real harm in the classroom and beyond? The rhythms and expectations of seminar—do the reading, show up on time, take notes, offer a few thoughts, rinse, repeat—that some students (and instructors) take for granted are for others the culmination of meticulous planning, preparation, and continuous adjustment according to circumstance. If we assume that every body in seminar has traveled an identical path to that particular seminar table and to doctoral education more generally, how many stories, revelations, and opportunities for attention and care are we missing? The consequence of overlooking so many layers of lived, embodied experience is a poorer seminar for everyone.

This leads to an even deeper line of inquiry: If one meeting of one seminar requires attention to so many dimensions of experience to ensure fairness and equity among all bodies, then how much thinking is required to extend that equity across an entire doctoral program? How much damage is done in the absence of it? As humanists, we have a special obligation to look closely for what we're missing. It is a prerequisite for recognizing our fellows in the fullness of their bodies and selves.

Stephanie Hannam-Swain recently provided one example of the hypercomplexity of having a body that exists in academia under threat of disregard or erasure. Writing for the *Impact* blog of the London School of Economics about life as a disabled doctoral student, Hannam-Swain notes the particular hazards of disclosing disability, existing on the often precarious border between being too disabled and not disabled enough, and navigating graduate school with a disability that is not immediately visible:

> For me, unless you know a lot about my condition—Osteogenesis Imperfecta Type III—you would be unaware of how stress and tiredness make fractures more likely or how easily fatigue can overcome me. You may understand that I fracture easily, but it's unlikely you know just how often or how often I carry on regardless because I have the same timescales and expectations of suitable output to abide by as everyone else. These issues and others like them are ones which I consider as "secondary" to my main impairment and to an extent I have the choice of when, to whom, and if I disclose them at all. I generally don't because people rarely know how to respond and the system isn't geared up to accommodate people who experience such fluctuations in health. I also don't want to risk falling into the "too disabled" category which could potentially damage my future career prospects.

The balancing act described by Hannam-Swain is unfortunately all too common in doctoral programs. And indeed, concerns about physical and mental health in graduate training are becoming harder to ignore.

An article published in 2018 in the journal *Nature Biotechnology* surveyed the mental health and well-being of 2,279 graduate students, 90% of whom were PhD trainees. The sample population spanned twenty-six countries and 234 institutions and included respondents across the academic disciplines; 56% of those surveyed came from the humanities or social sciences. The results of the survey were startling. The researchers found that graduate students are more than six times as likely to experience anxiety and depression as the general population (Evans 282). These experiences are almost certainly contributing to the high rates of attrition in doctoral programs across the country and beyond.

Data collected as part of the Council of Graduate Schools' landmark, multiyear PhD Completion Project found that the ten-year doctoral completion rate across all disciplines at American universities (both public and private) was 56.6% in the late 2000s, with considerable variability among research fields. While programs in engineering and the life sciences reported doctoral completion rates of roughly 63% within ten years of beginning graduate study, programs in the humanities fared significantly worse: only 49.3% of students achieved completion within a decade of study (Grasso 6).

No other longitudinal study as comprehensive as the CGS project has emerged in the last decade, but what literature is available suggests that the near 50% attrition rate in the humanities has not significantly changed. If anything, it seems to have embedded itself as a stubborn reality or even foregone conclusion in the profession. Leonard Cassuto, writing in 2013 in the *Chronicle of Higher Education*, wondered:

> What if doctoral attrition today were as high as 50 percent? We might expect that figure to perturb, disturb, and reverberate everywhere. As it happens, that 50 percent number isn't hypothetical—it's real. . . . That's way too high, but it hasn't exactly inspired picketing on the graduate quad. Why not?

There are far more urgent crises in our society that warrant picketing on the quad, yet we still do need to ask why the prevailing narratives and behaviors of our disciplines are driving so many students to abandon the field. Equally important is to ask how the training models enacted by one generation of academics might manifest in the approaches to teaching and advising held by the subsequent generation—that is to say, by those who successfully complete their programs and remain in higher education. If blind spots, biases, or other forms of disregard and critical inattention are transmitted to scholars-in-training, we must consider whether (or to what extent) these habits become part of daily academic life once these scholars have classrooms and colleagues of their own. If so, how many college students—the potential scholars of the next generation—might be (or have already been) alienated or pushed to the margins by nothing more than the repetition of inherited notions or unquestioned practices?

Quite simply, the future of the profession requires more bodies, and more bodily thinking—in humanities majors, doctoral programs, and across the workforce. To meet this goal, we must work toward eradicating all forms of prejudice, toxic work culture, and irrational expectations in our disciplines. More technical and radical than picketing on the quad, this project demands a novel framework for graduate education that centers the body, takes the body seriously. And it can't arrive soon enough.

The time has never been riper to rethink how to train the next generation of humanists. As gap years, "summer melt," declining national enrollments, and general attrition in undergraduate programs accelerate—and as many graduate programs have placed a freeze on admissions or radically reduced the scale of fellowship offers—the professoriate seems to be teetering on the edge of unsustainability, while the place of the university in American society is also uneasily shifting. Long before any COVID-related tumult, the worrying trends of corporatization, runaway borrowing, and fiscal austerity had already laid siege to the higher educational landscape, even as the academic labor market, especially in the humanities, extended its decades-long segmentation and contraction.

If indeed a crisis is upon us, then it is surely an occasion for bold thinking. The work of the humanities has rarely been more vital and more urgent, even as so many parts of the broader humanities ecosystem appear demonstrably imperiled. It is therefore incumbent on all members of the field—and especially on those most connected to the apparatuses of professionalization in their organizations—to consider how the pressing needs of this moment can best be met, while simultaneously ensuring the durability of the discipline for the battles yet to come.

One of the most obvious solutions to the problems at hand involves the broadest possible reappraisal of what constitutes a good placement for a doctoral student on the verge of entering the field. The sustainability of the humanities ecosystem—and the continued force of the humanities in public consciousness—requires that the next generation of humanities PhDs bring their energy and expertise to as many corners of society as possible. This will involve moving beyond the professoriate to find symmetrically meaningful work in a host of other environments: nonprofits, media, government, K–12 education, the private sector, nonfaculty university spaces, public-facing cultural organizations, and everywhere in between. This diversification of humanities worksites will lead organically to a greater democratization of knowledge, as more and more humanistic thinking will radiate beyond the traditional boundaries of academic departments, disciplines, and institutions, into all dimensions of civic life.

Yet if the work ahead demands a reorientation of humanistic endeavor toward a more global scale of impact, then those engaged in humanistic praxis have a particular obligation to consider how the next generation of humanists can be trained in a manner and spirit that maximally serves the public good. How then are we to make the humanities even more humane? I argue that we need a fundamental reimagining of our methods and models of training. We need a novel approach, informed by a heightened awareness of difference, that grounds the work of the humanities in the dignity and abundance of the human. For this, we must situate both our inquiry and our practice in the body as an original site of action, discourse, and knowledge. We must consider first and foremost how the body exists in the world, how it witnesses and bears meaning. We can begin by deploying a graduate training model that brings critical awareness to bodies—in society, in literature, in the classroom—as loci of narrative and as holders of truth. Such a model would grant to bodies not only visibility but also legibility, honoring the sheer presence of bodies in the world but also recognizing that bodily specificity, bodily difference, encodes a story and a history that matters.

What we are moving toward is a form of close reading, but one that is grounded in conscientiousness more than curiosity. The aim of such an approach is not to treat bodies dispassionately as autonomous objects of study but rather to encounter the bodies around us with reverence and with a heightened sensitivity to what makes them distinct, in terms of both their abilities and vulnerabilities. From this, we can produce a genuine ethic of care, an ethic powered by the understanding that the body is essentially implicated in humanistic labor—that it does not exist at a distance from intellectual production and therefore cannot be glossed over or erased; nor can it be tokenized or essentialized.

I am advocating for a more generous and empathic way of seeing, within a training paradigm that renders bodies legible in academic spaces and beyond. On a very practical level, enacting these shifts can be as simple as changing how students are treated throughout the course of their doctoral programs. One fundamental place to start is with program expectations regarding work-life balance. Creating formal departmental (and institutional) policies surrounding time off, including affording actual vacation time alongside sick and personal days, would help provide students with the necessary structures to protect their time and energy and remain in good physical and mental health throughout the many tribulations of doctoral education. The pandemic confers a special urgency to these concerns; departments and programs would be wise to use this moment to create a more generous and more durable work-life culture meant to remain in place permanently. While these issues regrettably exist across the whole of the American workforce—and every industry should feel compelled to further address them—higher education faces a particularly necessary reckoning in this regard.

Similarly, crafting, publishing, and upholding a formal policy on leave for parents or primary caregivers would achieve the crucial effect of both communicating that there is nothing abnormal or risky about building a family while in graduate school and ensuring that new parents or caregivers do not lose access to or support from their advisers and departments as they temporarily transition away from full-time academic work.

The horizon of these and other policies is the dismantling of the pervasive narrative that "good" doctoral students work ceaselessly and that taking breaks is a sign of intellectual weakness or inadequate commitment. Granting students valuable time to rest will reduce burnout and lessen anxiety. More importantly, the gesture affords students the liberty to manage their own lives, an appreciable conferral of dignity too often buried in the hierarchies of adviser-advisee dynamics.

Another important venue for this shift is in teacher training. In programs where teacher training does exist, the focus tends to be on building skills for delivering different types of content more effectively—how to teach a foreign language class versus a literature course, or how to teach rhetoric and composition to first-year students, for example. How often does training engage with the realities of bodies in the classroom?

New teachers may advance in their classrooms approaches they encountered in their own undergraduate classes or perpetuate received wisdom about teaching that may be uninformed, retrograde, or insufficiently nuanced. For example, when a new teacher parrots a familiar list of prohibitions—no laptops, no late arrivals, no late work, no negotiable grades or deadlines—they are ostensibly creating a culture of personal accountability as a core teaching practice. While admirable on the surface, such blanket interdictions may unwittingly reinforce layers of privilege or effect double standards in the classroom. How much do we assume about our students without taking the time to learn who and where they really are? How much do we know about what their minds and bodies have been through before they take a seat at our seminar table (or join us on *Zoom*)?

It is essential to incorporate such considerations into teacher training or pedagogy seminars so that doctoral students grow to address these concerns instinctively. In this way, as they gain footing as instructors, they will also simultaneously develop deep faculties of empathy for the members of the learning communities they serve. The ultimate result will be both stronger teaching and greater collegiality, a net benefit for students and senior colleagues alike.

An additional component of this shift concerns faculty members' approach to graduate training as a whole. Do faculty members frame the PhD program as positioning young scholars for a career exclusively in the professoriate, or is the charge more expansive? I venture that the ambitions of humanistic thought have always been broad enough to necessitate taking a more ample view, extending one's ambit of inquiry to encompass as much of the known and knowable world as possible. Indeed, humanistic thought is fundamentally communitarian; humanists are constantly considering how to better share the world, how to better exist among others. Humanistic praxis involves learning, enacting, and extending the codes of citizenship. In a practical sense, this means working toward being better colleagues and neighbors, among other roles that call upon our mutual affective bonds and obligations to those around us.

And this is where the final, most political shift must occur. Faculty members need to reevaluate and reframe their commitments to their institutional communities, taking more active roles in governance and service to ensure that the vital perspectives afforded by humanistic thought and praxis are not only included but amplified in conversations about what universities owe to the people who animate and enrich them.

The COVID pandemic has, perversely, thrust a paradox upon the profession. Since much of humanities scholarship lacks the site hyperspecificity of other research disciplines that rely on labs, special equipment, or geographically determined fieldwork, many scholars have been able to continue their projects remotely, even as colleagues in other fields have seen their work all but halted. This reality gives credence to the idea that bodies need not factor strongly in our work. And yet, over the last eighteen months, faculty members have rightly balked at the questionable compliance dynamics of many campus reopening plans, pointing out the very real attendant risks to health and safety. If in a time of pandemic, faculty members recognize the fragility of their own bodies in the classroom, must they not also acknowledge the bodies of their own undergraduate and graduate students? How can a professor's body matter while their advisee's body remains inert, invisible, or mute? Only a radical act can bring coherence to this moment. This act—of seeing, of making the body legible—must become an invocation for humanists to more thoroughly examine how bodies in academe may exist in tension as loci of both liability and privilege.

What would happen if humanities faculty members then used the knowledge gained through this act to motivate more active interventions on campus and beyond? I posit that the very same impulse held by humanists to decouple the mind from the body has also alienated the humanities from the university body politic. Perhaps our disciplines encode something of an innate resistance to faculty affairs and governance; we retreat into the life of the mind and let our colleagues from "harder" disciplines handle the drudgery of management and administration.

This impulse must be forcefully counteracted. We must throw our bodies into the work. Humanists are indeed uniquely qualified for the ends of administration—driving institutional equity and inclusion, strengthening community relations, making universities more humane.

Put simply: Humanists must take the work of citizenship much more seriously. It must become the animating principle of our pedagogy, our mentorship, our institutional stewardship, our professional personae. And it demands that we see and treat people in the fullness and complexity of their selves. This impulse must move beyond mere courtesy and approach something more urgent: the visibility and legibility of the body and the recognition of the dignity that inheres both in being-with (Heidegger 107–22) and in being seen.

Lastly, an embodied humanistic praxis will also greatly benefit the humanities ecosystem overall. More sensitive and generous approaches to doctoral training will ensure more positive holistic experiences in graduate school, which will allow young scholars to start their careers feeling more satisfied and optimistic about the state of their fields. This shift will not only enhance teaching and scholarship within the academy but will also preserve and even extend diversity and inclusion in doctoral programs nationwide. A training model that recognizes the innate sanctity and implicit difference of bodies will keep more of those bodies enrolled, simultaneously reducing attrition and demonstrating to publics both in and outside academia that getting a PhD is a workable life choice, thereby assuring the health of doctoral programs for the future.

For faculty members, bringing an embodied way of thinking to professional responsibilities will also strengthen institutions by iterating cultures of genuine compassion and making universities more accountable in their commitments to serving their student and other community stakeholder populations.

A final consequence of this shift is the long-term impact on intellectual environments beyond higher education. As more new PhDs enter the workforce and enact this praxis in their own professional lives, they will be able to make meaningful and lasting contributions to an increasingly diverse set of spaces across the whole of American society.

Yet none of this is possible without the commitment of faculty members at all levels, from the nuts and bolts of program administration to the grander, less tangible work of redefining professional expectations and reframing the social value of humanistic training. A substantial portion of this work will inevitably extend beyond office hours and class time. Professors should consider how to bring an embodied praxis to department meetings and committee work, to the faculty senate, and to the editorial and advisory boards of publications, associations, and learned societies.

Reimagining doctoral education in the humanities as an expanded study of citizenship—a crash course in world-sharing and being-with—might transform academia's one-body problem into something else entirely. Instead of perpetually erasing the scholarly body from the narratives and the physical sites of humanistic labor, the profession may at last be able to recognize the body as an uncontested presence and an essential locus of value. From here, a novel, more supple view of the humanities can take hold, one in which our work and our bodies are held as intimately connected and in which both are seen as worthy—of attention, of care, and even perhaps of joy.

NOTE

1. Recent well-publicized incidences of sexual assault and harassment perpetrated by faculty members against graduate and undergraduate students at institutions like New York University and the University of California, Santa Cruz, are a powerful reminder of how the environments and expectations of doctoral pedagogy and training can habitually expose students to unacceptable levels of risk.

WORKS CITED

Cassuto, Leonard. "Ph.D. Attrition: How Much Is Too Much?" *The Chronicle of Higher Education*, 1 July 2013, chronicle.com/article/ph-d-attrition-how-much-is-too-much/.

Evans, Teresa M., et al. "Evidence for a Mental Health Crisis in Graduate Education." *Nature Biotechnology*, vol. 36, no. 3, 2018, pp. 282–84, https://doi.org/10.1038/nbt.4089.

Grasso, Maureen, et al. *A Data-Driven Approach to Improving Doctoral Completion*. U of Georgia / Council of Graduate Schools, 2009.

Hannam-Swain, Stephanie. "Understanding the Additional Labour of a Disabled PhD Student." *LSE Impact Blog*, London School of Economics, 28 Nov. 2017, blogs.lse.ac.uk/impactofsocialsciences/2017/11/28/understanding-the-additional-labour-of-a-disabled-phd-student/.

Heidegger, Martin. *Being and Time*. 1927. Translated by Joan Stambaugh, State U of New York P, 1996.

Reed, Matt. "Two Bodies, One Job." *Slate*, 3 Oct. 2013, slate.com/human-interest/2013/10/academia-s-confounding-two-body-problem.html.

———. "The Two-Body Problem Revisited." *Inside Higher Ed*, 31 Jan. 2018, insidehighered.com/blogs/confessions-community-college-dean/two-body-problem-revisited.

Schuman, Rebecca. "On My 'Job Ad Grade' for Sewanee." *Pan Kisses Kafka*, 29 Sept. 2013, pankisseskafka.com/2013/09/29/doubling-down-on-my-job-ad-grade-for-sewanee/. Accessed Feb. 2018.

Humanities under Quarantine: A Reflection on Isolation and Connectivity in Graduate Education

Yevgenya Strakovsky

On 13 March 2020, Georgia Institute of Technology, like many universities across the country, shut down its campus in response to the COVID-19 pandemic. This essay takes the nationwide quarantine of 2020 as a starting point for a reexamination of traditional practices in humanities graduate education, particularly the role of the body and physical space in graduate research, teaching, and advising. This essay is deliberately a time capsule. It was written between March and August 2020, during what we might call the "high quarantine" at the beginning of the COVID-19 pandemic—at the height of uncertainty, precarity, and isolation across the globe. To the extent that this essay feels anachronistic, it is for the purpose of capturing this unique moment of isolation and using that visceral experience to reflect on how the culture of individualism and the psychology of human connectivity have shaped the humanities.

This essay offers a complementary exploration of Anna Westerstahl Stenport and Richard Utz's case study in this volume of the master's program in global media and cultures at Georgia Tech, where I served as associate director of graduate studies and career education in the School of Modern Languages. Stenport and Utz offer an image of the graduate program that the School of Modern Languages envisioned before COVID-19: an intensive twelve-month experience that prepares students for "real world" humanities. In the hope of avoiding academia's tendency to self-replicate, our team and faculty community aimed to prepare our students for roles in communications, community engagement, diversity and inclusion, international business development, and the public sector. The 2019–20 academic year saw the first cohort of students pilot the program, starting their studies in August 2019 with the plan of completing coursework during fall and spring, defending a project prospectus in April, and completing a final project for an August 2020 graduation.

This essay seeks to reexamine the role of physical closeness in the humanities, particularly in our traditional approaches to graduate education. The global quarantine has revealed the myriad ways that closeness can be constructed and reimagined. Transcontinental movie nights, extensive phone conversations, and coordinated *Zoom* dinners have created strange new imagined spaces of intimacy. The quarantine has also revealed the limits of intimacy in a disembodied world. I will share some of the strategies we implemented to grapple with the sudden absence of the closeness that had become a core foundation of our program. These challenges became particularly acute as campuses began to inch toward reopening and we realized that we needed to maintain social distancing practices to ensure the safety of our community.

COVID-19 was first identified in China, and China was the first country to implement a nationwide quarantine, on 23 January 2020; the World Health Organization declared a "global health emergency" one week later (Schumaker, "Coronavirus"). One after another, countries began issuing social distancing and stay-at-home orders, in the hope that cutting off all physical contact between people could contain the rapid spread of infection and keep death rates at bay (Schumaker, "Timeline"). As those orders took effect locally and internationally, colleges and universities transitioned into fully remote instruction, eliminating embodied physicality from the college experience, albeit replacing it with virtual access into highly private spaces such as bedrooms and family homes. The rest of this essay examines the effects of this sudden transformation both in the humanities, where the subtleties of communication form the basis of our pedagogical practice, and in the university, where space serves a pedagogical function to create accidental educational encounters. It asks as well what this unusual experience can teach us as scholars in the humanities about our work—its meaning; its value; and its capacity for joy, engagement, and sustainability.

Academia and the Private Sector: Two Visions of Humanities (April 2020)

The pandemic revealed the strange role of the body in the professional traditions, limits, and possibilities of humanities work. A program that was designed as an intervention in the status quo revealed the humanities as steeped in a tradition of disembodiment and perceived physicality as a means of breaking through systemic stagnation. As COVID-19 shut down operations in March 2020, the nationwide travel restrictions, limited access to resources, and collective trauma of the experience disrupted this trajectory, challenging students to redesign their master's projects for remote completion (which sometimes involved changing their project goals or extending their time to degree). Acknowledging the role of the body in academic work has forced scholars to reckon with the unequal ways in which academia treats different bodies. Conversely, conducting humanistic work in an embodied way connects formerly disparate spaces, audiences, and discourses.

Embodiment, it appears, sits at the innovative edge of our profession. It is both powerfully transformative and highly vulnerable to institutional inertia, and it is critical that we not lose this form of innovation. The body is also emerging as a marker of individual agency as institutions attempt to dictate the physical whereabouts of the bodies of students, faculty members, and staff members who continue to participate in the university system. Our newest challenge as educators is to sustain the benefits of embodiment and its capacity for innovation while we also struggle to protect the safety and health of our constituents in an ongoing and growing pandemic.

While preserving the nuance and complexity of rigorous humanistic inquiry, the program design team turned to the private sector as an interlocutor in designing our graduate program. This was not only because we firmly believe in preparing humanists for high-stakes leadership roles but because the private sector, in the wake of the past century's collective traumas, is actively faced with the need to address inequities and create visible, tangible social good. During the process of reimagining the humanities for the private sector in our curriculum, conversations with our industry partners showed that employers increasingly look to the humanities for expertise in navigating the nuances of human closeness.

Recent shifts in psychology have revealed the pervasive power of closeness and meaning not only to improve health but to transform teams and companies. Organizational behaviorists have responded by calling for greater attention to the role of culture and connection in the workplace (Coyle 11). To quote the Florida-based consulting firm Gapingvoid Culture Design Group, a case study in the MS program's required career course, "Culture is the greatest business challenge of our day . . . [and] data is NOT a solution" (Home page). Gapingvoid's signature product, the "culture wall," is bona fide visual art: alongside consultation on purpose, meaning, and community, the firm's artists create a collection of paintings that represent a company's values in imagery and language. The private sector increasingly looks to the humanities for what Christian Madsbjerg calls "sensemaking," or the capacity to transcend "thin data" to access intuitive, aesthetic, emotional, or historical meaning (Madsbjerg 14). However, in engaging with the private sector for internships and guest speakers, we repeatedly noticed the disconnect between companies' interest in human connection and the insufficiency of our profession's detached frameworks to respond to this interest.

Despite a long history of grappling with the most profound of human emotions and experiences, the humanities as a profession—particularly in traditional graduate education—has a meager relationship to closeness in its real-world forms: physical proximity, teamwork, and intimacy. In the academic humanities, physical proximity isn't typically examined as a significant factor, particularly in the process of research. The humanities trade in the memories of experience—diaries, archives, typed manuscripts, performances—not in experience itself. Language is our traditional currency. We commune with dead poets and forgotten events. We deconstruct and reconstruct life-changing stories of love and war, using nothing but our words. According to the cultural myth of the "life of the mind," the true scholar is driven by intrinsic motivation: a thirst for knowledge and a glowing desire to make sense of a problem—whether to speak truth to power or to understand a thing of beauty.

The Life of the Mind: Disembodiment, Dissertations, and Disciplinary Ideals (May 2020)

The cultural ideals behind humanities research models emerge from the introverted philosophers who popularized the life of the mind as a foundation for education—the German Romantics of the late eighteenth century. This philosophical ideal is one of the foundations of the modern research university, as imagined by Wilhelm von Humboldt and others in this circle of discourse. The *Naturphilosophie* ("natural philosophy") of the German Romantics foregrounds the ideal of the lone genius struggling to achieve transcendental objectivity by understanding beauty or truth. In the works of Romantics like Friedrich Schelling, Friedrich Schlegel, Novalis, and Johann Gottlieb Fichte, beauty ultimately manifests itself in nature; thus the Romantic genius is at his core a scientist-artist—one who immerses himself in the inexpressible sublime truth of nature and struggles to express this beauty back to society in the form of writing, painting, music, or philosophy. Indeed, as Robert Richards argues, the Romantics conceived of scientific inquiry and artistic production as related and even simultaneous activities.

The journey of the Romantic artist-scientist is often a lonely, disembodied one. Novalis offers a parable of scholarly self-actualization in his unfinished novel about knowledge and beauty, *Die Lehrlinge zu Sais* (*The Students at Sais*). A key frame narrative in the work, the fairy tale "Hyazinth und Rosenblüthe" ("Hyacinth and Rosebud"), foregrounds the journey toward enlightenment as a solo, disembodied venture that emerges from within. The world of this fairy tale is ethereal and timeless, and Hyacinth is at once human and a flower with no distinguishable physicality. A prototypical *schöne Seele* ("beautiful soul"), Hyacinth is pulled from the safety of his home and out into the vast world by an invisible, powerful force: a yearning to know the Truth, the Temple of Isis, "die Mutter der Dinge" ("the mother of all things"). Hyacinth must abandon Rosenblüthe to journey through the world, asking fields of flowers for directions, following the call. No one offers him assistance; on the contrary, "manche lachten, manche schwiegen, nirgends hielt er Bescheid" ("some laughed at him, some were silent, nowhere could he get a response"; 80). Hyacinth finally reaches the altar by detaching from his body in a dream, "weil ihn nur der Traum in das Allerheiligste führen durfte" ("because only the dream could have led him to the holiest place"; 81).

The pure individualism and Cartesian intellectualism that define Hyacinth's journey also undergird the premises of modern education as conceived in the seminar model of the nineteenth-century research university, which emerged concurrently and in direct communication with Romantic discourse and has persisted in humanities graduate education today. While collaboration is a logistical necessity in the STEM fields, the humanities have been slow to incentivize collaboration, holding onto the single-author monograph as the true measure of a scholar. Beyond co-organizing conferences and writing individually on overlapping topics for an edited volume, scholars in the humanities have few institutionalized forms of substantive collaboration available to them and must work within an incentive system that discourages shared intellectual production.

While often untenable in the context of financial and family obligations, the extended, unstructured isolation of the late-stage humanities PhD is the default curricular expectation. Radically unstructured time, sometimes stretching for months or even years without significant deadlines or end points, is the signature feature of dissertation-writing in the humanities. My own dissertation-writing included a two-month archival visit to Zurich, Switzerland, where my *Hochdeutsch* (formal or "high" German) was not the local language, making in-person conversation largely impossible. I spent the majority of that summer at one of three tables: writing in my apartment, reading manuscripts in a sixth-floor library, or uploading teaching statements to *Interfolio* in the deserted indoor dining room of the *Rathauskeller* ("city hall café").

Ultimately, Novalis's parable subverts its own Cartesian mind-body dualism. Removing the veil on the altar of Isis, Hyacinth discovers the face of his beloved, Rosenblüthe, whom he left behind, and she "sank in seine Arme" ("sinks into his arms"; 81). Love, we learn, is the final driving force and medium of transcendental enlightenment. Whereas it is an ethereal, disembodied love for nature that drives Hyacinth into the pursuit of knowledge, it is through the physical and emotional reunion with his beloved that Hyacinth crosses into a state of enlightenment. Although Hyacinth achieves clarity by passing through a disembodied state of existence, his reward is corporeal: "Hyazinth lebte nachher noch lange mit Rosenblütchen unter seinen frohen Eltern und Gespielen, und unzählige Enkel dankten der alten wunderlichen Frau für ihren Rat und ihr Feuer; den damals bekamen Menschen so viel Kinder, als sie wollten" ("Hyacinth lived afterwards for a long time with Rosebud and with his happy parents and playmates, and countless grandchildren thanked the old wondrous woman for her advice and her fire; because back then, people could have as many children as they wanted"; 81). The disembodied journey of the artist culminates in the epitome of embodied heteronormativity.

In late March 2020, the students in our master's program returned from spring break to find themselves in a boundless, disembodied swath of time, stretching across days, punctuated by one or two daily video calls where their courses used to be. Our students were due to submit a prospectus to their advising committees by 19 April and to give their defense presentations between 22 and 25 April. They were then supposed to spend the summer completing their final projects. As the pandemic unfolded and disembodiment became an institutional requirement, I was surprised at how prepared I felt to explain to my students how to manage extreme professional solitude: how to set up a workspace, manage time, and maintain mental health in a highly unstructured environment divorced from the support structures of "normal" life. "It's easy to think you can write anywhere, because technically, you can," I wrote in a blog post on working at home, hoping to convey that the act of writing requires more physical infrastructure than society would have us believe. "[W]riters are notorious for working everywhere but the office: at home, on a couch, in cafes, in train stations, on trains, or even wandering through the park with a voice recorder" (Strakovsky, "Virtual Grad School"). Immersed in a disembodied vacuum of ongoing responsibilities, my colleagues offered the tricks they had used to generate imagined structures in place of real ones during their disembodied educations: designated work areas, productivity timers, writing buddies, and even the primordial reward systems of childhood—snacks and stickers. However, we also reminded students that these strategies were coping mechanisms for, not solutions to, the immersive precarity they would experience. "Chaos is okay," the blog concluded. "Creativity is messy. Adulthood is messy. The world is certainly not a tidy bookshelf. It's okay to lean into that chaos a little." From a distance, there was little I could offer except platitudes and communication channels. The global pandemic had revealed just how flimsy optimism could be in the face of extreme precarity and impenetrable solitude.

In order to allow students to graduate on time after travel restrictions had halted study abroad and stay-at-home orders had made interviews and filming impossible, we had to ask our students to submit contingency plans that reconceptualized their projects to extract all embodied components. What was striking about this process was both the ease with which we could articulate the act of disembodying a project and the profound sense of loss that accompanied this process. On 13 March, we announced:

> For those of you who planned to travel abroad this summer, you now know that all Institute-sponsored international travel has been cancelled. . . . [We as faculty members] can only deeply empathize, [knowing] what a profound role travel plays in our lives and our profession. [We] encourage you to reflect on what you found most interesting about the location, organization, or question you originally set out to explore, and to hold onto that core element as you adjust your project. (Strakovsky, "Updates")

Even as we mourned the transformative power of embodied learning that had shaped our own educations and careers, we operated under the assumption that the essence of a project could be extracted from the space in which it occurs. This assumption shaped student outcomes.

The process of requiring contingency plans revealed the role of embodiment in creating innovation within the humanities. As one might assume, the projects that could most easily continue without interruption were those involving traditional humanistic questions, practices, and texts. Two students translating Japanese manga and science fiction for English audiences did not need a contingency plan. A student in the Russian program, whose internship at a think tank in Tbilisi, Georgia, was canceled, converted his project to a research paper about current events in Georgian-Russian relations, transposing his writing desk "from Georgia the country to Georgia the state" to take on the challenge of drafting an academic article. A student in the French program, who had been interning at the Carter Center's Democracy Program, analyzing Congolese media and drafting communications for the initiative, continued her work with all the more urgency as the pandemic called for additional reporting. Writing, translation, and the analysis of mainstream media and policy are resilient to pandemics and budget cuts, just as they were to war and autocracy in centuries past.

In calling attention to embodiment, I do not want to downplay the value of the disembodied humanities. Indeed, some students shared just how much they enjoyed the opportunity to slow down and dive deeply into an idea. At the end of the day, writing can be very gratifying, and the disembodied humanities are both appropriate and conducive to specific formats of academic work. Moreover, the power of the written word to ring in our minds across physical barriers is all the more critical in a postfact world. The pandemic revealed the importance of information and humanistic skills in a crisis. As new health information became available, Atlanta's city government reached out to the School of Modern Languages to request translators to disseminate new policies and regulations to the diverse communities around the city, and several of our graduate students volunteered to help. The virtual landscape is also creating new opportunities in online production. As Georgia Tech began to reimagine how it could work internationally post-COVID, the institute's industry collaboration unit, Innovation Ecosystems, reached out to us for help in designing a bilingual English-Chinese virtual entrepreneurship course. We were thrilled to recommend a student in the Chinese program, who was ready to step into a fast-paced professional setting.

Embodiment and Social Justice (June 2020)

While it was gratifying to see the emergence of a new interest in the fields of communication and accessible education in this crisis setting, it was also very revealing to see that the projects that faced the biggest challenges were those that struggled to overturn unjust systems. For example, two students had planned to travel to Germany to produce documentaries on vulnerable populations, and both projects were significantly altered, not only in their format but in their essence. One of these students had planned to explore Afro-German identity and the means by which Afro-Germans create identity within their own community and articulate an independent cultural identity that does not rely on existing "in contrast to" the white German identity. She had planned to conduct research with the internationally recognized community organization Each One Teach One in Berlin while also doing an internship with the organization to plan the annual Afro-German Festival. With major events and all travel canceled, this project could not take place. When well-meaning faculty members suggested the alternative of a website or podcast, the student explained the importance of body language and physical space in her work. She argued that without the visual element and without the event, the project would not convey information and identity in the correct terms. This moment reminded me that the canonical forms traditional humanities scholars turn to for academic production are rooted in Western hegemonic culture and thereby affect even the types of questions we can ask. To preserve as much of the project as possible, this student's degree completion is being extended and the project is continually being reimagined as we continue to grapple with the tension between her vision and our institutional limitations.

The other aforementioned student had planned to document how climate refugees are portrayed in the media and to produce her own photo series as an example of ethical media coverage. Without the opportunity to travel to Germany, her project morphed into a collection of photo analyses focused on political refugee populations in Germany over a ten-year period. While she was able to make her argument regarding the importance of first-person narrative in visual media coverage of refugees, her project took on a canonical tenor. Its inquiry into climate change and climate action was set aside entirely.

My own dissertation adviser once reminded me that a degree project is not a magnum opus. I am confident that both these students will find a way to pursue the fundamental goals behind their projects, whether through delaying their degree completion or in a subsequent endeavor for which these projects were but a warm-up. My colleagues and I will certainly be there to advise them as alumni and as fellow humanists when that day arrives. Still, I can't help but take note that the projects most vulnerable to disembodiment were those aiming to reexamine and re-center nonhegemonic identity—to push the needle on representation, access, and equality. These projects relied most strongly on embodied research methods, precisely because they sought to document and uplift communities and identities that were not yet already represented in established discourse. Discourse analysis may be easily done from a desk, an armchair, or even a moving train, but expanding the circle of our attention and creating new language for that circle takes a deeper level of engagement as well as direct contact with inaccessible or underexamined spaces. Across the six language programs of the MS in global media and cultures, our students were drawn to the nontraditional opportunities offered by embodiment, both in social justice work and in career pathways. As emphasized by the other essays in this volume, the humanities have great capacity to be generative of new collaborations and new spaces that facilitate the public good. Embodiment and the positionality of the body are pivotal to that endeavor.

The Physiology of Connectivity and Building an Embodied Humanistic Culture (July 2020)

In the second part of this essay, I turn to the psychology of closeness and its proven importance for well-being. The humanities are decidedly individualistic, but psychology has demonstrated that strong relationships and interconnectivity are essential for well-being. Talking about well-being in graduate education must include a discussion of relationships between individuals. In our graduate program, we tried to create a collaborative environment that could push against this isolationism, and in this section, I consider the psychology behind that effort as well as what it looked like in practice—both in person and during quarantine.

Organizational behaviorists and psychologists observing contemporary humanists might warn that our professional ethos leaves us with only threadbare access to the fabric of human fulfillment, at least on a neurological level. The paradigm-shifting Harvard Study of Human Development, which observed 724 subjects' health over seventy-five years (1938–2008) to pinpoint which factors foster well-being, famously summed up its research in a single takeaway: "Happiness equals love—full stop"

(Vaillant). The "Harvard study" reflects a major turn in the health fields over the past half-century toward recognizing the critical importance of strong relationships in health and well-being. Following John Bowlby's foundational studies on emotional attachment in the 1960s, evidence has continued to increase that the human brain is not self-contained. Rather, humans are intrinsically relational. Our relationships are "a symphony of mutual exchange and internal adaptation whereby two mammals become attuned to each other's inner states" (Lannon et al. 63). In *A General Theory of Love*, Richard Lannon, Thomas Lewis, and Fari Amini argue that science and society must acknowledge human beings' inherent interdependence. They locate "love" in the limbic system, which allows the mammalian brain to perceive, co-experience, and care about others' emotional states. They posit "limbic resonance" and "limbic revision" as neurological intersubjectivity—that is, people in close relationships actually rewrite each other's brains as they begin to mimic each other's emotional responses to various situations, take on different roles and specializations in a team, and learn to recognize each other's survival needs. *A General Theory of Love* argues that relationships are not simply a source of joy and emotional richness but are also essential for health and have a physical manifestation. Once formed, the authors write, they exist in the body's neurology as tangibly as hunger, vision, or pain—a reality that has been brought into sharp relief during quarantine.

The interconnected brain flies in the face of canonical individualism. Humanistic education and higher education in general have failed to take this biological reality into account, leading to a culture that systematically prevents flourishing. Our neat philosophies of self and rubrics of personal success cannot account for the power of relationships to shape our actions and experiences. Those relationships—whether strong, dysfunctional, or unacknowledged—also populate the professional arena. In the popular business strategy book *The Culture Code*, Daniel Coyle argues that an organization's success depends on the ability to create a strong, cohesive culture and mimic the cognitive safety offered in a family unit (8). In alignment with the concept of limbic resonance, Coyle argues that this cohesion is built not just through shared ideals or purpose but through "a steady pulse of subtle behaviors that signal safety" (12). Like *A General Theory of Love*, *The Culture Code* urges us that the "protolanguage" of safety is physical ("proximity, eye contact, energy, mimicry, turn taking"; 9–10), and that human connectivity is embodied. Describing the teamwork of the Navy Seals, Coyle writes, "[I]t looks smooth and quiet. But . . . beneath the surface, communication is happening. It takes the form of invisible exchanges: Someone weakens, and the people next to him adjust their efforts to keep the log level and steady.... A conversation travels back and forth through the fibers of the log" (121). This same form of communication, located outside language and grammar, applies to the single-minded collaboration of a surgical team, a cast of actors in a play, or a group of students organizing a major event.

Whether with purposeful pedagogy or as an invisible force, the physiology of limbic resonance is as ubiquitous a reality in graduate school as it would be in any work environment. How does the psychology of closeness operate in the workplace, and how does our profession's jagged relationship to closeness and embodiment affect graduate school as a psychological work experience? Although humanities research is often described as a lonely, isolating endeavor, humanities practices are also entrenched in profoundly interpersonal models of pedagogy, such as the shared focus of a close-knit seminar group, the bonds between students surviving a study abroad, and the lifelong adviser-advisee relationship, built over years of quiet conversation. The physical spaces in which the humanities take place are private, personal, and immersive.

Even a traditional humanities seminar is readily shaped by body language, the mirroring of emotional states, and the latent power dynamics of students and professors. When we read aloud a passage that touched us deeply, our voice and our posture convey interpretive affect. If our classmates lean forward to hear us, we may feel safe enough to deliver a more immersed reading. If our voice shudders in an anxious moment, our classmates—sitting two, four, or six feet away—may sense this anxiety limbically, shifting the group's interpretation of the text ever so slightly. Alexander Pentland of the MIT Human Dynamics Lab suggests that subtle social signals such as mirroring, turn taking, and mutual influence are "as important as linguistic content in predicting behavioral outcome" and statistically predictive both in immediate events, like negotiations, and in long-term outcomes, like divorce, "sometimes months or years into the future" (Pentland). The graduate seminar, as a space of group interaction, can shape the direction of research interests, professional relationships, and, in turn, long-term career outcomes.

When I arrived in Atlanta, my colleagues were my first teachers in the practices that can foster inclusion in a humanities department: rank-neutral faculty meetings; an accepted habit of copying all group members on an e-mail; a culture of feedback and cowriting grant and curriculum proposals; regular social gatherings; announcing good news to the whole unit (whether it be a promotion, a new book, a new baby, or a staff award); and the creation of clear anchor spaces (locations and specific times reserved for School events). To me as an early-career, female, non-tenure-track faculty member, these small signals repeatedly conveyed that my work mattered and that I was part of a community.

When the School of Modern Languages launched the MS in global media and cultures, imagining a collaborative humanities practice was a latent but central component of a career curriculum that aimed to prepare students for a highly collaborative professional world. I would like to think that by coteaching core courses, co-advising each student, and codirecting the program in a team of three, our faculty modeled collaboration for our students. Our "Culture at Work" Graduate Research Assistantship (GRA) also appointed students to various community engagement roles that tasked them with engaging deeply with a specific audience over a sustained period of time and included a course (one credit per semester) in which students learned basic theories of empathy, organizational behavior, and community work. Our students discussed how concepts of cultural identity and narrative could apply to building cohesion and safety in a college dorm, in a corporate office, and in the graduate program they themselves were experiencing and indeed cocreating.

After we locked the doors to our building in March 2020, it was a challenge to re-create a semblance of this "collision-rich environment" (Coyle 23) online, and I cannot claim to have fully succeeded. We created two 24/7 video conference rooms and launched a weekly faculty memo and student memo for conveying important information, as this was an active period for admissions, summer enrollment, and final project review. To provide a sense of interpersonal closeness between students, we divided the cohort into three-person "writing teams" in the month leading up to their prospectus defenses. Writing teams exchanged drafts of their prospectuses, résumés, and ePortfolios; they were required to connect regularly and to conduct video rehearsals of their presentations. Teams were free to communicate however they wanted to, as long as they had a space to develop an in-depth understanding of each other's work and share in each other's experiences. Writing teams, we hoped, would offer consistent signals of safety through repeated exchange, creating the opportunity for limbic resonance and stronger support. Indeed, after a day and a night of rehearsals, I woke up on the day of my students' defense presentations to discover the distinct symptoms of pre-presentation anxiety, even though I had nothing at stake personally. Throughout the day, the entire cohort supported and collectively experienced each other's defense presentations. All students attended the presentations of their writing team members, and many chose to attend other talks as well, showing their concern for each other and the capacity to empathize across distances.

Coda: A New Incoming Class (August 2020)

As I conclude this essay, we are in the middle of a fully virtual orientation to welcome our second cohort of graduate students into the program. While Georgia Tech's campus will be open, the heart of our program will remain virtual to accommodate all students and faculty members, including those in high-risk categories and those who cannot enter the United States for visa reasons. We are keenly aware that orientation is a critical socialization process that can determine degree outcomes and that a departmental orientation is particularly important to adequately support underrepresented students in a program (Poock). Creating a sense of community and safety is our foremost challenge and priority in designing this orientation in a virtual environment.

Drawing on the embodied framework, the orientation emphasizes both shared space and relationship development. We created two space-relationship pairings to shape a robust community for students: an informal social media group paired with a peer mentorship program and a *Canvas* site paired with a two-week series of orientation events. Social media offered an informal socializing space and a touchpoint for questions while the *Canvas* site created a structured introduction to both the requirements of the program and the multifaceted community through multiple entry points: a fifteen-minute welcome video introducing the program's faculty and alumni, small-group video discussions bringing together faculty members and students within each language track, open-discussion seminars on topics like what to expect in a graduate seminar, and workshops with alumni, including a discussion of resilience and suggestions on confronting the challenges of graduate school. The *Canvas* site also provided several hangout spaces: 24-7 video conference rooms for each language group and for the whole program as well as discussion boards and e-mail lists so students, faculty members, and staff members can easily get in touch. The workshops aim to create open lines of communication between students, faculty members, and alumni, and to foreground the act of connecting—speaking, chatting, meeting—as an essential mode of being in the program.

Thus far, students have been responding positively to the orientation. It has been gratifying to see how excited faculty members are to welcome students and participate in the process; statements like "We're so excited that you're here" and "Don't hesitate to reach out" echo again and again in faculty introductions with a redundancy I am keen to preserve. Although it is only the illusion of proximity, students seem to be feeling a sense of belonging, at least according to our peer mentors, who report that students have expressed a sense of "reassurance" and shared other positive feedback.

I do not yet feel like I know the incoming class. But the 2019–20 academic year has taught me that closeness takes place in space and over time. Over the past two years, I have had the privilege of working closely with several faculty members, staff members, and students to conceptualize and put into practice a model of humanities education that embraces collaboration. Three or more times a week for almost two years, we gathered in various configurations at a trapezoidal table in a small room adjacent to the lobby of the Modern Languages building, designing flyers and marketing materials, editing the program website, putting stacks of flyers into folders, restocking the candy and swag for distribution at grad school recruiting fairs, reviewing the admissions database, negotiating GRA positions with other campus units, planning the course schedules, creating faculty retreat presentations, writing the student handbook, and planning events and guest lectures. We also conducted advising sessions, consoled anxious visitors, wrote stories of student success, and tried to solve problems we had never anticipated. We developed a shared language and a culture of care that seeped into the student experience. It is unlikely that I will ever share this kind of proximity with the incoming cohort; some of us are not in the state of Georgia at all. However, I have faith that we will find other pathways to professional closeness and meaningful collaboration. Our limbic systems are designed for it, and so is, I hope, our program.

WORKS CITED

Coyle, Daniel. *The Culture Code: The Secrets of Highly Successful Groups.* Bantam Books, 2018.

Home page. *Gapingvoid Culture Design Group*, gapingvoid.com/. Accessed 20 July 2020.

Lannon, Richard, et al. *A General Theory of Love.* Knopf Doubleday Publishing Group, 2007.

Madsbjerg, Christian. *Sensemaking: The Power of the Humanities in the Age of the Algorithm.* Hachette Books, 2017.

Novalis. "Die Lehrlinge zu Sais." *Gedichte: Die Lehrlinge zu Sais*, edited by Johannes Mahr, Philipp Reclam, 1984.

Pentland, Alexander. "Social Dynamics: Signals and Behavior." MIT Media Laboratory Technical Note 579, Oct. 2004.

Poock, Michael C. "Graduate Student Orientation: Assessing Needs and Methods of Delivery." *Journal of College Student Development*, vol. 43, no. 2, Mar.-Apr. 2002, pp. 231–45.

Richards, Robert J. *The Romantic Conception of Life: Science and Philosophy in the Age of Goethe.* U of Chicago P, 2002.

Schumaker, Erin. "Coronavirus Declared Global Health Emergency by WHO after 1st Person-to-Person US Case Reported." *ABC News*, 30 Jan. 2020, abcnews.go.com/Health/world-health-organization-decide-coronavirus-global-health-emergency/story?id=68639487.

———. "Timeline: How Coronavirus Got Started." *ABC News*, abcnews.go.com/Health/timeline-coronavirus-started/story?id=69435165. Accessed 28 July 2020.

Strakovsky, Yevgenya. "Updates Regarding Institute Transitions." Modern Languages Graduate Program, 13 Mar. 2020. *Canvas* announcement.

———. "Virtual Grad School 1: Tips for Creating a Great Work-space at Home." *Advising Blog*, Graduate Program in Modern Languages, web.archive.org/web/20210927093944/https://grad.modlangs.gatech.edu/blog/virtualgradschool1.

Vaillant, George. "Yes, I Stand by My Words, 'Happiness Equals Love—Full Stop.'" *Positive Psychology News*, 16 July 2009, positivepsychologynews.com/news/george-vaillant/200907163163.

Joy and the Politics of the Public Good

Stacy M. Hartman and Bianca C. Williams

"What changes would we have to make to doctoral education if the emotional wellness of our students were at the center?" Bianca posed this question to a room of students and faculty mentors during a session of the PublicsLab seminar at the Graduate Center, City University of New York (CUNY), in February 2020. In response, there were smiles, sighs, furrowed eyebrows, and blank stares; one student let out a "Yes!" in affirmation of the question. Bianca continued, "How might we train students differently—as humanists and social scientists—if we viewed their wellness as essential to their teaching, research, writing, and communication of knowledge?" After a few moments of silence, a student suggested that doctoral students would be fully funded and receive appropriate pay, as the lack of funding negatively affected health and wellness. Other students offered commentary about the types of mentoring they needed as they navigated the stress-inducing and often hidden rules of doctoral and disciplinary training. A faculty mentor discussed some of the structural barriers to coteaching and research collaborations with colleagues, students, and community members, acknowledging that the tenure and promotion process often penalized faculty members for this shared labor and knowledge creation. Throughout the discussion, participants talked about the ways various systems of oppression in higher education, like racism, sexism, and ableism, created an environment that led many to feel anxious, depressed, overwhelmed, disheartened, insecure, and incompetent.

However, the conversation hit a turning point as we, the authors of this essay, asked participants what had brought them to graduate school and why they were pursuing doctorates. Eyes lit up and voices became animated as participants spoke of the hometowns and communities they wished to serve, the research inquiries that had led them down exciting rabbit holes, the activism they had engaged in, the skills they wanted to acquire in order to address particular issues, and the changes they wanted to make in higher education and in various industries. As people tapped more deeply into their motivations, joy became mixed in with the heaviness in the room. Students and faculty mentors spoke transparently about being forced to push their initial motivations aside in order to fall into line with what is traditionally valued and rewarded in the academy. But they also shared stories about the work in service to multiple publics that had brought them joy.

This conversation about wellness, affect, public scholarship, justice, and doctoral education is essential to the work of the PublicsLab. The PublicsLab is a center focused on transforming humanistic doctoral education and providing graduate students with the professional development and support necessary to practice scholarship—particularly public scholarship—effectively. Here, Bianca, as faculty lead, and Stacy, as director, encourage graduate students, faculty members, and practitioners to trouble the oft-assumed boundaries between "the academy" and "the public" and to lean into the values, desires, commitments, and beliefs that made them want to pursue research in the first place. Over the past two years, as we have supported students in their public scholarship, we have been dedicated to paying attention to their affective experiences during the doctoral process. We recognize that their emotional wellness is crucial to their academic journey, particularly to their experience of joy. At the PublicsLab, preparing students to be great scholars requires us to take public scholarship seriously while also recognizing that emotional wellness and joy are necessities for doctoral education.

The PublicsLab was founded in 2018, when the Graduate Center received a $2.26 million, five-year grant from the Andrew W. Mellon Foundation intended to "transform doctoral education for the public good" ("About"). The PublicsLab sponsors a robust slate of events and internships that serve the wider Graduate Center community. We also run a regranting program for departments with ambitions of transforming doctoral curricula to better serve the public good. But the centerpiece of our program is an interdisciplinary fellowship, composed of students from across the humanities and humanistic social sciences. PublicsLab fellows spend a year working together in community to consider the philosophy, mindset, theories, methods, and practices of public scholarship, which they then put into practice the following year through projects and internships at external organizations (see "Public Fellows"). As evidenced by their responses to the question of what had brought them to graduate school, many of the fellows have strong community connections and feel a deep-seated urge to uplift their own communities or to work toward a more just society in general; hence their projects are almost invariably justice-focused in some sense. Students have worked from their interest and knowledge in areas such as educational justice, legal justice, environmental justice, and human rights, to name only a few. As faculty lead and director, we provide mentorship and continuity, but the students are the driving force and the moral compass of our project. They hold us accountable and shape the program in ways that neither of us could have ever expected.

It quickly became clear when we began working together to create the PublicsLab that we shared a set of values related to acknowledging and centering the emotional wellness of our students. Bianca's 2018 book, *The Pursuit of Happiness: Black Women, Diasporic Dreams, and the Politics of Emotional Transnationalism*, examines happiness as a political and oppositional act for Black women and highlights Black women's agency in the pursuit of happiness. Stacy's dissertation looked at affect and moral reasoning and posited postmodernism and the rise of the hermeneutics of suspicion as an emotional response to fascism in post-1945 Germany. As scholars, we are both committed to taking seriously the emotional dimensions of life inside the academy.

Making emotional wellness a central tenet of the program has been a means of resisting what Stefano Harney and Fred Moten have called a "professional and critical commitment to negligence" (41) in the academy. Furthermore, we emphasize the affective dimensions of graduate education—the affective labor involved in teaching, mentoring, and, yes, even administering a program like this one. This interest in affect is connected to how we—the program's administrators and fellows alike—have come to think about "the public good" as something more radical than the project's original mandate would suggest.

Drawing on Harney and Moten's essays in *The Undercommons: Fugitive Planning and Black Study* and on the cultural theorist Sara Ahmed's *On Being Included*, we here consider the ways in which the PublicsLab engages in "the undercommon refusal of the academy of misery" (Harney and Moten 118); how it attempts to center "study," as Harney and Moten conceive of it; and how, in doing both these things, it seeks to create a doctoral education that is social, joyful, and committed to justice.

Defining the "Public Good"

The question of what, exactly, the public good *is* is one we have encountered frequently in the last two years. What public—or publics? Whose good? Do we mean "a public good," as in public ownership, or "for the good of the public"? And who are we, administrators and fellows, to decide what's good for anyone? Are we not, ourselves, a public?

"Public good" often appears to be a politically neutral phrase, although many institutions long considered to be "public goods" in the United States have become politicized, from the Centers for Disease Control to the postal service. Our mission statement conceives of the work of the PublicsLab less "as a public good" than "for the public good." The shift in language from a noun to a verb implies that the university is in service to and yet still separate from a broader public and invokes vague, comforting feelings without encouraging too much examination of the relationship between the university and its publics. Furthermore, it does not force the university to examine the racism, sexism, and classism inherent in its institutionalized assumptions about what constitutes good scholarly work. The assumption is that doing service work for the public is good and may be impactful, but, as it remains marginalized at many universities, it is not viewed as the "real" work of the university and therefore seems unthreatening at first glance.

In short, "the public good" as a phrase hides the fact that so much of what we do in the PublicsLab is about addressing systems of power. Work that addresses systems of power is not politically neutral. It is justice work, and it is deeply, unapologetically political. For something to be "a public good" or "for the public good," it must face, understand, and address the inequities that are prevalent in the public and within publics. Centering racial equity and social justice is essential to doing work that is effectively public and good.

If we understand that working for the public good is political, then it becomes easy to see how the programming, institution building, and knowledge production we do is closely aligned with what the academy labels "diversity work." It is true that not all who work for the public good do so with a critical eye toward racism or any other form of oppression. However, because of our values and research interests (and those of our fellows), we bring specific political commitments related to justice, equity, and anti-racism to our work at the PublicsLab. We are constantly asking questions about who benefits from particular histories, narratives, and methodological choices; who has access to which resources; which types of knowledge are valued or dismissed; and which communities get erased and why during the doctoral education process. We engage in similar conversations about access, belonging, difference, and power as diversity workers in other parts of the university. Ahmed writes, "Diversity workers work from their institutional involvement. Diversity practitioners do not simply work *at* institutions, they also work *on* them, given that their explicit remit is to redress existing institutional goals or priorities" (22). As we participate in mentoring and curriculum changes that challenge the power differentials underlying traditional doctoral education, we find ourselves frequently working on the Graduate Center and higher education more broadly. Though the mission statement declares that our focus is on the public good (with our lens facing outward), in reality, much of the PublicsLab labor leads us to do significant work on higher education (with a lens focused inward).[1]

This work on the university requires us to address not only the ways in which higher education has failed but also the ways in which it has succeeded in perpetuating unjust systems of power even while it critiques them. It is possible, if you are white and working with a predominantly white student population, to take the mission of the university itself for granted as fundamentally good, if flawed in its implementation. It is possible, if you are white and working with a predominantly white student body, to not see, or ignore, the ways in which the university harms particular students who are racially marked and marginalized. However, at the Graduate Center, the student population is more racially and ethnically diverse than at some other predominantly white institutions, and within this community students are often aware that their relationship to the university is different from that of their white peers. Students of color drawn to the PublicsLab are frequently vocal about their experiences with, and analyses of, the inequities within higher education. If one takes seriously the affective, emotional dimensions of life inside the academy, and hopes to center emotional wellness for one's students—especially students of color, queer and trans students, first-generation immigrant or college-educated students—then it is impossible, or at the very least unconscionable, to ignore the harm that the university can and does do.

To be clear, very little of this was conceived of in the grant whose language still defines the PublicsLab to various publics. It is not wholly obvious from looking at our website, for example, that the PublicsLab supports and promotes not only *public* work but specifically *justice* work. Part of our project in this essay will therefore be a public rethinking of the PublicsLab's mission statement to encompass the development of our own thinking about the institutions in which we are embedded and our at-times fraught relationship to them.

Our Starting Point: The PublicsLab Mission Statement

Mission statements are a curious genre. Ahmed notes that "mission talk" is "'happy talk,' a way of telling a happy story of the institution that is at once a story of the institution as happy" (10). Such statements leave no room for ambivalence or for critique of the institution itself. They are, in effect, the very opposite of what Harney and Moten attempt in their essay "The University and the Undercommons."

Harney and Moten always come at the undercommons sideways, out of the corner of their eye, rather than head-on, as though it might vanish if one ever tried to look at it squarely. They describe the undercommons as the imaginative home of the subversive (Black) intellectual. It is the university's "refugee colony . . . where the work gets done, where the work gets subverted, where the revolution is still black, still strong." It is born out of an ambivalent or even adversarial relationship between the university and the intellectual, an acknowledgment that an institution is incapable of love or care. Harney and Moten write:

> But certainly, this much is true in the United States: it cannot be denied that the university is a place of refuge, and it cannot be accepted that the university is a place of enlightenment. In the face of these conditions one can only sneak into the university and steal what one can. To abuse its hospitality, to spite its mission, . . . to be in but not of—this is the path of the subversive intellectual in the modern university. (26)

The question, "What is the undercommons?" is probably the wrong question altogether. "Where is the undercommons?" doesn't quite work either. "Who is the undercommons?" seems closer to the truth—that the undercommons exists primarily in scholars' relationships with each other and in their relationships to their own institutions. It encompasses the "Maroon communities" of "composition teachers, mentorless graduate students, adjunct Marxist historians, queer management professors, state college ethnic studies departments, closed-down film programs, visa-expired Yemeni student newspaper editors, historically black college sociologists, and feminist engineers" (30).

The undercommons emerges out of ambivalence toward and critique of the institution and as such has no mission statement. The PublicsLab was conceived as having a mutually beneficial relationship to the Graduate Center, so it would be going too far to call it a true undercommons. And yet what has emerged in the recruitment of the first and second cohorts, and over the course of the first two years of study, is that the PublicsLab is, for many of our students, a refuge from the supposed refuge of the university. It is a place where they come to escape the neglectful aspects of their programs and where the experiences of students of color and queer students are foregrounded in a way that they are not in the wider university.

This work is not evident in our mission statement. The PublicsLab mission statement, as presented on our website, is pulled more or less from the grant proposal, with only light editing, and was institutionally coauthored by a committee on which neither of us sat. It reads as follows:

> The PublicsLab has two broad goals. The first is to ensure that The Graduate Center's humanities doctoral programs prepare students for careers both within and outside of academe. The expertise required for humanistic inquiry is vital to understanding the world around us. Through fellowships, internships, workshops, and curriculum enhancement, we strive to provide students with skills and opportunities that will allow them to thrive in academic and non-academic professions.
>
> The second goal is to encourage doctoral students and faculty to engage in scholarship that is accessible to the public, deepens our understanding of burning issues, and might even spur social change. The PublicsLab seeks to incubate and promote socially-engaged learning and creative, community-based research and to attract scholars who are committed to generating new knowledge that contributes to the key issues of our time. ("About")

The lack of allowance for critique and ambivalence in mission statements makes them troubled and troubling documents for those of us undertaking organizing work in the academy. There is no room in this mission statement to note that, while it is perhaps true that humanistic expertise is vital, the push for PhD "career diversity" is rooted in the current academic job market crisis for humanities and social science students. It also cannot acknowledge that the CUNY system, with its overreliance on adjuncts, contributes to that crisis ("Facts"). There is no space in this mission statement to note that the Graduate Center has suffered from severe austerity, along with the rest of CUNY. Although multiple CUNY campuses are regularly named in the top ten in the United States for upward social mobility (Reber and Sinclair), the state and the city have deprived the institution of the resources necessary to do its work for years now. CUNY is a public university that serves a vast and diverse student body, and yet even as that student body has grown and diversified, public support in the form of taxpayer dollars has diminished ("Addressing"). To describe these conditions is not proper "mission talk."

What is especially curious about the construction of the PublicsLab mission statement is that the two goals are separated out so distinctly, when they are in fact closely intertwined. As leaders of the program, we aren't inclined to distinguish the preparation for public scholarship from the preparation for careers beyond the academy. Preparation for public scholarship *is* preparation for careers outside the academy, and not only because it involves learning new skills and ways of communicating. Thinking about public scholarship as not only translational but foundational and critical—not only an add-on but a requirement—transforms that scholarship, and it raises the ethical stakes of the work in ways that may lead students down a variety of pathways, both inside and outside the academy.

And yet we are aware that the tenure and promotion system of the university does not value work that is *too* public. The prestige economy of higher education resists work that is relevant, accessible, or activist and often punishes scholars who do it, especially scholars of color and queer scholars. It does so by denying or delaying tenure, leveling empty but damning phrases such as "lack of academic rigor" at them in justification.[2] Such accusations of poor quality—difficult if not impossible to refute either in dissertation defenses or in the tenure and promotion process—are rooted in assumptions about who does public work, what that public work does, and, indeed, who the public is. If the public at large is presumed to be unintellectual (or even anti-intellectual), then work done with them must also be less intellectually valuable.

Even more curious than the split between these two goals, however, is the phrase "might even spur social change." We detect in this phrase a note of ambivalence—rare, as we have said, for a mission statement—about whether work conducted within the bounds of the university can spur "social change." This ambivalence is revealing. First, it marks the desire not to overpromise and underdeliver, as no one wants to be held accountable for "spurring social change," which is difficult to measure in terms of programmatic success. It also belies a very real concern about the relevance of humanities work, as well as the desire not to appear "too political" in the project's reach. More subtly, however, this ambivalence may mark uncertainty about what "spurring social change" might do to the university itself. The result is a palpable anxiety on the part of the institution.

Resisting Neglectful Professionalization

The reason for this anxiety becomes increasingly clear as one spends more time considering the depth of change that a substantive commitment to "the public good" might bring to a university. Much in the same way that a substantive commitment to diversity would be transformative and disruptive, for the university to insert itself into public life (beyond preparing a workforce for deployment or catalyzing social mobility) would transform the university into something it does not yet recognize. The university would have to take up a different set of responsibilities and priorities and dedicate itself to a form of education that is hallmarked by care.

    Imagining such a scenario would be easier if the relationship between neglect and professionalization were not so clearly about the imbrication of the university with capitalism. The university has traditionally been a refuge for those who wish to avoid the more overtly brutal forms of capitalism, and yet it has always produced a workforce for capitalism. It has done this by encouraging a highly individualized and isolated form of scholarship. Achievement within the university is individual; this is especially true in the humanities, where single-authored work counts above all else. Therefore, while the humanities think of themselves as antiprofessional (if not unprofessional), they remain quintessentially professional by Harney and Moten's definition: "It is professionalization itself that is devoted to the asocial, the university itself that reproduces the knowledge of how to neglect sociality in its very concern for what it calls asociality" (40).

    It is our view that professionalization need not be neglectful but that neglectful professionalization within the academy, and especially within graduate education, is, in Ahmed's terms, institutionalized. It has become "second nature" or "natural" (24); neglectful professionalization has receded into the background and become—like institutional whiteness, or, indeed, in conflation with institutional whiteness—business as usual. It becomes obvious only when someone or something comes along to disrupt it, triggering a sort of affective immune response. The disruptive element—often a scholar but sometimes a program or even an emerging discipline—is told that they are not the right "fit," or they are not performing scholarliness correctly. Their work is too creative, too public, too collaborative, too practice-based. It is "unprofessional" and it does not belong in the university.

An astonishing number of students, especially queer students and students of color, receive such messages, either implicitly or explicitly, in the first two years of their PhD programs. Many of them leave, to the detriment of us all. Some stay and work for change but do so too often at the expense of their physical and mental well-being. Whether they stay or leave, they are frequently seen as unprofessional and unmotivated or as unsuccessful in navigating perfectionism or impostor training.[3] Instead of viewing these disruptions as opportunities to engage in deep reflection about disciplinary and departmental values, or taking steps toward institutional change that incorporates caring and innovative ways of knowledge-making, the academy carries these narrow, neglectful notions of professionalization forward, with little recognition that at the core of this type of professionalization is institutional whiteness.

Oriented in opposition to neglectful professionalization is Harney and Moten's conception of "study." Harney and Moten conceive of "study" as inherently social. In an interview with Stevphen Shukaitis, Moten says,

> When I think about the way we use the term "study," I think we are committed to the idea that study is what you do with other people. It's talking and walking around with other people, working, dancing, suffering, some irreducible convergence of all three, held under the name of speculative practice. . . . The point of calling it "study" is to mark that the incessant and irreversible intellectuality of these activities is already present. (Harney and Moten 110)

Study, in Harney and Moten's conception, is not institutionalized. It is social, based in care, disruptive, and "unprofessional"—or perhaps "more than professional" (30). To reorient professionalization within the academy toward the social would be to reorient it toward care, affect, and equity.[4]

Harney and Moten's concept of study and the ways in which it subverts and resists institutionalized neglect inside the academy bears some resemblance to Kathleen Fitzpatrick's concept of "generous thinking." Generous thinking, Fitzpatrick says in her book of the same name, is "a mode of engagement that emphasizes listening over speaking, community over individualism, collaboration over competition, and lingering with the ideas that are in front of us rather than continually pressing forward to where we want to go" (4). This idea of generous thinking reconceptualizes the university "not as a giant nonprofit organization, focused on the fiscal sustainability required to provide services ... but instead as a site of voluntary community—a site of solidarity—forged with and by the publics we seek to engage." This reconceiving of the university would allow us "to begin to develop new models, new structures, that could help all of us reconnect with and recommit to a sense of the common good" (13). If we can reassert our values, we can successfully transform the university, bringing about what Fitzpatrick refers to as a "paradigm shift" in higher education toward a model that is neither based on elite research universities nor on blunt workforce preparation for a capitalist economy. Rather, the university as Fitzpatrick imagines it would be a community "grounded in an ethic of care" (208).

Fitzpatrick's ideas are inspirational and attractive for those of us who have identified a lack of care as one of the major problems within the university. Indeed, Fitzpatrick's work and the PublicsLab were conceived in the same spirit, and our current mission statement resonates with much of what Fitzpatrick has to say. But while Fitzpatrick shares with Harney and Moten a sense of the possibilities of prosocial forms of learning and living, she doesn't embrace their skepticism about the university as a place where such forms of learning and living are universally possible. Fitzpatrick's work reflects the conviction that although the system is broken, it wants to be reformed, even transformed. Her use of the words "reconnect" and "recommit" implies that there was a period in the history of the American university when institutions were committed to the common good. Fitzpatrick does in fact cite that halcyon time in the middle of the twentieth century, when universities briefly had sufficient funding from state and federal governments (191–92).

The story that Fitzpatrick tells about the "Golden Era" (Boggs et al.) of the American university is familiar from the field of (white) critical university studies and the work of scholars such as Christopher Newfield. In contrast, Harney and Moten, and others writing about higher education—particularly scholars of color—resist the urge to rehabilitate the university. Abigail Boggs, Eli Meyerhoff, Nick Mitchell, and Zach Schwartz-Weinstein argue in "Abolitionist University Studies: An Invitation" that this way of thinking, endemic to critical university studies, elides the systemically racist and exclusionary history of American higher education; it ignores that many if not most universities were built on slavery and that the origin story of land-grant universities is rooted in the seizure of land and the displacement of Indigenous peoples (see also la paperson; Wilder;

Porter; and Williams et al.). By conveniently forgetting the extent to which government support for the American university of the mid-twentieth century was tied to national defense and the Cold War, this narrative also has the effect of distancing the institution from "genocidal domestic and foreign policy." Abolitionist university studies underscores the ways in which this narrative about the midcentury public university "relies on a periodization . . . that produces the appearance of justice by cropping out the violence constitutive of the institution itself," and it retells the history of the American university as one of violent accumulation—of capital, of land, and of labor, including slave labor (Boggs et al). Such an institution, these scholars argue, may not be redeemable or recuperable.

In the first PublicsLab seminar, held in the spring semester of 2019, a number of students of color offered a strong critique of *Generous Thinking*. Though Fitzpatrick cites Black scholars such as bell hooks and Tressie McMillan Cottom and offers scenes from her classroom, the students felt that experiences like their own in the academy and pertinent scholarship from disciplines like Black studies were erased or not taken into account. They felt that many of the ideas of solidarity, collaboration, and the centering of the public that anchor Fitzpatrick's framework of generosity had been theorized and advocated for in decades past by Black organizers and scholars who had been punished and marginalized within academic spaces precisely because they encouraged these practices. Students were frustrated in two different ways: first, they felt that only certain people with racialized, gendered, and classed privileges were able to practice Fitzpatrick's generosity in a way that would be recognized as valuable by the academy, even though others without those privileges had been practicing and advocating for it for years; and, second, they felt that people of color's critiques of texts, disciplinary practices, and doctoral training were often righteous and that Fitzpatrick's call for generosity would be used by others with more power to silence, ostracize, and dismiss them.

In the end, these students argued that the absence of a critical lens toward race and racism in Fitzpatrick's discussion of generosity (in contrast to the explicit analysis of race in Harney and Moten's work) demonstrated how even some of the most well-intentioned efforts at making the academy more inclusive and welcoming could result in exclusion, neglect, and further marginalization. Through this critique, the students questioned us as leaders of the PublicsLab about our commitment to equity and generosity and held us accountable. That seminar taught us some powerful lessons about the different positionalities and critical lenses students brought to the PublicsLab and served as a reflection point that made us revisit how we practiced our values and commitments in future courses and programming.

Taking all this into consideration, we are left with a number of difficult questions: What does it mean to work within and on an institution that should not or perhaps cannot be rehabilitated? How do we imagine study and generosity in ways that do not reify the institution itself or reproduce past and present inequities? Finally, if the institution will never care for us in the ways we need and want it to, then how do we ensure that we care for each other?

The critiques that PublicsLab fellows frequently offer about the university contain elements of the critiques offered by Harney and Moten, Boggs, Meyerhoff, Mitchell, Schwartz-Weinstein, and other scholars of color; the fellows are all too aware of the ways in which the system is functioning as intended—in ways that do harm, even violence, to them. And yet they find themselves inside the university anyway. Some students are there because they wish "to sneak into the university and steal what one can" (Harney and Moten 26), but for others, the decision to remain—at least for now—contains a complicated and at times painful hope that the university *can* be transformed. Although this dual perspective is not currently foregrounded in the mission statement of the PublicsLab, we believe it should be. It is precisely within noninstitutionalized spaces like the PublicsLab that this sort of tension can be navigated and that the potential for true transformation exists. It is our intention to foreground this tension in our new mission statement.

Centering joy and equity in the mission of the PublicsLab requires us to focus on process rather than product. Our original mission statement clearly articulates the two broad end goals of the project: to prepare doctoral students for a range of careers and to support scholarship that engages the public, with the tenuously expressed hope of spurring social change. However, it is in making decisions about how to accomplish these goals that we are able to create opportunities for more joy and greater equity in graduate education. The PublicsLab therefore has the goal of providing graduate students at the Graduate Center with the opportunity for study, in Harney and Moten's sense.

Centering Joy and Equity: The New Mission Statement of the PublicsLab

Public scholarship requires students to think of their work as a social and collaborative endeavor in which different forms of expertise are valued equally. We model this by providing a space for students to be their own selves and to build on what they already know rather than assuming a blank slate or an empty vessel. Students bring with them commitments to their communities, to their politics, and to their families. We support students as they explore ways of fulfilling these commitments through their scholarship. We do not ask students to disentangle their identities and selves from their academic work but rather acknowledge that academic work rooted in community, identity, and politics is often more rigorous, more sustaining, and more publicly relevant than work that is not. We demonstrate this by regularly asking ourselves and our fellows during class sessions and programming, "Who is your community? To whom are you accountable? How does your research demonstrate this commitment?"

We are collectively committed to the idea that no one knows everything and that cocreating and cothinking allow us to create new knowledge together. We are committed to building a generous and trusting space that includes practicing public humanists from outside the university. In inviting practitioners to join us, we honor the different personal and professional choices that PhDs have made and acknowledge the many and varied needs and desires each of us has. We learn from the diverse and creative ways these practitioners produce, communicate, and teach their knowledges.

We make space for ambivalence, doubt, and critique of our own methods, purpose, and institutional engagements. We engage in a generative and thoughtful process of experimentation as a community. We make visible different forms of labor, including the care work and emotional labor that are necessary for generosity, and we acknowledge the uneven distribution of such labor across lines of race, class, and gender. We advocate and organize, in small and big ways, against the systems of power that enable these inequities to continue. By rendering visible the dysfunction that is inevitably present in any relationship between an individual and an institution, we are able to reimagine that relationship as one that is more generous, more nurturing, more equitable, and more joyful.

As we write this, it is summer 2020, and life at the Graduate Center and in New York City more generally has been completely disrupted by the COVID-19 pandemic. Only a few weeks after the seminar discussion in which we talked about centering joy and wellness in graduate education, we were all sent home to continue the semester in isolation from one another. Our students have been able to meet only virtually since March

2020. CUNY was hit harder by the first wave of COVID than any other university system, suffering thirty-eight reported deaths of faculty members and staff members as of this writing (Valbrun). Furthermore, the nation has been roiled by a renewed conversation about race, policing, abolition, and the systemic undervaluing and dehumanizing of Black lives.

In such times, we have all rediscovered, everything is heightened. Both privilege and inequality become more apparent. The consequence of decades of neglect of CUNY on the part of the state and the city—neglect that is itself a consequence of systemic racism—has become heartbreakingly obvious through its impact on students who do not have abundant family and community resources to fall back on. Discussions about access to health insurance that would have been unthinkable at either of our own doctoral alma maters have become a daily occurrence as we scramble to meet the most immediate needs of as many students as possible.

Under these circumstances, we at the PublicsLab have found ourselves revisiting the question that hangs over every grant-funded initiative: institutionalization. To become institutionalized has many advantages, the most obvious of which is funding. But it is more than that; when an initiative is funded not by grants but through the institution where it lives, something novel is brought from the margins into the center. It is deemed "mission critical." Institutionalization allows for longevity, the retainment of staff, and stability. However, it also has the effect of making something less visible. "When things become institutional, they recede," Ahmed writes. "To institutionalize *x* is for *x* to become routine or ordinary such that *x* becomes part of the background for those who are part of an institution" (21).

The fact that our initiative is not institutionalized yet in a traditional (or fiscal) sense is useful or even essential in this: since the PublicsLab isn't taken seriously yet by some at our institution, the community is able to hold on to joy, generosity, and care. All three concepts are connected to students' being invited and encouraged to bring their whole selves with them to their study if they so desire. We make room for their whole selves, even as we recognize that for some, this may not feel safe just yet, especially during a pandemic that has rocked our worlds. For, as we discussed elsewhere in this article, these whole selves are not seen as unproblematic by the institution. "Study," in Harney and Moten's sense, is subversive.

Even at the most basic level, if these whole selves are invited, then the institution must be prepared to respond to the needs that will arise. Responsiveness is certainly easier when there are resources at our disposal.

In April 2020, while the lumbering bureaucracy of CUNY struggled to respond to students' needs, the PublicsLab was able to implement an emergency grant program within weeks to help students whose publicly oriented research agendas had been completely disrupted by the pandemic. Some of these grants covered what we traditionally think of as research expenses, such as stipends for study participants or new technology. But some of them covered costs that fell well outside the traditional bounds of that category—child care, for example, or the cost of housing in New York City relative to where a student had intended to live over the summer. This consideration of students' whole lives would have been far more difficult, if not impossible, under conditions of institutionalization.

It would be going too far to say that we conceived of our community of fellows and their faculty mentors with Harney and Moten's principles in mind, or that we were deliberately resisting institutionalization. Instead, we came to the project hoping to create a community where doctoral students felt supported in their work and professional lives; where wellness was centered and people felt nourished intellectually, physically, and emotionally; where we were generous with each other and our publics; where hierarchy was as flat as possible and prestige was not the coin of the realm; where we had fun and engaged in activities that were intellectual, social, and joyful. We wanted to strip away the performative, professionalizing, neglectful aspects of doctoral study and create a community where a diversity of positionalities and therefore a diversity of scholars were nurtured.

Things that are possible on the margins are not always possible in the center. At the PublicsLab, we have embraced the notion that research can be affective, justice-focused, and transformative, and we believe that new knowledge often comes from practices based on collective brainstorming, asking good questions, and experimentation rather than an individualized, linear process. Moreover, we have both come to question, especially under COVID-19, as we watch administrators at CUNY campuses make cuts in anticipation of austerity measures (Lerner), whether institutionalization is always a step in the right direction.

This is a difficult reckoning. Marginalization is painful in many ways and choosing to remain joyful on the periphery feels counterintuitive. But power is not only present in the center, and so much of the influential work being undertaken on the margins, by those marginalized, in various publics and communities deemed unimportant, proves that to be true. When change comes, it often does not come from the center; rather, change happens on the margins, and then, through careful organizing, moves inward.

NOTES

1. We hesitate to use the framing of inside and outside, because we spend a great deal of time trying to complicate this binary that anchors so many conversations about the academy and publics. While literal or figurative barriers often block access to universities, spaces between these two sites are sometimes more porous than many imagine. Throughout the CUNY system, some students, staff members, and faculty members come from marginalized communities or other publics that CUNY imagines it serves. These CUNY community members may face institutional barriers to equitable access to power and resources within the university system; nevertheless, they frequently fight to ensure that their voices, and those of the publics they represent, are included in the system's mission and affairs. The boundaries of inside and outside are always in flux, blurred, and contested. As a result, we encourage students to remember that the academy itself is a type of public—one that is often deciphering whom it is speaking to and with as well as to whom it is accountable.

2. Patricia A. Matthew's edited volume *Written/Unwritten: Diversity and the Hidden Truths of Tenure* delves into this phenomenon in detail. In particular, Matthew notes that "it is often difficult for faculty in more traditional fields to fully appreciate and assess the value of scholarship in emerging fields" (xii). This is true for interdisciplinary academic fields but perhaps even more true when a colleague's work is explicitly public in nature.

3. Mike Mena, a PhD candidate in anthropology at CUNY, encourages researchers to use the phrase "imposter training" instead of the traditionally used "imposter syndrome" because it draws attention to the racist and elitist practices that undergird academic training, which often marginalize and disempower students of color, queer students, and working-class students ("What").

4. For more on prosocial forms of professionalization, see Jenna Lay and Emily Shreve's essay in this volume.

WORKS CITED

"About." *PublicsLab*, Graduate Center, CUNY, 13 May 2020, publicslab.gc.cuny.edu/about/.

"Addressing the Underfunding of CUNY, New York's Engine of Mobility, Innovation, and Economic Support." *Office of the New York City Public Advocate*, 6 Dec. 2019, www.pubadvocate.nyc.gov/reports/addressing-underfunding-cuny-new-yorks-engine-mobility-innovation-and-economic-support/.

Ahmed, Sara. *On Being Included: Racism and Diversity in Institutional Life*. Duke UP, 2012.

Boggs, Abigail, et al. "Abolitionist University Studies: An Invitation." *Abolition Journal*, 10 May 2020, abolitionjournal.org/abolitionist-university-studies-an-invitation/.

"The Facts about CUNY Adjuncts: Why an Increase in Adjunct Pay to $7,000 Is Essential to Student Success." *PSC-CUNY*, Professional Staff Congress, 2018, psc-cuny.org/sites/default/files/FactSheet_7K_Final.pdf.

Fitzpatrick, Kathleen. *Generous Thinking: A Radical Approach to Saving the University*. Johns Hopkins UP, 2019.

Harney, Stefano, and Fred Moten. *The Undercommons: Fugitive Planning and Black Study*. Minor Compositions, 2013.

Hartman, Stacy M. *The Ethics of Emotion: The Dialectic of Empathy and Estrangement in Postwar German Literature and Film*. 2015. Stanford U, PhD dissertation.

la paperson. *A Third University Is Possible*. U of Minnesota P, 2017.

Lerner, Ben. "The Backward Logic of Austerity Threatens America's Most Vibrant Campus." *The New York Times*, 26 May 2020, nytimes.com/2020/05/26/opinion/cuny-cuts-ben-lerner.html.

Matthew, Patricia A. *Written/Unwritten: Diversity and the Hidden Truths of Tenure*. U of North Carolina P, 2016.

Porter, Lavelle. *The Blackademic Life*. Northwestern UP, 2019.

"Public Fellows." *PublicsLab*, City U of New York, 2023, publicslab.gc.cuny.edu/mellon-humanities-public-fellows/.

Reber, Sarah, and Chenoah Sinclair. "Opportunity Engines: Middle-Class Mobility in Higher Education." Brookings Institution, 19 May 2020, www.brookings.edu/research/opportunity-engines-middle-class-mobility-in-higher-education/.

Valbrun, Marjorie. "CUNY System Suffers More Coronavirus Deaths than Any Other Higher Ed System in the U.S." *Inside Higher Ed*, 23 June 2020, www.insidehighered.com/news/2020/06/23/cuny-system-suffers-more-coronavirus-deaths-any-other-higher-ed-system-us.

"What If 'Imposter Syndrome' Is a Racist Concept? Let's Talk: Ethno-VLOGraphy, Ep. 2." *YouTube*, uploaded by Mike Mena, 30 Jan. 2020, youtube.com/watch?v=32xKvwrQjLg.

Wilder, Craig Steven. *Ebony and Ivy: Race, Slavery, and the Troubled History of America's Universities*. Bloomsbury, 2013.

Williams, Bianca C. *The Pursuit of Happiness: Black Women, Diasporic Dreams, and the Politics of Emotional Transnationalism*. Duke UP, 2018.

Williams, Bianca C., et al. *Plantation Politics and Campus Rebellions: Power, Diversity, and the Emancipatory Struggle in Higher Education*. State U of New York P, 2021.

Radical Collegiality and Joy in Graduate Education

Paul W. Burch, Brooke Clark, Sonia Del Hierro, Meredith McCullough, Kelly McKisson, and S. J. Stout

Among the members of any professional group, collegiality is by no means a given. Within the specialized world of graduate education, interpersonal cohesion cannot be at the top of a department's recruiting criteria. However, collegiality is a prerequisite for the well-being of individuals and universities alike—although not always in the way that institutions might expect or desire. As students in an experimental, introductory graduate course at Rice University, we fostered a praxis of radical collegiality and precarious joy. We amend the traditional definitions of "collegiality"—companionship and cooperation between colleagues who share responsibility—and of "joy"—pleasure arising from a sense of contentment—to argue for a form of relationality that has the potential to reimagine graduate student well-being. We define *radical collegiality* as a generative, potentially aberrant, and interpersonal flourishing that can run counter to administrative forces; additionally, we define *precarious joy* as a satisfaction derived from facing difficult realities together.[1] We do not draw a causal relationship between these two terms, but we talk about them together, as each continuously shapes the other. We use these terms to articulate and also respond to the environment of crisis in the humanities.

Humanities graduate students work in a seemingly clear and loud discourse of crisis. As Geoffrey Galt Harpham notes, "[C]risis has become a way of life" and even the "rationale" for humanistic study itself in recent years (22). To be clear, humanities graduate students—who likely have been humanities undergraduates and continue to be part of the contingent labor force of humanities education—know well the many flavors of crisis in our ecosystem.[2] We constantly read reports noting the current statistical possibilities or impossibilities of securing tenured or full-time employment in our fields. We continue to train ourselves to enter these eroding academic markets, filling our CVs and portfolios with evidence of both competency and innovative interventions in our respective disciplines. In the model of neoliberalism, graduate professionalization often treats knowledge like a commodity, students like clients, and colleagues like competitors with whom we must contend for increasingly part-time and low-wage positions (see Giroux).[3]

Without downplaying the urgency of these crises, we argue that higher education has always relied on *crisis* as a ubiquitous term that can obscure more than it clarifies; the question is, crisis for whom? As Kyla Wazana Tompkins recently asked, "Is *your* crisis in the humanities *my* crisis?" (419). Taking a long view, we remember how universities have been founded on the physical and ideological legacies of enslaved labor, and, in our own discipline of literary studies, the work "has always been and continues to be, disproportionately, to uphold an Anglo-Saxonist tradition that while productive of some major critical movements seems barely able to ethically respond to our current moment" (Tompkins 419). We wonder how to hold power accountable while working within these disciplines and universities throughout these various crises. In the ongoing COVID-19 pandemic, colleges and universities, including our own, slash budgets, halt graduate admissions, eliminate majors, and terminate members of the staff and faculty, including those with tenure (see Hubler). As COVID-19 cases were on the rise, our cohort was able to operate remotely, albeit from inadequate work environments. Meanwhile, the labor of university maintenance staff members continues to allow for our own, even as their numbers are reduced; all the while, university endowments sit untapped, in some instances growing (Onyechere). We question the impact of our work because of the disconnect between the stakes of our analytic inquiry and the material constraints of our capitalist realism. If we are to live and thrive in humanities ecosystems, and, most significantly, if we accept the role of reproducing the university, then when does our humanistic critique become merely a mode of inquiry that is, in effect, passive?[4]

To think through this question, we cocreate this piece on graduate education rooted in our perspectives as graduate students at a private, well-funded institution. Our position is complex and contradictory because we are vulnerable to these crises but also share uneven, privileged access to institutional resources. We are shielded and supported in ways that others in graduate humanities education are not: our English department matriculates small cohorts (an average of six students), supports students with a nontiered stipend structure for five years, and requires minimal service, including two semesters of teaching-assistant work and one semester as instructor of record. It is important to remember that these are the conditions from which we work and speak and that these conditions, in part, allowed our collegiality to flourish. Simultaneously, graduate education has the potential—bears the responsibility—of adapting our humanities ecosystem with graduate student well-being in mind. Supported by our experiences in our departmental introductory graduate seminar, ours is an argument for necessarily precarious joy, embracing a radical collegiality that we propose would open possibilities for the future of graduate education in the humanities.

This essay speaks against the discourse that, in calling itself crisis, forecloses options for us and for the ecological health of the humanities.[5] For Kyle Whyte, "an epistemology of crisis involves . . . solutions that can occur quickly, maintain the current state of affairs, lack any sense of realism, and further entrench power" (61). Like Whyte's alternative, an "epistemology of coordination" based on relations, we speak toward joy that, as Kandice Chuh proposes, "inheres . . . in the fact of being, and being together" (168). We offer precarious joy and radical collegiality as critical terms for speaking toward the possibilities of the otherwise in graduate education. We are buoyed—both anchored and lifted up—by the call of Chuh to "continue to proliferate the unlearning of inherited ways of knowing and being . . . to be ever attentive to the complex ways in which power operates to dis/organize life" (168). This chapter argues for a collegiality that offers a critical adjacency, that is founded in play, and that conditions the possibility of another university.

Critical Adjacency

Graduate students are positioned adjacent to the institution—both instructors and not instructors, students and not students, employed but not protected—whether recognized or not by themselves or the university at large. Yet graduate students are rarely taught how faculties and administrations function and interact. Entering Rice University's English PhD program in 2017, our cohort was the first to engage in an experimental introductory, two-seminar sequence focused, in part, on institutional awareness and negotiating the profession. Cotaught by four faculty members, these courses invited us to discover the various ways in which literary scholars, the English department faculty, and the university operate. After providing a brief survey of literature contextualizing the crisis in the humanities, our professors asked us to imagine our own fictional English department and to construct an undergraduate literary curriculum for our imagined institution. Beyond a general outline of course expectations and learning outcomes, including a presentation to the Rice English department at the end of the term, there was no established protocol for how we might undertake this project. The mere existence of this required, three-credit-hour course provided us with a unique intellectual space and an uncommon amount of time in which to examine and experiment with our position in the institution. In this unscripted space, we created our imaginary university, Ecalpon U (read backward: No Place).

Through devising a fictional university and English department, we created a collective imaginary adjacent to our home institution, writing an undergraduate curriculum as though it were speculative fiction. We soon decided that our work should be bound by realistic, institutional limits. Negotiating these limits, we both practiced and pushed at the structures that condition possibilities for curricular design and implementation—a process that, in turn, sparked our trajectory toward radical collegiality. We learned about how faculty members relate to one another on educational, academic, and administrative levels by constituting our own English department, rehearsing traditional departmental structures, serving as chair and vice-chair, holding committee meetings, and presenting individual and group reports. To truly inhabit these roles, we implemented voting procedures, minutes, and Robert's Rules of Order—a parliamentary procedure toward consensus with lots of yea-ing and naying. To map our operating methods and overarching ethos, we adopted and revised Rice University's English department bylaws and crafted a departmental mission statement, emphasizing a commitment to advocacy and community. As we imagined ourselves within a department, we negotiated producing a dream curriculum within the boundaries of a realistic university, including faculty politics and constraints. With this new understanding of departmental processes, we were able to produce a curriculum that troubled the edges of a traditional undergraduate English degree.

This act of imagining our university was productive in itself, because the exercise required us to reflect on what we value most about our discipline and its implementation. What ideals and pedagogical concepts would we prioritize most when designing our curriculum—periodization, textual diversity, student-centered pedagogy, or academic freedom? Our curricula emphasized personal growth, open dialogue, flexibility, and mentorship for Ecalpon English undergraduates. We integrated outward-facing course options, including a public-facing pedagogy specialization; proposed an introductory roundtable class; and engineered varying pathways through our undergraduate degree, including a range of honors options and a choice between traditional theses and flexible capstone portfolios. The process helped bring into focus the unique utility of utopic envisaging and speculative modeling—modalities of work that we suggest should be added to existing graduate curricula.

While certain elements of our final curriculum were insightful and convention-flouting, time and again this speculative work led us back to questions of ingrained disciplinary limitations. Despite our attempts to produce a creative curriculum, we still found ourselves mired in the traditional nomenclature of survey courses: "pre-" and "post-1800," nationalist categorizations, and questions of canon. In particular, we were concerned about the ways in which jumping through the preordained disciplinary hoops of "British," "American," and "World" literature would continue to inscribe ideologies of American exceptionalism, colonialism, and white supremacy as norms of our students' intellectual growth. With their own experiences crafting syllabi in mind, our professors noted students' and parents' expectations of a traditional combination of scope and specificity: a schooling in the "classics" as well as the requisite presentation of American and British cultural and territorial histories and their relationship to literary production. Additionally, if we insisted on a greater range of authors than typical of such survey classes, we should bear in mind the reinvestment of time and labor that would be required of most instructors to undertake these revisions and the universities' necessary material investments in faculty hires.[6]

These discussions and debates ultimately brought us back to our institutional present: the nationalistic and hegemonic limitations and expectations modeled in ourselves, Rice University, and the academy more generally. That we were unable to circumvent these patterns of curricular reproduction in our imaginary work required us to face the institutional role that humanities scholars play in reinforcing cultural and territorial colonial norms. Our answer to one such problem was to qualify our British and American literature survey courses with the prefix "Ideas of."[7] For example, a course titled "Ideas of America: Literature

Before 1800" leaves the door open for divergent interpretations and questions of nationalistic frameworks. But, as la paperson outlines in *A Third University Is Possible*, being able, or willing, to critique systems of power from within the university is not innately anti-colonial or decolonial. Indeed, la paperson sees "critique" as most often doing the work of "second worlding universities," those "genteel," humanistic institutions that live within "first worlding universities," and helping them "actualize imperialist dreams of a settled world" (xiv–xv), tacitly reinforcing norms, such as "fees, degrees, expertise, and the presumed emancipatory possibilities of the mind" (42). Our ultimate compromise regarding survey courses reflects the dynamic to which la paperson speaks. While semantically elegant, our renaming was an easy way out, no more than a gesture in the direction of something more radical.

Ultimately, this essay is not a treatise on a radical overhaul of undergraduate English curricula. Rather, it is a discussion of how the tasks and conditions instituted by our graduate course helped our cohort become an adjacent network of joyful, mutually supportive questioning and resource sharing that moves within and beyond the bounds of the university. As our seminar required us to contend with the entrenched limitations and colonial underpinnings of the typical survey course we would eventually be teaching, we developed an appetite for pedagogical critique as a part of our shared collegial network. This collective questioning continued even when no one asked us to do this work, demonstrating how collegiality can become radical when its networks are adjacent to, but by no means neatly positioned within, the institution from which it has emerged. In 2020, we entered our fourth year, having taken our department's pedagogy seminar and prepared our required courses as instructors of record. When the university radically altered its operations to manage the impact of COVID-19, we already had a valuable support network in place. We felt like we were not facing challenges alone; further, this collegiality made us more willing to take risks. We continue with the process of bending categories such as "American," "British," and even "Literature"; we attend mock classes to help one another prepare lectures and class activities; we share a constant stream of materials back and forth across e-mail and *Google Drive* folders; and we plan collaborative classes with one another. In short, when facing the challenges of the classroom, both political and logistical, we have continued to see our work as collaborative rather than as that of siloed individuals with privatized materials. At the current moment in humanities education, this radical collegiality can be vital in helping graduate students continue to bend the parameters of the institution, even as institutions demand exploitative levels of labor without equitable resources.

The position of critical adjacency that emerged out of that introductory seminar has given rise to reflexive self-training, which responds to, augments, and, in some cases, resists the official training we receive elsewhere. More important than the Ecalpon curriculum were the modes of collaboration and imagination we developed. Working to create a collective imaginary, more for each other than for our professors, we devised methods of working together that emerged from, moved parallel to, and retained the potential to pull away from the existing institution. In this way, the experience furnished us with an institutional bearing and practical skills that invite our participation in the work of la paperson's "third worlding university," where "decolonizing dreamers who are subversively' part of the machine themselves . . . wreck, scavenge, retool, and reassemble the colonizing university into decolonizing contraptions" (xiii). The radical collegiality we advocate for, and benefit from, can increase the likelihood that humanities graduate programs generate such subversive wreckers, scavengers, and rebuilders. The space and resources afforded us at Rice University and by the curriculum design of our introductory seminar clearly supported our development of a radical collegiality. It is vital that humanities graduate coursework makes space and time for this kind of relationality to flourish.

The collaborative methods and affective networks we devised to meet the seminar requirements created a space adjacent to the university that helped demystify internal department workings and the mechanics behind academic developments. As graduate students, we take courses and read publications by faculty members and peers, but the labyrinthine systems behind this work remain opaque. Left unexplained, this opacity papers over the processes of research with the myth of romantic scholarly genius—a myth that generates imposter syndrome, or even imposter training (see "What"). First-generation students, in particular, feel the effects of this opacity most keenly. For our cohort, this space has persisted and allows for systemic thinking rarely done within coursework. It also helps equalize inevitably uneven institutional awareness. Our enduring networks are not seamlessly integrated into the university's structures but instead operate both within and outside the usual expectations of graduate school. As we enter our fifth year, the adjacent position of our collegiality has proved an enduring and radical trait, surviving multiple crises, from Hurricane Harvey to the COVID-19 pandemic, and persisting through the ever-present uncertainties within and beyond academia.

Play and Joy

This section reflects on our methods of shaping and sustaining our radical collegiality to demonstrate how graduate pedagogy can nourish networks of support among graduate students. Critical adjacency is precarious as a positional standing in academia, but it also is playful in its indeterminacy and its refusal to see graduate student life and its future as settled. The constant slippage of critical adjacency embraces the certain and uncertain place of graduate students while underscoring the possible playful connotations residing within it. J. Allan Mitchell writes, "Play recreates itself moment-to-moment as a volatile field of interplay, veering among the elements" (340). Like critical adjacency, Mitchell's orientation of "play" does not play well with institutional logic: the changing from "moment-to-moment" in a "volatile" manner runs counter to the institution's propensity to stay the same. However, Mitchell's characterization of play does speak to humanities graduate students' place in the university: "veering among the elements" of financial insecurity, a dissolving job market, a lack of institutional support or even acknowledgment, a constant reassessment of our careers in academia and beyond, and a sometimes harmful interrogation of our own selves. Mitchell's version of play also spotlights the playful constitution inherent in humanities graduate students' peripheral yet central positions in the university. This position, at once adjacent to and critical of the university, is one site of our fostering of collegiality: we find joy together because we are in this uncertainty together. While much of our movement as graduate students appears to be passive, to the institution and even to ourselves, we can and do actively form a collective of care and awareness, despite the noise of individualism and competition filling academia's air.

Within graduate education, play and joy might initially seem to be ubiquitous terms that signify a lot while potentially pointing to nothing. Administering bodies, especially within the neoliberal or increasingly corporate university, valuing marketable skills over philosophical inquiry, tend to align play and joy with not only a floaty optimism but also an escapist character. As approaches to collective critical work, play and joy might appear as utopic responses to the unending pessimism that humanities departments publicly and legislatively undergo—as nice feelings with no critical charge.[8] However, play and joy inflect, form, and saturate the humanities' analytic work, and they can renegotiate how we approach our individual and collective methodologies in graduate education. Many monographs in our discipline challenge their readers through playful prose styles; repeated referential loops and shimmery use of language are common in our readings and reveal play's established presence in the humanities. This style of play diffuses across our experience as a cohort, a simultaneously performative and authentic collective; playful work frames our thought, pedagogy, and community and enacts precarious joy.

Our collegiality is both somewhat organic and constructed, but this seemingly contradictory nature opened us to playful modes of work and working together. Collegiality, and indeed friendship, must be carefully maintained while wading through the logistical minutiae of everyday life and general institutional operations. So how did our collegiality develop and, more importantly, survive three meetings a week and hours of extra administrative work? Remembering our first year's minimal service requirements, its low-competition environment, and the loose structures of the introductory seminar's curriculum, we point to our time together and the play that infused our performances of institutional structures. The unfamiliar formalities resembled inherited costumes we were trying on, testing lines like actors performing parts. We regularly strayed from the script and kept returning to it as a kind of game in which "seconded" began to sound like "bingo!" Taking the work seriously meant recording minutes and noting clear tasks. Memos of the general silliness that gave those meetings energy are interspersed through the fifty-four pages of minutes—in, for example, encouraging notes like "We are good at voting on stuff." We also established a relaxed and accessible practice of resource-sharing as our modus operandi. In particular, our shared *Google Drive* folder, inaugurated during our introductory seminar, remains a key intellectual repository and a welcome venue for running jokes and whimsical excursions. The implications of this balance between playful performance and everyday face-to-face contact, along with the networks this work created, become more profound as we advance further in the degree.

This slippage between "play" and "reality" meant a recurring joke during that introductory seminar was that we actually were, surreptitiously, founding our own secret college on Rice's quad. As we created our own imaginary department, a common question became "Wait, which university are we talking about?" Returning to the work of la paperson, our playful envisaging of a separate institution, with its own parameters and rules, took increasingly radical forms. Not only does Ecalpon U persist in the parasitic and deconstructive manner that la paperson outlines but as individuals have left the program, and our network of contacts continues to extend beyond those affiliated with the university, our experience of institutional parameters has become less rigid. We have colleagues and friends and peers, some of them formally enrolled in the institution and some of them not, but all in *our* university, a flexible, imaginative, and supportive space, linked to but not governed by Rice University. The fact that this network of interpersonal play and attuning persists across official university boundaries suggests one way that courses such as our introductory seminar might set graduate students on a path toward decolonial work. Requiring graduate students to play with the boundaries of the university allows for the persistence of a sense of porousness that might contribute to an actual opening up of the university, disrupting its patterns of exclusivity, knowledge impartation, and accumulation.

The time we invested in fostering a playful and thoughtful collegiality continues to influence our navigation of real-life institutions. Since the course's end, we have come to see this endeavor as a process of becoming attuned, or sensitized, not just to one another but to our positions in a system. Sensitivity to workplace structures and colleagues also extends outside the university; thus, this attunement prepared us in our precarity, even before the pandemic and our interactions with the ever-plummeting job market. Like joy, this contingent awareness emerges from our radical collegiality precariously. Attunement to ourselves as individuals and as a group, to departmental functionings, and to academic administrative aims is precarious within an environment seemingly on the verge of collapse.[9] In this atmosphere of risk and uncertainty, we found joy by actively carving out our own space in our way. The course was partially a performance as a class but was also a community playfully forged beyond the course's parameters. The seminar was a beginning, but certainly not an end, to our attuning to each other alongside social and personal challenges. In our openness to learning and unlearning from one another, our radical collegiality takes the unseriousness of play seriously in humanities graduate education. The play and joy infused into radical collegiality can serve as a method of explicitly recognizing the collective critical work that already happens and will continue to do so, if humanities education allows for these spaces of play to endure or even occur. Through play, we can precariously push against bureaucratic forces and crises while joyfully pushing and pulling up ourselves and others along with our work.

A Radical Collegiality

We argue that the collegiality we have developed is radical in that it is able to be disruptive rather than only complicit. While learning the histories of academic institutions, we practiced and debated how to critique and disrupt those inherited structures. Throughout our work together, we have asked ourselves how our collegiality—inside the bounds of academia, in the service of professionalization, and under the guise of innovation—can diverge from reproducing the structures of critique that neglect the social. Stefano Harney and Fred Moten identify this problem, asking, "Does the questioning of the critical academic not become a pacification? . . . [D]oes the critical academic not teach how to deny precisely what one produces with others, and is this not the lesson the professions return to the university to learn again and again?" Harney and Moten counter this position of negligence with "a nonplace called the undercommons—the nonplace that must be thought outside to be sensed inside . . . wary of critique, weary of it, and at the same time dedicated to the collectivity of its future, the collectivity that may come to be its future" (38–39). Like the potential of what Harney and Moten call the undercommons, a kind of sociality and building work can take place within a practice of radical collegiality.

Key to our development of radical collegiality was making a kind of "nonplace" through taking institutional space, a disruption spilling beyond the bounds of the classroom. As we continued our collaboration on Ecalpon U, we increasingly inhabited department and university common areas and other accessible, porous, sometimes necessarily secret spaces difficult for the registrar to get ahold of or even categorize. Under the guise of Ecalpon U, we negotiated meetings with members of the departmental staff and faculty. We grew confident in these physical spaces and in speaking with administrators. While we worked toward the nebulous course assignment, we engaged in nonproductive social acts just as often. This practice in particular—using space and time to move adjacently to the goals of the institution—has stuck with us. We claim this practice as establishing the conditions for necessary disruption and affirm the precarious joy within this work. Though kindling a "nonplace" can feel uncomfortable, this is our revision of joy and collegiality: it is not always pleasant. Our disruption was thrown into relief when we were told our collaboration was "weird" and wouldn't last, that we should "just wait" for the inevitable falling-out, and that our "own" individual work was our "real" work. This pushback is the neoliberal institution vocalized through our instructors and our peers, people we like and trust. The university would like our work to be profitable, efficient, smooth. Our collaboration is often rough, time intensive, not sustainable.

Because sustainability and productivity are not the goal, radical collegiality has the capacity to foster a collective awareness that can counteract the pitfalls of institutional gratitude. Too often, it is expected that graduate students will merely be grateful: for example, to have funding or to work on research with lauded academics. At our well-funded, private university, we are reminded frequently to be grateful that we have more than graduates in other programs, and we have internalized that voice, policing and repressing our own critiques and judgment. Ultimately, this institutional gratitude cultivates an expectation of compliance. We are primed to think of the needs of the university, and those in positions of power within it, before our own.[10] This expectation of gratitude coincides with exploitative and violent cases of sexual harassment on college campuses. In the Me Too era, crowdsourced documents listing thousands of mostly anonymous reports of sexual harassment demonstrate rampant abuse by faculty members.[11] Many of these reports identify that exact expectation of gratitude: star professors show seemingly genuine interest in their students' work while predatorily crossing physical, verbal, emotional, and psychological boundaries, implicitly demonstrating their power to advance or end student careers.[12] We can counteract institutional gratitude with radical collegiality by continually investing in a collegial unit as a support network adjacent to the institution. The critically adjacent work of radical collegiality can include sharing stories and evidence, establishing witnesses and networks of support, and developing strategies to respond to trauma and retaliation before harassment becomes "egregious" in a community (Hill). This work is already being done yet remains consistently undervalued and unrecognized by the institution. Graduate student bodies across the United States have been working together against institutional gratitude by staging protests and walkouts, setting up mutual aid funds, or sharing open letters and petitions.

The radical part of our collegiality can also respond to the unforgiving teleology of graduate school. Progress to degree relies on diminishing financial, social, and emotional support, often punishing graduate students for deviating from the strict teleology. This rigid process is part of the neoliberal university's investment in churning out clientele. Radical collegiality can augment this experience by encouraging us to be sensitive to one another, to listen to one another, even when the conversation is difficult, and, most importantly, to attune to risk. Being sensitive to one another and to risk is not necessarily a deviant practice in humanities education but currently seems like an uncharacteristic one. If we know that positive peer groups and communities reduce tendencies of isolation, perfectionism, and procrastination, then we also posit the intervention of radical collegiality as a creation of cofuturities, both academic and personal, professional and otherwise. Without practices of interdependence, dissertation isolation is more likely. From one perspective, radical collegiality means safety in numbers with a cohort refrain of "We're going to make it"—"it" being the completion of our degree and "we" being our cohort members, dragging, carrying, and nurturing each other through professional and personal obstacles. For vulnerable students, radical collegiality can establish a peer group that explicitly and implicitly deems one's work necessary, one's personhood important, and one's presence welcome.[13] From a different perspective, a radical collegiality pushes back on the idea that progress to degree is more important than individual needs and well-being. This form of peer networks can support a decision to drop out of a program and the increasingly inevitable pursuit of a nonacademic career. With established modes of caring for and with each other, our collegiality extends beyond academia's bounds and helps us find joy in one another, no matter how precarious, uncertain, or unsettled matters are or become.

As we continue to reflect on our introductory graduate seminar and its ongoing effects, we end with a question: Does this introduction to the profession of literary studies provide a platform from which we can critique the neoliberal institution, or do we risk being absorbed into the object of critique?[14] In a way, learning how to adopt appropriate industry poses within the institution is an important outcome of professionalization. Already in relation to the university, graduate students benefit from understanding how institutional expectations shape an academic department. In fact, the somewhat invisible work that maintains a functioning department is often meant to remain hidden, simply the nature of the university, part of the unexamined background in our ecosystem. Our seminar made visible these mechanics, and this denaturalizing had a distinct effect: rather than becoming completely absorbed into the neoliberal machine, we became sensitive to its operations. We continue to acknowledge the effects of this dangerous proximity—an articulation, itself, that is important work.

Our argument is not a defense but rather an expectation: radical collegiality will be necessary for unlearning and relearning. It is not a defense, because that would assume the crisis, or an offense, in the sense of aggressive, competitive innovation; rather, radical collegiality is a bricolage creation that arises on site, through play and interpersonal relation. We try our own motions, contingent upon our collective, that are risky but also exciting. China Miéville finds possibility in "motion that seems for a moment quite new, but that we realize we have seen before. When we watch bats crawl. Faced with unusual difficulties, certain animals move in deeply strange, unfamiliar ways, ways that seem abruptly alien, and/but that remain absolutely theirs" (184–85). We repurpose like this, taking what we have and remaking it, using it to crawl along, to make something happen, weird but together. Radical collegiality forces us to understand that interdependence and moving differently are not only things to ask for but conditions that should be assumed.[15] As the university moves beyond tenure-track faculty positions, this repurposing helps reimagine a thriving humanities ecosystem.

"If we are to develop political vision," Donna Haraway suggests, "some sense of living and dying with each other responsibly . . . I think the practice of joy is critical. And play is part of it. I think that engaging and living with each other in these attentive ways that elaborate capacities in each other produces joy" (252–53). If we are to persist in these violent, unequal systems, Haraway suggests that play and joy are "critical." By joy, we do not mean the imperative to be happy. Indeed, we are cynical and know that happiness can be a shiny distraction. In "The Uses of the Blues," James Baldwin helps us think about making joy from an experience of struggle or from within a system that tends, at best, toward exploitation. "Joy," Baldwin argues, "is a true state, it is a reality; it has nothing to do with what most people have in mind when they talk of happiness" (57). For Baldwin, joy comes from the realization and acceptance of experiences of life that may be full of anguish. His picture of humanity involves joy and incremental steps toward that joy (66). For our cohort, precarious joy emerged incrementally from the collegiality fostered among six people. Ecalpon U was not a high-stakes project but a high investment in each other. Our collegiality was built slowly and gradually, so it is easy to miss or mistake its value. Rather than merely a course outcome, our collegiality is a radical place for our realities to be voiced with the joy of being heard. With this project, we crawl toward joy.

NOTES

For their guidance and support, we thank our seminar leaders, Betty Joseph, Alexander Regier, Emily Houlik-Ritchey, and José Aranda, who gave us the space to experiment and grow. And we are thankful to the Rice English department for encouraging this collaboration.

1. When we began this essay in 2018, these difficult realities referred to Hurricane Harvey, declining humanities enrollments, and the collapsing academic job market; they have now come to include an ongoing global pandemic that has further exacerbated the challenges we face together.

2. These crises include underenrollment, under- and exploitative employment, lack of political praxis, and lack of academic freedom. These claims have

been put forward by a variety of sources with differing agendas, many of which we are suspicious of. For example, we might ask, Academic freedom for whom?

3. We also note the statement by the American Association of University Professors that, today, over seventy percent of instructional positions in American higher education are non-tenure-track, and more than half of all faculty positions are part-time ("Background Facts").

4. Here, we follow Stefano Harney and Fred Moten in thinking about possibilities for subverting structures of conquest even as our labor maintains sites of expert individualism.

5. As Maggie Berg and Barbara K. Seeber note, "The discourse of crisis [both] creates a sense of urgency . . . which makes us feel even more powerless in the face of overwhelming odds . . . [and] also inadvertently encourages passivity: if it's too late, why bother?" (11).

6. We are asking for a structural change here, but we also note the unequal resources individual professors have available to put toward these revisions, even at a privileged, private university. As Tompkins argues, the arguments over literary curriculum "are not method wars: these are resource wars. Every 'war,' if we even want to use that term so loosely from here on out, is going to be a war of resources pretending to be something else" (419).

7. We thank our colleague Elena Valdez for conceptualizing this phrasing with us.

8. For a critique of the assumed apolitical nature of minor feelings, see Ngai.

9. See Stewart for a similar use of this critical term. Stewart defines "atmospheric attunements" as "palpable and sensory yet imaginary and uncontained, material yet abstract. They have rhythms, valences, moods, sensations, tempos, and lifespans. They can pull the senses into alert or incite distraction or denial" (445).

10. See for example, Solomon and Luther's discussion of an academic culture of favors. See also Ahmed on the importance of being "ungrateful" (*Living* 246).

11. On a recent visit to Rice University, Anita Hill explored Me Too's potential for significant social impact through such steps as progressing intersectional coalition building, establishing procedures prior to an "egregious" peak of sexual harassment, preparing for and expecting retaliation and hostile environments, and—quite simply—firing people.

12. For a detailed individual account of this implicit power and its overlap with sexual threat, see Solomon and Luther.

13. Students of color, in particular, can benefit from a graduation-oriented support group; according to recent MLA studies of humanities graduate students in their third through tenth years, "only African American and white doctorate recipients show completion rates over 50% at year 10. Hispanic doctoral students have an especially low ten-year completion rate of 37%" (MLA Office of Research 2). Across graduate degrees, "on average, over half of all black graduate students leave their programs of study before completion compared to 25% attrition . . . of white students" (Sullivan i).

14. This question is adapted from Ahmed, who writes, "I want to think about . . . how critiques of neoliberalism can also involve a vigorous sweeping: whatever is placed near the object of critique becomes the object of critique" ("Against Students").

15. Critical disability studies reminds us there are many ways to be able, many ways to do a thing: "Disability is part of the reality of living in a body—any body"—no body innately knows the way to do the thing, and no body can do the thing by itself (Taylor 142).

WORKS CITED

Ahmed, Sara. "Against Students." *feministkilljoys*, 25 June 2015, feministkilljoys.com/2015/06/25/against-students/.

———. *Living a Feminist Life*. Duke UP, 2017.

"Background Facts on Contingent Faculty Positions." American Association of University Professors, aaup.org/issues/contingency/background-facts.

Baldwin, James. "The Uses of the Blues." *The Cross of Redemption: Uncollected Writings*, by Baldwin, Vintage Books, 2010, pp. 70–81.

Berg, Maggie, and Barbara K. Seeber. *The Slow Professor: Challenging the Culture of Speed in the Academy*. U of Toronto P, 2016.

Chuh, Kandice. "Pedagogies of Dissent." *American Quarterly*, vol. 70, no. 2, 2018, pp. 155–72.

Giroux, Henry A. *Neoliberalism's War on Higher Education*. Haymarket Books, 2014.

Haraway, Donna. *Manifestly Haraway*. U of Minnesota P, 2016.

Harney, Stefano, and Fred Moten. *The Undercommons: Fugitive Planning and Black Study*. Autonomedia, 2013.

Harpham, Geoffrey Galt. "Beneath and Beyond the 'Crisis in the Humanities.'" *New Literary History*, vol. 36, no. 1, 2005, pp. 21–36.

Hill, Anita. "From Social Movement to Social Impact: Putting an End to Sexual Harassment in the Workplace." 25 Mar. 2018, Baker Institute, Rice U, Houston, TX. Lecture in Gray/Wawro Lecture Series in Gender, Health and Well-Being.

Hubler, Shawn. "Colleges Slash Budgets in the Pandemic, with 'Nothing Off-Limits.'" *The New York Times*, 26 Oct. 2020, nytimes.com/2020/10/26/us/colleges-coronavirus-budget-cuts.html.

la paperson. *A Third University Is Possible*. U of Minnesota P, 2017.

Miéville, China. "A Strategy for Ruination." Interview. *Boston Review*, vol. 42, no. 4, 2017, pp. 180–90.

Mitchell, J. Allan. "Play." *Veer Ecology: A Companion for Environmental Thinking*, edited by Jeffrey Jerome Cohen and Lowell Duckert, U of Minnesota P, 2017, pp. 340–54.

MLA Office of Research. *Data on Humanities Doctorate Recipients and Faculty Members by Race and Ethnicity*. Modern Language Association of America, 2010.

Ngai, Sianne. *Ugly Feelings*. Harvard UP, 2005.

Onyechere, Faith. "Columbia Reports $310 million Increase in Endowment during Pandemic while Smaller Schools Flounder." *Columbia Daily Spectator*, 22 Oct. 2020, columbiaspectator.com/news/2020/10/22/columbia-reports-310-million-increase-in-endowment-during-pandemic-while-smaller-schools-flounder/.

Solomon, Dan, and Jessica Luther. "In Academia, Professors Coming On to You Is on the Syllabus." *Splinter News*, 6 Aug. 2018, splinternews.com/in-academia-professors-coming-onto-you-is-on-the-sylla-1826669829.

Stewart, Kathleen. "Atmospheric Attunement." *Environment and Planning D: Society and Space*, vol. 29, no. 3, 2010, pp. 445–53.

Sullivan, Nicole. *Mentoring and Educational Outcomes of Black Graduate Students*. 2015. Clark Atlanta U, PhD dissertation. *ETD Collection for AUC Robert W. Woodruff Library*.

Taylor, Sunaura. *Beasts of Burden: Animal and Disability Liberation*. New Press, 2017.

Tompkins, Kyla Wazana. "The Shush." *PMLA*, vol. 136, no. 3, 2021, pp. 417–23.

"What If 'Imposter Syndrome' Is a Racist Concept? Let's Talk: Ethno-VLOGraphy, Ep. 2." *YouTube*, uploaded by Mike Mena, 30 Jan. 2020, youtube.com/watch?v=32xKvwrQjLg.

Whyte, Kyle. "Against Crisis Epistemology." *Routledge Handbook of Critical Indigenous Studies*, edited by Brendan Hokowhitu et al., Routledge, 2021, pp. 52–64.

Notes on Contributors

Paul W. Burch, Brooke Clark, Sonia Del Hierro, Meredith McCullough, Kelly McKisson, and S. J. Stout are currently writing and working in Houston, TX, though they have lived all over the United States as well as in England and Australia. While many of them are completing PhDs in English at Rice University, they have also been actors, adjunct laborers, editors, food service employees and managers, scotch connoisseurs, and teachers. Respectively, they have presented at various conferences on petroculture, modernism, Chicana studies, Victorian studies, ecocriticism, and medieval literature.

Todd Butler is dean of the College of Arts and Sciences and a faculty member in the Department of English at Washington State University (WSU). A prior president of the MLA's Association of Departments of English, he was also the founding director of WSU's Center for Arts and Humanities, which organizes the university's Publicly Engaged Fellows program. More recently, Butler was also the recipient of a grant from the Spencer Foundation to establish a network of western land-grant institutions committed to linking the humanities and agricultural extension programs.

Alex Christie received his PhD in English from Loyola University, Chicago, in 2019. During his time as a graduate student, his research and teaching focused on ethics, futurity, and posthumanism in late twentieth- and twenty-first-century literature and culture. His work has appeared in *Configurations*, *ASAP/J*, and *Real Life Mag*.

Katie Dyson received her PhD in English from Loyola University, Chicago, in 2020. Her academic research focused on narrative, ethics, and reading in modernist fiction. Her work was featured on the inaugural episode of the *Modernist Podcast*, "Modernism, Women and Feminism," and has been published in *Pedagogy*.

Tabitha Espina is a postdoctoral teaching associate at Northeastern University, having previously taught at University of Guam, Washington State University, and Eastern Oregon University. She has published in *College English*, *Race and Pedagogy Journal*, *Asian Studies*, *Humanities Diliman*, *Pacific Asia Inquiry*, *Oregon Humanities*, *Humanities Washington*, and *Micronesian Educator* and has publications forthcoming in volumes from Duke University Press and the University of Pittsburgh Press. She has presented her work throughout the United States and in eleven other countries.

Will Fenton is associate director of the Center for Spatial and Textual Analysis (CESTA) at Stanford University and the editor of *Ghost River: The Fall and Rise of the Conestoga*. He earned his PhD in English from Fordham University in 2018.

Manoah Avram Finston studied English and French literature at the University of Chicago and later completed a PhD in French literature at New York University. A former MLA Connected Academics Fellow, he works in academic administration at Columbia University, where he is currently associate university registrar.

Stacy M. Hartman is currently an independent scholar, researcher, facilitator, writer, project manager, and consultant. She served as director of the PublicsLab at the Graduate Center, City University of New York, from 2018 to 2023. Previously, she served as inaugural program manager of Connected Academics at the Modern Language Association. She holds a PhD in German from Stanford University and has presented widely on career education for humanities PhD students and the humanities ecosystem.

Elizabeth Hodgson is professor of English literature at the University of British Columbia. Founder and faculty coordinator of the PhD co-op program, she has presented and published widely on this initiative. She has also published two monographs and many articles on gender and spiritual culture in the English Renaissance.

For the past thirty years, **Marcia Halstead James** has taught part-time at the undergraduate and graduate levels while pursuing a full-time career in nonprofit fundraising, mostly for the arts. She holds degrees in English literature from Mount Holyoke College, the University of Oxford, and Yale University.

Jenna Lay is associate professor of English and director of the Eckardt Scholars Program in the College of Arts and Sciences at Lehigh University. She was previously director of graduate studies in the English department, during which time she served as project director for Lehigh's NEH Next Generation PhD Planning Grant and led workshops on graduate education at the Modern Language Association's ADE and ADFL Summer Seminars.

John Lennon is associate professor of English at the University of South Florida, where he serves as director of the graduate program for the English department. His research is principally concerned with how marginalized individuals exert a political voice in collective actions. He is author of *Conflict Graffiti: From Revolution to Gentrification* and *Boxcar Politics: The Hobo in Literature and Culture, 1869–1956* and coeditor of *Working-Class Literature(s): Historical and International Perspectives*, volumes 1 and 2.

Teresa Mangum is a professor of gender, women's, and sexuality studies and English and director of the Obermann Center for Advanced Studies at the University of Iowa (UI). She is principal investigator for the Andrew W. Mellon Foundation–funded Humanities for the Public Good initiative, working with members of UI's faculty, staff, and student body to design an experiential, interdisciplinary humanities certificate and master's degree that will prepare students for social-justice-oriented careers.

Donald (D. J.) Moores, a writer, editor, anthologist, and professor of English, is the author of numerous scholarly articles and conference papers as well as several books. He was coeditor of *The Eudaimonic Turn: Well-Being in Literary Studies* and is the author of *Mystical Discourse in Wordsworth and Whitman: A Transatlantic Bridge* (2006), *The Dark Enlightenment: Jung, Romanticism, and the Repressed Other* (2010), and *The Ecstatic Poetic Tradition: A Critical Study from the Ancients through Rumi, Wordsworth, Whitman, Dickinson and Tagore* (2014).

Jennifer New is former associate director of the Obermann Center for Advanced Studies at the University of Iowa (UI). She oversaw the center's communications and many of its community-facing programs. For nearly a decade, Jennifer guided the annual Obermann Graduate Institute on Engagement and the Academy in collaboration with faculty codirectors. She also directed the Humanities for the Public Good Summer Internship program, which places UI graduate students with site partners for eight-week intensive project work and professionalizing workshops.

David Pettersen is associate professor of French and film and media studies at the University of Pittsburgh, where he also directs the Film and Media Studies Program. He is the author of *Americanism, Media and the Politics of Culture in 1930s France* (2016) and *French B Movies: Suburban Spaces, Universalism and the Challenge of Hollywood* (2023).

Tiffany Potter is professor of teaching at the University of British Columbia. Specializing in eighteenth-century literatures, she has most recently published *Approaches to Teaching the Works of Eliza Haywood* (2020) and classroom editions of *Oroonoko* and *A Life of Mrs Mary Jemison*. She was awarded Canada's 3M National Teaching Prize in 2020.

Katina L. Rogers is the author of *Putting the Humanities PhD to Work: Thriving in and beyond the Classroom* (2020). She codirected the Futures Initiative from 2014 to 2021 and now consults with colleges and universities to design and implement creative, sustainable, and equitable structures for graduate education. She holds a PhD in comparative literature from the University of Colorado, Boulder.

Emily Shreve is associate director of academic transitions in the Academic Success Center at the University of Nevada, Las Vegas, where she coordinates and teaches in a first-year seminar program focused on acclimation to the university community and major and career exploration.

Sidonie Smith is Lorna G. Goodison Distinguished University Professor Emerita of English and Women's Studies, University of Michigan, and past president of the Modern Language Association (2010). Her major research interest is in autobiography and life writing studies, with specialties in women's life writing, life writing and human rights, and a range of contemporary genres of life writing in textual, graphic, performance, and online media. Her books include *A Poetics of Women's Autobiography: Marginality and the Fictions of Self-Representation* (1987); *Manifesto for the Humanities: Transforming Doctoral Education in Good Enough Times* (2015); with Kay Schaffer, *Human Rights and Narrated Lives* (2004); and, with Julia Watson, *Reading Autobiography: A Guide to Interpreting Life Narratives* (2002; third revised edition forthcoming in 2024) and *Life Writing in the Long Run: A Smith and Watson Autobiography Studies Reader* (2017).

Richard Snyder is assistant professor of English and communications at Northwest University and associate director of the Electronic Literature Lab, where he also functions as metadata specialist for the Next— a combination museum, library, and preservation space for born-digital literature that was honored with the Electronic Textual Cultures Lab's 2022 Open Scholarship Award. He has published in *Digital Humanities Quarterly* and *The Journal of Marlowe Studies*, and his creative work has been featured in *The New River Journal*, *Taper*, and *The Virtual Museum of Posthumanist Art*.

Anna Westerstahl Stenport is professor of communication studies and dean of the Franklin College of Arts and Sciences at the University of Georgia. She served as dean of the College of Liberal Arts at Rochester Institute of Technology from 2021 to 2023 and is an expert in transnational media studies with a focus on the Arctic and Nordic regions. A regular contributor to the national conversation on the purpose and significance of liberal arts graduate education at venues such as the Association of American Colleges and Universities and the Modern Language Association, she also served as a member of the executive committee of the MLA's Association of Departments of Foreign Languages from 2017 to 2020.

Yevgenya (Jenny) Strakovsky served as associate director of graduate studies and career education at the School of Modern Languages at Georgia Institute of Technology from 2018 to 2021, where she managed the launch of the school's first-ever graduate-level program. Her research explores the cultural history of human flourishing in literature, psychology, and philosophy from 1750 to the present as well as its legacy in the liberal arts and career education. Strakovsky recently joined the Fletcher School of Law and Diplomacy at Tufts University as associate director of executive education.

Richard Utz is senior associate dean for faculty development in the Ivan Allen College of Liberal Arts and professor in the School of Literature, Media, and Communication at Georgia Institute of Technology. His scholarship centers on medieval culture; medievalism; the interconnections between humanistic inquiry, science, and technology; reception study; and the formation of cultural memories and identities. He is author, editor, or coeditor of twenty-one book-length publications and more than 130 essays and reviews on topics ranging from medieval studies to humanities in the twenty-first century.

Veronica T. Watson is professor in the Department of English and served as director of graduate studies in literature and criticism at Indiana

University of Pennsylvania. She holds a PhD from Rice University and teaches and publishes on African American literature, Southern American literature, and critical race and critical whiteness studies.

Bianca C. Williams (she/her) is associate professor of anthropology and faculty lead of the PublicsLab at CUNY Graduate Center. Exploring race, gender, and Black women's affective lives in higher education and organizing communities, Williams is the author of *The Pursuit of Happiness: Black Women, Diasporic Dreams, and the Politics of Emotional Transnationalism* (2018) and coeditor of *Plantation Politics and Campus Rebellions: Power, Diversity, and the Emancipatory Struggle in Higher Education* (2021).

Laurie Zierer is executive director of PA Humanities, where she has led the organization's recent shift to humanities-centered community building, youth development, and participatory research. She is an alumnus of Leadership Philadelphia and a graduate of the Nonprofit Executive Leadership Institute at Bryn Mawr College, and she holds a BA in English from Temple University, an MA in rhetoric from Penn State, and certificates in fundraising and executive administration from the University of Pennsylvania's College of General Studies.